DRIVE ON!

DRIVE ON!

A SOCIAL HISTORY OF
THE MOTOR CAR

L. J. K. SETRIGHT

Granta Books
London

Granta Publications, 2/3 Hanover Yard, Noel Road, London, N1 8BE

First Published in Great Britain by Palawan Press Ltd 2002

This edition published by Granta Books 2003

A CIP catalogue record for this book is available from the British Library.

1 3 5 7 9 10 8 6 4 2

ISBN 1 86207 628 6

Typeset by M Rules

Printed and bound in Great Britain by St. Edmundsbury Press, Bury St. Edmunds, Suffolk.

CONTENTS

A Preamble   vii

PART I: AN HISTORICAL REVIEW

1   To 1895   3
2   1896–1905   17
3   1906–15   35
4   1916–25   43
5   1926–35   57
6   1936–45   73
7   1946–55   87
8   1956–65   103
9   1966–75   117
10   1976–85   131
11   From 1986 . . .   143

PART II: THE YOKE AND THE SPUR

1   Extortion and Distortion   159
2   Small Expectations: The Decadent History of a
    Decaying Idea   169
3   Scapegoat and Idol   177
4   The Liberator   185

PART III: THE FACE OF THE EARTH

1	The Big City	195
2	Somewhere to Stop	211

PART IV: THE TURN OF THE WHEEL: REVOLUTIONS IN TECHNOLOGY

1	The Nature of Revolution	221
2	ForWarD	227
3	The Can . . . of Worms?	235
4	The Popular Front	243
5	Re-inventing the Wheel	251
6	Inconstant Mesh	259
7	Tyres and Timing	267
8	Fear of Flying	277
9	Fluid Power	287
10	Computer Control	297
11	The Air Inside	305
12	Four-wheel Equality	315

PART V: PERSONAL EFFECTS

1	Making a Start	325
2	Changing Gears in Changing Times	333
3	What to Wear	345
4	Sport	353
5	Arts and Fashions	375

Appendix: Timescale	391
Index	400

A PREAMBLE

Great abilities are not required for an Historian . . .
Imagination is not required in any high degree.

SAMUEL JOHNSON (via Boswell), 1763

HISTORY IS INCOMPLETE. Nobody knows all of it; no one, if he did, could ever tell all of it. No greater number, however they tried, could ever agree on all its content.

So this little book is just a taster. There is more, much more, vast and immeasurable, that might justifiably be incorporated in it. The social history of the motor car is infinite in its ramifications – which is to say, again, that none could write it all nor read it. Had this little book only succumbed to its author's temptation to include a chapter on roads, for example, it would have to be twice its present size, for the subject of roads is worth a book in itself. Yet, as every driver knows too well who has encountered the sheep, the pedestrian, the truck, the cyclist or the occasional level crossing for frogs or locomotives, the road and the car are not co-extensive.

The car, being a partial expression of the individual who gains freedom in it, does not share limits with anything or anybody. It does, however, suffer limits, imposed by its own deficiencies or others' wills, and that is part of its social history no less than of its technical background.

The study of what the car has done to society has attracted some interest among a few serious writers, and among an unholy rabble of activists; but they have invariably taken a view that has been either geographically too narrow or historically too short. The study of what society has done to the car has been virtually overlooked, but it is just as important an aspect of the story. The unfolding and interaction of political, scientific, technological, migrational, agricultural and domestic histories will be shown to have affected the course taken by the car in its development, to have distracted and delayed and debased it. It will be seen that it is no fault of the car that it has failed to keep its initial promise, nor that it has been accused of evils beyond all reasonable guilt.

To hint at the limitations suffered by the motor car must lead at least to some veiled criticism of the obsessive enthusiasm often devoted to the motor car. There are those to whom the machine has become a god, prompting a reminder that 'the idols of the nations are silver and gold, the work of men's hands . . . Those who trust in them will become like them' – that is to say, futile. However, if this book should enlarge the interest of the motoring enthusiast so as to embrace or at least explore such matters as architecture and chemistry, mathematics and poetry, physics and fashion and all the other subjects that it will show to be relevant, that will be no bad thing. In the study of the car, as in life itself, though nothing may matter all that much, yet everything matters.

To write a chronological account of it all would result in something impossibly complicated, cross-referential, and decidedly heavy going. Instead, a chronological table – relating motoring developments to what happened contemporaneously in politics, art, economics and the standard of living – is offered as an appendix, while the text of the book is composed in a series of parallel sections each of which explores a certain theme.

It is freely admitted that there are repetitions in this book. They are not here merely to demonstrate the theory so well expressed, in *The Hunting of the Snark*, that 'what I tell you three times is true'. In fact the principle of threefold iteration is soundly established as part of the schoolteachers' art, pithily expressed by one practitioner in the formula 'First you tell them you are going to tell them, then you tell them, then you tell them that you have told them'. However, the reiterations in my text are sometimes merely duple, sometimes manifold. In any case I consider them justified by the intricacy of the relationship between the car and many superficially unrelated aspects of the human life through which it passes: something relevant to the subject matter of one chapter may be equally relevant to that of another, and is not to be denied its additional place.

For example, Napoleon's journey from Vilna to Paris in 1812 crops up in more places than one. So it should, for it is relevant in all those places. It may occasion some surprise that a history of motoring should delve so far back, but it could be argued that it should start even earlier. We have to consider the ground upon which the motor car first tentatively set its wheels, the civilisation that laboured to give it life. I find good grounds for arguing that modern times began in 1800, the year in which Volta created his electrical pile, in which the patent protection enjoyed by Boulton & Watt for their primitive steam engine ended, and in which the Napoleonic Wars began. If that be the beginning of modern times, it must also be the beginning of the motor car, the time of fertilisation if not of parturition.

And yet, can we not see the potential of it even earlier? Is the revolution it brought about not discernible in the revolutions that took place back in the 18th century? I cannot trace the one without noting the lessons of the others; and I say so – more than once.

There really is nothing wrong in repetition. Truth, opinion, even a mere felicity of expression, must bear more than one iteration. The serious student of Setright's works over the past forty years may note the occasional fragment of earlier output in this book, though now amplified or qualified by additional material. This is entirely proper, as may be seen by analogy to music, where composers from Bach to Shostakovich (with particularly strong supporting argument by Prokofiev) made repeated use of what they had already written. If what I have said before seems to be right still, then where it is relevant I must say it again.

So I say again that this book is incomplete. It would have to be true of the half-dozen most recent years, which as always cannot be seen in perspective until they are more distant. It is true also, and especially, of one aspect of motoring history that this book will not address in detail. The chapter headed 'Sport' is not a history of motoring sport at all, but an account of the influences that beset it. Of histories recounting in stupefying and technically quantified (though rarely technically qualified) detail the events of more than a hundred years of contention, confrontation, contumacy and controversy masquerading as an ennobling activity, we have had more than enough, in books by Setright and by countless others. We need no more. Perhaps the relevant chapter in this book will show why we need no more.

What we do need is a book to show us – especially those of us too young to remember – what good and evil things have been done to, with, for, and by, the motor car. I would like this to be a book that the enthusiast for motoring can read with pleasure, the critic with growing understanding, the historian with some surprise, and the scholar with satisfaction. It should also occasion, amongst such diverse readers as industrialists, accountants, politicians, advertising agents, media people, civil servants, and sporting promoters, not a little embarrassment, wonder, or shame.

See how it strikes you.

PART I

AN HISTORICAL REVIEW

CHAPTER 1

TO 1895

The things that made the Dark Ages so dark – the isolation, the lack of mobility, the lack of curiosity, the hopelessness . . .

LORD KENNETH CLARK, *Civilisation*

THE SOURCES OF INVENTION AND the tributaries of discovery seldom flow directly or rapidly towards those reservoirs of employment wherein pragmatic men acknowledge the genius of their prognostic mentors. The ancient Chinese invented fireworks, for instance, long before the Emperor Augustus invented the fourth of July or even the fifth of November.

There are some who, history being the interminably interpretable thing that it appears (actually it is a perfectly simple algebraic entity, being the product of time and geography, but that is another matter), would argue about attributing the calendar to Augustus, since he demonstrably failed to get it right. They would say that we should give the credit to Pope Gregory, or the Emperor Julius, or King Numa Pompilius, or most convincingly to Rabbi Hillel haKatan; yet we need hardly worry, unless we are Russians, in which case it might be embarrassing to concede that the October Revolution really took place in November.

Likewise we need hardly worry about who invented the motor car, unless we believe the commentator R L Bruckberger who wrote, in his *Image of America*, that 'Ford's revolution is far more important than Lenin's.'

How was Ford's way paved? What constitutes invention, and when does a horseless carriage become a motor car? There is a strong current move to proclaim the originator of the species as Karl Benz, whose petrol-engined three-wheeler was running well enough in 1885 for it to be driven into a wall. This opinion, backed by the corporate and commercial pride of Daimler-Benz AG (Gottlieb Daimler's motorised carriage did not run until 1886, but his son set his trousers on fire driving a petrol-engined bicycle in the previous year), as well as by the *furor Teutonicus* of the Nazi party after coming to power in Germany in 1933, appears to have as its sole foundation the fact that Benz was the first to make a motor car as a commercial venture. However, dissenters could find grounds in patriotic fervour, coreligionist pride, anti-capitalist zeal, steam-age sympathies, or mere cussedness, for asserting that the first was Hammel in Denmark in 1886, Delamère-Deboutteville in France in 1884, Markus in Austria in 1870, Lenoir in France in 1863, or Brown in England in 1824. All these built vehicles propelled by internal-combustion engines, but the earliest were gas engines[1] of one sort or another, and it is to Siegfried Markus – inventive, scientific, Austrian, Jewish, and brilliant – that the garlands go for the first petrol-engined car. He made himself four of them in succession, but with no thought of engaging in trade: like Hammel and Lenoir, he made them for his own use and his own amusement.

The first recorded use of the word 'petrol' (one bought the stuff from apothecaries in those days) was by a German in 1876, and it attracted little notice in the burgeoning age of steam. Surely what mattered was not the propellant fuel, but the fact that the vehicle was propelled by mechanical rather than animal agents? If so, again, who was first? Certainly not Oliver Evans, the American who launched the steam dredger he had built for Philadelphia by belt-coupling its engine to one of the wheels of the undercarriage on which it rolled from factory to harbour. Certainly not the Englishman (if Cornishmen will forgive the expression) Richard Trevithick, one of whose advanced non-condensing high-pressure steam engines propelled a carriage up Camborne Beacon on Christmas Eve 1801: one could hardly say of him that he had 'lit a flame that would never be extinguished' – though by forgetting to put out the boiler-furnace fire when he stabled the vehicle for the night, he caused carriage and building both to go up in smoke. Perhaps not even the Frenchman Nicolas-Joseph Cugnot earned the distinction, often though he be given it for creating a couple of steam-powered artillery tractors in 1770–1, the second of which was driven into a wall. Cugnot's vehicle may thus have created a tricycle precedent for Benz to follow, but it seems that the steam vehicle itself was not unprecedented: Padre Verbiest, a member of the Jesuit mission to Peking, sought to impress the Emperor of China by making a steam-driven[2] carriage a century before Cugnot.

---

1 Why this airy dismissal of gas engines, which were structurally and functionally so like the gasoline (or 'petrol') engine? To carry a gas in ample quantity is difficult, even today, much technology being necessary if the gas is to be compressed, cooled, condensed, and contained. In contrast gasoline (the proper word for what we commonly call 'petrol' in those parts of the world where English rather than American is spoken) has an extraordinarily high energy density: there is more latent energy in a given weight of gasoline than in the same weight of most high explosives. Given reasonably efficient machinery, a little gasoline can take one a long way.

2 There is some suggestion that the mechanism was a steam turbine.

It was a hard life, and sometimes a short one, for the youngsters riding the Pony Express.

Who truly did it first, and whatever it was, hardly matter to us now. What is more important is to remember that the petrol-engined motor car – or even the gas-engined variety – did not present to the world any startlingly new notion of horseless motion. Just a hundred years before Benz drove his vagrant three-wheeler into a wall, James Watt was elected to the rolls of the Royal Society, while John Loudoun MacAdam, lately returned from fourteen years' service in his uncle's New York counting-house, was beginning private experiments in road construction. It was in large part thanks to these two, and to the Napoleonic roadbuilder Pierre Trésauguet, that England and France enjoyed for the most part of the 19th century not only the world's best roads but also the world's busiest steam traffic.

The first self-propelled vehicles antedated the petrol motor by a very long time. Working models of steam-driven carriages for road locomotion had been built[3] as early as the 18th century. At about the time when the first passenger train service had started, an engineer named Walter Hancock[4] built a steam-driven carriage which proved itself on various routes and then plied for hire between London and Stratford. Such pioneers (there were a number of others plying on assorted routes) suffered occasional accidents and encountered severe obstacles – most consistently from the drivers of horse-drawn transport who, fearful of their livelihoods, resorted to simple obstruction and old-fashioned harassment whenever they encountered a steam vehicle. They were sometimes a greater danger than either the machinery or the state of the roads, which were often in worse fettle than when the Romans had quit them.

The railways were more important at that time. Indeed, their rapid development extinguished the hopes of the road-haulage steamers. Yet it was steam which mattered most, steam which mattered more than anything since the invention of printing, by achieving something that not even the Reformation nor the Renaissance nor the Age of Reason had been able to accomplish: *it was the power of steam which abrogated what had been one of the fixed conditions of life.*

For over 4000 years, since the invention of the wheeled chariot by the Sumerians, the maximum speed of land travel, over distances greater than a man could ride on horseback in a day, was about 4.8mph. Even the Emperor Napoleon, travelling post-haste from Vilna (where he had left his army after leading it to a safe retreat from Moscow) to Paris in 1812, could not better this average speed, taking 312 hours for his journey of 1500 miles[5]. Even on the highly developed coaching routes there was no hope of significantly changing what had so long been thought immutable, even though some English posting-houses boasted ostler teams who were

---

3 By Murdock and by Symington. Trevithick did it full-scale at the turn of the century, numerous others in the next 50 years.

4 His brother Thomas independently discovered (or deduced) the principle of the vulcanisation of rubber in the same year as Charles Goodyear discovered it (accidentally, according to legend) in 1839 in the USA. Nothing has ever been more vital to the evolution of the car.

5 The Emperor Julius Caesar, who worked himself harder than most dictators, would sometimes travel as nearly non-stop as possible, by night and by day, sleeping in his horse-drawn coach. By this means he could cover the 550 miles from Rome to the Rhône in six days, only a little slower than Napoleon.

as professionally adept as the best modern motor-racing pit crews, changing a team of four horses and getting the stage-coach on its way again in less than a minute.

Such people were less than happy about the rivalry offered by the steam carriage. The Turnpike Trustees[6] heaped loose stones across the Glasgow-Paisley road in 1832 to deter the Steam Carriage of Scotland Company from maintaining its service. One of the carriages suffered a shattered rear wheel in attempting to break through, causing it to capsize and rupture its boiler: the five people killed would have been distinguished as the first road casualties, had not one of Hancock's steam-omnibus stokers rashly wired down a safety valve to get more performance a couple of years earlier, blowing himself up with his boiler.

Steam was to produce other disasters too, not all of them so explosive. The miseries of industrial towns were magnified when steam powered their factories, and in some ways the 'railway towns' were just as bad; but the wonders that the railways accomplished were of more general benefit to the health and general prosperity, and moreover to the freedom and enlightenment, of society as a whole.

Steam achieved no less on the high seas: within ninety years of the first working puffer, the *Charlotte Dundas*, appearing on the Clyde in 1802 (earlier steamboats had been merely experimental, like all the cars before the Benz), the Atlantic could be crossed in one-tenth of the fastest time under sail. Likewise ninety years after Stephenson's triumphs in County Durham, the railways had achieved the same tenfold increase in average speeds for journeys that had formerly been limited to the average speed of Sumer and Napoleon.

Here was the secret of the political unification of the large new states – American and European – which congealed or accreted in that industrious and revelatory century: as frontiers were pushed outwards, a land ten times larger in linear dimensions *and accordingly 100 times greater in area* could be brought within the range of prompt communications from the centre of government.

The motor car was to achieve something more, when it picked up the torch that the railways eventually proved unfit to carry any longer. Whereas the political and economic effect of the railways was to offer society a certain consolidation, the motor car offered particularity, so that any member of society with such a vehicle available could at last choose his own starting point and his own destination, link them by his own choice of routes, and make the journey either alone or in company of his own choosing. Another fixed condition of human life was thus lifted: an individual could now shun isolation, could enjoy independent mobility, could indulge his curiosity and

The hand-cranked petrol pump is a good deal newer
than this Abbé's primordial Panhard-Levassor.

hope. Steam may have brought us into the Machine Age, but it was the motor car which brought us out of the Dark Ages.

It had to be a 'petrol' car. Steam could never have accomplished it, lacking the convenience, the practicality, the small-scale efficiency, of the still incomparable petrol-burner. Only in the USA did it take any appreciable time to deter the steam-car fanatics: eventually the distances, and the winters (when water turned to ice) of America persuaded even the most romantic or conservative steam enthusiast of his folly.

---

6 The British government, having put the burden of maintaining minor roads on local authorities, farmed out the responsibility for major roads to private enterprises. These were the turnpike trusts, which were supposed to carry out all necessary repairs to the roads under their charge, and which certainly charged tolls for all vehicles that passed. Similar systems were tried elsewhere, notably in America.

Steam practice in fact was a serious handicap to the development of the motor car: too many of the engineers in the then-young industry thought in steam terms, assuming (like Edward Butler, who patented an otherwise clever[7] petrol tricycle in 1884) that direct gearless, clutchless transmission from piston to driving wheel by simple connecting-rod would work satisfactorily, assuming that steam-engine valve timing would be appropriate, and so on.

Industrial gas engines, stationary affairs used for factories and pumping-stations, had more in common with steam than with petrol, and likewise burdened the car with their influence. The early Benz, like many others, had a transmission redolent of factory practice, where a stationary engine drove shafts up amid the ceiling rafters from which belts drove machines or let them idle by running them over fast or loose pulleys. (My father's London factory, doing exquisite precision work in light alloys in the 1930s, still had this primitive kind of power-transmission system when it was bombed in 1941.) The Diesel was to come much later and has yet to prove satisfactory. As for electricity, there were more than a few little battery-operated runabouts doing errands in some cities (there were electric 'Hansoms' in New York City, while in London the Harrods van fleet remained exemplary for decades) but their short range (not to mention the dwindling performance as the batteries ran down) was crippling; in any case, electricity still needs the same sources of energy and modes of power generation as the others, being nothing more than a means of power transmission, though most people have not yet awoken to this fact. That great engineer Sir Charles Parsons was rightly considered to have wrought wonders when he created the first modern turbine in that same 1884: it ran at a stupendous 18,000 rev/min, but the generator coupled to it only produced about 100 watts.

Still, there in the turbine was a clue, linked to the definition of 'power' as *the rate of doing work*: revolutions per minute were the key to the greater revolution, a fact which Gottlieb Daimler alone seems to have recognised so early. His former boss, Dr N A Otto, devised the first practical four-stroke petrol engine in 1876, but forbade Daimler's horseless-carriage experiments; Daimler went off to do it himself, at the age of 49, and did it. It may have been his obstinacy in retaining the abysmal incandescent-tube ignition system that forced him to run his engines faster than others, but 800 rpm was very fast by the standards of 1884 crankshafts.

What a lot passed through the minds of the thinking engineers in that crucial ten-year span! Otto's concept of the four-stroke engine started them off in the realisation that the conventions of the steam engine need not be followed too closely.

There was a wonderful parallel in music, on which the musicologist Hans Keller once commented while giving a radio talk on the notebook techniques of Beethoven and Brahms, with special reference to the latter's first symphony over which the composer struggled for two decades: 'All those years of muddle and error and stupidity, and then – the great leap forward into genius!'

Brahms did at last produce his first symphony, in 1876 – the very year in which Otto crystallised his four-stroke engine. With that Rubicon crossed, progress was rapid: by 1885 Brahms had produced his further three symphonies. Brahms was his own master: Daimler had to quit Deutz before he could enjoy the same risky independence, but in that same 1885 he made his engine, proved it in a timber-framed bicycle test-bed, and was ready to instal it in a car (or anything else, for that matter) by the following year.

Daimler's cars, when they appeared, were unworthy of his engines, being merely carriages deprived of their hay-takers; Karl Benz (whose career had many striking similarities to that of railway pioneer George Stephenson) built less adventurous engines, but they did have electric ignition and were mounted in purpose-designed chassis. Both kinds should have prospered faster than they did, but Vested Interest was ready and able to impede them.

Nobody, I suspect, noted the omen of 1884: in that year was founded the Fabian Society, named in celebration of Fabius Cunctator, the dictator who had earned his nickname for his unpopular but effective delaying tactics in defending Rome during its second Punic War. *Delaying tactics!* The pioneers of the motor car were beset by them on every side.

Surprisingly for a young and progressive nation, America had a share in the opposition. An early joke on the subject: *She*: 'It must be fine to be a motorist.' *He*: 'Alas, young lady, many people think it should be fine and imprisonment.' Even as late as 1909, the US Senate heard in a speech by Senator Joseph W Bailey of Texas that 'If I had my way, I would make it a crime to use automobiles on the public

---

7 Obtaining his patent in 1884, a year before Daimler's, Butler built a much improved version in 1887, the same year as Daimler's car; but it was in many respects far more modern than the German. It had rotary valves for inlet and exhaust, for example; it had electric ignition, foot brake, foot clutch, and a surprisingly modern float-feed carburettor which antedated that of the supposed pioneer Maybach by five years. Butler had another, minor, claim to fame as the originator in Britain of the word *petrol*: Frederick Simms maintained a less justifiable claim to it, but (like Maybach) he was better supported by a publicity machine.

highways . . . Perhaps the time will come when horses will be educated to the point where they will not be afraid of automobiles; but I doubt that, for I have not yet seen the time that I was not afraid of them myself.' Early American objections in fact concentrated upon the evident use of the automobile, then a seriously costly luxury, as a tool for the aggrandisement of the rich; as soon as the machine became available to the middle-income bracket, the opposition dwindled.

Not so in England, where opposition to the motor car was always worse than elsewhere[8] – where, indeed, it was to become ingrained in British political thinking. Consider the plight of Edward Butler and his petrol-engined tricycle which so richly deserved further development. England was no place for that; the emancipatory Bill which was to relieve British motorists of at least some of their intolerable burden was not to reach the Statute Book until 1896. By that time Butler, cruelly hounded by the police (and, perhaps as a consequence, henpecked by his wife), had felt obliged to give up; in that same year his vehicle was broken up for scrap.

The railroads look dense in parts of this map, but the vast scale of the USA left plenty of space for the motor-roads that would be needed.

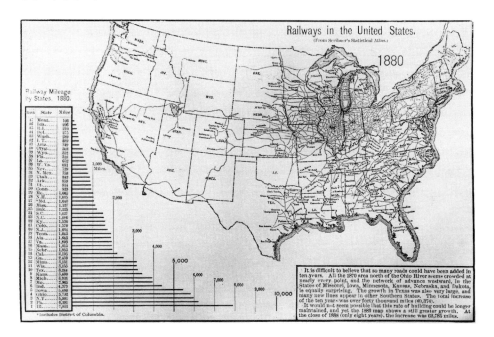

That disabling legislation had been in existence since 1861, when the British Parliament hit upon a simple stratagem whereby legally to confound all motor vehicles. An Act was passed purporting to attend to the dangers of large steam-powered agricultural machines which needed occasionally to venture upon the country lanes; but the way it was worded cunningly contrived to manacle the motor car for half a century. The original Locomotives on Highways Act of 1861 had imposed limiting dimensions on such traction engines, a 10mph speed limit, and the first road tax. In 1865 Parliament presented a revised version, whereby the speed limit was cut to 4mph in open country, 2mph in towns, and a crew of three was stipulated for each vehicle – a driver, a stoker, and a man to walk ahead carrying a red flag to warn of its approach and help calm jittery horses. As it stood, this legislation effectively scuppered the steam carriage (examples of which had proved capable of as much as 30mph[9]) and barred the way for any worthwhile petrol-engined successor; and as it stood, so it stood for a long time, the only concession being when an amending Act of 1878 relieved the man walking in front of the need to carry a flag.

Within a decade, it was becoming obvious that a new breed of vehicles had been born, to which the strictures that might have been appropriate to a 15-ton traction engine hauling a two-ton load were not relevant. Government – for reasons shortly to be examined – continued reactionary, but under increasing pressure (notably from Sir David Salomons[10] and the Hon. Evelyn Ellis MP – not to mention one Harry J Lawson, to whom we shall return). Parliament eventually conceded that 'light locomotives' were something different. What the motor-minded were to welcome joyously as the Emancipation Act in 1896 recognised a class of road machines weighing less than three tons, which were exempted from the rule about 'three persons in attendance', and were supposedly free to travel at 12mph.

Why had Victorian Britain been so hostile to the motor car? Why did legislation so deliberately handicap the use of horseless carriages on the roads? Was it, as has been suggested, because Britain was a nation of horse-lovers who could not bear to

---

8 Holland, alias The Netherlands, runs it close.

9 Their engines may have been capable of it, but their wheels, as yet denied the benisons of the pneumatic rubber tyre – it had been invented by Scotland's young Robert W Thomson, who patented it in 1846 – were not capable of sustaining anything like that speed.

10 It was this famous Jewish philanthropist (and owner of a Peugeot) who organised Britain's first Motor Show, in the grounds of his house near Tunbridge Wells.

see that 'noble' animal supplanted? It was not. If we had truly loved the horse, we would have done everything possible to relieve it of the abject slavery to which it was bred. The horse suffered bitterly on our country roads and in our city streets: toiling overburdened up slippery hills, whipped when it fell, killed (usually without much finesse) if it could not get up, it lived in filth and could not help but plaster our streets with filth[11]. The flies which fed on its ordure carried diphtheria which killed more children than ever our motor cars did. We claimed to love children, too[12].

The real reason for keeping the self-propelled vehicle at bay was that a very large and influential number of the people's representatives in Parliament had taken the trouble to acquire financial interests in the railways that had so transformed the country. Running them, dealing in the land often compulsorily acquired to build them, building large speculative housing developments around them (whole suburbs were thus created), all were immensely lucrative business, and Members of both Houses waded wallet-deep in it. Road transport could have ruined their fortunes.

The desire to avoid rocking the boat was expressed elsewhere, too. In Baden in 1893 Benz, about to launch his first four-wheeler, was given official notice that a 12 km/h (7.5mph) speed limit would be imposed on country roads, and would be halved within town limits and around sharp corners. In Prussia, an old law prohibiting 'occupied premises' above a boiler was interpreted to outlaw steam cars. In New York (which had a law like Britain's Red Flag Act until 1901), a city alderman proposed to outlaw petrol. In France, on the other hand, the doctrine of *laissez-faire* was endorsed with enthusiasm.

Whether because of the state of their roads or the state of their minds, the French welcomed the motor car unreservedly. Little steamers had been popular for some time, made by Panhard & Levassor, De Dion, Serpollet and others. The Peugeot family, manufacturers of corset stays, cropping tools and coffee grinders, had recently diversified into the bicycling movement: it was more popular in France than anywhere else but England, breeding an enthusiasm for modern roadgoing machinery that was soon to make these two countries the greatest in motorcycling. That enthusiasm led the French naturally to cars, too, and Armand Peugeot built his own steamer. Panhard told him he would do better to use the new Daimler petrol engine (Panhard had acquired the French agency and patent rights through marriage), and soon Peugeot was the first to sell petrol cars commercially in France.

Panhard was close behind, but he took time to study how best to exploit the new engine. He worked out what became the *système Panhard*, the classical front-to-rear ordering of radiator, engine, friction clutch, sliding-pinion gearbox (*c'est brutal*, he admitted, *mais ça marche!*) and final drive to the rear axle. It was ready at the same time as the first *Sherlock Holmes* story, and it set a pattern in 1891 that was to dominate motoring for most of the ensuing century.

In the land which kept that pattern most prevalent, there were then only about 150 miles of roads that were better than mere American dirt. By 1893, however, two Springfield brothers named Duryea had run a successful prototype car, a lightweight affair with a single-cylinder engine. Two years later, America boasted its first 'great motor race': there were two entrants. One, an imported Benz, retired with its driver frostbitten by the Chicago blizzard; the survivor and winner was a two-cylinder Duryea horseless buggy, which was then put into production in Illinois. At last America had an automobile manufacturing company that had been founded for the purpose . . .

France had, at last, a proper motor race. The Rouen Trial of 1894 had been inconclusive; now there was a 732-miles race from Paris to Bordeaux and back, the first of the heroic and finally tragic series of Paris-based races which were to stimulate development, design, and sales, throughout mainland Europe. Offshore England was still unemancipated – catching up would take 60 years – but in 1895, as well as reeling over the Jameson raid and writhing over the trial and sentence of Oscar Fingal O'Flaherty Wills Wilde, there were signs of the emergence of 20th-century thinking: the London School of Economics was founded, and England had its first Motor Show. The show to see in Paris was the new *cinématographe* of the brothers Lumière, but all the talk was about the truly great motor race, which had attracted 46 starters. The leader all the way to Bordeaux and back had been Emile Levassor driving single-handed his firm's new two-cylinder Panhard, to complete the round trip in 48 hours and 48 minutes. That corresponded to an average speed of 15mph – more than three times faster than Napoleon, while relying on a very different and much more accessible kind of power. No accomplishment could better display the new independence of the man in the street.

---

11 In 1898 the annual conference of Municipal Engineers was held in Birmingham, and it resolved in connection with the congress of the Sanitary Institute 'that the introduction and use of efficient motor vehicles should be encouraged by county, municipal, urban and other authorities, in view of the fact that the extended use of such vehicles would contribute to the general improvement of the sanitary condition of our streets and towns . . .'

12 And dogs; yet when we find a car that we thoroughly dislike, we describe it as a dog. We are a strangely hypocritical lot.

CHAPTER 2

1896–1905

Change is not made without inconvenience, even from worse to better.

RICHARD HOOKER

IT TOOK REMARKABLY LITTLE TIME, once Benz and Daimler had severally made a proper start on it in the fruitful valley of the Neckar, for the motor car to proceed from conjecture to concept. If the most successful encapsulation of that concept was the *système Panhard,* which in 1891 broadly outlined the morphology of the machine, then it took only another decade for the details to be settled. They were settled with sufficient authority to dismiss for ever the notion of the car being merely a horseless[13] carriage, with sufficient authority for them to be comfortably accepted for sixty years and scarcely even questioned for thirty.

Whether they were right is another matter. If the combination of electrical transmission and front-wheel drive, demonstrated in the Porsche Lohner at the beginning of the 20th century, had captured the imagination of the masses as effectively as it impresses today's retrospective critic, how much sooner might the motor car have satisfied the needs of those masses?

According to Herbert Spencer, who had written his *Social Statics* not long before, progress was a necessity, a part of nature. It was not yet in the nature of society, however, that the masses should even be in a position to consider what their vehicular needs might be. In the second half of the 19th century, illiteracy in England had dropped from 35 to 3%, but England's record was very much better than most other countries could boast: so the masses hardly had the education to understand the problem. In the last year of that same century, Rowntree (the chocolate maker, and an earnest Quaker) found that 28% of the people of York lived below the subsistence level, and ten years earlier Charles Booth (a shipping magnate with a conscience) had found 31% of London's 4.2 million were likewise living in abject poverty – and this at a time when England seemed the most prosperous nation on earth: so the masses hardly had the means to order what they needed. In fact the motor car was not yet a necessity to them; their priorities lay elsewhere. All they could do was to take note of

Big Albert Marquis de Dion and (beyond him) little Georges Bouton, his engineering partner, on their 1894 steam tractor, the fastest finisher in the Paris–Rouen competition. With a semi-trailer for its passengers, this may be the originator of the modern articulated truck. It also shows how motoring pioneers clung to the traditions of the horse-drawn carriage.

what the cars were like that the privileged few were playing with, and mentally file a desire to do likewise in due course.

The view of the French social historian François Bédarida was widely shared: *The motor car had become a symbol of the new modes of ostentatious consumption. A luxury object, rarely put to any useful purpose, it served amid noise and dust only to impress the vulgar crowd in town and village.*[14]

---

13 There was a rich young Parisian lady who caused something of a sensation in 1901 by being driven along the boulevards of her city in a carriage pulled by a pair of sleek black cows, evidently well trained for the duty. This caused some perplexity among the police, for the lady insisted with some reason that her vehicle qualified as a 'horseless carriage'.

14 *A Social History of England 1851–1975* (translated by A S Foster), Methuen, 1979.

Pedal-cycling was always a somewhat sporting fashion, but one could remain ladylike aboard the petrol-engined De Dion Bouton quadricycle.

Rarely put to any useful purpose, indeed? What better retort to this than the classic 'What is the use of a new-born child?'[15] Uses would be found; meanwhile, those who could afford it derived a lot of pleasure from it. The socially adventurous of the upper classes, and the intellectually curious of the middle classes, might not spend too much time forecasting the motorised liberation of the working classes from their virtual imprisonment; but by seeking for themselves a new emancipation from the strictures imposed by history and horseflesh on their mobility, they pointed the development of the motor car in a direction which may not have been ideal but was decidedly useful. Indeed, by spending as much as they did upon it, they were in effect paying for the development of the motor car to which the common man might one day aspire.

It certainly cost a lot. Maintenance cost a lot more, and the cost of tyres[16] (which lasted only a few hundred miles) was appalling. Admittedly there were relatively cheap ways of going motoring: nothing did more in Europe to spread the taste for motoring than the little and easily managed De Dion engines which were to be found (sometimes as pirated copies) in little motorised quadricycles and tricycles galore. Their chassis were often English, for Coventry had become the centre of the cycle industry, merely because anti-motoring legislation in England was so ferocious that an appetite for the road could only easily be met by a pedal-cycle. France had been as enthusiastic in its bicycle-building as England, but unlike most other countries France had taken the petrol engine – German though it might be – to its bosom, and no motorised feat could be too outrageous to be appealing.

Speed limits were being eased, here and there. Germany was tough, Switzerland worse (one of the more Calvinistic cantons maintained a ban on Sunday motoring until 1927), and the supposedly United States differed quite a lot, with limits of 40, 35, 20 or 15mph in some of them, and a healthy desire to cover a lot of ground quickly enjoying the support of country common-sense in others. The best that horsey England could do was to pass in 1896 what became known as the Emancipation Act: the 'man with the red flag' had already gone (the flag had, to be more precise), and now the speed limit was raised from 4 to 14mph – which the Local Government Board promptly reduced to 12mph.

There was more to the so-called Emancipation Act than that. It provided, for the first time, Construction and Use Regulations, with some remarkable rules. Rubber tyres, for example, whether pneumatic or solid, had to have smooth treads. Motor cars (which under the Act were 'light locomotives') were to be so constructed as to 'consume their own smoke', in marked contrast to the freedom of railway locomotives to vent coal-smuts all over the land. Never mind; motorists felt themselves liberated, and on 14 November 1896 they celebrated 'Emancipation Day' by gathering in London and driving thence to Brighton. At least, that was supposed to be the idea;

15 Benjamin Franklin, when asked what was the use of a new invention.

16 When tyres were solid, any rubber soft enough to provide cushioning would be worn away very rapidly. When they became pneumatic, they were much more durable, subject only to the random incidence of punctures. Omnibus companies provided the necessary details: solid tyres on a London bus cost 4d per mile, pneumatic tyres performing the same duty at 0.1d per mile.

but the event had been organised by the aforesaid Harry J Lawson, and at least one of the participating cars reached that seaside resort via the good offices of the Southern Railway Company . . .

In retrospect we see that the event celebrated the supposed end of a period of imprisonment from which British road users would never be wholly free. In America, at the same time, Alexander Winton's second car had been timed at 33mph over a mile, and he drove his third the seven hundred miles from Cleveland to New York just to show that it was no mere sprinter.

America was clearly the place where the motor car could develop fastest, though not where the fastest cars would be developed. Building itself a classless society in which money would be the main determinant of social status, it was achieving a remarkable balance between the Revolutionary ideals of the French[17], to whom equality mattered more than liberty, and the traditional ideals of the English, who prized liberty above equality. With its population swelling at a fantastic rate as refugees flooded in from torn and cruel Europe, and yet with more work to be done than there were people to do it, America made money by applauding money-making, and soon had an enormous number of people able to afford some sort of motor car. Add the circumstance of embracing enormous distances which demanded some faster and more flexible form of transport than had hitherto been available – the railways were at best only a network, and over such vast areas the mesh could only be coarse – and it becomes understandable why America, so recently jumbled by the Civil War of 1861 and so self-righteously keen on fraternity, on the brotherhood of man, was the car's breeding-ground.

Detroit became its effective centre by chance. Ransom Eli Olds was going to set up his car factory in Newark, but on the platform of Detroit station he met a copper miner named Smith who offered to finance him if he kept his business there. Business did not exactly prosper (his first cars were too big and too costly) but things changed in the aftermath of the fire which gutted his factory in 1901. The only thing saved from it was the prototype of a little buggy-type car with a scroll-curved dashboard, hauled out of the blaze by timekeeper James Brady[18]. It was all that was left for Olds to make, by farming the work out to local firms, but it became a great success: orders for 1000 were captured after a drive across Canada from Detroit to New York (in less than eight days) by tester Roy Chaplin[19].

What made the success of the little Curved Dash Oldsmobile so important to the future of the American industry was that farming-out of work. It gave local industries an interest in what Americans were already happily calling the automobile, in emulation of the French and despite the protests of etymologists who despised the mongrel word. The names of the contractors were to become household, as in the case of John and Horace Dodge, whose machine shop built transmissions for Olds. Most notable of them all was the firm which built the engine, Leland & Faulks: from developing precision machine tools for Springfield and for Colt (the firearms business was the first to inherit mass-production methods from the Connecticut clock-makers), Henry Martyn Leland went on to higher things with toolmakers Brown & Sharpe, fathered the universal grinder, and then in late middle age began to show the motor industry what marvels machine tools could work. Henry Ford, with whom he had a brief association, may have popularised mass production, but it was Leland who taught it, and by 1902 he was in charge of Cadillac, doing well by doing good.

Ford's first two firms (Cadillac was the second) had in their failures failed to warn him that he was out of place in the high-price market, where Colonel James Packard reigned. Ford saw the light in time, and instead of trying to outdo Cadillac he resolved to undercut Oldsmobile . . .

While America was building a future, Europe was making history, and Britain was finding itself once again in a frightful muddle. Inspired by an ageless unwritten Constitution in which the Common Law[20] enshrined all their hard-learned practical safeguards of corporeal freedom, safety, and enjoyment of property, the British still set much store by liberty[21] – and liberty and the motor car, as we should learn, belonged together. But not yet. There were scarcely enough cars in Britain to count – and, before they could proliferate, Harry J Lawson meant to ensure that they should do so under his aegis. A bicycle-maker turned company-promoter, he had learned

---

17 *Liberté, Egalité, Fraternité.*

18 He later became Mayor of Detroit.

19 He later became US Secretary for Commerce. Olds must have been gifted in choosing employees.

20 Such of it as had survived. There is far less of it remaining today.

21 The police everywhere assumed an unwarrantable authority to interpret the law as they chose. An instance is afforded by the *Automotor and Horseless Carriage Journal* for July 1899: 'On July 3rd while Mr J Scott-Montagu, MP., was about to enter the gate of Palace Yard on his Daimler motor vehicle, he was stopped by the police and refused admission. In vain the Hon. member claimed that he was only following the example of other Hon. members who have dispensed with horse traction. The reply was forthcoming that there are autocars and autocars, and it was suggested that, while a motor driven by electricity meets the approval of the Office of

during the recent cycling boom the techniques for displaying another great British freedom, the liberty to separate a fool from his money.

At the end of the previous decade, a young engineer named Frederick R Simms (no fool, but his earnestness then hinted at naïvety) met Gottlieb Daimler and acquired the Daimler rights for Britain and most of her colonies. Since Britain's restrictive laws prevented effective demonstration of the car on her roads, he took to the waterways, using a motor launch to show off the Daimler engine; enjoying a decent trade in subsequent launch-conversions, he felt emboldened in 1895 to import a Cannstatt Daimler (the first into Britain) – and was soon approached by Lawson's syndicate, which was anxious to acquire the rights to all cars in Britain. Lawson floated the Daimler Motor Company, and began promoting the new cause, making free use of the new magazine *The Autocar*[22] which had been set up as his organ of propaganda.

Early in 1897 Henry Sturmey, the editor of the magazine and a director of Daimler (which made him an affront to journalistic ethics), set out on an epic drive to demonstrate the abilities of the car. The Daimler company had begun by importing complete cars from Daimler and from Panhard; their first 'production' models were assembled copies of the current Panhard, but might be badged as MMC (the Motor Manufacturing Company, which built the bodywork) or as Daimler. Sturmey's 3½ horsepower 'Daimler', carefully prepared by the factory at Coventry, was driven to John O'Groats at the northern extremity of Britain whence, in 17 days (but only 93½ hours' actual driving time) it reached the other extremity at Land's End, with nothing worse than a couple of complete brake failures to its discredit.

Enormous publicity attended the trip. It must indeed have done much good for the cause, since motoring thereafter began to flourish in Britain; but it did little to help the thousands of investors whom Lawson had successfully mulcted of a huge amount of money. Juggling the shares and accounts of a multitude of companies belonging

Works, a vehicle which depends upon oil for its propulsion stands in a very different category. There was nothing for it but for the Hon. member to leave his motor outside the gates and to cross Palace Yard on foot. Mr Scott-Montagu very properly resented this high-handed and improper behaviour on the part of the police. Ultimately an apology was tendered, and in future the Hon. member will enjoy the same rights and privileges as other owners of vehicles.' As it happens, that Hon. member's son drove the same car, 100 years later, into the House of Commons Yard once again, to prove an historical point – and he (that is, Lord Montagu of Beaulieu) took the precaution of bringing with him the Speaker of the House. As many a failed candidate may admit, getting into Parliament is not easy.

to his syndicate (including Humber, Beeston, Daimler, Coventry Motor, the London Electrical Cab Company, and MMC), Lawson also used the courts to attack any pioneer manufacturer whom he saw as infringing the patents he had bought. He drove one such man to suicide, and showed no remorse when boasting of his vindication. Perhaps he felt some later: he and his major crony Hooley were prosecuted for fraud, and Lawson was given twelve months' hard labour.

The motor trade has had a bad reputation in Britain ever since[23]. The focus of public suspicion is the dealer, but in the past there has been equal censure of the industry's factory workers and management, and it has doubtless been equally merited. The impassioned enthusiasts who believed that they had something to contribute to the evolution of the car were very few, and most of them were business failures. The men who succeeded were mostly inspired not by progress but by a rapacity and parsimony which for some time justified the continued activity of the trades unions, born into a very different world in about 1824. It also explained why the bosses were not too keen on having very clever engineers or accountants around, who might spot what they were up to and spoil it all. What has been a cause for widespread dismay – the low pay and social standing of senior engineers and managers in Britain – may well be a product of these early days of entrepreneurial roguery. At any rate it explains why, in engineering design and business skills, the British motor industry has always deserved so much criticism.

With the manacles removed, the motor car began to flourish in Britain at last, as it had already been flourishing in France and in Germany. Manufacturers sprang up everywhere, but then and there Britain became a car-importing nation, avid for the proven products of continental Europe. Most British makers were content to copy these, to produce them with (or sometimes without) licence, to improve upon them only in minor details[24]. Some of them produced original designs, but many were mere assemblers, buying components from the specialist manufacturers who had seen opportunities for expansion by diversification into the new industry.

The evolution of modern technology that had made the Industrial Revolution

---

22 The oldest motoring magazine in the world but bereft of its definitive article, *Autocar* survives to this day.

23 In their 1967 song 'She's Leaving Home', the Beatles sang of the parents' dismay at the thought that their daughter had gone to meet 'a man from the motor trade'.

24 That was how Henry Royce started.

truly a Revelation was most evident in metals and mechanical engineering: there were two-thirds of a million such workers[25] in 20,000 establishments that were prospering, notably in and around Sheffield and Birmingham – and it was Coventry, satellite to the latter, which was home to many of the firms that had become purveyors to the booming pedal-cycle business a little earlier, and were mentally most adapted to the next phase in making the people mobile. These were the places to which a new car-maker would despatch his most trusted engineer, with a shopping list for proprietary engines, transmissions, axles, wheels, steering boxes, chassis pressings (though some cars still had wooden frames), oilers and gauges and a multitude of bits. As well as his list, the engineer would be given a very tight budget (such minions were not expected to stay at the better hotels while on these errands), and an awareness that some component manufacturers would look after his own personal interests better than others.

Though it caused a minor hiatus in design and development, at a time when the country's best brains could have impelled the evolution of the car at a great rate towards something cleverer and more forward-looking than the merely horseless and excessively steam-inspired designs which were common, this hunger for production – this desire to have some sort of car now, rather than wait for anything better – did have beneficial effects. It meant that, as well as the sprinkling of very rich men lording it in some powerful and tyre-hungry Napier or Panhard, there was a more extensive stratum enjoying new-found mobility aboard some modest little single-cylindered tricar or quadricycle, which could be bought and maintained more cheaply than a pony and trap. Mobility – without which there could be no curiosity, no hope – was no longer the prerogative of the 'carriage folk'.

Admittedly, the working and lower-middle classes had a railway system available for their travelling, a system which had transformed Britain in three-quarters of a century and cobwebbed it with lines ostensibly to everywhere. In fact the railways only served trade, whether for workers going to the factories, or gentlemen going to the City, or coals going to the furnaces. A few trippers' services took families to the speculatively built seaside resorts, but there was very little real choice. If you want to discover what steam and the railways really did for Britain, you should read about life in the conurbations that depended on them. Read Alexis de Tocqueville[26] on Manchester in the mid-19th century, for example. When British 'Tommies' endured the filth and squalor of the trenches on the Western Front in the Great War of 1914–1918, was it much different – give or take a military hazard on the one hand, an industrial hazard on the other – from the misery in which their grandfathers might have lived, in one of the growing and proliferating industrial towns[27] which were adding their own feculence and stench to the railways' grimy web? Disease killed more of our servicemen than did high explosives in that war; it raged no less at home.

From all this, the motor car – the blessed *private* motor car – offered escape. It might only be for half a day a week, but it was an escape which offered hope. It did not take long, in those days, to drive out of town and into the countryside; the transition was the more salutary for being the more sudden. The ribbon development which made the task so much longer and more dismal did not come until the 1920s, a joint product of buses[28] and of those speculative builders (again!) who have been one of the curses of England.

The upper strata of Britain's nobility and gentry may have been blissfully unaware of all this. Hippophiles almost to a man, they generally gave the motor car very little support; but their counterparts on the mainland of Europe were of a different mind. There, motoring's sporting aristocracy ('Unless my car will do 80mph', said King Leopold of Belgium, 'it is of no use to me') were avid motor-racers. The years from 1896 to 1903 saw a succession of scandalously dangerous road races, usually from Paris to another city (Marseilles, Amsterdam, Berlin, Vienna, and finally the abortive Madrid affair), and prompted the construction of purpose-built racing cars.

Most of them were giants, but it was a lightweight which taught the most salutary lesson: fastest of all in the Vienna race was the Renault running in the lightweight category. It only had about 40bhp, but for all its comfortable size it weighed only 1200 lb. The big cars weighed a ton, but could not compete with this finely balanced design of Louis Renault, the man who was winning popularity in the market place with live-axled cars that were so much cleaner and quieter than the

---

25 There were half a million miners, and their numbers had doubled in half a century. For that matter, the population as a whole was increasing faster than anywhere else in Europe.

26 As you may at the beginning of Part 3 of this book.

27 By 1896, 75% of the population of Britain lived in towns; 40% of the population lived in the 24 biggest towns. Men died, on average, at the age of 44.

28 The motor omnibus burgeoned rapidly, making its appearance on the London streets in 1905. In 1913 London General buses covered 55.5 million miles.

familiar chain-driven brutes, however better their suspension. His brother Marcel reached the finish at Vienna so far ahead of the field and of expectations that he had to wait for the officials to turn up and meet him there.

What an object lesson! In the USA the Empire State Express had set a speed record for locomotives in 1893 at a remarkable 112mph, a record which stood until 1905 when the Pennsylvania Special ran three miles at 127mph. If these were brief sprints in special circumstances, then in England one could rely on regular schedules to average 50mph on the London–Cheltenham train, or reach 90 behind Gooch's *North Star* [29]; yet 20mph in a car was deemed an offence against the human body, against G-d, and against organised society – in ascending order of seriousness. German attitudes were not much healthier, but here was this Frenchman making light of a 5000ft Alpine pass to reach Vienna seven hours faster than the Arlberg Express!

There were Germans in the sport, too, and representatives of what might be called the other half of Greater Germany, which was the Austro-Hungarian Empire. One of the latter used to do well in the events of the Nice Speed Week (a race, a sprint along the Promenade des Anglais, and a climb up the hill to La Turbie) where the cream of society flocked each winter. The diplomatic Emil Jellinek, Austro-Hungarian Consul in Nice, moved in these high circles, and drove heavy Daimlers at high speeds with good results[30], all of which made him exceedingly influential in the sale of cars to the polite and prosperous. The only handicap he encountered was the Teutonic name of Daimler, distasteful to the French; so he insisted that the new Daimler model for 1901 be named after his daughter . . .

The son of a distinguished Hungarian-born rabbi, Jellinek led an adventurous early life, later settling for some time in Morocco, where he swept up a beautiful Sephardic bride – and that is how the car came to be called Mercédès[31]. How would Hitler have reacted as he paraded in the world's most German car, forty years later, had he been told that it was named after a rabbi's grandchild?

How, for that matter, would old Gottlieb Daimler have reacted to the car itself? He had died with the 19th century, unable to see further (Benz, tired after years of living on the brink of disaster, was merely unwilling to go further, and had to be forced into retirement from his firm in 1903), and his assistant Wilhelm Maybach was at last able to realise some of his engineering ambitions.

The 1901 Mercédès 35hp that Maybach created was more than merely ambitious: it was authoritative, more completely definitive than anything in the next fifty years. It had a positive gate-change instead of a vague quadrant for the gearlever, it had a honeycomb radiator instead of a snakepit of gilled tubes, it had steel chassis members instead of flitched wood, and it had timed inlet valves instead of automatic ones – and they even had variable lift (instead of a throttle) to control the supremely flexible engine. It prescribed the pattern for cars in such detail that it is still recognisable today as the first modern motor car.

The impact of that first Mercédès on the motoring world was terrific. After a failure at its first appearance in February 1901 for a race in Pau, where it suffered transmission troubles, it completely dominated the Nice Speed Week a month later, winning more or less everything for which it was eligible, at speeds far higher than had been recorded in past years. The most successful example of the several taking part was driven mainly by the fastest of the professional drivers, Wilhelm Werner[32], and was the property of Baron Henri de Rothschild, but was entered by one 'Dr Pascal', which was actually the pseudonym under which the good and lively Baron made his services (he was a leading figure in medical research) available free of charge to the hospitals of Paris.

What impressed the socialites in Nice as much as anything was to see the winning Mercédès a quarter of an hour after it had won its event, now transfigured from a dusty stripped racing two-seater into a gleaming and fully equipped touring four-seater for its well-dressed occupants to parade through the town. Surely, if the iron fist could be so readily gloved in velvet, this must be progress? Of a sort; but it could be argued that if, ahead of the brilliant technician Maybach, that brooding genius Dr Frederick Lanchester had been able to persuade crass businessmen to manufacture his superlatively scientific car of 1895, the progress Spencer thought so necessary would have been much faster. What is more, the intellects which were

29 From 1847, when he was only 21 years old, Daniel Gooch served as locomotives superintendent for the Great Western Railway until 1864. In the following two years he was in charge of the laying of the first pair of transatlantic telegraph cables, between Britain and the USA, for which he was awarded a baronetcy.

30 Driving one with sadder results, Daimler works driver Wilhelm Bauer had his grossly top-heavy Canstatt Daimler overturn and kill him on the hill near La Turbie. It was this mishap which prompted Jellinek to demand of Maybach a car that was longer and lower, as well as more powerful.

31 The accents remained until Daimler merged with Benz, a rather lengthy operation which was completed in 1926.

32 He later became chauffeur to the Kaiser.

seeking future paths of development for mankind would have got along with the new notion of motor cars a good deal more happily.

Town and road planning were the two most important matters that were left to trail in the wake of motoring development instead of advancing with it. Things could so easily have been otherwise: it was in 1898 that Sir Ebenezer Howard proposed 'garden cities' for the future. He could not then have foreseen how naturally the private car and the pretty town might be mutually suitable and supportive. The car allowed people to see beyond the confines of the old refuse-dump towns, to hope for a soothing blend of rural felicities and urban facilities, if not for themselves then for their children to inhabit.

The earliest architectural planners were unaware of the need to provide for the

The idea of 'garden cities' was first propounded in 1898. By 1913 the first of them, Letchworth, was taking shape like this.

car: in 1904 there were but 8000 cars in Britain, one for every 4750 people. The zeal which saw Letchworth, first of the garden cities, begun within a decade of Howard's book, did not extend to providing a multitude of garages for the citizens; but by 1910 there would be 53,000 cars (only 770 people per car) and they should when the time came have been noticed. In another three years, their number would double. One more year, and we would be at war.

Architecture in Britain was to some extent served by Luddites, fondly believing in some sort of revival of folk art to which the products of modern engineering bore no relevance. On the whole, like civil engineering and most of the social sciences (Havelock Ellis published *The Psychology of Sex* in 1899), it was populated by intellectuals – but in the motor industry they were very rare indeed.

Their absence has indeed been conspicuous throughout the century[33]. Before the giant corporations grew beneath the bean-counting surveillance of accountants and business-school graduates, most car firms were run by jumped-up mechanics who had somehow promoted themselves off the factory floor. Many were intuitive mechanics, some of them were gifted, but unfortunately too few had the sense to see that aggrandised mechanics was all that they were.

Most notable of that few, among the many who styled themselves 'engineers' while staunchly setting their faces against the progress that real engineers should have made, was yet another middle-aged man, F H Royce. His electrical machinery had a high reputation, and he was shocked to find how rubbishy cars were when he bought one. His success in making the same sort of car vastly better by making it properly[34] came to the attention of the Hon. C S Rolls, a sporting gentleman who was

---

33 In the 1930s William Morris, later Viscount Nuffield, would tolerate no varsity men on his staff at Morris Motors. When he discovered that some of his engineers were graduates (a status that candidates learned was best kept secret if one sought a job), he had them summarily dismissed. He was not alone among industrial magnates in fearing to employ men who might be cleverer than he, but this attitude persisted into the latter half of the century more in Britain than elsewhere.

34 The firm's motto became *Quidvis recte factus, quamvis humile, praeclarus*: whatsoever be properly done, however humble, is noble. It would not have been F H himself who established the Latin. Educated people of the time were familiar with what the historian Gibbon described as 'the decent obscurity of a learned language', and Royce's company secretary, De Looze, was fond of quoting Latin tags, which only drew forth some of Royce's considerable store of vulgar invective: having had very little education himself, he hated the use of alien tongues. It was probably Johnson who persuaded him to accept the Latin motto.

making a pretty penny by selling French *teuf-teufs*[35] to British toffs; and the association of these two unlikely partners led astonishingly quickly to the appearance of a very light and very fleet Rolls-Royce in the 1905 Tourist Trophy.

Royce knew his job, and did it well: his car was the fastest in the Isle of Man that year. Rolls did his job rather less than well: selling was one thing, but snap changes in a Rolls-Royce gearbox were another, and he retired with stripped cogs in the first lap, leaving the firm's very competent professional driver Northey to come in second. But the R-R man who knew, and did, his job best of all was the business director, Claude Johnson, upon whose judgement the firm's prosperity was really founded.

The year 1897 saw not only the Diamond Jubilee of The Widow of Windsor but also the foundation of the Automobile Club (later the RAC) of Great Britain, and Johnson was its secretary. In 1900 he had shown his organisational ability, his judgement, and his good taste, in running the 1000 Miles Trial which did as much as anything to put motoring on the British map. His tact was much exercised, too, as when he arranged for riders to pilot the convoy of competing cars by bicycle around the outskirts of Buxton. The Derbyshire spa regarded itself as a place where ailing gentlefolk came for the restoration of their health: as a town devoted to this preservation of life, it would not countenance the presence of that monstrous engine of death, the private motor car!

The public motor omnibus, which catered to a clientele several fortunes removed from that cultivated by Rolls and his peers (for example the Chevalier de Knyff, a deservedly popular racing driver who was also a director of Panhard), made its appearance on the streets of London in 1905, the year when Sinn Fein was formed. Before long, bus accidents would account for the major proportion of road casualties; but by that time, though high European society[36] would not have ceased to play its part in the evolution of motoring, wide American society would have a stronger influence than ever. The arrogant conduct of the wealthy motorist there in the USA[37] was already prompting severe political misgivings in Woodrow Wilson: 'Nothing has spread socialistic feeling in this country more than the use of the automobile.' Louis Renault, remembering the cheap little De Dion engine in his 1898 prototype, might raise an eyebrow at such views; but it would be another nine years before the entire French nation gave thanks for the salvation of Paris from *les sales Boches* by the 'other' unforgettable six hundred[38], *les taxis de la Marne*. In 1905, the motor car was not yet the servant of all men – nor yet the master of any.

---

35 The expression is pure onomatopoeia, but it really is what the French called the puttering little cars of the very early days.

36 Nowhere were the obligations of the upper classes more stressed than in Germany, where it was unthinkable that in any international event the nation should be represented by anyone of less than noble stock. In 1903, when it fell to the Automobil Club von Deutschland to field a team of three Mercédès for the race in Ireland for the Gordon Bennett Cup, they refused permission for them to be driven by professionals, however competent: the honour of Germany could only be decently upheld by those who were *hochwohlgeborene* – of high birth. By some curious process of elimination, this meant that Germany's honour had to be upheld by two Belgians, the Baron Pierre de Caters and Camille Jenatzy, and an Englishman, Mr Foxhall Keene. Jenatzy won the race, which proved something or other.

37 The venerable British medical journal *The Lancet*, which had in 1902 been indulging an occasional enquiry into cars suitable for General Practitioners, saw fit to interrupt a seriously professional discussion of such matters as the transmissibility of bovine tuberculosis or the use of radiotherapy in treating cancer to publish this diatribe from its New York correspondent:

'The automobile has gained for itself a very bad name in America among the community at large. In New York the craze for automobiling has become an intolerable nuisance and also a source of grave public danger . . . The people of the United States are much given to boasting of the freedom of the country, but when this freedom takes the form of trampling upon the rights of other citizens it is hard to say where the advantage of it comes in. Freedom too often is allowed to degenerate into license here, and in no country have private rights to be preserved by such incessant struggle as in the United States. The owners and drivers of automobiles have too long been allowed flagrantly to disregard the rules of the road, for although a few traversers of the law are arrested occasionally, the punishment meted out to them seldom or never is in proportion to their offense . . . Again, such portentous evil-smelling machines as some of the large racing automobiles should not be allowed on city streets. Gaudy, noisy, and malodorous, they are a terror alike to pedestrian and horse and have greatly helped to render the already crowded and bustling streets of New York an abomination to the nervous citizen. Many automobilists have exhibited so cynical an indifference and so brutal a disregard for the rights and feelings of the remainder of the population . . . etc, etc.' As usual, the USA led the world.

38 See 'The Charge of the Light Brigade' by Alfred Lord Tennyson.

CHAPTER 3

1906–15

Hos successus alit; possunt, quia posse videntur

VIRGIL

IN THE EARLY DAYS OF DADA, the painter Raoul Hausmann produced a collage entitled *Tatlin at home*. Tatlin was a Russian artist and architect, prominent in the Productivist school; Hausmann wanted to show 'the image of a man who had only machines in his head'. In an American magazine he came across a picture of a man who, for no apparent reason, reminded him of Tatlin[39], and that picture became part of the collage, with the skull stripped open to reveal the mechanisms within. It was right that a car's steering gear should have been among those mechanisms: the man in the magazine was Henry Ford.

Egregious though he was, Ford was representative of the men who flocked into motor manufacture in the third decade of motoring's history. They were mostly mechanics, unschooled and scientifically naïve. The decade began and ended with the greatest papers of Albert Einstein; but while he was demonstrating that, with every revolution, the hub of a wheel aged faster than the rim, they were still debating whether the spokes should be of wood or of metal. They were not to be presumed brilliant because they were successful; they succeeded because they were mechanics, in an age when the masses, at all levels of society, were mechanically ignorant. Scientists would have made motor cars quite differently, had they demeaned themselves enough to try it; and their customers and backers would have been frightened off, as Lanchester's had been. The mechanics stood closer to ordinary men, could reach out a hand and lead them gently into the future instead of confronting them with it.

There were exceptions, most notably in Germany and Italy. Rudolf Christian Karl Diesel had passed out of the *Technische Hochschule* at Munich with the most brilliant examination results in the institution's history; but his influence on the motor car was not to be felt until long after his disappearance from the ship carrying him to Britain in 1913 to advise the Admiralty. We do not know whether he fell, or was pushed, or jumped; but we can see how the purity of his theoretical work was corrupted by some of those practical English vandals whom the Industrial Revolution had created.

The Turin School of Engineering was perhaps even more distinguished than its Bavarian counterpart, and from it were recruited the members of that truly brilliant team of designers who helped to make the capital of Piedmont also, for a while, the capital of the motor industry; but it was more important that the founders of Fiat in 1899 had been a group of young aristocratic gentlemen and businessmen, sharing a brand of intellectual socialism which showed them how to capitalise on the artisanal and arsenal resources of the sociological phenomenon that Turin then was. They too had been imbued with the spirit of the Industrial Revelation (although it came rather late to Italy), and would be ready to lead the people as soon as the time arrived when they could be led gently.

Revelations and revolutions were all the causes and effects of the time. Three great revolutions – the Industrial (or English) Revolution which began in 1760, the American which began in 1775, and the French in 1785 – had formed a triad, disharmonised by the Napoleonic Wars to produce a 19th-century cadence which was to be either resolved by the Russian Revolution of 1917 or dissolved by the greatest revolution of all, the Great War of 1914–1918.

Everybody could see these two cataclysms coming, but nobody could bear to look forward to them. Instead, they looked back, gilding their lives with what conservatism had taught them to esteem, while steeling themselves for what rejectionism was to bring. The steamships they most admired were those redolent of

---

39 Vladimir Tatlin was not exactly short of cogs and ratchets in the brainbox himself. When the new revolutionary government in Russia wanted a post-war monument to the Third International (founded in Moscow in 1919 to rally the communists of the world behind the victorious Russian communist state and to inspire revolution worldwide) he designed an extraordinary metal structure 1300 feet high, a dynamic revolving spiral which embodied the very essence of revolution. At its base was a cube, a conference room, which would revolve once a year; above that, a pyramid containing offices would turn on its axis once a month; on top of that, a cylinder rotating once a day would be a centre for administration and propaganda – which can of course reverse its message in an hour or even every minute. This triumph of Constructivist aesthetics was never built; the authorities were suspicious of it, and instead academician Shchusev provided them with a stolid solid-looking mausoleum which, being no fun at all, sat heavily on its site to express the suppression of the spirit, the heavy-handed oppression that was to characterise the new regime, as eloquently as Tatlin's proposal expressed earlier revolutionary aspirations.

sail; the public buildings they most admired were those reminiscent of cathedrals; the cars they most admired were those of 'the carriage trade'. It was thus entirely appropriate that 1906 should have seen the launching not only of the first *Dreadnought* but also of the first 40/50hp Rolls-Royce.

Like Tatlin and Ford, Royce had a head full of machinery – but none of it was allowed out until every known convention had been applied to its perfection, and only when convention had been exhausted was anything unconventional to be considered. The 40/50, which became famous as the Silver Ghost, was thus entirely ordinary in its administration and equally extraordinary in its execution, the one and only car that in its own times could truly be called the best car in the world.

That fact – or c   f   *   were numerous Frenchmen, not to mention dignitaries and heads   launay-Belleville its equal – did not automatically   olls-Royce to all who could afford one. The most   es looked somewhat askance at the Rolls-Royce, cc   image (the result of various competition ventures   ind suspecting its buyers of being a little raffish.

When the 40/50   mber 1906, it was one of 434 different models disp   0 to £2500. Earlier that year the new four-cylinde   iritain for sale at £125, while the dismayed British   ieap could be any good. The laws of supply an   ell enough understood and expounded by Ford

'The automob   ipite of its price because there were more than en   ited output of the then new industry . . . The automobile of the present is making good because the price has been reduced just enough to add sufficient new customers to take care of the increased output . . . The automobile of the future must be enough better than the present car to beget confidence in the man of limited means and enough lower in price to insure sales for the enormously increased output. The car of the future, the car for the people, the car that any man can own . . . is coming sooner than most people expect . . . The market for a low-priced car is unlimited.'

A car for the people! Here was revolution indeed, one for which the classless, rootless – and, when it came to material novelty, fearless – American people was hungry. They would not wait for roads to carry them, for fortunes to pay for them, nor for knowledge to understand them; they wanted them now, and therefore they wanted them cheap and simple. In 1902 the USA had one car to every 1.5 million citizens; in 1905 it had one to every 65,000; by 1908 the proportion would be one to every 800. In 1906, the USA supplanted France as the greatest manufacturer of cars.

Widespread economic depression hit most manufacturing countries in 1907. Italy, which had built 8870 cars in 1905, was left with only 20 brands out of more than 60, of which 40 had their homes in Turin. Despite this, 1907 and 1908 were technically enterprising. In Germany, Daimler used an overhead camshaft to operate all the valves of a Mercédès. In France, Sizaire improved their independent front suspension to an acceptable sliding-pillar form, and ran an engine at 4000 ft/min mean piston velocity, a speed that has inexplicably remained the conventional limit ever since[40]; Levavasseur devised petrol injection into the ports of an aero-engine (the Wright *Flyer* had a more rudimentary form of injection when it made the first powered flight[41] in 1903); and Houdaille brought out hydraulic suspension dampers. In England, the Skinner brothers made the first constant-vacuum carburettor, the SU; and the Ferodo firm (founded by a man named Frood) dismissed all the trials of everything from leather to camel-hair by establishing asbestos as the best material for lining brakes. In Switzerland, Büchi invented the turbocharger – specifically for diesel engines, be it noted. In the USA, Lee Chadwick made a centrifugal supercharger to improve the breathing of the six-cylinder engine in the latest of his high-priced, high-quality cars. It was all adventurous and enterprising, but none of it was more so than the event which outweighed all others in 1908, the launch of the mass-produced $850 Ford model T.

---

40 In the 1990s Honda raised this limit (even in what were ostensibly touring cars) by 20%, but outside the reckless realms of racing no other manufacturer has seemed avid to do likewise.

41 So much, in the overdone business of who did what first, is a matter of definition. The author is not merely questioning how one defines fuel injection; but the reader might usefully consider the relative importance of the first powered flight and the first man-carrying flight, both of which took place long before the Wright Brothers' 1903 effort – and what, among all the prescriptive requirements of distance and height and control, constitutes *flight*?

It looked too flimsy to endure the tribulations of life in the American wilderness, but its exiguous structure was deceptive. Ford's quest for better materials had led to the use of vanadium steel and of heat treatments which so enhanced the properties of the metal that lightness could be combined with strength. Production efficiency was as tirelessly sought, and production accelerated all the way, reaching 2000 cars a month in 1909. Rather than transport whole cars all over huge America, Ford took to dispatching them in 'knocked-down' parts to assembly plants from Los Angeles to Long Island, and then to his first overseas plant at Trafford Park, Manchester, where Britain's first industrial estate had been as significant a creation as Hampstead Garden Suburb, initiated in 1907, two years before the passing of the Housing and Town Planning Act. Trafford Park built 3081 cars in 1912; Detroit built 82,400, whereas the entire British motor industry made only 23,200.

Producing cars on Ford's scale had far more effect than the mere eventual provision, as had been forecast earlier by William Durant, of half a million cars for the American people each year. Ford's annual orders for material included 12 million billets of hickory for wheel-spokes and 400,000 hides of leather. Think what the first of those meant to the timberlands of America, or what the second meant to the meat trade centred not very far away in Chicago. Then think what effect such commodity orders might have on the deals done with smaller customers.

The economies of scale were being recognised as clearly as they were being demonstrated. Durant's group, General Motors, had been dragged down by some of its duller constituents until the bankers had to take over in 1910 and eject him. In 1912, with a new president, named Nash, and a new works manager, named Chrysler, and shorn of the loss-making companies, GM made a superb recovery. One of its most profitable members was Cadillac, which in 1912 introduced the electric starter[42]. The car for the people would get it soon – and then women might aspire to be included among the people.

It may not be true that it was the self-starter which brought women into motoring. It was the fancy new magneto, or the alternative battery/coil ignition system, that made cars hard to start; with the older trembler coil, the task was often easier. Still, the electric starter meant far more than Aquila-Italiana's novelty of aluminium pistons, or Peugeot's deployment of two overhead camshafts operating four valves per cylinder, both of which developments also occurred in 1912. But the year before, Ernest Rutherford at Cambridge University had proposed a new model for the atom; and the year after, resorting to Max Planck's quantum theory, Niels

Bohr had solved the one doubt that beset Rutherford's proposition, and gave us the atom's modern image. The idea was not exactly a self-starter (the problem to be explained had really been that the atom should not be a self-stopper) but it was destined to take us a lot further than anything from Cadillac.

Yet Cadillac found a place ahead of atomic science in the annals of warfare. An armoured fighting vehicle based on a Cadillac chassis proved very effective in dealing with guerrillas on the Mexican border in 1915, and there were armoured cars in Europe before that. On the whole it was the heavy commercial vehicle that was seen as being likely to prove useful in war; bus and lorry chassis were recommended for adaptation, just as they had been for service with fire brigades some years earlier, with Daimler in Germany taking great pains to determine exactly what was wanted before building special-purpose vehicles in their truck works at Marienfelde.

The lorry and the omnibus were two most eloquent expressions of the idea that the motor vehicle should serve the people. The taximeter cab was perhaps another; and it was the first to do notable service to the nation. It all happened so quickly, once the trigger had been pulled on a fateful midsummer Sunday in Sarajevo[43]. Trotsky called war 'the locomotive of history', and what did that mean but movement?

Things moved very fast throughout July 1914; and when, her ultimatum to Germany having expired on 3 August, Britain rushed to the defence of Belgium, the German advance did little more than falter. Within a month, the army of von Kluck was at Meaux and ready to storm Paris, where five battalions of infantry were mustered at *les Invalides*. Desperate General Gallieni, promising the meter fare plus 27%, requisitioned all the taxis of the capital, a matter of 600 little two-cylinder Renaults. Into the valley of death drove the six hundred, or at least as far as Nanteuil,

---

42 There were self-starters earlier, mostly pneumatic. The most remarkable examples were fitted to the three very special and very large cars made (in 1908 and 1909) to Imperial order by Delaunay-Belleville for the Czar of all the Russias. Although fitted with vast and opulently heavy bodies, and powered by huge 11.65-litre engines, these cars could be started in gear and sent on their way without sound or hesitation. The important thing about this instant and noiseless getaway was not that it was at once impressive and decorous, but that for the Czar the moment of departure was always a time of danger, and any hesitation might provide an opportunity for an assassin. Lesser cars by Delaunay-Belleville, for lesser customers, had smaller air tanks, charged at lower pressure.

43 The Archduke Ferdinand was assassinated in the street. It was not the reason for the Great War; it was the occasion for it.

ferrying soldiers all through the night for a dawn attack that flung the surprised Germans back.

The car of the people never played such a part again. Staff cars were altogether higher-class affairs – Crossleys, Rolls-Royces and Vauxhalls[44] for the British, Mercédès for the Kaiser – because the light cars which had proliferated in Europe in the last prewar years, in an approach to popular motoring, were too frail and too hopelessly unreliable for the ardours of the Western Front. What Mr Winston Churchill demanded of the new Land Ships Committee in 1915 (when the production of private cars in Britain was stopped) was some kind of 'traction engine with feet' to straddle the trenches and break the armies' deadlock. The tank, which emerged a year later, was eventually to change the pattern of warfare; the car of the people could not. The people were too terribly pinned down: ancient warfare might not have been, as Arnold Toynbee suggested, the sport of kings, but it had never been the scourge of common people that it had now become.

For a quarter of a century, the people of Europe would be haunted by the memory of that relapse into barbaric depravity. It was a war that set aside Trotsky's dictum about locomotives, for it was a war of position, not of movement. It was, as Paul Valéry put it, a war fought by 'the man in the street dressed as a soldier'. Part of that dress, for that war of mud and laceration, of vermin and shellshock, was the steel helmet which the British infantryman euphemistically called his 'tin hat'. While Henry Ford went on making his Tin Lizzie, Tommy Atkins had a new use for vanadium steel.

---

44 When Field Marshal Allenby took possession of Jerusalem in December 1917, it was a Vauxhall that carried him to the city wall – and might have carried him through the gate, had not an aide tactfully pointed out that a previous saviour had entered riding a humble donkey. Allenby took the hint, dismounted from his car, and walked through the gateway.

CHAPTER 4

1916–25

Diversity is the propellor of evolution.

BRONOWSKI

INHERITING THE POSITION UPON THE death of Warren Harding in 1923, Calvin Coolidge became the 30th president of the United States of America, and was to preside over the nation through one of the most buoyant economic periods in all its history. He was not, however, the true author of what became known as the Coolidge prosperity; that was actually founded on America's industries (not least Ford's) being unscathed, and her credit being vastly enlarged, by the Great War.

On 5 March 1916 Britain introduced conscription: 6 million Britons were called to the colours, and another 3 million from the Empire. At the Somme alone, 400,000 would be lost in gaining about three miles' advance on a 20-mile front. As for the private motor car, now 30 years old as a feasible proposition, its production and use were stopped so that Britain could concentrate her efforts more single-mindedly. America, on the other hand – and, in more senses than one, on the other side – could not be summoned across the Atlantic and into battle for another thirteen months: in 1915 pacifist Henry Ford celebrated his millionth Model T, the US industry as a whole produced more than a million motor vehicles, and the pace was maintained if not quickened in the next year – and the year after that.

Despite the 'conscientious' objections of Mr Ford, Britain did get Model T chassis for military duty, which they did well; but, until the USA joined the war, they could only be obtained from Ford's overseas plants, two of which (in England and Ireland) were hardly in a position to refuse. The motor vehicle of the Great War was often no more than an ordinary car, sometimes adapted, sometimes not. There were lorries too, in those days well behind the car in technical evolution[45]; and there was the tank.

Without the motor industry, the tank could never have happened: the idea was as old as Leonardo da Vinci, but neither the age of muscle nor the age of steam had been able to make it viable. The age of internal combustion did it, and the tank

A German transport column advances near Bapaume in March 1918. Apart from the staff-officer's car, almost everything is horse-drawn. The German army was still making extensive use of draught horses (and even occasionally of oxen, for pulling heavy artillery) 27 years later.

in turn did something else, which was to liberate the 'poor bloody infantryman' from the sickening stasis of the trenches, the final stalemate of frontal pedestrian warfare. The horse could not do it; in fact by this time most of the horses, so thick on the ground at the start of the war, were under the ground. The aircraft could not yet do it. The warship, useless except to guard supply routes, may even have made matters worse. The tank, a glorified armoured motor car, eventually broke the nauseating deadlock (*You've never seen rats until you've seen rats that were born, and fed, and grew, in human flesh*) of which Passchendaele was the most ghastly example.

The motor vehicle did other things in that socially most revolutionary of wars. Most of them can be passed over, but one thing remained when the war was over: it

---

45 Like the omnibus, the lorry was still condemned to run on solid tyres.

Citroën half-tracked vehicles crossed the Sahara when that undertaking still seemed impossible, in the winter of 1924–1925. It was a cause for celebration and, as in this poster, an opportunity for contemporary art.

had enabled multitudes of common men to experience and understand the motor vehicle, to see that it was something that could quite possibly figure in their future lives. Those who thought that the standard of living was a political matter came back to their 'land fit for heroes' disillusioned and bitter; those who thought it a matter of industrial progress had reason to be confident of the car in their future.

The Great War brought a pause to the evolution of the motor car. During that pause, the war did wonders for technology; a remarkably large proportion of those wonders were to advance communications, of which the motor car (by giving an individual or a group the mobility to go and learn, or to go and tell) was a part that profited exceedingly. Marconi's first radio transmission[46] had only been four years before the war, and for a long time the radio (like the telephone) would be something that only the relatively well-to-do would enjoy. In Britain and most of Europe, that was still true of the car, too, and the tremendous advances in materials and machining, in tribology and production technology, that had been spawned most lavishly by the new aircraft industry were applied with enthusiasm and occasional understanding to the betterment of the car that only the better-off could enjoy.[47]

In the USA, people were simply not prepared to wait; they would wait neither for roads nor for instruction, neither for research nor for refinement. Coolidge was to promise them 'a chicken in every cooker, a car in every garage' – but they would not wait for garages either. They wanted cars, and they wanted them forthwith.

That was when the American car acquired its now traditional characteristics. It had to be capable of working, and keeping on working – no matter how badly – in an environment that could be far more hostile than anywhere in Europe. It had to endure not only the meteorological and topographical hazards of north America, but also to endure the casual abuse and the stubborn ignorance of that proudly independent fellow the American man. Nobody was going to tell him how to drive (indeed, there might be nobody within a hundred miles who knew how to) and he was not going to

---

46 How elegantly does Marconi's example illumine the long evolutionary chain from abstract theory to substantial practice! Marconi built upon the work of Hertz (b.1857), who first generated electromagnetic waves artificially. Two years before Hertz was born Gauss died, having provided for him by applying mathematics to electricity and magnetism. The mathematics came, via the theoretical work of James Clerk Maxwell who was an approximate contemporary of Gauss, from Leibnitz early in the 18th century.

47 The rest had to make do with public transport, which was by now a combination of railway train and omnibus. Its hazards and frustrations were sometimes acute even then, as *The Times* reported on 7 October 1919 of the conditions in London on the day after the end of a rail strike: 'In the morning, many people resolved that walking to town would be quicker than waiting for Underground or suburban trains. Long queues were formed at stations. Trains were crammed. Some passengers saw three go out of the station before they could find room on a fourth . . . In the evening, both tramway-cars and omnibuses were again the objects of the familiar struggle . . . The scene on Blackfriars-bridge in the middle of the morning was marked by a volume of goods traffic . . . The length of the bridge was occupied . . . by drays, lorries, wagons, and carts, in double lines of three and four abreast. Without being particularly clever in his calling, a gymnast could have crossed the road by the vehicle tops, so tightly were they packed together.'

read about it in books: when the American army came to Europe in 1917, the US government (which at that time was finding it difficult enough to coerce its soldiers into brushing their teeth, a practice alien to the USA) discovered for the first time how alarmingly illiterate their nation was.

The car had to endure all this abuse and more: fuel that varied in quality, in ways that were not understood but were grossly evident, from the west coast to the east; rutted roads that tore the wheels off any car with a track other than 56½ inches – the same as the railway gauge of Britain; and mechanics whose qualities were the greatest variable of all. So the domestic car became a big open tourer with a lot of suspension travel, very little in the way of brakes or steering finesse, and with a large engine so low-tuned and incredibly flexible that all the multitudes who could not shift gears did not need to – and with the corollary that it was a fearful gas-guzzler. One supposed authority warned that, because of the thirst of the ever more prolific car, the world was likely to run out of petroleum in 1932[48].

So in 1920 there were 9 million cars in America, while in England (which mustered only 78,000 at the end of the war) 40% of the cars on the roads were Model T Fords, flooding in at the rate of 33,000 a year. Taxation smartly put a stop to these imports, but the American industry carried on unchecked by such trivia.

The extraordinary thing was that people were insisting on buying cars even though times were perilously hard. Whether it was the euphoria of 1919 that was responsible, or the influenza epidemic of the same year which killed more people world-wide than the Great War had done, the twenties began – as they were to end – with a terrible slump. It hit Japan and then America in 1920, Britain and Germany (the latter already tortured[49] by the Gallic iniquities of the 1919 Versailles Treaty) in 1921; ruin struck almost everywhere that was not already ruinous – unemployment was never less than one worker in ten[50] in Britain throughout the whole period between the two world wars – but, grunt as they might under these fardels, people insisted on buying cars. The car manufacturer could say what Matthew Boulton, in partnership with James Watt to make steam engines, said to Boswell in 1776: 'I sell here, sir, what all the world desires to have – power.'

Selling was what mattered, when production was gathering such momentum. The motor industry became by far the most important customer of the advertising industry, made it rich, encouraged it to be clever, and provided experience which enabled it to apply its newly honed skills to the selling of all manner of consumer goods, with incalculable effect upon the standard of living. In some countries the two industries backed each other so effectively that motor manufacture became the most important segment of industry. This was hardly yet the case in Britain, where in 1925 a notable piece of political misjudgement prompted revaluation of the pound and a return to the gold standard, the idea being that Britain would revert to her traditional role as international broker, growing rich on the world money market rather than by industrial production. Even so, there were 134 different British makes on show at Olympia in 1919, most of them despicably ramshackle.

Standards were higher in France, where the 1919 Paris Salon had a month earlier revealed some superb engineering. Far and away the best example was the new H6B Hispano-Suiza from the firm that had revolutionised aero-engine design during the war, but in everything except sheer quality of manufacture the new Delage (and perhaps Italy's Lancia) could outface any other nation's offerings to the carriage trade, including the Rolls-Royce.

Was it the long straight roads of France that encouraged her manufacturers to produce the finest headlamps, as they did then and for another sixty years? One needs a decent memory today to recall the supremacy of lamps by Cibié and by Marchal, but in those days the legendary illuminators were those by the famed aeronaut Louis Blériot. By 1920, and thanks as much to the progress made in electrics by the Americans as to that made by the French in optics, electric lamps were becoming the norm, already pushing light before some three-quarters of the world's cars.

When the first cars had taken their first faltering sallies upon the road, they did so only in daylight. It was only to get them home after dark, in the event of some not unexpected breakdown, that cars before 1900 often carried candle-powered carriage lamps. The oil lamps which supplanted them were not much better, though they survived a remarkably long time as auxiliary side- and rear lamps, and finally as the so-called 'opera lamps', fancy coloured and cut-glass things used as courtesy lamps to assist someone alighting from a car in the dark, supposedly outside a theatre. What really cast a light for serious driving, though, were acetylene lamps.

---

48 Experts are saying such things still. Stupidly, we believe them still. Almost certainly there will still be petroleum when we no longer need it.

49 One of their problems was a lack of crucial materials. Such German cars (there were not many) as could be exported in 1918 went from their makers without tyres on their wheels.

50 Unemployment in Britain reached its peak, affecting one worker in five, in 1932.

These relied on the principle of dripping water onto pieces of calcium carbide, the reaction producing acetylene gas which could be ignited with a match, whereupon it burned with a brilliant white light. This, it was claimed, was the nearest thing to artificial daylight; but daylight never smelled so intriguing and exciting as acetylene. One might have to proggle the jets at the focus of the reflectors with a slender but stiff wire to clean them from time to time; one might have constantly to fiddle with the water valve to ensure that the supply never failed nor flooded; but the light was something at which to wonder. The paraphernalia of carbide and water tank and valve might be built into the structure of the lamp together with the reflector and jet, in which case the thing was known as a headlamp; or, as an alternative much preferred for high-powered cars in France and America, the gas generator might be mounted on the running board where it was much more accessible to the driver, while a long rubber tube carried the gas to the burners in the lamps proper, which were then known as projectors. Sometimes of vast proportions, often of brilliant performance, the best acetylene lamps might be the nearest practical alternatives to the electric-arc searchlight for a motor vehicle. They were the visible sign of a fast and powerful car[51], at a time when speed and power were the automobilistic paraphrase of fame and riches.

What was more important was what was happening at the other end of the gamut, where an absolutely brilliant little man (petulantly described by Louis Renault, the even tenor of whose meanness had been grievously disturbed, as *le petit Juif*) had set about mass-production in the style of Henry Ford. This was André Citroën, erstwhile chief engineer of Mors and more lately the wartime saviour of France's ammunition industry, who had in months set up Europe's first real line-assembly plant[52] and took 20,000 orders at the 1919 Salon for his Type A tourer (which incidentally was the first low-priced car to embody electric lighting and starting), satisfying half of them within a year. His affairs went so well that in 1922 he took over Clement-Bayard and began production of the three-seater 5CV, the eternally admirable Cloverleaf, a light car designed to endure the bestial servitude imposed by the French peasantry and so good that Opel hurried to build it under licence as the Laubfrosch.

It was less influential than an even lighter car which emerged in England that same year. The idea of a real car in miniature was not new (Peugeot, Singer, and others less notable had tried it) but Herbert Austin saw how to take trade from the makers of the ghastly little cyclecars, and the unsociable motorcycle-and-sidecar combinations, that had provided the only hope of mobility for the impoverished working-class Briton. Occupying the same space as a combination, the 1922 Austin Seven was a real car; at £165 it was sure of success; and by its pert adequacy (though in some respects, such as its fierce clutch and feeble brakes, it was barely adequate) and its enticing example it gave hope of emergence from the dark for multitudes all over the world. It was built under licence in France (Rosengart), in Germany (Dixi, later BMW), in the USA (Bantam) and even in Japan, where Datsun, with an episodic history so far distinguished only for its opportunism, got back into car manufacture with it. They sold three abroad in 1925 – the first Japanese car exports . . .

Perhaps never, and certainly not until the 1960s, was there so fruitful a time for car design as in those racked and roaring early twenties. The Great War had forced the pace of engineering progress, especially in aviation, in ways from which the motor industry could subsequently profit for years. In fact the very existence of the aeroplane helped the car: when the car was the very newest thing, people were wary of it as something experimental and hardly a sound investment, but once the aeroplane had taken over as the extensor of human ambitions, the car became quite acceptable.

What developments there were! New materials proliferated, notably Y alloy (which started in Germany, was developed in the USA, and was finally perfected in Britain's National Physical Laboratory) and the Elektron magnesium alloys (which followed precisely the opposite route!), while the increased use of nickel in steels and electrical alloys, as well as for plating, made those few countries which had plenty of

---

51 As early as 1927 they were supplanted in this by the electric Lucas P100, a headlamp of serious brilliance which remained in the catalogues until the 1950s. The '100' was alleged by unscrupulous marketing men to represent the candlepower achieved; the 'P', believe it or not, indicated that this fine-looking construction of brass and glass and silver was intended for Posh cars!

52 His factory on the quai de Javel in Paris was a model of enlightenment, not least in its thoughtful provision for the women who began to do so much factory work during the war, many of them (when there were so many men who were sadly missed) remaining after it. There were groceries and other shops on the premises, crèches for little children, and proper medical facilities. Considering the scale on which he worked, there was probably never an individual industrialist as great or as good as he, though certain corporations such as Fiat and the Japanese came to exercise a similar paternalism.

it (such as Canada) suddenly richer. Plating itself was enriched by the commercial availability from 1925 of chromium[53], destined to do as much for the embellishment of cars as for the development of hard and stainless steels. There was an intensive study of engine balance and vibration (American engineers were outstanding in this essentially mathematical work, Rolls-Royce abysmal), and of lubrication and bearings – with Bugatti's steel-backed shell bearings for his aero-engines the source of salvation for future high-output car engines.

What mattered even more than the commodities, as always, were the people. The war had made millions familiar with machinery, and made thousands keen on engineering; it was the early post-war engineers who really did wonders. The most brilliant team of mechanical engineers in the industry was in the Fiat design office up to 1922, after which the rest of Europe enticed many of them away to lead and inspire future generations under other brand names; but America, despite an overall low standard, had a smattering of men who approached genius.

Duesenberg's hydraulic brakes were actually the idea of a Scot named Loughead (inevitably corrupted to Lockheed), and Wright's sodium-cooled exhaust valves were thought up by an emigrant from Newcastle (via Coventry, where he worked for Siddeley) named Sam Heron, the inventor later of the Heron head[54]. But it was America's own Walter Midgley who discovered the use of tetraethyl lead as a petrol additive for suppressing knock (incidentally creating new problems for makers of valves, seats, guides and spark plugs) in 1922. In five years another gifted American, GM's 'Doc' Kettering (who gave us the standard ignition system), would hit upon isooctane as a blending agent, following Midgley's work and leading to a coherent octane-rating system.

In the meantime, the man in the street – and especially the rural American street – was more impressed by what he could see than by what he might fail to hear. In 1923 GM and DuPont together evolved nitrocellulose[55] spray painting: at once, bodies could be mass-produced much faster and cheaper[56].

This was most welcome to the man in the street because the street itself was no longer so blindingly dusty. The friable water-bound surfaces of old had proved incapable of enduring motor traffic; the dust that rose in the wake of every car was more unpopular than any emission of which the car has since been accused. Methods of top-dressing varied all over the world: oil-bound road surfaces worked in California, bitumen was spread everywhere, and each locality tried to use local materials. Germany's blue basalt blocks were noisy but had surprisingly good wet grip, whereas the natural rubber tyres of the day skidded as though on ice in south-west England, where Bridport pebbles from Dorset were rolled on to road-top tar and wore to a fine enduring polish. The tarred woodblock streets of London[57], greased by oil-droppings and horse-droppings alike, were made even more treacherous by the lacing of tramlines which still served those who could not yet afford to drive themselves.

But the dust had gone. Motoring was cleaner, and except in the hottest regions such as Italy and the southern states of America the closed car began to offer more attractions to the everyday user. One still had to dress up for warmth (the heater was yet to come, though too much heat sometimes filtered up through the floorboards of many a rattletrap), but one could dress smartly and in ordinary clothes. And there was a new way of building car bodies, a way that made the saloon more attractive still, that had been introduced by yet another brainy American engineer, a Philadelphia graduate by the name of Edward Gowan Budd.

Specialising since his youth in the technology of pressed steel, Budd had plenty of experience ranging from pulleys to Pullman railcars. As good a salesman as an

---

53 Chromium had been discovered by a French chemist, Louis Nicolas Vauquelin, as early as 1798. The pressures brought to bear on technology by the Great War led to its use for coating projectiles, and when swords were later turned into ploughshares there was uncovered a huge market for this brilliant material. Many a purist found its decorative use repellent: Gabriel Voisin, who always yearned for the integrity of his cars to be beyond reproach, declared that he woud not use chromium plate until Cartier sold artificial pearls.

54 In essentials this comprised a flat-bottomed cylinder head, bearing perpendicular poppet-valves, beneath which the necessary combustion-chamber space was shaped as a depression in the crown of the piston. It enjoyed some popularity in cars of the 1960s.

55 All over the world, but especially in the great arsenals of war, there were factories languishing that had once been busy creating high explosives. Their basic workstuff was nitrogen, worked up into such products as nitro-glycerine and the more manageable cellulose nitrate or guncotton. Life might be at their mercy in guns and bombs, or reshaped with each blast that divests a quarry or diverts a river; and mercy is in the life-support from the fertilisers which are their close chemical relatives, or life itself enlivened by the chemical 'dopes' such as nitro-benzene used to enhance the power of a racing engine. They are all part of the nitrogen cycle which makes our food grow in the ground and makes us rot in it.

56 By drying so very quickly, nitrocellulose paint needed no resting-time in the storehouses where bodies painted in the old way had to be accommodated. In effect this space no longer had to be rented – or alternatively it could be put to more profitable use.

57 Setright nearly fell off when his Ariel Arrow motorcycle, new in 1960, skidded on the last of these woodblocks, in the Marylebone district.

engineer, he had persuaded Hupp in 1909 to adopt car-body panels pressed in the same way as the Budd steel railroad car bodies had been; but his most important success was in selling the idea on a far broader scale to Dodge, the first company to commit themselves to the principle for large-volume production. The first examples were open tourers for 1916, each built up (Budd was a master of welding technology too, and was mainly responsible for the adoption of arc welding) from about 1200 stampings, and there were 70,000 ordered for that year. By 1917 he had devised an all-steel 4-door saloon body, and when this went into production in 1919 it was the most important thing that happened in the motor industry in the entire decade. It did well for Dodge, who achieved record sales, and it did well for Budd, who found himself sympathetic to the assiduous wooing of André Citroën in France and William Morris in England. Morris, trying to undersell Austin and the rest, joined Budd in forming the Pressed Steel Company in Cowley, and soon found he had the answer to his problem.

The supercilious would sneer at these 'cheap tin boxes' for thirty years or more, but the engineering of those boxes was better than what had gone before them and was the foundation of the modern unitary-construction car. Add the new marvel of sprayed cellulose paint, and the man in the street would look no further. This was the era when, more crucially than in any other, the design of the car was determined by what the customer in his ignorance knew he wanted, rather than by what the engineer in his isolation thought he should have. It was the era when prejudice, ignorance, ambition and penury fixed the pattern of the motor car for so long that it could never entirely break the mould later. The common man was obsessed with his new little tin god, and understood but poorly what went on beneath its shiny skin.

There were always some uncommon men to be found, and to be pleased with elegant chassis and refined behaviour. The early twenties offered all manner of delights for such discerning customers, for whom knowing the radiators of Bugatti and Bentley was just the beginning. In Italy, while Fiat toppled the existing gods of Grand Prix racing with a series of dazzling new designs all growing out of the 1921 straight-8 which set the pattern for nearly all racing engines for decades to come, Lancia created a long-legged tourer so unconventional in every detail and so remarkable in every motion that the best of other road cars were to take years catching up with it: the 1923 Lambda was undoubtedly his masterpiece, and one of the most distinguished and meritorious cars of all time.

It probably mattered less, and certainly made much less commercial impact, than a car which made its debut in the USA in 1924. Leaving his vice-presidency of GM even quicker[58] than he reached it, Walter P Chrysler took over the ailing Maxwell company, kept it afloat, and then produced something that was the almost perfect compromise between European fastidiousness and American appetite. It had a high-compression engine with six cylinders, for goodness' sake, and a lovely tubular front axle which bore (as did the rear) hydraulic brakes and dampers. It was smart, it was fast, it was smooth and reliable (fully pressurized lubrication of all engine bearings was not all that common in those days, for instance, nor were aluminium pistons, but the Chrysler Six had both) and it made the new Chrysler Corporation $50 million in its first year. You buy a Ford for cheapness, went the new maxim, a Chevy for style, a Chrysler for engineering. If you bought anything else, whatever it was and wherever you were, in 1925 it hardly mattered very much: the American public, seeking to create new gods, had created giants.

In Italy it was less easy to see which had been the intention and which the result. Fiat might have employed the best team of engineers in the industry, as suggested earlier; but it also engaged the best architects to give expression to the best ideas of modern times, the best artists to depict in advertising posters and elsewhere the outcome of such brilliant engineers working in such stimulating buildings. Quite the most outstanding of all those buildings was the factory built on the edge of Turin, the company's birthplace, at Lingotto. Here was evidence of real civilisation in industry, a factory building in which mere economic necessity was dismissed as an inadequate criterion, a factory which declared that what was desirable was considered more important – and which implied that the same approach might have been taken in designing its products.

Seen in close-up, Fiat's Lingotto factory was an instructive and entrancing display in reinforced concrete ribbing, on the underside of each floor, of the lines of stress concentration in the structure. Seen as a functional whole, it was a remarkable conduit for line-assembly production, work beginning with basic components on the ground floor and continuing up spiral ramps to successive floor levels until the finished cars emerged on the roof, which was a test track with 'banked' or

---

58 Alfred P Sloan Jr, then head of General Motors, noted that Chrysler (of whom he thought highly) banged the door as he left.

Fiat and architect Matté-Trucco together created at Lingotto the most eloquent testimony to all that functional beauty, imaginative process, and modern materials, could mean to the burgeoning motor industry.

superelevated turnings at each end. Seen from a distance, from the air, it had the proportions, the decking and the clearly defined superstructure, of a great and ultramodern ocean liner. This breathtaking building, the work of Giacomo Matté-Trucco, was in action in 1919 and complete by 1923, and for a decade no other factory building – none of the Bauhaus jobs in Germany, nor the Boots pharmaceuticals factory at Beeston near Nottingham – could hold a candle to it. Certainly no mere car-factory approached its standards: other car-makers might claim that their products displayed the same visionary modernity as could be seen in the best of contemporary architecture, but only Fiat held fast to the conviction that art, like style and taste and manners, is to be cultivated in the home rather than picked up in the street.

CHAPTER 5

1926–35

The artist has always tried to reach the impossible with the least visible effort, and thus when he does succeed he makes the impossible practical, meaning within the reach of everybody.

PAUL JACQUES GRILLO

THE ROOTS OF THE MODERN MOTOR CAR – what it is, what it does, what it means – took hold shortly before motoring began its second half-century, and did so in three places. Radical revision of the motor industry, of its objectives and of the internal and external means whereby it pursued them, took place in the USA. Radical realignment of the place of the car in society was most notable in England. Radical regeneration in car design, deriving from notably recreational advances in technology, was remarkable in Germany.

This is not to say that significant developments did not occur elsewhere. They did, all over the world, because the whole world was eventually affected by the consequences of the economic slump which began with catastrophic suddenness in New York's Wall Street stock exchange in 1929.

Not long president, after Coolidge (perhaps aware of the earthquake pending beneath his feet) had suddenly announced his disinclination to continue in office, the famous erstwhile engineer Herbert Hoover had triumphantly trumpeted the end of poverty, assuring the American people that they had arrived on 'a plateau of permanent prosperity'. Just a month later, in one of the most bleak of all Octobers, all manner of records were sadly shattered: the first time 12 million shares were sold, it took more than four hours for the ticker-tape machine to catch up with the dealings. Hopes were shattered, and lives too; and as the shock-wave spread from its American epicentre to topple the stoutest of men and the bravest of commercial edifices in progressively remoter trading centres, the car was just one of many industrial projectiles that were forced to change course.

It was astonishing that the American car industry was able to weather the storm so well. But for the gigantism of General Motors, things might have been otherwise; and the size and strength of GM might have been inadequate, but for the life-or-death struggle forced upon it by the earlier slump which proved the Corporation's mettle.

In 1934 the majority of family cars could scarcely reach 60mph, and the land speed record stood at 254. In a brilliant and beautiful engineering collaboration between Fiat (who did the engine) and Macchi-Castoldi (responsible for the rest) the world speed record was raised in the air to 440.

Coming out of retirement, Pierre S duPont took over the presidential reins from founder William Durant, and by 1923 he had wrought sufficient miracles for him to be able to retire again, handing the reins to one of the quietest and most successful revolutionaries of all time, Alfred P Sloan Jr. If duPont stopped GM dying, Sloan made it live; and by 1926 he was making it very lively indeed. It was a lively time for American car-makers: the number of cars on the roads of the Union rose by a million a year to reach 19.7 million in 1929, a year in which the American industry made a record 4.5 million new cars.

A large number of those were Chevrolets, large enough to make Richard H Grant, transferred from Delco Light to promote GM's baseline brand, the top salesman in the USA. He figured in a tale (recounted by Maurice Olley, the Rolls-Royce man who came to GM and created the new sciences of ride and handling) which illustrates how GM sat tight and weathered the Wall Street storm. In 1932 Olley campaigned for the adoption of independent front suspension, at the same time as another department was working on a steplessly variable transmission. Early in 1933 both teams were ready to demonstrate their achievements to the bosses, driving Sloan and the others in a brace of i.f.s. Cadillacs and a Buick with the new transmission. Olley's account of the subsequent discussion was eloquent of the strain they were all suffering:

'. . . in March 1933 there was not a bank open in the United States, and anyone who owned a farm was thankful that at least he could eat. Under these circumstances Dick Grant's reaction was not surprising. He turned down the transmission, and the hundred dollar cost that went with it, as something that a Buick buyer could very well do without. "But", said he, "if I could have a ride like you've shown us for a matter of fifteen bucks, I'd find the money somehow." '

Where once there was only the twittering of birds on the marshes, observed the advertisements, there is now the roar of machinery. This was reckoned a good thing in 1931, and so was this Model AA light truck, the first vehicle to emerge from Ford's new English factory at Dagenham.

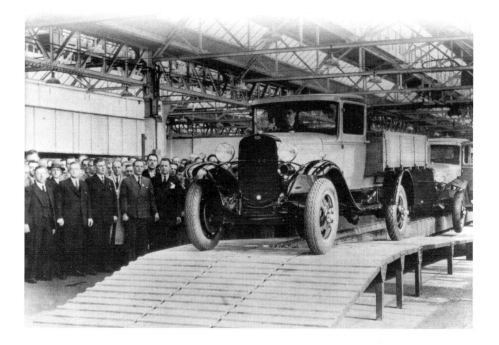

Ford hired a small army of thugs as strikebreakers. During the Prohibition era, organised crime had become Detroit's second biggest industry; in 1937 the underworld could provide all manner of services . . .

In November 1933, as evidence that the money had been found (and it meant a courageous commitment of millions), 1934 model GM cars from Cadillac down to Chevrolet appeared at the New York Show with independent front suspension.

Some European cars had had it for years[59], and it was on the east side of the Atlantic that the first really notable step was taken towards automatic transmission, when Daimler in Britain installed the fluid coupling (invented in 1907 by Föttinger) together with the Wilson 'Preselector' self-changing epicyclic gearbox behind the 12 sleeve-valved cylinders of the stately Double Six. The fluid coupling had been used in bus transmissions since 1926 – the year when Fiat designer Fornaca invented the

---

59 Sloan had been impressed, and approached André Dubonnet whose patented i.f.s. was one of two types initially fostered by GM before they settled for wishbones.

Parking attendants go back a long way. This 1933 Morris Minor is going back in its home town, Oxford.

strut suspension of which the modern MacPherson variety is merely a development.

Comfort and convenience were now paramount in the American customer's priorities, once he had decided how much he could spend on his car. In 1927 Packard, whose V12 engines had been inspired by a Sunbeam aero-engine imported at the start of the Great War, introduced hypoid bevel gears in the back axle to lower the transmission line and reduce or remove the hump that its tunnel raised in the floor of the cabin. Stutz briefly tried power-assisted steering in that same year, but the American woman was not yet doing that much driving and the American man was not yet ready to admit that his muscles might not be up to any task.

His brain/limb coordination was a different matter: easy gear-shifting won his instant approval. Cadillac introduced synchromesh (based on a design by Thompson) in 1928, and by 1932 it had spread throughout GM even to Vauxhall, and incidentally to Rolls-Royce. In the old Model T Ford the gears had been epicyclic and therefore in constant mesh, but the Model T was dying from Ford's insistence on never changing it.

Henry Ford showed his colours most truly during the later slump and during ensuing labour troubles[60], when he was seen capable of being truly vicious; but already in the middle of the 1920s he was proving unable to reconcile his ideas of what the people should be buying with the facts of what people actually wanted to buy. Obstinately he kept the Model T coming down the line[61], but it was becoming increasingly difficult to move it any further. The line stopped in 1927, after 15.5 million had been made (a production record that was not to be beaten until the long years of the Volkswagen[62]), and the Model A Ford which followed several months later was blandly conventional.

The Dodge brothers had also insisted that they would never change anything, and had been forced to recant in 1923. It was on that evidence that GM argued the merits of an annual model change to stimulate sales.

Indeed, selling accounted for three of the four most important new factors which transformed the practices of the American industry in the mid-1920s. Only one of these, as they were listed by Sloan, had anything to do with the design of the car, and this was the closed body, which not only expanded the use of the car by making it a practically comfortable all-year-round vehicle, but also added substantially to the price the customer was prepared to pay. The other three factors were purely marketing techniques without any engineering foundation: the annual model change, instalment selling (beginning in 1915, it reached 65% of new car sales in 1925), and the trading-in of used cars.

It was a great time for new ideas. Aldous Huxley was not to publish his *Brave New World* until 1932, the year in which Rutherford and his colleagues set about splitting the atom; but already in 1926 keen photographers were turning to the extraordinary new and small Leica camera, designed by Oscar Barnack who saw how to exploit the length of 35mm film stock in a 'miniature' camera that would be able to use wide-aperture lenses and fast shutter speeds. The next fifteen years would see the golden age of black-and-white photography, featuring not only a new and

---

60 The huge scale of organised crime in the USA could not entirely be accounted for by its activities countering Prohibition, though it was estimated that Prohibition itself cost the nation much more than the Great War had; and by 1929 bootlegging, employing fifty thousand people and grossing over $300 million a year, was Detroit's second biggest industry. Professional criminals specialising in violence also found trade in the labour racketeering industry, in which the unions and the employers both hired gangs of thugs to reinforce their arguments. It was a highly organised business.

61 Assembly time for the Model T had been cut by this time to 5.8 hours, from 12.5 in 1910, by persistent application of Taylor's time-and-motion theories.

62 In terms of longevity, if not of production quantities, certain Fiat models did very well. The Nuova 500 ran from 1957 to 1975, its successor the 126 from 1972 to 1992, and the 1980 Panda was still going in 2000.

journalistically candid style but also expressions of the architectural and surrealist ideas currently suffusing the art world.

That was not the only development involving 35mm film: in 1927 there was the first sound film at the kinema. In that same year came the first solo flight by Charles Lindbergh across the Atlantic[63]. A year earlier still, R H Goddard fired the first liquid-fuel rocket, an event which history may judge more significant than the work of Dr Otto just fifty years previously. And in Britain, large portions of which were cloaked in poverty, the TUC in that same 1926 had the idea of calling a general strike of all workers as an expression of solidarity with the miners, whose latest grievances were contributing to an average of 45 million working days lost in industrial disputes each year from 1919 to 1926.

Iam nova progenies demittitur ab alto: *the return of Germany to GP racing in 1934 was marked by astonishing new displays of modern technology. One was the Auto Union, designed by Porsche from the ideas of Rosenberger, and here driven by Varzi (ahead of Chiron in an old-school Alfa Romeo) on the very fast circuit at Pescara in the 1935 race for the Coppa Acerbo.*

On page 67: *With all the lavish spectacle typical of Nazi occasions by 1935, Hitler opens the first stretch of the Frankfurt–Darmstadt Reichsautobahn, taking the salute from a supercar bearing the name of a grand-daughter of an Hungarian rabbi.*

Inspired by the Russian Revolution and organised from what was nicknamed 'Red Clydeside' (Glasgow), left-wing militants had been demanding better conditions even while their brothers were falling on the Western Front, but the General Strike of 1926 was a debacle for organised labour – the parliamentary follow-up was not repealed until 1946 – and collapsed, a total fiasco, in less than two weeks. One of the most important agencies in breaking the strike, by ensuring the mobility of the people and the supply of their necessities, was the motor vehicle. Lorries, buses, and cars[64] galore deprived the strike of its intended impact, their drivers and passengers demonstrating the moderation of a majority who preferred social peace to social war.

Life in Britain did not thereby become easier; but life in Britain was changing, and would continue to change, so fast that it was hard to find proper criteria whereby to judge it. A vast redistribution of industries and people was taking place: the traditional area of industry was in decay, while new sectors expanded elsewhere. Northern England, South Wales and the Scottish Lowlands produced half the national output in 1924; by 1935 their share was only 37%, about the same as London and the Midlands. In the same period, output per head grew by a third, faster than in the Victorian heyday.

Many of the products were new and sophisticated, while traditional things such as cotton and ships dwindled. The most extraordinary fact, evident in the USA but even more marked in Britain, was that despite mass unemployment there was actually a rapid rise in the average standard of living, because the wages of those at work and the salaries of the middle classes rose proportionately with productivity and the growth of the economy. British households bought 38,000 vacuum cleaners in 1930, 410,000 in 1935. No less urgently, they bought cars, with an insistence that may have seemed suicidal but was probably self-preserving.

---

63 The same journey was to be made in one-tenth of the time in 1961 by the prodigious delta-winged Convair Hustler bomber. This American performance was put into a shocking perspective by a Russian one in that same year, when in half the time it took for the Hustler to cross the Atlantic, Major Gagarin orbited the planet in the first manned earth satellite.

64 There were no newspapers, so the government issued its own daily broadsheet to keep the public aware of what was going on. The delivery of it to provincial centres was entrusted to a fleet of high-powered upper-crust cars (almost all of them either 40/50hp Rolls-Royces or 30/98 Vauxhalls) volunteered and driven by high-powered upper-crust gentlemen. They were not expected to observe speed limits, and some of them had a quite adventurous time running the gauntlet of pickets.

The cars on British roads numbered one million for the first time in 1930. Not all were truly British cars: GM, having failed to acquire Austin, bought Vauxhall in 1927, and in 1929 Ford began work on their big new factory at Dagenham. Two years and £5 million later, it opened; but sales were poor, because existing Fords were not suitable for Britons who were poor. In a frantic burst of creativity, Ford designers threw together an inspired if horrid little hack known as the Model Y, which was gratefully rushed into production and promptly gave a tremendous fillip to the 8–9hp category which was to dominate sales for years to come. Morris made a blatant copy of it, but Ford were the first to pare the price down to £100.

At the same time as the Y, and just as quickly, Ford dealt with another more domestic problem. Sales in the USA were suffering because the Chevrolet had six cylinders. Henry Ford, publicly blustering 'I've got no use for a car with more spark plugs than a cow has teats!', privately tried to design a five-cylinder engine[65], but was not a good enough engineer to manage it (indeed he was not really an engineer at all, however well he might rate as a mechanic), so he decided that he must have a V8. It was not to be an elaborate affair with separate blocks, as other American V8s since the 1907 Hewitt had been; he did what others said was not feasible, creating a monobloc of cylinders and crankcase. In 1932, the buyer of the new Ford V8 could believe that he was experiencing what advertisements assured him was 'the greatest thrill in motoring': none but the wealthy could have known such vivid acceleration.

The taste for it was very rapidly acquired, the first million examples being sold by June 1934 with another million in the following year: soon all American Fords were V8s (there were meaner engines for heavily taxed Europe, and from October 1934 a V12 from Ford's Lincoln division for those who would pay twice the cost of a Ford V8 for the luxury and distinction of the Lincoln) and all American motorists demanded similar performance. They did not so much want their motoring to be fast, though the Ford could reach 80mph, as they wanted it to be easy.

The same was true in Britain. The priorities were the same. Price came first, comfort next, appearances third. Engineering mattered little; roadholding, handling, speed and other dynamic properties seldom mattered at all. As the manufacturers strove to satisfy these demands, a new cynicism expressed itself in car design. Radiators grew more and more imposing; bonnets were tall, and sometimes outrageously long, echoing the proportions of steam-locomotive boilers and signifying corresponding power, even though the engine caught cowering in the shady shallows when the bonnet was lifted might be the most pusillanimous little low-compression

side-valve affair that could conceivably propel the car. The chassis was often exiguous, the suspension rudimentary, but the passenger compartment would have plenty of legroom and the exterior would be as ostentatious as possible. It was disgusting, albeit for explicable and possibly good reasons, and although the industry's products have never since been as consistently awful – not even in America – as the majority became in the 1930s, motoring has never wholly recovered from the blight which then settled on it.

In Germany things were different. In Germany, in the 1920s, things were so bad that they could only get better. When an able and proud nation is humiliated, it exerts itself strenuously to regain self-respect, as most brilliantly exemplified by Japan in the last third of the nineteenth century. Germany, what was left of it, suffered intense humiliation in the 1920s: the blind vindictiveness of the 1919 Treaty of Versailles not only set Germany an impossible economic task but also denied Germany the means whereby to try to accomplish it.

In the autumn of 1923 the mark had been quoted in Cologne at 12,000,000,000 to the dollar. The fact that an artificial era of prosperity followed, from 1924 to 1929, was explained by economic adjustment associated with American loans.

The money was used bravely, but not always wisely. Theoretically unified for more than half a century, Germany still thought and acted internally like the lot of little states and principalities it had formerly been, each influenced or directed by its own oligarchs. Thanks to native skills and a high standard of education, engineering undertakings abounded in every town, and there were car manufacturers from Aachen to Zwickau; but because of interstate rivalry and its influence on bankers, commercial thinking was confused. All too often, each little town wanted to produce something that would outshine the Mercédès, and such firms as did not seek that glory were content to regurgitate foreign designs. That was how Opel became the biggest of them in the 1920s, making copies of the Citroën 5CV until they fell into the hands of GM in 1929. That was how BMW graduated (if that be the word) from motorcycles to cars, making the Dixi Austin 7 from 1927. To be respectable, however, one had to rival the Mercédès – though even Benz had stopped doing that, the two pioneer companies having amalgamated, after years of bickering, in 1926. There was no Henry Ford, no Giovanni Agnelli of Germany to proclaim the advent of popular motoring; that would be the task of a political leader.

Some such man was bound to emerge in the years that followed. In 1929 the loan repayments had to begin, but then the slump which spread from Wall Street made that harder than ever. The German gloom was only relieved after the elections of July 1932, and at the end of the following January the old Weimar Republic was finished. In its place was born the Third Reich, which was promised to last for a thousand years but instead consumed millions of people; but, as Hitler came to power[66], the figures that mattered to the German nation were printed in marks on the newly stabilised currency.

As Hitler arrived, others (usually because they were Jews) had to leave. Max Born, for example, was evicted from his chair of theoretical physics at Göttingen, where he had inspired so many pure scientists. Adolf Rosenberger fled from the consultancy where he had inspired his somewhat impure engineering partner Ferdinand Porsche. It was Rosenberger, who had worked with the Rumpler and Benz 'teardrop' cars, who persuaded Porsche of the virtues of rear engines and all-round independent suspension, which suited Porsche's torsion-bar patents very nicely. So when Hitler asked through Auto Union for a Porsche-designed Grand Prix car to accompany the Mercedes-Benz team he had commissioned to display German merit to the motoring world, Porsche had ideas ready; and when Hitler asked him directly to design a car for the people, he had substantially the same ideas ready for that too.

In Italy, as Mussolini himself remarked, they did things rather differently. As the Germans muscled into motor racing, the Italians could not keep up with them, but they already had cars for the people: in 1934 Fiat had a new small saloon, the Balilla, that was to sire one of the most prolific lines of Europe. In the same year, an exceedingly clever Fiat engine driving a pair of contra-rotating airscrews through coaxial crankshafts propelled the MC72 seaplane to a new world record of more than 440mph.

Aviation was the best way of advertising engineering merit. Wonderful things were happening: a four-day mail service from Germany to Buenos Aires, a passenger service taking little more than four hours from Berlin to London by *Luft Hansa* (still two words, then), the first stratospheric balloon flight, new structural methods which cleared the way for aerodynamicists to do what they wanted, new alkylation processes yielding better fuels, direct fuel injection (in a Daimler-Benz inverted V12 aero-engine), a new generation of high-performance airliners from Boeing and Douglas in the USA, a whole string of gaudy wonders broken only by the horrors which accompanied the death of the airship. There was potentially more horror in the overt revival of the Luftwaffe, prompting England in 1935 to begin rearmament and to invent radar while Italy, still smarting from defeat at Adowa in 1896, dropped bombs on Abyssinia. And it all mattered to motoring, for aviation was the source of most of the technical developments from which the car (the European car, if not yet the American) profited, be it a Rolls-Royce or a Renault.

Most, but not all. In France there was a man who made his own way, and thus made the way literally smooth for the people, a man whose name had shone in 250,000 lights from the Eiffel Tower in 1925. Since 1926 he had extra factories in Belgium, England, Germany and Italy; and in 1933 he set about demolishing his main Paris factory and building a new one able to make 1000 cars a day – while somehow maintaining production of 360 a day in the midst of the reconstruction. *Le petit Juif* had determined to introduce a front-wheel-drive car, a stiff squat Budd body with an independently sprung wheel at each of its pressed-steel corners. It would be quite fast, quite economical; it would enjoy unprecedented stability, undying fame; it would stay in production for a whole generation, father a whole new genus of popular cars; and it would cost him his livelihood, if not his life. The Citroën 7CV *Traction Avant* took rationalist France by storm when it appeared in 1934.

Other nations, with other characteristics, had other problems. By 1935 the world car population was 35 million and was bound to bring changes. In Britain, where the motor vehicle had provided wonderful opportunities for the speculative builder, the 'built-up areas' it had encouraged were subjected to new speed limits before Parliament passed a toothless Restriction of Ribbon Development Act. In America, where there was more scenery to spare beyond the fringes of the towns, the first parking meters were set up in Oklahoma City. And in Germany Hitler, once again 12 years in Mussolini's wake, opened the first Autobahn[67]. He had hit upon a way of bringing employment to the men of the nation: the shovel, shouldered manfully by many a man who had never previously handled anything more hefty than a file or a fountain-pen, was now the badge of full employment. Hundreds of thousands of Germans were put to the state-inspired and state-controlled task of building modern motor roads. That was the true beginning of the Autobahn system; it was even the means by which the Nürburgring race-track was built.

In the USA the new president, Franklin D Roosevelt, had hit on the same stratagem in his campaign to distribute some of the nation's wealth (or credit) to those who lacked the chance to earn it: part of his huge programme was to take 3 million unemployed youths off the streets and set them to planting 10 million trees and building a vast mesh of highways.

In 1922 (the year before Italy's first Autostrada was opened), Benito Mussolini had become dictator of Italy and embarked upon a foreign policy calculated to reduce the influence of France. Was it coincidental that the rise of Italy and the decline of France, in motor racing generally and Grand Prix racing in particular, could be seen to have begun in that very year? Undoubtedly the Fascist government that he headed encouraged the Italian motor industry to celebrate the alleged emancipation of the Italian people, but it is very doubtful whether this encouragement took any very substantial form. When Hitler, not a driver[68] but a knowledgeable motoring enthusiast, took charge of Germany in 1933, his approach was very different, as foreseen by Mussolini: *I should be pleased, I suppose, that Hitler has carried out a revolution along the lines of ours. But they are Germans, so they will end by ruining our idea.*

---

65 Whether he could not count, or was too shy to look a cow straight in the udder, is to this day debated. It seems that his mistrust of sixes stemmed from the failure of his six-cylinder Model K in 1906.

66 Adolf Hitler had a lot to say for himself, but one quotation may be particularly revealing in this context: 'I regard Henry Ford as my inspiration.' Well he might, as much for his ideas as for the ruthlessness with which to carry them out. Several passages in *Mein Kampf* – the credo that he wrote while in jail – were taken almost verbatim (subject to translation) from the *Dearborn Independent*, the Ford newspaper put out by Henry Ford's private publishing company.

67 Once again we have to contend with matters of definition. The Germans had built an expressway in the suburbs of Berlin back in the 1920s, but that Avus dual-carriageway was hardly a motorway as we understand the term.

68 Things were different in the Mussolini household, where son Bruno proved himself not only a successful combat pilot but also a competent sporting driver with a particular penchant for the Lancia brand.

CHAPTER 6

1936–45

silent enim leges inter arma

CICERO

HOW MANY PEOPLE KNOW OF the Hispano-Suiza only through that rhapsodic passage in a Michael Arlen novel, where he refers to it 'as supplied to his most Catholic majesty'? A good many more, no doubt, than know that the first model to be associated with the King of Spain actually bore the name Alfonso.

It may be felt that a fellow who admires the Hispano-Suiza cannot be entirely bad. On the other hand it would be a mistake to assume that, merely because he shares one's enthusiasms, he must be a good fellow. Hitler, even though he could not drive, was a motoring enthusiast; Lenin was a Rolls-Royce enthusiast; Dillinger[69] was warmly appreciative of his Fords. As for King Alfonso XIII, he may have been – by the standards of princes, if not of prelates – superlatively Catholic but, as kings go, he was not very competent.

His background was less than helpful: he was born after the death of Alfonso XII, and the Queen acted as regent until he reached his teens in 1902. That was the year when Marc Birkigt built his first car for the firm that was reconstituted as Hispano-Suiza in 1904, the year when Henry Royce built his first car. Birkigt went on to much better things, doing the best of them in Paris so that the Allies enjoyed the use of the superb 20mm machine-cannon which he designed for aircraft; but for Alfonso things grew worse and worse until by 1931 he had to go – though not as kings generally go, for he left his country without abdicating his throne.

Thus the stage was set for the Spanish Civil War which broke out in the spring of 1936, at a time when motoring had just completed its first five decades. That war, brought to an effective conclusion in 1939 by the scarcely challenged participation of the Fascist countries (not least because Britain and France, probably wisely, acted on their priority of keeping the war contained in Spain rather than allowing it to spread), conditioned Spain to bend the laws of neutrality so as to lend the utmost aid to the Axis powers in the world war which followed. What prevented Spain from overtly joining

An instructor, himself trained in the Earl of Cottenham's effective new police driving school at Hendon, explains from his Lagonda the technique for running a bandit (in a Wolseley) to earth.

the war was an abject dependence on oil that could only be obtained from the Allies. Whereas artillery and the machine gun had made the Great War a war of mud and blood, the internal combustion engine made the Second World War a war of petroleum.

While war was so much the topic of conversation, keeping the peace remained a matter that worried individual countries. In Britain, the general feeling was that the

69 If ever there were an example of prison serving to corrupt its inmates, John Herbert Dillinger must be a good one. Having deserted the US Navy, he was caught in the foiled hold-up of a grocer, and spent several years in jail – where he learned from inmates the craft of the bank robber. Upon parole in 1933, he promptly became the most famous bank robber in US history, famous as much for his escapes from detention as for his success in relieving banks of their contents. In a fine example of the bare-faced effrontery of which American criminals of the period were so proud, he actually wrote to Henry Ford explaining how suitable Ford cars had proved for his purposes.

speeding motorist (and the occasional criminal who used cars for his purposes) was a greater and more noticeable threat to civilised peace and quiet than any notion of riot or bloodshed. Police forces were not doing too well in their supervision of the roads, their drivers too often showing themselves no better, and sometimes worse, than other road users. In 1937 the Metropolitan Police, the London force whose lead was commonly followed by the county constabularies, therefore invited Lord Cottenham to be the civilian adviser for the training of police drivers.

Lord Cottenham was a man who delighted in performing handbrake turns through his gates, and had a decade earlier been a member of both the Alvis and the Sunbeam racing teams. His aim of perfection was here to be expressed as a technique of advanced driving assimilable to a police constable's intelligence yet fail-safe and fool-proof, and he established it effectively for an advanced course for drivers in the fast-response Flying Squad, the undercover Q Division, and the Traffic Patrols. He promptly reduced the police accident rate by 70%, while improving their functional efficacy in other respects – so much that his teaching was to be exported to police forces in many parts of the world. Today the best police drivers (choose your country) are real experts, as are some of the specialists who teach anti-terrorist soldiers or even VIPs' bodyguards; but it was from the police training grounds on the edge of the old and famously pioneering Hendon airfield, close to London, that it all began.

The British police in those days, and long after, relied on an extraordinarily compelling personal authority and went unarmed. In too many other countries, though, the police already appeared to be paramilitary services, bringing to the streets that atmosphere of war which filled the newspapers with foreboding. Preparations for what was now a certainty went on everywhere apace, with the motor industry playing a leading part that it knew would remain profitable.

When war is so widespread as the internal combustion engine made it after 1939, it is most intriguing to examine the behaviour of the neutrals. Switzerland, for example, sent jig-borers to Ford's Urmiston shadow factory near Manchester where Rolls-Royce Merlin engines were being made in unprecedented numbers; these essential machine tools were dispatched via German-occupied France because the Swiss insisted on their right as neutrals to supply any and all belligerents – and Germany, in dire need of Swiss machine tools too, was forced to agree. This pious sanctification of the laws of commerce and the name of Mammon gave the lie to the English legal maxim *inter arma silent leges* and its Ciceronian source which implied that when there was war there was no law.

For an even stricter insistence on the priorities of big business, consider Opel: throughout the war, even after the USA had entered it, the German company continued to remit a due share of its profits to the parent corporation in Detroit. One of Opel's most successful lines during this period was their *Blitz* three-ton truck, introduced in 1937 and so satisfactory in wartime service that Daimler-Benz were made to produce it instead of their own L3000S truck in 1944. Technically the *Blitz* had a lot in common with the British services' Bedford and the Americans' Chevrolet trucks, all three being products of GM engineering; the millions who fought so bitterly for some notion of freedom or dominion were not supposed to see that in some measure they were all fighting for General Motors.

Until December 1941 the USA remained neutral in theory, though as sympathetic practically to the allies as Spain and others were to the Axis. Thus the American motor industry could maintain full steam until 1942, and it profited enormously from the opportunity, producing well over 4 million cars in each of its last two peacetime years. At the same time, to meet the needs of other nations already at war, its output of military vehicles and other munitions soared; and so, in natural and joyous correspondence, did the national economy.

The shock to American self-esteem that had earlier been brought about by the embittering depression which followed the 1929 Wall Street Crash was as profound as perhaps any country ever suffered, even Germany in the 1920s. In 1933, as Hitler took powers to revive Germany, the new F D Roosevelt administration proposed a New Deal with the twin objects of putting the Union back on its feet and keeping its new president in his seat. A chaos of frantic expedients tacked together, of compromises hastily effected whenever resistance grew too strong, the New Deal did at least recognise the probable cause of the slump: the nation's vast 1920s wealth had not been distributed widely enough to maintain healthy consumption, however avid the appetite. Things had not changed much from the days when the average factory worker earned about $500 a year while an industrialist like Andrew Carnegie enjoyed a tax-free income of more than $20 million. No wonder that America's successful cars were all essentially cheap, so that the new motorists grew up accustomed to crudely simplistic machinery from which the dynamic virtues expressed in the best European cars were absent but not missed.

Now the New Deal sought to cure the depression by placing income in the hands of consumers. Government spending in support of this crusade was more important than balancing the budget; the administration became reconciled to the

The gimmickry of new cars is not new: just look at the list of features in the 1939 Chevrolet range.
'Knee-action riding system' is a salesman's expression, meaning independent front suspension.

idea of a chronic deficit. The gamble was successful: by 1939 the economy had regained the 1929 level. There were still 8 million unemployed, because the population and the labour force had grown since 1929; all that was needed now to boost production and employment was the war which the far-sighted must have seen coming. With it, economic expansion was tremendous: the gross national product rose by 61% between 1940 and 1944, *per capita* consumer expenditure rose by 12%, and the elementary mechanical foundations of the private car began to be overlaid by the trappings of conspicuous luxury.

In 1938, when Nash introduced what they called 'air conditioning' (it was merely an elaborate heating and ventilation system; true air-conditioning arrived with the Packard range in 1941), GM showed their first 'dream car', a two-seater convertible styled by Harley Earl for the coil-sprung Buick Roadmaster chassis. Buick and Oldsmobile made a half-baked semi-automatic transmission available a year earlier (at the same time as they installed torque-converter transmission in buses), and by 1939 GM had its Hydra-Matic transmission with fluid coupling and self-change gearbox in some cars. That was the year of the 15-millionth Chevrolet, with optional steering-column gearlever, and a year later there was a fastback coupé to exemplify the newly expansive and exhibitionist styling which, far more effectively than invisible mechanical improvements, was seducing custom. Seldom had American isolation been so splendidly exuberant.

Neither that insularity, nor the theoretical neutrality, could long survive. They were not threatened by events across the Atlantic but in the Pacific, where an even more theoretical neutrality had been travestied since 1931, in Manchuria and elsewhere, by the undeclared wars launched by a wildly expansionist Japan. The League of Nations proved quite unable to patch up the Manchukuo affair – there are some who insist that it was this failure, rather than later ones of the League, which made the Second World War inevitable – and by 1937 the Japanese pitted themselves against China.

Since 1867 the Meiji dynasty had rapidly modernised feudal Japan; by the turn of the century the nation was remarkably industrialised and exceptionally well educated. Compact and cohesive to the point of being cluttered, Japan had no urgent need for cars, although DAT and Datson and Datsun had made some at various times after 1912; it was only in 1935, under the new Nissan name[70], that they set off in a new direction, and instead of making their own versions of the little Austin Seven began to emulate American practice with a large 75mph 6-cylinder saloon that owed much to assistance and tooling from Graham (erstwhile Graham-Paige) of Detroit and, when it appeared in 1937, not unnaturally looked like the Graham Six. In that same period Toyota, seeing opportunities for diversification from the textiles machinery business (and a forthcoming demand for factory facilities appropriate to the needs of war) offered their first car, which looked rather like the Chrysler Airflow.

One of their sub-contractors was a former garage proprietor and racing driver, Soichiro Honda, who was trying frantically to learn how to make piston rings. The first batch he thought satisfactory was produced in November 1937, but it took time and toil to reach Toyota's standards. When he did, Toyota backed him; he went on to make airscrews, a fortune, and history . . .

All that Britain seemed to be making in those late 1930s was faint deprecatory gestures. There was prophesy, however, in the poetry of Louis MacNeice:

> . . . *new*
> *Patterns from old disorders open like a rose*
> *And old assumptions yield to new sensation;*

What was for years despised and derided as weak-kneed pacifism can now be seen as brilliantly diplomatic playing for time, so that when the war that everybody knew was coming could no longer be postponed, Britain would bear up-to-date arms. By allowing the munitions industry to idle in the twenties and early thirties[71], Britain could gamble on a technological leapfrog which gave it Hurricanes, Spitfires, and radar, in the nick of time. The motor industry in particular was commissioned to produce engines of war, with hardly a known car-maker lacking some shadow factory playing Vulcan at the elbow of Mars.

Whether the people were yet ready for their ordeal was hard to tell. Nowhere was there such soul-searching, such racking of the conscience, as in England approaching the brink of war. People began to read more: the first modern paperbacks, Lane's sixpenny Penguins, had appeared in 1935 and had a noticeable slant towards the political left; his Pelicans, two years later, made a broader culture more broadly accessible than ever before – as did the high-toned BBC under that high-minded giant Lord Reith – and millions began to read as never before[72]. In the poetry of the period they learned how they, the common men and the uncommon, would soon respond :

> *He held the right opinion for the time . . .*
> *When it was peace, he was for peace;*
> *When it was war, he went.*

Books were cheap; motoring was not. The £100 car was now a Ford reality, but a gallon of good petrol cost an hour's wages for some men who thought themselves lucky to be working at all. The car was not yet a means of going to work, for which the cobweb of railways and bus routes provided with a snug slow certainty that seemed to pervade so much in Britain then; the car was a means of escape, and the need to do that, to go out for a drive into the country at the weekend (Sunday, for many who worked a six-day week), was enough to drive buyers into the showrooms at all possible costs.

The cars that most of them bought were quite awful. Their bodies were heavier than before, prinked-up echoes of English carriages and American grossmobiles trimmed with the wood and leather that were deemed necessary expressions of the smug certainties of British social ambition. Old-fashioned girder chassis flexed independently of bodies and soggy steering, being modernised only in having their engines further forward than in the past; and what soulless engines most of them were! Beneath those tall and deliberately imposing bonnets, each fronted by a chromed radiator shell that had to be distinctive but was usually derivative, was a humble little affair, small in the bore and long in the stroke because of the taxation on piston area. For all the length of stroke, the engine was not tall: it was usually side-valved, because in those days of primitive mineral-based lubricating oils regular decarbonisation was a necessary chore that most shoestring motorists regarded as a do-it-yourself job. Driver's manuals in those days carried explicit illustrated instructions on how to lift the head, remove encrusted coke, grind-in valves, and put everything together again; some of them included instructions on relining brakes.

If their propagandists were to be believed (as in those days they often were), it was the Germans who were making cars consistent with modern times. The motorists of Europe reeled in astonishment when they read about the latest Auto-Union and Mercedes-Benz Grand Prix cars, the fastest and most powerful ever known. High-strength alloy steels and lightweight aluminium and magnesium alloys accounted for their ability to combine unprecedented power with a maximum dry weight of 750kg, under the formula which prevailed from 1934 until the end of 1937. To these metallurgical marvels were added the sorceries of the fuel chemists and the popular new magic of streamlined bodies; but what captured the imagination most strongly were the clever new systems of independent suspension.

Those systems look anything but clever today, but in 1936 the swinging half-axles at the rear and the short-travel wishbones or trailing links at the front of the German racers seemed marvellously sophisticated. Then in 1937 Mercedes-Benz gave their latest racer, the fastest and most powerful of them all, a De Dion rear axle,

---

70 The original name of the company in 1911 was the Kwaishinsha Co: DAT, its first car, is the Japanese word for 'hare'. In 1925 the firm merged with another and in 1930 produced another car, the Datson, or 'son of Dat'. This was a marketing mishap: in Japanese, 'son' means 'ruin'. Next year they changed it to Datsun, before the company took on the name Nissan in 1934.

71 The turning point came in May 1935, when the British government realised that appeasement and disarmament were propositions as hopeless as had been the paying of the Danegeld, some 1100 years earlier. From this point onwards, while statesmen saw that things were looking bad, industrialists found that things were looking up: rearmament was the salvation of the economy. It gives a new slant to the old idea *si vis pacem para bellum*.

72 Much popular literature in France (and elsewhere in Europe) had never been anything but paper-backed. For that matter, there were English-language paperbacks in the 1880s: early editions of some of Kipling's stories were published in this form in India for keeping passengers engrossed during their long railway journeys there.

This Fiat Millecento, new in 1937, was destined to become one of the most influential cars of all time.

and it seemed that there was no limit to their cleverness. In fact Horch had incorporated a De Dion axle in a road car two years earlier, and Miller in the USA had done it in his racers earlier still; but the propaganda machine was taking no notice of them. The W125 Mercedes-Benz, with longitudinal compliance in its front suspension and hydraulic dampers all round, was a new elaboration of Maurice Olley's published notions (still only a few years old) of high moment of polar inertia for roadholding to match its 600bhp performance. It dominated the 1937 GP season, just as the 3-litre V12 models would in 1938–9, latterly with 2-stage supercharging.

It was true that Mercedes-Benz road cars did offer some good things at that time, but theirs was a confusing range (they could not decide between front or rear engine for their 170 model, and offered both; the public was in no doubt at all!) and made little contribution to motoring for the people. Germany's only real pointer to the future, in terms of a rigid structure with independent front suspension and an efficient ohv engine in a lightweight (and easily cleaned) body, was the BMW 328 sports car, which deserved most of the praise and laurels that came its way from 1936 onwards. Other German cars were often interesting (especially Adler, Neander and Maybach) but not often convincing.

A similar flurry of experimentation disturbed France, where the front-drive Citroën, the only real harbinger of the future, was well into production. The Hotchkiss Grégoire, featuring not only front-wheel drive (of which Grégoire had been the most persistent advocate since his Tracta days) but also unitary construction in light alloy, was a small car that could have saved us a couple of decades had the war not intervened; but the real flavour of future driving was first made popular in Italy.

More modern, more refined, more useful, and more affordable than the 328 BMW, the Fiat 1500 which went into full production in 1936 brought new concepts of beauty and efficiency to everyday motoring. It had a backbone chassis with Dubonnet independent front suspension, a short-stroke ohv 6-cylinder engine, the cleanest production saloon body yet seen, and a better brakes-to-weight ratio than family cars commonly enjoyed. It was followed in short order by the 500, the endearing little Topolino, and then in 1937 came one of the most noteworthy cars of all time, the new Fiat 1100, the Millecento.

Originally styled in the same fashion as the 1500 and the 500, the Millecento endured so long in production that it could scarcely be recognised as the same car when it finally ceased in 1970. At various times in between it had sometimes looked as nasty as its Renault contemporaries, it had been adopted by Simca, it had provided the basis for countless Italian sports cars including the first Ferrari (not to mention the dainty and delicious Gordini racers), and above all it taught the man in the street just how good an ordinary car could be. It was frugal, it was fast, it had better handling and roadholding and braking than most sports cars, and it was entirely intelligible. If it had any real rival, that must have been the 1937 Lancia Aprilia; but one had only to compare their prices and their sources to see that the rivalry was not real.

If Fiat had made nothing but the Millecento, they could still have been regarded as universal providers, by establishing a set of standards by which people could judge other cars. Never mind who, some time between never-mind-when and 1901, was the father of the motor car; if Henry Ford the mechanic was the father of the popular car, Dante Giacosa the engineer was the father of the modern car.

His new Fiats were widely sold, right from their start: the 1500 cost £298 in England, where people perversely paid more for a Humber 12 Vogue or a Lanchester

10. Italy was the place where cars were really appreciated, though, and the Italy of Mussolini – for all its corruption and its confused ambitions – seemed to be thriving. The Germany of Hitler was evidently well on its way to doing the same; but what were the prospects for popular motoring there? Politics now dictated the direction that applied science had to take: the Führer's patronage of the Volkswagen made it an expression of *Kraft durch Freude*, strength through joy. The KdF Volkswagen was not to be merely a people's car, it was to be the German People's Car. The fact that its designer, the greatly overrated Ferdinand Porsche, had 'borrowed' most of its concepts from the much cleverer Tatra designer Hans Ledwinka of Czechoslovakia[73] was just another inconvenient fact to be suppressed.

But there was no suppressing the Volkswagen. The people of Germany were thirsting for it. In America there was a car for every 5.6 people, in New Zealand one for 10.5, in France one for 24.5, in Britain one for 30.6, in China one for 13,123; the world-wide average was 66. When would the Germans go from strength to joy? It was delayed, but for good reasons, the Volkswagen finally being released to the market in 1939 just before the inevitable war was at last begun; and then of course it had to be adapted to wartime service, which it did brilliantly. The Kübelwagen went nearly everywhere.

There was another car that went further. In 1940 the US army issued a specification for a four-wheel-drive quarter-ton truck for what were described as command reconnaissance duties. The order was won by Bantam, the firm that had made Austin Sevens under licence, but they could not produce it in the quantities required and were pipped by Willys-Overland, who found ways of bending the rules to admit their own design. In the end the design was an amalgam of Bantam and Ford ideas superimposed on the Willys basis, and for a while the vehicle was made by all three firms. It became the General Purpose vehicle of the army, and from those initials came the name Jeep.

No name was better known for any wheeled vehicle during the war, for which Willys built the cobby little 'blitz buggy' as fast as one every 80 seconds. Total wartime production ran to two-thirds of a million, and everybody who drove one was impressed. In North Africa the exchange rate was one Jeep for any two or more other vehicles, and it was the Jeep rather than the Daimler Scout Car (itself a prodigious performer, and very sophisticated with its disk brakes and fully reversible driving) which prompted no less a personage than Feldmarschall Erwin Rommel to direct that captured allied vehicles were to be used where possible for front-line duties, German vehicles being relegated to supportive tasks for which their inferiority was less of a handicap.

It was a long and hard war[74], but this is no place to summarise it, unless it be in the words that Edith Sitwell wrote during the terror of the London blitz:

Still falls the rain

In the Field of Blood where the small hopes breed and the human brain

Nurtures its greed, that worm with the brow of Cain.

It was a war in which the motor industry played an enormous part. In America it produced 2.8 million trucks and tanks, while in England it was not for nothing that Coventry was so seriously assaulted by the *Luftwaffe*. It was a war in which the ignorant learned what the high-speed petrol engine could do after half a century of development from Daimler's first, a war in which the confined learned to travel. Alas, after walking the long firelit night, we found the dawning daylight was still smoke-laden; the stinging in our nostrils warned us that there were years of austerity still ahead.

Austerity: the very word conjures up the memory of high-minded narrow-visioned politicians striving to maintain wartime discipline despite post-war euphoria, telling us that we could not have cars until other more basic needs had been satisfied. They were probably right, but they expressed themselves very badly, and were

---

73 Although Porsche found it convenient at one stage of his career to adopt Czech nationality, Ledwinka always considered himself an Austrian. Though the two men were born not far from each other in Danubian country, and were both technically citizens of the Austro-Hungarian Empire, the motions of artificial political boundaries at various later times made them Germans or Czechs.

74 Despite the paucity of vehicles on the roads of Britain during the war, when tyres were practically unobtainable and fuel was either denied or rationed with understandable stringency, the accident rate was appalling, possibly the highest ever known in the land. The blackout, imposed to handicap enemy aircraft, was held responsible, *nemine contradicente*: with one headlamp extinguished and the other blinded by a regulation mask through which three or four shallow horizontal slits allowed only a miserable glimmer to pass, there was every chance of a nocturnal accident on roads that were everywhere unlit.

Some figures issued in 1943 by the *Civil Defence Journal* told part of the awful truth. Casualties in the UK armed forces for the first two years of the war amounted to 145,012; casualties on our roads for just 1942 numbered 147,544. During March 1943, 298 were killed in air raids, 529 on the roads; in that same month a further 439 were injured in air raids, 9238 on the roads.

There used to be a simple basic summary of skilled road usage, proposed by the police driving school at Hendon, and the second half of it was particularly apposite: Be in the right place, in the right gear, at the right speed – *and if you can't see, don't go!*

probably correctly suspected of being right for the wrong reasons. Britain suffered purchase tax to dissuade it from buying cars, France had its own weird fiscal methods of doing the same, and even in the USA (where the industry was granted permission to resume the building of private cars as soon as the European war was over, less than three years after their production had been halted) there was governmental interference. For Japan and Germany, as should have been obvious, there was no hope . . .

What about the Volkswagen? It could be put into production quite quickly; the KdF initials would have to be left off, but nothing else needed to be changed. Or did it? William Morris, long known as Lord Nuffield, toyed with the idea of using the VW works to build Morris cars as well as VWs, or instead; but finally he rejected the idea. The British Control Commission could not make up its mind, and invited a study by the industry. An engineer from Humber was deputed to go and see what it was all about; he came back and reported that the VW was a hopeless machine, absurd in its design and inappropriate in its abilities to meet the needs of the coming years. A deputation of engineers from Australia came and reached a similar conclusion.

Some people never learn. Others learned very quickly to forget what had always previously been knowledge. A wartime cartoon by an American artist in a British paper showed a couple of American soldiers in a Jeep, climbing some precipitous slope somewhere in high Europe and coming face to face among the rocks with a mountain goat or chamois bearing the most incredulous expression ever to fill the space between horns and beard. Said one of the Americans, *'Say, how the hell did he get up here?'* Halfway through its long journey, the motor car had already arrived: it had caused a new set of facts to be taken for granted.

CHAPTER 7

1946–55

For now I see Peace to corrupt no less than war to waste.

MILTON

'THE SOCIETY OF MOTOR MANUFACTURERS and Traders Ltd is happy to be able to present the long-deferred 33rd Exhibition of the series which originated in 1903. The arrangements for the 1939 event were of course discontinued on the outbreak of war, and the revival successively announced in 1946 and 1947 was postponed by reason of the fact that the circumstances of the industry precluded any distraction from the objectives of the development of post-war designs and a concentration on Export trade . . .

'The emphasis of the Exhibition, from the point of view of British manufacturers, is on export, since approximately three-quarters of present car production must be ear-marked for overseas. The number of cars available for the home market must be very much smaller than was the case before the war; consequently, while the supreme attractiveness of the exhibits may whet the appetite of hundreds of thousands, it is regretfully the case that the pent-up demand associated with the short supply still means that only a minority of essential users in the home market can be satisfied as yet.'

Such pomp and prosaic circumstance might not be found opening the catalogue of a modern motor show, but in 1948 it was commonplace in daily business and commercial correspondence, full of ultimos, proximos, esteemed favours, and a pox of inappropriate capital letters. If it served to mask true feelings or cloud real issues, so much the better: with the industry striving for volume and minimising the variety of models, there were so few cars to be displayed that much of the Earls Court space was given over to motor boats and caravans. It would have looked even more sparse had not the Treasury and the Board of Trade graciously permitted some foreign cars to be put on show, just to make it nominally international; but it was made clear that those beautiful French and bloated American specimens were strictly for exhibition only. For a resident of the UK to buy a foreign car, at a time when the nation was in international terms bankrupt, would have been treason – and the idea of buying a German or Japanese car would have been as unthinkable socially, in the aftermath of the war, as it would then have been inadvisable technically. Apart from those roguish Americans and ravishing French, the only foreign car exhibited was the Alfa Romeo.

Like most of the others, it was an old design. The urgent priority was to make cars, not to improve them. A few manufacturers – among them Rolls-Royce and Riley, the latter now in the chill and enervating grip of Nuffield but still making their own deep-breathing and lusty long-stroke engines – were in the happy position of having ready new designs that had been shelved at the beginning of the war, but even that recipe did not always work. In 1946 the British had been promised the £200 Kendall, sensibly very light and economical and initially with a three-cylinder radial engine in the rear, soon revised to a front-drive derivative of the prewar Grégoire/Aluminium Français; but the factory, intended also to make tractors and sponsored by Denis Kendall MP, only made 200 before closing.

Tractors were emphatically on the 'essential' list. The internal combustion engine had relieved the horse of its agricultural burdens as completely in the war just past as of its military duties in the war of the previous generations. Its next task was to relieve the railways of their supremacy in transport, except in the USA where it had already done so[75]. America was now fully motorised (though to judge from the clamour for new cars after just three years' abstinence, one might hardly believe it) and had graduated from the drive-in cinema to the drive-thru bank and the vast shopping mall on the outskirts of town.

The outskirts themselves were spreading as the centres of cities were opened up to speed traffic through. America had room for this; Japan could not even think about it[76]; Britain and Europe had to take desperate measures, with the centres of cities emptied by bombing and the country emptied by urbanisation. By 1950, 98% of the UK population was confined to 65% of the land area, 40% of the people being jammed into the six biggest conurbations. Compared with the end of the Great War, London had sprawled to three times its size, yet in the same time a million people had

75 What appears to have been a joint operation involving one of the major oil companies and one of the major motor-manufacturers who, with a third partner, together bought up and made redundant many urban railroads and stations, doubtless had some contributory effect.

76 The streets of Tokyo accounted for only one-tenth of the urban area.

left (or been bombed out of) its centre to live near its rim. An eighth of the population of France packed Paris. And then they all began to demand cars.

Architects and officials found it hard to see what was coming and to cater for it. France, in the grip of communism but somehow prevented by a national sense of style from committing the worst atrocities of totalitarian ugliness commonly seen in the more truly totalitarian buildings (one hesitates to use the word 'architecture') of eastern Europe and the USSR, had embarked on a wild programme of workers' flats as seen through the distorted lenses of middle-class art. Britain, where Town and Country Planning had been invented, at last had a uniform system for the whole country with the passing of the 1947 Act, but had already taken the brave step of instituting the New Towns. There were to be 29 of these, and the first dozen (mostly around London, starting with Harlow) were created with impressive speed; but, halfway through the programme, revisions had to be made to accommodate the car. The architects had reckoned on one garage to every ten dwellings; hastily the ratio had to be adjusted to house five times as many cars.

The cost of war, and the social vendettas pursued in its political aftermath, had readjusted the distribution of wealth. Between the Munich *Anschluss* of 1938 and the start of the Cold War in 1947, the top 84% of Britain's privately owned capital had been spread among 53% more people, reaching more than one person in ten over the age of 25 years, while the proportion of the population (in the same age group) with enough to buy a car rose from 18 to 25%. Not that the car was any longer the preserve of capitalists: in another three years, half the nation's hire-purchase debt had been accrued in the purchase of cars.

The Americans had been through all this earlier. By this time, they had so many cars that (allowing for a few toddlers sitting on their mothers' laps) the whole nation could have been carborne simultaneously, even if all their cars had been two-seaters. They had acquired more expansive tastes, however, as a result of being sold status with their cars: the bigger, the better. The flashier, too: Buick's 1950 radiator intake grille will never be forgotten, and may never be forgiven. That was the year of the GM automatics; a year earlier, a crude side-valve V8 took over from the old V12 in the Lincoln range; but it was two years earlier still that the most important thing happened, when Raymond Loewy (who had taken over the styling of Studebakers in 1940) produced the two-ways Champion, a Janus of a car whose wraparound screen made it hard to tell which was the front end and which the back.

Delighted to have a car which did not look like a face-lifted 1942 job, the

Americans happily and mercilessly rejected anything that was truly new under the skin. The Tucker, the Kaiser and others got short shrift. Emerging from the war healthier and wealthier than all bar maybe a few Swiss and those expatriate Germans who, before or after the war, had managed to settle themselves in South America, the euphoric Americans begged to be taken for a ride, and the big four manufacturers gladly obliged. This was the era of the worst of all American cars, the most inane and most inept amalgamations of superfluity and inadequacy ever to bring into question the intellectual credibility of a whole nation. Only a few rebelled, but the number swelled rapidly as drivers of standard Detroit behemoths found themselves being outwitted and outmanoeuvred by 'pesky little furrin automobiles' which seemed to have decorative octagons in even greater numbers than hexagonal nuts.

The MG, rushed into production soon after the war ended, was sold almost exclusively for dollars. By no means the high-performance car that it looked, the TC Midget still behaved so very much better than American cars in everything but straight-line acceleration that it earned proselytes as fast as profits. There were other more modern and much better new cars produced in Europe in 1946 – the Cisitalia, which frankly acknowledged its Fiat components, and the Ferrari which did not – but the MG TC was cheap to Americans, and was being sold to them as hard as anything the hard-pressed dollar-hungry British industry could make.

Not for the first time, government was trying to exploit Britain's motorists and motor industry by penal taxation and cramping legislation. The austere regimen imposed for the sake of economic recovery ought to have made things hard enough: petrol was rationed (even bread was rationed, something that had never happened during the war) and tyres were almost impossible to obtain. Most other things in short supply could be procured on the black market, bureaucracy thus making immoral quasi-criminals of most of us and encouraging car dealers in particular to risk the unsavoury reputations they duly acquired.

Things were worse on the European mainland where, once again, there was reason to fear a revolution that, like Saturn[77], would consume each of its children in turn. Every possible French industrialist was accused of complicity with the Germans: Louis Renault died in prison after a succession of nightly beatings, and his company was nationalised. In Germany it was assumed that everybody was criminal: the entire output of the VW factory (1785 in 1945, 10,020 in 1946) was allocated to the British army of occupation; Russia had plundered all the factories east of their border, and now America tried to grab what was left.

BMW should have had nothing left. On 11 April 1945 Hitler had ordered all their production facilities to be destroyed, but director Kurt Donath ignored the order. He did it again in October of the same year, when one Eugene Keller Jnr, deputy commander of the US garrison in Munich, had ordered the dismantling and destruction of the factory, anything usable to be shipped to Detroit . . . Not until 1948 did the occupying powers concede that, as a step up from making cooking utensils and simple agricultural machines, BMW might at least return to making motorcycles.

At a higher level, the Americans were far more constructive. In that same 1948, the Marshall Plan was implemented, at an estimated cost of $15,000 million and some risk of inflation. A professional soldier since 1902, George C Marshall was chief of staff throughout the Second World War, afterwards applying his strategic thinking to the economic recovery of Europe. In a Harvard address in 1947 he set out his plan for financial assistance to such war-shattered countries of Europe as would be prepared to work with it, and thus he laid the foundations for the integration of western Europe, earning the distinction of being the first military man to receive the Nobel Peace Prize. The recovery of the European motor industry, especially in Germany, could never have been so rapid without him.

One of the plan's attractions to the USA was that it would help to contain the spread of communism. What the nation's strategists did not see that year was the trouble brewing up in another quarter. Britain, having made irresponsibly irreconcilable promises to both the Jews and the Arabs about the future of what all three parties considered the Holy Land, washed her hands of the whole affair in 1948, refused to cooperate with the United Nations Commission, and very suddenly and quickly withdrew from her mandated Palestine. Equally quickly, the Jews joyously proclaimed the State of Israel, on 14 May. On 15 May, no less happy that the opportunity had at last arisen and confident in their ability to make the most of it, the surrounding Arab nations invaded with the expressed intention of eliminating Israel. Their persistence in this aim, and their incompetence to achieve it, was to lead to a series of Middle Eastern crises which would shake the smugness out of the world's economists and crack some of the best-laid foundations in the motor industry.

Was the future then clear to see? George Orwell thought so: his *1984* was published in 1949, the year of the Atlantic Pact which begat NATO, the year of the devaluation of sterling, and much more romantically the year of the Jaguar XK120. It was a revelation of a new era to see the team of three – red for Walker, white for Johnson, blue for Bira – spurn the rest of the field in the production-car race at

Silverstone that summer. Chastely beautiful as they stood in échelon at the pits, the Jaguars rolled and pitched obscenely through the corners, but the paradox was resolved by the silken 6-cylinder hum which proclaimed their supreme speed along the straights. How memorable to be present[78] at the beginning of something that was clearly going to last a long time!

Something even longer lasting made its appearance in France that year, when Citroën unveiled the 2CV upon which they had been working since the prewar prototype had been recovered from its hiding-place. It was such a car – a car of studied utility, remorseless economy, and irrefutable logic – as millions of folk had wanted since 1945; millions would still do well to have it today. Across the border in Germany, however, the car of other folk had at last been liberated: in 1949 the VW factory was decontrolled, and soon the Volkswagen, shorn of the stigmata of *Kraft durch Freude* and destined to become a legend as the Beetle, the car that never changes shape, began to take over all the export markets of the world.

The man who took all the credit for the VW still owned a factory in Stuttgart, and now he was in a wonderful position to make a car bearing his own name and relying heavily on VW components. The Porsche 356 was very pretty, aerodynamically the cleanest car of 1950 (it was even better than the Bristol 401), and a most convincing blend of speed and economy. It also demonstrated once again that Porsche had a huge blind spot where suspension was concerned; but the enthusiasts would never admit it, so Porsche and VW together went wagging their tails into the rosy dollar-rich sunset.

Had they been heading the other way, they should have seen a clouded sunrise. After so brief and uneasy a peace, war had broken out in Korea in 1950. It was to last 37 months, at the end of which South Korea would have gained 1500 square miles and lost a million civilians. American losses would amount to 33,647 servicemen and $18 billion, proudly dismissed or sadly missed as appropriate. Theoretically it was not America but the United Nations which were running the war, but – apart from the hapless Koreans themselves – it was the Americans who were most involved. At home

---

77 Pierre Vergniaud, quoted in Lamartine, *Histoire des Girondins,* 1847.

78 Setright stood at the entrance to Beckett's Corner to watch this race. It would be useless to stand on that same spot now: the place has changed, as motor sport has changed, becoming an industry *sui juris.*

Precursor of the Renault Espace and all other MPVs of 'modern' times was the Vauxhall-related Bedford Dormobile, which seemed awfully modernistic in its styling when it was new in the early 1950s.

they consoled themselves with the conviction that they were the world's most powerful nation and therefore were bound to win; and their addiction to power was never better served than by Chrysler, who in 1951 presented a 5.4-litre V8 with opposed inclined valves in part-spherical combustion chambers, the rugged high-performance engine which shot to fame as the Hemi. It was America's most powerful car engine, destined to grow bigger and more incredibly powerful with the passing years, and to prompt such retaliation from GM and Ford as to usher in the age of the muscle cars, America's proudest.

It showed how nonsensical was the boardroom opposition which would not allow designer Dante Giacosa to put an engine larger than 1.4 litres in the new Fiat of 1950, despite the firm's desire to sell well in the USA. In Britain, Ford showed what was really wanted in 1951: their new Consul and Zephyr were cleanly styled, simply constructed, and had engines just that crucial amount larger than their rivals'. The lesson of the V8 had not been forgotten, and as Britain gave way to a perfervid enthusiasm for motor sport, highly tuned Zephyrs began to make their presence felt in competition.

One of the most memorable features of the Consul/Zephyr design was its adoption of that cunning form of independent front suspension, the MacPherson strut. The MacPherson bit (the man was an Australian, but he sold his idea in the USA) was no more than a rational simplification of strut suspension, something that Giacosa had devised (on a basis provided even earlier by his predecessor Fornaca) before the war. Meanwhile, the man who was to devise his own kind of strut suspension for rear wheels, Colin Chapman, was a cheerfully shrewd young slave-driver whose objective thinking had produced a most disturbingly roadworthy piece of gossamer which had simply slaughtered all opposition in 750 Club racing. The Lotus 3, surely second only to the Issigonis Lightweight Special in its thoughtfulness, set this determined cocksparrow on his way to fame and fortune. Soon he would be winning much bigger races.

The most important race of all was still the 24-hour sports-car event at Le Mans. The cars which competed were still recognisable, covetable, and sometimes practical, road cars, but everybody who knew of the legendary performance of Daimler-Benz before the war (and that meant everybody in motoring) took a respectful step back when a revolutionary new Mercedes-Benz was dragooned by the firm's master psychologist and racing manager Alfred Neubauer into winning at Le Mans, as it did at Berne and in Mexico. The gullwing doors of its closed body were what showed it to be a thing apart, but those who thought about its true spaceframe chassis and its fuel injection could see that if Daimler-Benz did return to Grand Prix racing, they would do it as conclusively as ever.

Grand Prix racing was in the doldrums. The prewar cars had been used up; Lampredi's unblown 4.5-litre Ferrari had at last beaten Colombo's blown 1.5-litre Alfa Romeo; the highly touted V16 BRM had been a failure. Still the sporting craze continued, ever more compulsive; and while Britons were newly wild about Jaguar and Lotus, the Americans who had been lately weaned on MG Midgets were now buying from Europe everything from sports cars to Beetles. Indeed, to some Americans the Beetle was a sports car.

Somehow it dawned upon the American manufacturers that while the big standard domestic sedan – with its three-abreast front bench seat made practical by a steering-column shift lever if not by a two-pedal automatic transmission, and a big lazy engine that never needed much gearchanging anyway – might be effective for doing the weekly shopping at the mall, for regular boring business trips, and for a night of heavy petting at the drive-in cinema, it might not serve all the other purposes of the newly inspired American motorist.

Somehow the dollars that were being lavished on imports must be redirected into domestic coffers. Chrysler's Hemi was not the answer that they sought; its styling was too clumsy. General Motors were first to hit upon the solution, creating America's own version of the sports car, the Chevrolet Corvette, which was to appear in 1953 – the year when the disk brake made its sensational debut at Le Mans[79], allowing the C-type Jaguar to beat the 4.9-litre Ferrari. Compared with something like the 300SL Mercedes-Benz, the Corvette was pathetically primitive; but even the 300SL had a faint air of olden times when it was new in 1952, for that was the year in which the De Havilland Comet went into service.

The world's first jet-propelled airliner made all other vehicles look silly. It even made contemporary jet fighters look silly: an RAF ground controller at Sopley[80] identified the Comet in some final shakedown trials over the Channel one spring day in 1952, and asked the pilot if he would mind being the target for a practice interception by a brace of Vampires. The pilot obliged, and the controller brought the fighters in on a perfect course for a final tail-chase – only to hear their leader howl in dismay as the Comet suddenly accelerated away and left the RAF standing. People began to think that the gas turbine, despite its then heavy fuel consumption, was the future power-plant of cars, too.

The nationalist revolution in Egypt might have given them some clues. Alas, the future threat to oil supplies was not fully recognised at the time; some people were more taken with the fact that, in the year of the Comet, London had at last got rid of its trams[81]. What should have attracted their attention most of all was that Japan at last was rid of occupying forces: loathed and feared by the Americans who had moved in, back in 1945, the Japanese had been encouraged to adopt the standards and practices of the USA, and by 1952 had become favoured friends and trading partners.

Poor in natural resources, Japan always had to import most of the raw materials for the goods it exported – iron ore from Malaya and India, oil from Saudi Arabia and Kuwait, assorted minerals from Australia and almost everything else from the USA. There could be no better incentive for the earnest application of their superior intelligence, and both their products and their marketing developed fast. Hino began to make the Renault 4CV under licence, but Datsun copied the Crosley, a really small American car built by a small young firm (Powell Crosley was a radio pioneer) using one of the cleverest of all engines, a 722cm^3 fabrication originally intended for the US Navy. Toyota went their own way: they had built but 215 cars between 1947 and 1952 (neat cars with backbone chassis and some of them with disk brakes[82]), but after the occupation ended their production boomed, to reach 8500 per annum in 1955. Japanese economic growth was almost fissile, the nation's rate of recovery defying comparison with anywhere other than West Germany, and the USA was a good and ready market.

In sharp contrast to Japan and Germany, Spain was in poor shape. Centuries of misrule, following the disastrous mistake whereby they exiled all their clever men (Arabs and Jews alike) in 1492, had left this once rich nation almost exhausted of

---

79 A year earlier, the victory of a C-type Jaguar equipped with disk brakes went almost unnoticed in the 12-hour sports-car race at Reims. This was intentional; although a works car, it was privately entered so as to conceal its purpose as a development vehicle.

80 Then a rather advanced radar station a few miles inland from Bournemouth on the south coast. Setright served there at that time as 'Ops B', assistant to the chief controller.

81 The trolleybuses were dismissed too. Daft idea that they were (the system was devised in the 1880s by an American named Leo Daft), they were put into London service in the 1930s after tests had highlighted their quietness and speed: a prototype undergoing acceleration tests proved able to spin its driving wheels inside their tyres! Trolleybuses shared with the trams not only great theoretical advantages but also a crippling disability which was discovered during the wartime air-raids on London: inflexibly committed to the route of their electrical rails or overhead wires, they could not be diverted in any sort of emergency.

There once was a man who said Damn!

It is borne in upon me I am

A creature that moves

In predestinate grooves;

I'm not even a bus – I'm a tram!

82 Those British firms such as Jaguar and Jensen who claimed to be the pioneers of disk brakes were not telling the truth, though they may possibly have been ignorant of the truth. The most expensive Chryslers had disk brakes on all four wheels in 1949. Earlier efforts, not sustained, were made by AC in 1919 and by Lanchester in 1903.

natural resources, and the Civil War of 1936–9 had left it in a chaos from which six years of profitable neutrality in the Second World War had not redeemed it. Yet in 1951 there issued from Barcelona a car of the most refined design and most exquisite manufacture that had yet been seen. Designed by the intellectual Spanish engineer Wilfredo Ricart (late of Alfa Romeo, where his presence made Enzo Ferrari redundant) and made regardless of reject-rates by apprentices to the ENASA truck company in a factory that had once produced the Hispano-Suiza, the rare and costly Pegaso was modestly explained: 'We are a poor people making jewels for the rich.'

That contrast was more stark where the war had more recently made its wastes. Germany in 1952 was phenomenal[83]. The shop windows in a city such as Cologne looked terrific; but if one stood back and looked up, the upper storeys of the buildings could be seen to be still empty shells gutted in the air raids a decade earlier – and they could be seen even in the middle of the night, for floodlit rebuilding went on everywhere without pause. Women worked the fields, and even pushed the ploughs; their men, those that were left of them, were working with steel and cement[84].

The greatest producers of cement were the Italians, with as much rebuilding to do as anybody because their lovely land had seemingly been fought over by everybody. Here was another country urgently needing to expand foreign trade, and it did so fourfold; but its motor industry never lost sight of its responsibilities to its own people, even though that might hamper exports. Having perhaps misguidedly become a republic after the war, Italy was politically unstable, and this delayed the appearance of her economic miracle. Accepting the shortage of cars and the generally low standard of living, the populace worked and waited with characteristically genial sobriety (the world's biggest wine producers, the Italians nevertheless share with the Jews the distinction of being the least drunken of all people in greater Europe); but if the volume of their products was not yet remarkable, the volume of ideas was.

Italy was the world leader in design, not only of cars but also of furniture, clothes, tunnelling machinery and buildings. The stress-patterned concrete and hyperbolic paraboloids of the architect Nervi excelled in functional beauty; how many visitors to the Turin Motor Show ever looked up to admire them, though? There was so much to see on the ground, where the couturiers to the world's motor industry held court.

The Italians are also the world's leading Egyptologists, but they got into much less of a flap than Britain and France during the evacuation of Suez in 1954. It was the American government which put the kibosh on what might have been a most interesting military operation there, while the American people were getting into a lather about the new Ford Thunderbird. It was Ford's answer to the Corvette, or rather a fellow combatant in the fight against imports: the advertising agents called it a 'personal car', and popular motoring took off with the idea.

If the two-speed Corvette seemed simple compared with the 300SL, Ford's crude T-Bird was positively coarse compared with the Mercedes-Benz which brought the three-pointed star back into Grand Prix racing's *Grandes Epreuves*. Technically the most admirable cars yet built, they won everything except friends: the second-class brains populating the sporting scene resented the firm's sheer authority. When guest driver Levegh's[85] sports version metamorphosed into a magnesium bomb full of petrol, benzol and alcohol, and slaughtered scores at Le Mans in 1955, public opinion seemed to demand that they remove themselves from the scene. Opinion in some places, notably Switzerland, was that the accident provided a long-awaited opportunity to proscribe motor racing entirely.

When autumn had softened the agonies of that horrific summer, France had cause to rejoice again in *l'automobilisme*. She had created a car, a production car meant for the ordinary man in the street, sublimely endowed with such complexities

---

83 It cannot be denied that they worked hard. Even so, there was something astonishing about what they managed to achieve with what was, after all, a limited amount of American financial aid. Only decades later did we learn that they possessed substantial further financial resources, mostly garnered by appropriating the property of the 6 million Jews they had exterminated, these funds being during the war prudently lodged in the strictly businesslike privacy of Swiss banks.

84 All this could be confirmed from the personal experience of Setright, who in 1952 as part of a NATO exercise was given charge of a group of airmen to take to Wahnerheide, near Cologne. Emerging from the railway station at night, and looking across the square (almost empty of traffic) towards the looming bulk of Cologne Cathedral (which sadly had not been unscathed in the bombing) he saw strategically and even artistically parked beneath a lamp outside it a gleaming Mercedes-Benz 300 saloon: it seemed to represent all that many British secretly admired about the German revival. A slightly different picture of our hosts was presented by the former SS barracks in which we were accommodated: strongly built and well finished, they enjoyed the luxury (denied to the British by reactionary building bylaws) of mains water pressure for all fixtures and fittings in the ablutions; but an anteroom to the officers' mess was furnished with a substantial vomitorium, where German officers who had reached their limits at dinner could pump ship before returning to the table for further drinking.

85 Levegh was a *nom de guerre*, a device popular among racing drivers before the war and especially among the French. His real name was Bouillon.

The most modern car of the 20th century, the new Citroën DS
was the centre of attraction at the 1955 Paris Salon.

of execution and refinement of conception as made the bristling technology of the racing Mercedes-Benz appear merely the laborious handicraft of gifted mechanics. The Citroën DS was an engineers' car, the thinking man's car, far and away the most modern car in the world, not only in 1955 but for at least 15 years until another even cleverer Citroën should emerge from the closeted brains of that most uncompromisingly logical of design teams.

The DS should have had a flat six engine, either water- or air-cooled and with either a carburettor or fuel injection, when it first appeared. It should have acquired active suspension before it gave way to the CX. These things, though readied, were just too much for the firm's production resources, alas; but it was more than enough that the original DS already had powered high-pressure hydraulics to serve the brakes, the steering, the clutch, the gearchange, and the self-levelling suspension. It also had perfectly progressive nitrogen springing, disk front brakes (Citroën's own), automatic load-sensitive lock-inhibition for the rear brakes, Michelin X radial-ply tyres (that particular revolution began when the X became the standard fitment on the previous model), a detachable roof of translucent resin-bonded glassfibre, front-wheel-drive stability, and a drag coefficient rivalling that of the slippery little Porsche coupé.

No car had ever been cleverer. No car was ever braver. The DS should have inspired the world to embark on a new course of motor engineering, to accept and advance the new standards that Citroën had set. All it did was to gratify the desires of 1.3 million people, to stimulate a lot of arguments, to expose a great deal of ignorance, and to stand as a lasting reproach to the rest of the industry whenever we compared what they were making with what, on the evidence of the DS, they should have been making. If it achieved no more than that, it was not the fault of Citroën; it was the fault of everybody else.

CHAPTER 8

1956–65

Is it gone for ever? I'm not certain. But I tell you it was a good world to live in.

GEORGE ORWELL

JOHN OSBORNE'S *Look Back In Anger* seemed timely enough when it was published in 1956. There is seldom a time when a newly emancipated generation does not condemn the generation which begat it; but there has seldom been such emancipation of a generation as was seen in the decade which followed, and seldom so much to be later condemned. In a decade dominated by Khruschev, distinguished by Kennedy, and nearly doomed by Johnson, such things were done as were to be lamented a long generation later. It was a guilty lamentation: at the time, most of us – not the Hungarians, not the Vietnamese, not the Pedestrians' Association, but most of us – thoroughly enjoyed ourselves.

It was not just Mary Quant's (and Courrège's) miniskirt, which did not lift to usher in a mood of revelation until about 1964. It was not just Beatlemania, which did not soar to chords of modal revolution until about 1963. It was just a sense of present or impending prosperity, in which apparently everybody (except, paradoxically, Berliners) was on the Spree.

Khruschev raised his wall across Berlin three years before Englishwomen raised their hemlines; but hallowed rights of passage had been challenged as early as 1956 by his Egyptian protégé Nasser, precipitating yet another Suez crisis. Notice was thus served that the oil-burning world was at the immediate mercy of the oil-producing world: Italy and Germany set about building economical but ineffectual bubble-cars, while Britain, starting the world's first atomic power station at Calder Hall, served what the world's 19th-century thinkers should have seen as notice to quit. If they did not recognise it as such, they could not mistake the sign in the skies of 1957, when the USSR sent up Sputnik, the first satellite.

Motoring enthusiasts, who seldom look above the horizon, had their own marvel to ponder. The Cooper Formula 2 racer, with its engine behind the driver in a crude but compact and light chassis, was doing wonders in Formula 1 events. This

1.5-litre car won eight of the ten first-class F2 races of 1957, and with a slightly larger engine it began to appear on the leader-board amongst the élite of 2.5-litre F1 contenders. There was another Elite of 1957, the ravishingly beautiful new Lotus coupé which promised a new paradise of reinforced plastics and Costin aerodynamics[86]; but while the young Lotus company struggled to make ends meet, Cooper made the ends of its car so neat in balance that by 1959 the GP version carried a new World Champion. So fast-burning was racing's revolutionary fervour that, after the beginning of the 1961 season, we should only ever see one more front-engined GP car in the lists – and that was the four-wheel-drive Ferguson, which sowed the seeds of what eventually looked like becoming another revolution . . .

The very air was heady with change. Over Los Angeles it would change to smog at the slightest provocation, prompting the legislators of California to introduce measures which would lead to the Clean Air Acts of 1965[87] and thereby offer America's starved minds the opportunity to become engrossed in another witch-hunt.

The comptrollers inside Ford were preoccupied, however, with their own hunt, one that Wilde might have described as the unspeakable in pursuit of the indelible: they wanted to know why the 1958 Edsel had been such a red-inked and unforgettable disaster. According to the marketing experts, the gross and pretentious Edsel should have been just what the status-seeking customers wanted. Certainly the extravagance of contemporary American cars pointed in that direction; but while people undoubtedly were in the mood to spend lavishly, the Jonesmanship of the early 1950s had taken subtle turns. People no longer spoke merely of *status*; each now cultivated his *image*, and the cult was fostered by an advertising industry prospering as never before.

Prodigal Americans were not the only devotees of this cult; profligate Britons

---

86 Glassfibre-reinforced plastics were introduced to aircraft structures in the wing fillets of the De Havilland Comet, the world's first jet-propelled airliner. Frank Costin had been working for De Havilland on the Comet before doing the shaping of the Elite for Lotus, proving himself one of the finest exponents (in Setright's view there was none better) of aerodynamics in car design in his time.

87 Britain had its own clean air legislation a decade earlier, aimed with impressive success at the historically notorious pea-soup fogs of all its principal towns. By proscribing the open coal fire, it precipitated the rush to adopt central heating in a country once notorious for its reluctance to have anything to do with it. The car, as will be seen, helped.

made it almost a culture. Most of them, their Prime Minister Macmillan announced[88] in 1957, had never had it so good; in 1958 they happily responded by buying more than a million cars (which was a record) and more than a few copies of Professor Galbraith's new book *The Affluent Society* (which was not).

Another million cars on the 191,000 miles of roads in Britain sounded altogether more serious than the issuance of the 50-millionth Ford upon the 3.5 million miles of US roads in 1959. Europe could not challenge such figures: France enjoyed or abused 766,000 miles of roads, the UK ranked second, Germany mustered 151,000 to come third, but the whole of Europe (exclusive of the USSR) had a total of 2 million miles – less than four times the length, though probably more than four times the area, of the roads of Japan. As yet, the Japanese industry was not hell-bent on filling any of them: ten years earlier, it had made more than 50,000 trucks but only 2000 cars.

Pending the imposition of a new balance from the east, the west found its own corrective measures. Radar succeeded in its first conviction of a speeder in Lancashire in 1959 (he was fined £3), while a more gross form of antisocial behaviour in Cuba was checked by the rising (essentially popular but politically less so) of Fidel Castro. In the world of motoring (a flatter world, with more limited horizons) the most salutary corrective for galloping elephantiasis and galloping consumption ever seen rolled out of the BMC factories on ten-inch wheels that for a while had worried Dunlop sick: suitably incredulous but improperly unconcerned, the world beheld the Mini.

More foolhardy than brave, more pure than simple, the Mini was more truly *a car for the people* than any previous pretender to the title, since an unprecedented 80% of its volume was habitable. To some it was as zany as the elephant jokes then in circulation (How do you get four elephants in a Mini? Two in front and two in the back!), to others it was a temple of sociability (How do you get 71 people in a Mini? Two in front and *soixante-neuf* in the back!), but to the dullard majority it was something to discuss, not to buy. They had been happy to take as many Morris Minors as could be made (and would keep them in production for many years to come); but that Issigonis design, in circulation since 1948, had proved much more than it looked. This new Issigonis design looked what it was – adventurous and iconoclastic as well as utterly sane – and that combination was too much for the timidity of the average man.

Knowing far less about motor engineering than he would ever admit, the man

Whenever times were hard, BMW always depended on the motorcycle market. After this little
piggy came to market, their production of motorcycles became voluntary rather than compulsory.

in the street was thoroughly befuddled by new developments. He had found it hard
enough to believe in tubeless tyres, which had been introduced in large numbers, both
in Britain and America, in about 1956 (though Goodrich had tried to do it years
earlier); he had not a clue about the steel-belted radial-ply concept[89] embodied in the
Michelin X, and the advantages of the new fabric-belted radial-ply Pirelli Cintura

---

88 He is often misquoted as saying *You never had it so good,* but in fact that was the
Democratic Party slogan in the US election campaign of 1952. What Mr Macmillan said to his
party members in a conference on 20 July was *Let's be frank about it: most of our people have
never had it so good.* On that very same day, a Vanwall driven by Tony Brooks and Stirling Moss
won the British GP, the first British car to do so since 1923.

89 Michelin deserved all credit for developing the idea, but the idea itself dated back to 1913
when two British engineers named Gray and Sloper patented all the essential features. Had the
Great War not intervened, the idea might have enjoyed more prompt attention.

were beyond his comprehension. As for buying a Mini, that was much too risky; he would rather hang on to the reprehensible old banger that had miraculously served him adequately (and occasionally served him right, though he might not survive the experience) until these new-fangled things had been around for a few years and proved themselves. Meanwhile there were plenty of things on which to spend his money . . .

He had started going abroad for holidays. He spent a lot on pet-foods: dogs, cats and canaries in Britain consumed a sum equal to two-thirds of Britain's overseas aid to underdeveloped countries. Most important of all, he had to have a television set, a bigger and better one than his neighbour's. One household in 15 had a set in 1951, one in four by 1955[90]; by 1960, it was two out of three. Britain, having started first, had a big lead in television, which the USA strove to follow; but it was in some of the smaller countries that this new and dangerously persuasive medium of communication was most aggressively cultivated. The Cuban rebels made telling use of TV; as for pioneering Britain, the graph of television statistics matched the graph for the number of students in higher education, and that in turn matched – with uncanny accuracy – the rising curve for crimes reported to the police.

Not usually reported was motoring's most common crime, that of using a dangerously ramshackle car on the highway: Britain's Ministry of Transport instituted annual testing in 1960, initially for cars that were ten years old. Not surprisingly, sales of new cars took an upward turn: between 1955 and 1960 the number of cars on British roads jumped from 3.5 to 5.5 million. Not many were Minis (the car had done more for the language than for BMC) but people were getting the message that cars ought not to be excessively big. In the USA, delayed response to the Suez crisis took the form of compact cars (compact by American standards!) and aluminium-alloy engines, of which the new Buick/Oldsmobile 3.5-litre V8 looked most promising. The ironfounders of America fought back, proving that with new materials and technology they could cast thinwalled iron blocks no heavier than thickwalled aluminium ones, and cheaper: the industry gratefully returned to the devil it knew, and that was that – except that GM persevered with a radically modern compact car which, with its air-cooled boxer engine in the independently sprung tail, was obviously inspired by the continuing success of the VW Beetle. There were sports versions, and in time a turbocharged one; the 1960 Corvair was full of promise.

One of the things which made 1961 a very full year was the 5-millionth VW. The economic recovery of West Germany continued at an amazing clip, though the

Bavarian government had to bail BMW out of a financial crisis. German car production and exports continued to prosper, and although people were emigrating in large numbers from all European countries, Germany was well supplied with 'guest workers', mostly from Turkey. Even more amazing things were happening even further east: already the world's greatest motorcycle maker, Honda introduced a car for the first time, and characteristically its engine was happy to run at 8000rpm. What was more to the point was that the Japanese motor industry, having quietly made itself the sixth largest in the world, was now expanding rapidly.

There were fears of fissile developments just over the water in Vietnam. In the aftermath of the troubled postwar years when (in decreasing order of righteousness) Britain, France and the Netherlands ran into difficulties with their colonies in the Far East, Vietnam looked likely to become a communist stronghold. By 1961 the guerrilla warfare was so troublesome that President Kennedy dispatched General Maxwell D Taylor to assess and advise; Taylor's counsel was to send several hundred US specialists to train and support the South Vietnam forces, but it was not to be long before others had boosted that trickle to a flood, with a hideous war the inevitable consequence.

Should the troubles spread, Britain had at least an insurance against difficulties with Malaysian rubber. Close to the refineries at Fawley, the petrochemical industry had set up a big new plant making synthetic rubbers which had wonderful properties absent from the natural tree-sap product. For some time Avon had been using some of these synthetics to make the grippiest motorcycle tyres ever known: riders were delirious with joy as they discovered such competence on wet roads as they had never dreamed possible. Dunlop set out to do the same for cars, making a big soft-riding tyre for big opulent cars (the expense always associated with new technology meant that it was bound to be a costly tyre) which they called the Elite. They miscalculated

---

90 It was the coronation of HM Queen Elizabeth II in June 1953 which accounted for such meteoric sales. It may be an illuminating comment on the replacement of the horse by the internal combustion engine that, as Princess during the Second World War, Her Majesty had learned to drive army trucks. It was an even more illuminating commentary on the standards that were unconsciously assumed by people in those days that, when families gathered to watch the coronation on TV, they dressed in their best clothes to recognise the occasion.

it badly: people were driving faster, the tyre was overheating, and premature failures were rife. It took Avon to find a disarmingly simple way of capping a cool-running high-speed tyre with a 'cling-rubber' synthetic tread. Before long the same safety was brought to the most humdrum of cars, and the man in the street began to take notice.

The high-speed tyres arrived in the nick of time. Britain's first[91] motorway, the M1, opened in 1961, and by the end of the year we all knew what car was king over it. Not even the XK120 in its time created such a furore as the new Jaguar two-seater, the fabulous E-type. If one really wanted to cultivate one's image, no other car could do as much for it as this most symbolic of them all.

The E-type did something else: it effected a new emancipation. At a typically Jaguar price, a modest price comparable with that of the Lotus Elite and far below those of Aston Martin or Ferrari, it enabled a man (or, better still, a woman) to discover that to drive at 140mph or more did not require the abilities of a superman (or, perish the thought, a superwoman) nor the wealth of a Croesus. In a sense, the E-type destroyed the very images it created: its sheer availability and its simple driveability achieved a salutary debunking of the mythology of speed. Once that had been done, many more very fast cars came into being, until sheer speed became commonplace. For those who wanted the image but not the reality, anything on wheels could be given a fancy steering wheel, a rev-counter, a matt black interior and a fashionable form of tailpipe trim; it then qualified for a GT[92] badge and entitled its owner to speak with authority on anything from Lanchester to Lotus.

He would be expected to defer to Jaguars when speed was the topic, but not all men were thus deferential – least of all the American driver Dan Gurney, whose 7-litre Ford Galaxie dismissed all the race-prepared Mk 2 Jaguars in a 1962 saloon car race at Silverstone. A crisper and more compact Ford Falcon came within a whisker of winning the Monte Carlo Rally two years running. If Jaguars could be beaten on the track, and the formidable Mini-Cooper S could at least be challenged on the road, perhaps the Americans truly had something? Obviously the old order was changing: one had but to contemplate the new Coventry Cathedral . . . What the Americans had, in that same 1962, was 2 million Chevrolets – and the Cuban rocket crisis, deftly solved not by the President but by Robert Kennedy. In Germany, the BMW crisis was ended by the launch of the *Neue Klasse*, the boxy 1500 which started the firm on a course from which they have never since dared to deviate. In Britain, Ford were innovative under the cover of convention: having satisfied themselves that making a Mini could never be profitable (BMC had had to find out the hard way), they wooed the man in the street with a saloon that carried the same four people in a hull much more loosely packed. The Ford Anglia 105E of 1960 was noted for its reverse-rake rear window, but in due course it was admired for its strong and free-revving little engine, whose short stroke and free breathing were to make it the basis of many a competition car.

Three years later Ford brought another new car to the market, this time a full four feet longer than the Mini but still a four-seater. The Cortina, aimed with unerring accuracy at the British family motorist, was an historic if lamentable success, but like the E-type it did good in a special way: it pioneered a new kind of air-blending heater with fresh-air ventilation of a standard never previously known.

Ford were soon to cheapen their system, but everybody else copied it. It was the logical thing to do, after the tyrannies of the old-fashioned cooling system had been overthrown a year earlier when the Renault 4 pioneered the sealed coolant circuit and the Bristol 407 pioneered the thermoswitched electrical radiator fan. People would no longer tolerate having to dress up to go driving in inclement weather: even the British, surely the least likely people on earth, had started to adopt central heating in their houses, and the clothing trade had been forced to adapt to this new circumstance; why not the motor industry?

The fashion trade – it went far beyond mere clothing now – was an absolute riot, from Beatle haircuts to boots. The French were rather sniffy about it all, having lost their supremacy, and derived considerable satisfaction from vetoing the British entry into the Common Market on the grounds that the UK was little more than a satellite of the USA. This could not have been quite correct, for in 1963 the fashionable thing to do in the USA was once again to participate in the purchase of 2 million Chevrolets. They were very fashion-conscious cars, emphatically full-sized in the full

---

91 The first to be taken seriously, that is. The very first British road to meet motorway criteria was the Preston bypass, just eight miles long, opened in December 1958. The motorways soon showed up the deficiencies in current car engines: many manufacturers had to take emergency action to replace old-fashioned white metal bearings with the modern steel-backed thinwall variety, an idea stolen by Vandervell from Napier but originating long earlier in Bugatti's Great War aero-engines.

92 *Gran Turismo* – the expression from which the initials are derived was first coined in Italy in the context of a 1750cm^3 Alfa Romeo of 1929.

American meaning of the term: the Impala was 17½ feet long. At least it kept its engine in the front to drive the rear wheels: so did the admirable new Fiat 124, which celebrated the reconstruction of Fiat by that most businesslike academic Vittorio Valetta. Amazingly stable and incongruously lively, the 124 was a superb piece of engineering in an unprepossessing body, the start of a dazzling decade for Fiat, and not to be mentioned in the same breath as the Cortina by any but the most dully uncomprehending denizens of Dagenham.

Brave BMC were not yet finished. Issigonis had gone further, with the help of Dr Alex Moulton, and created the only true super-Mini, the Morris 1100. Never a cult car or fashion object as the Mini had become[93], the 1100 was elegantly proportioned and cleverly sprung on Moulton's interconnected Hydrolastics; few people raved about it, but it remained a best-seller in Britain for a remarkably long time. It deserved success everywhere, but where else would a buyer give a second thought to anything from that strife-torn corporation?

A smaller British car that deserved far more success than it achieved was the Hillman Imp. It had an exquisite little die-cast aluminium-alloy engine, a turbine-smooth overhead-camshaft derivative of the Coventry Climax 'racing fire-pump' engine[94], in the tail; its suspension was calculated to ensure consistent understeer, despite the engine location, up to 0.7g; it had great bodily strength through excessive bodily weight; and it had some trivial teething troubles with its cooling system and its pneumatic throttle-pedal (a nice idea which deserves revival), so it came a commercial cropper. The Rootes Group had built a fine modern factory for it near Paisley, one of the only two decent examples of modern architecture then to be found in the entire Scottish desert, but the effort (and the qualities, if that be the word, of their locally recruited workforce) had cost them too much; Chrysler had to take a large stake in the company in 1964 to save them from extinction. The first step towards the complete Chrysler take-over which was to follow later, it cannot have done Chrysler much good at all; they should have been fighting off the GM onslaught in the US, where once again 2 million Chevrolets were sold in the year.

Did the sheer size of those things appeal to the expanded consciousness that the drug subculture had made fashionable? If bigger was better for the happy hippie of the swinging sixties, there were some very formal Germans who would not have wished to be associated with any such thing, but who were nevertheless very proud to be seen in the latest and longest *Grosser Prunkwagen*, the Type 600 Mercedes-Benz.

There was little space left for them in Britain, where the year's car sales reached a record total of 1.87 million: 600,000 of those were exported, but still the roads were crowded. There was a record traffic jam, too, measuring 35 miles from Torquay to Yarcomb.

Most of the travellers involved were heading for their summer holiday resorts. Things were very different when a new record was set on the recently opened M6: a frightening pile-up involved more than 100 vehicles and caused 123 casualties, though only three deaths. People were outraged: cars were too fast and too dangerous, roads were too indulgent and excessive. In fact the new motorways against which ecologists inveighed were proving not only to have a far better safety record than any other roads, but also to constitute undisturbed nature reserves for many species which came to live on the fringes and the central strips, prey only to the kestrels which also came to live there and were counted at a pair per half-mile[95]. And it was not the cars which were too fast, it was the drivers who were too stupid – but what social animal, under the impulsion of a cultural imperative, will stop to consider such an argument? In America things were much worse: the combination of inept unschooled drivers in rear-engined cars with swing-axle rear suspension had proved lethal, and the Corvair was now being pilloried.

The VW Beetle came in for some stick too, even though the subtitle of the book which cashed in on all these troubles declared war only on the American industry. As sales of the book *Unsafe at Any Speed* soared and the controversy raged

---

93 The tide of popularity really turned in favour of the Mini in 1964, when the sporting Cooper S version – new in 1963 when it triumphed in the Rallye des Alpes and in the Tour de France – won the Rallye Monte Carlo. Thus proven a giant-killer, the car's prowess could no longer be doubted, and it rocketed to fame by association with the famous as much as by further sporting successes, numerous though these were.

94 Wartime experience had shown the fire services the need for a mobile pump unit light enough for two men to carry. Coventry Climax responded with an uncommonly efficient little four-cylinder engine which in due course found its way into a variety of lightweight sports cars and eventually grew enough to be a successful Grand Prix engine.

95 Something in the air prompted the kestrels to disappear when the coming of exhaust catalysts made us start using unleaded fuel. Nature eventually found a balance, as nature always does, and after some years the kestrels returned. Either they were tougher or fuel additives had changed again.

ever more widely, the author Ralph Nader showed what American lawyers are too often made of: he suppressed judicious objectivity in favour of profit, seeing for himself a new role as demagogic leader of a consumers' rebellion, with the jealously hated motor industry once again cast in the role of villain, tyrant, and money-grubbing trampler on the faces of the poor and unsuspecting. He did it very well, very profitably, very convincingly: in next to no time, neither the industry nor the government knew whether crash statistics mattered more or less than toxic emissions. All they knew was that unless they arrived at Utopian perfection in both, and that promptly, the law courts would pretty soon be redistributing all the money not in Fort Knox.

Secretly, both the industry and the government saw ways of turning the situation to advantage. The flood of new legislation on emissions and safety standards did at least as much to keep foreign competition at bay as it did to make American cars better. The Swedes soon followed their example, and the Germans, and the Japanese, even the Australians, all taking to heart the cynical Tom Lehrer lyric about the Old Dope Peddler 'doing well by doing good'.

None of this hypocritically high-principled skulduggery stopped two-thirds of a million Britons from flooding through the Earls Court turnstiles for the London Motor Show in 1965. Nor did it stop 2 million Americans from buying Chevrolets yet again. It did not stop a lot of young Americans from confirming the popularity of the new and stylish sporty-car that Ford had offered them in the Mustang. It did not stop the Summers brothers from setting a new speed record for wheel-driven cars, at more than 409mph in their pencil-slim Goldenrod powered by four compacted Chrysler Hemi engines[96]. It did not stop the new Ford GT40 from upsetting the established order by winning the long-distance sports-car race at Daytona, nor did it stop Honda from toppling the Grand Prix establishment by winning the Mexican race, the last GP of the season and of the 1.5-litre formula.

None of the fuss about fuel shortages was abated when Britain announced that she had found natural gas in the North Sea. By no means all of those who deplored the loss of life on the roads agreed with Britain's abolition of the death penalty. Not all of those who proclaimed equal rights for all mankind were happy to see a turbanned little Sikh, Joghinder Singh, score a runaway win for Volvo in the tough East African Safari Rally; they were even less pleased when Mr Joghinder later completed his hat-trick in Datsuns.

On the other hand, Britain's large population of Luddites expressed some satisfaction when a non-motorist known as Mrs Barbara Castle but recognised in some quarters as Minister of Transport told us that we were to suffer a 70mph limit even on our newly beloved motorways. An equally large section of the population, the Gullibles, believed her when she said that it was an experimental measure and would only be temporary . . .

---

96 How much simpler and purer than the absurdly complex and costly British car, *Bluebird,* which had with so much effort set the previous record!

CHAPTER 9

1966–75

If Detroit is right . . . there is little wrong with the American car that is
not wrong with the American public.

JOHN KETAS

THE CAR WAS NEVER BESET by such a crisis as that which transformed it and the world in this decade. It was not one of those common crises that arise from the desire of some class or some nation to slit an adversary's purse or throat; it was not even one of those more mysterious (but, according to Keynes, no more necessary) disorders that the capitalist world always capitalises as The Economic Problem. It was a crisis of conscience – and, even now, it may be too soon to offer thanks for having come through it satisfactorily.

The decade began brightly enough for the motoring world, with Ford justifying the frantic disbursement of $15m by at last winning the Le Mans race[97]. The American motor industry had plenty of money, after all: in the previous giddy year it had produced a record 9,305,561 cars, while Japan had made only 696,176 – even fewer than Canada. Production was soaring everywhere, for the car had become a status symbol more urgently sought than ever before, by people who found status harder and harder to achieve. The poor Papuan might assert himself with nothing more than a boar's tusk thrust through his nose, but the rich westerner needed at least a ton of painted and powerful metal, and even then suffered the chagrin of seeing his neighbour blowing the same note on an apparently identical trumpet. Cars, unlike noses, were mass-produced for the common man, and what they really did for his status was to make him more and more common.

This was less true in Europe than elsewhere, for the enthusiasts of Europe were better educated in the niceties of motoring than elsewhere, and were correspondingly more demanding of progress. It was a great time for technological novelty: stereo gramophone records[98] were now taken for granted, and in 1966 the Hovercraft went into service just 11 years after Cockerell first thought of it. In that same year an intelligent and perceptive young racing Texan named Hall (working in secret cahoots with GM) created a car that was forced down by airflow as sternly as the Hovercraft was held up: mounting a large inverted wing above the rear of his Chaparral sports-racing car caused a strong downforce to be generated aerodynamically, increasing the grip of the latest low-profile tyres that Firestone had developed for racing and that would in 1966 find their way into F1 racing[99].

The flurry of technical innovation continued. In 1967 NSU produced the sweetest, smoothest and most encouraging car that had yet been seen, the Wankel-engined Ro80; this development was echoed by the similarly engined Mazda, while all manner of other makers from GM to Rolls-Royce made noises of intent to do likewise. In 1968 Jensen produced something no less revelatory of the future, the four-wheel-drive FF; but the echoes of this have proved to have a much longer reverberation period, and there is still food for thought in the fact that the customers of the late 1960s bought the cheaper Jensen Interceptor because, although it was not nearly as good, it looked almost identical.

The FF was perhaps the only British car to set new standards at this time, although the healthy domestic market absorbed 1.4 million new cars in that Jensen's natal year; the Jaguar XJ6 so widely acclaimed a year later merely confirmed the market value of old standards. In other fields such notions were treated with grave suspicion: it was in 1968 that Britain abolished theatre censorship. We had finished with the era of the angry young man; we had, we thought, almost finished with that of the unleashed adolescent, who believed that society had made him a god when it had really made him an idol. Swinging '66 was a time of intense conviction, all too soon to give way to serious doubt. In China, where the Little Red Book of Chairman Mao suddenly

---

97 This was the event at which the winning American drivers showed their class by spraying the crowd with the champagne in which their victory was supposed to be toasted. The vulgarian display of disrespect for this princely drink, nowadays a commonplace of riotous victory-podium behaviour, stems from this original and deplorable example.

98 The industry had learned to make them of vinyl, because the nastily brittle shellac formerly employed was made from an insect from south-east Asia and supplies were now difficult to obtain. It was all to the good: the best of the new LP records, if played through high-quality apparatus, sounded better than anything that has yet been achieved with the digital compact disc.

99 It took the F1 world two years before they could catch up, wings beginning to sprout from their single-seaters in 1968. Hall's next step was to make a Chaparral (the 2J, known as the sucker car) that functioned like a reversed-flow Hovercraft, generating even more downforce and doing it at all speeds. Racing people resent the intrusions of the clever, and the principles of the 2J were ruled out of motor sport everywhere.

Held down by air: the vast rear wing of the Chaparral transmitted its downforce directly to the hubs of the rear wheels, which was intelligent but in other hands structurally dangerous.

appeared in millions of hands, the Cultural Revolution was already starting.

A different and more indelible red began to stain hands in Vietnam. The USA dropped its pretence of acting as expert advisers to the anti-communist faction there, and the two sides rushed together into a combat calculated to prove, by slaughter and attrition, which was the finer ideology. The Vietnam war was to go on getting worse and worse for years and years, and every evening it came home to America on television. While their young men in Vietnam grew more and more vicious and dissolute, the folks at home felt their anger change to guilt. Those who could find an anodyne in bread or circuses did so to excess; those who could not turned their self-examination to a series of cultural witch-hunts, the environmentalists and the safety campaigners joining forces to pillory the motor industry while the government, relieved to see how this counter-irritant distracted the people from contemplation of more painful but more distant happenings on the far side of the Pacific, did everything to encourage them.

The space race served the same purpose, until in 1969 Americans proved that they had the Right Stuff by visiting the moon. On their return, President Nixon announced (with what has become typical presidential effrontery) that it had been 'the greatest week in the history of the world since the Creation'. Britain, still nursing hopes of joining the EEC, felt something similar about the retirement of Charles de Gaulle; but in Britain, too, consciences were beginning to be nagged by television each night[100], recounting the violence that broke out in Ulster over issues much older than those in Vietnam.

At least there was evidence that conflicts of arms did not have to be chronic. In 1967 the situation in the Middle East had become acute, as President Nasser of Egypt made a new bid for leadership of the Arabs. He mobilised his troops on the Sinai border, ordered the UN peacekeepers to leave, blockaded the Straits of Tiran, and invited support for the war that would wipe out Israel. Syria, Iraq and even Jordan[101] closed in to share the triumph. Israel dealt summarily with them all in six famous and occasionally miraculous days, but observers were left with the uneasy thought that three-fifths of the world's known oil lay beneath Muslim states, and that in future there might be difficulties in obtaining it.

The American motor industry had no thought for that morrow. It had to deal with emissions laws which threatened to grow ever more stringent, starting in California and culminating in the Clean Air Act of 1970. California suffered a unique climatic pattern along its coastline, where layers of stagnant air frequently settled along the slopes of the picturesque mountain ranges parallel to the shore. The normal flow of fresh air could be inhibited by these stagnant blankets, leading in large urban areas (notably Los Angeles and San Francisco) to a rapid build-up of fumes identified as coming from the famously dense traffic there. Never mind that most of the ambient foulness in the atmosphere, coming as it did from such sources as factories and power stations and natural vegetation, was no fault of the car; society decreed that the car

---

100 The spreading seduction of the gogglebox was nowhere better quantified than in addicted Britain, where figures showed that the average adult watched it for four hours every evening.

101 King Hussein was one of the bravest and best of men, but on this occasion he did not dare to be left out.

should put it right. The measures that had to be taken had to be quick ones, and they dismissed fuel consumption as irrelevant.

American engines began to be festooned in auxiliary pipework for exhaust recirculation or catalysis, which meant the disappearance of lead from gasoline and the abasement of compression ratios. Fast idling, poor throttle response, low power and high temperatures began to make the American engine thoroughly unpleasant; defensive engineering to deal with crash-safety legislation did the same for the rest of the American car. In the mid-1960s it was beginning to be good; now, worried America turned on it viciously and forced it to be bad again.

It could have become better, had American industry not been so defensively forceful in trying to maintain a dominance that it no longer deserved. In 1972 Honda created a new small car, small enough for it to have been thought beneath the contempt or even the attention of American customers. Then, to the incredulity and shock of the American industry, Honda inserted in that small car a small engine that might have begun a revolution – but which instead triggered all musterable forces of repression.

It was in the USA that the Civic thus powered was marketed, with the most shattering effect on the motoring scene. America was held fast in the grip of the pollution scare, with new legislation demanding a drastic cleansing of exhaust emissions by 1975. Every car manufacturer, domestic or otherwise, had protested that what was being asked was impossible – except Honda, who created this new engine (they called it the CVCC) to meet these future requirements, and offered it in the Civic. The American people loved it, and with it learned to love Hondas; but the despairing American industry, unable to match Honda engineering, persuaded the legislators to recant. No longer would the law insist on inherently clean-burning engines; instead it required the fitting of bulky and costly[102] catalyst chambers to scrub some of the harmful constituents out of conventionally foul exhaust gases.

In fact the catalytic converter performed no atmospheric miracles: no processes took place in it that could not and eventually would not occur naturally in free air. All that catalysis did was to accelerate the processes of nature, but by preventing the concentrations of contaminants that nature would deal with rather more slowly, it offered prompt treatment at a price that those who would profit reckoned people would pay. That is why all our cars have to be corrupted by catalysts today, including Hondas – despite which Honda engines are still the world's cleanest, as well as the world's liveliest.

The milkman delivers; the battery-powered milk float obstructs. So, to be fair, did the milkman's horse before it; there has at least been some progress.

In Britain, where memories are long and foresight is discounted, those who could be bothered to consider the problem at all reasoned that the electric vehicle was the answer. They thus proved that they had not understood the question, since the electricity (blandly assumed to be something one found in batteries) had to be generated somewhere; but they triggered a mild explosion of quite futile little battery-driven horrors to add to the existing collection. It was in truth a small collection, but

102 At least, as the US government appreciated, the money would be spent in the USA, where Johnson Matthey (the precious-metals arm of General Motors) were ready and anxious to supply the world with catalysts. As noted elsewhere, the General has a flair for winning battles by fighting on both sides.

a distinguished one: in 1967 Britain had 55,000 battery-electric vehicles on its roads –
most of them were milk floats, but there were also fire tenders, trucks, buses and mobile
shops – and that quantity was greater than could be found in all the rest of the world.

Italy was having its troubles too, but the growing social unrest had not yet
interfered with the revival of merit in Italian cars. Fiat, sometimes using Autobianchi
to test the market, was breeding new marvels faster than gestation seemed possible,
but none was more significant than the Fiat 128 of 1969. Modest in size and brilliant
in detail, it was this car which confirmed the pattern for all popular manufacturers to
follow. Citroën had in 1934 made the front-wheel-drive car work; BMC had made it
fun; with the 128, Fiat made it good, resolving all the problems of erratic steering,

The ever-adaptable car: used as barricades during the Paris student riots.

tricky handling, noise and tyre wear and balance and habitability which had come to the surface in the previous generation. The 128 had modest dimensions, brisk performance, decent economy (which still mattered to Europeans) and unprecedented road manners; it also had front-wheel drive, a transverse engine, an overhead camshaft, radial-ply tyres and several other things that likewise have since been adopted by every serious maker of popular cars.

No manufacturer was ever more serious than Citroën, and none[103] ever displayed more contempt for what was popular. The 1970 Citroën SM was a low-drag, high-density demonstration of what could be done for the modern car by systems engineering. This discipline had become very highly developed in the dauntingly complex machinery of aviation; it was a much simpler aid to modern flight, the rocket engine, which that year drove Gary Gabelich across the Utah salt at 622.41mph, so that man could now proclaim that he had exceeded 1000 km/h on wheels. The Citroën GS, of that same year, was no rocket, but it shared with the SM the best steering geometry[104] ever built into a production car. Production was what was amazing about the GS: to mass-produce a car with powered hydraulics for self-levelling, ride height control, and braking – not to mention a most elegant air-cooled flat four engine, an immensely strong gearbox, an aerodynamically exceptional body, and detail felicities beyond number – would have been beyond the ability of half the world's mass-producers, and beyond the comprehension of the other half. If the SM demonstrated systems, the GS demonstrated logic; and if the Fiat 128 has been inadequately acknowledged as the most influential car so far, the Citroën GS deserves appraisal as one of the most meritorious.

One which seemed among the bravest was the Fiat X1/9. It had been tacitly assumed by the industry at large that new requirements for crash safety (including rollover tests) would for ever destroy the market for open cars. Creating a wonderfully small but extremely strong (and therefore heavy) hull structure that would stand up to all these requirements, and employing engine and running gear from the 128, Fiat

---

103 Until the firm was acquired by, and ground under the heel of, Peugeot, whose irrational and obsessive boss Jacques Calvet demonstrated that he was by nature as well as by career a politician.

104 Zero caster, zero camber, zero kingpin inclination: with so many corruptive influences removed, any messages conveyed by the steering were likely to be true.

defiantly put on the market a two-seater sports car with the engine aft of the cockpit and substantial roll-over protection above it. Delighted first by the removable rigid roof (which slotted into place above the engine compartment) and then by the superbly agile handling of the little car, such customers as could take it seriously at all loved it to distraction.

The evidence of some concern for economy and the preservation of driving pleasure, on the part of the French and the Italians, showed that the whole of the western world had not all been tarred with the one brush. A look at the average *per capita* income for 1970 reveals more: for the USA it was $4285, when even Kuwaitis managed only $2814, just $65 more than the West Germans. A Frenchman made $2490, a Briton $2031, a Spaniard $985; in Bangladesh it was just $53.

The American used his wealth with ease: it took him 17 weeks' work to earn the price of his new car. It still does, but in the mean time his country's economy became as unstable as all the others. The collapse of Keynesian economics was not just due to the insupportable cost of the Vietnam war; it was the breakdown and rearrangement of social structures that made the terms of the Bretton Woods[105] agreement no longer tenable. So the USA came off the gold standard in 1971, two years before the crises that everybody would later blame for all recessions, and inflation began to run riot. In this climate the car producer catches a cold: US industry had managed only 6.6 million cars in 1970 – and it is productivity, as much as wage levels, which determines inflation.

Japan was the new productivity champion. From 0.88 million cars in 1966, her output shot up to 2.06 million in 1968. That incredible growth rate was sustained: in 1972 the figure reached 4.02 million, having passed West Germany the year before to make Japan the world's second largest car-maker.

Britain, although suffering as much as some of the others, had cause for some optimism in 1970: oil was found nearby under the North Sea. By the beginning of 1972, de Gaulle was dead and Britain was in the Common Market; by the end of that same year, another 1.7 million new cars had been registered. Optimism was more widespread by that time: Henry Kissinger, perhaps the busiest man of the decade, declared that peace was in sight in Vietnam – something towards which the USA had been working for some years, even in its invasion of Cambodia in 1970. At the start of 1973, the Vietnam war ended; at the end, American car production totalled 9.7 million, an all-time record.

They were not the sort of cars over which to rejoice. European industry was not yet in the grip of such stringent legislation as in the USA, but it was already bad enough, and worse could be seen to be on its way. While there was yet time to produce a good and individualistic design, Citroën did so yet again: 19 years after the debut of the DS (which would have won the London–Sydney Marathon Rally if it had not been deliberately smashed off the road by agents of a rival team), the Citroën CX was a new and wonderfully refreshing expression of the very same concepts that had made the DS an inspiration for every rational product-planner.

It looked like excellent timing, but it turned out to be disastrous. The beginnings of another world-wide crisis interrupted what should have been a charmed life for the big Citroën – and nobody could be blamed for not seeing it coming, since Egypt had learned the folly of telegraphing its punches. On Yom Kippur (the highest of holy days, upon which even the most lackadaisical Jew feels impelled to withdraw from the workaday world) the Egyptian army jumped the Suez Canal and attacked Israel. Syria, with help from other Arab states, came in at the other end. Caught off balance, Israel took twelve days to defeat them all – but the Arabs had another way of waging war . . .

The Middle Eastern oil-producers suddenly raised their prices by no less than 70%, and restricted supplies to certain countries whom they considered to have favoured Israel against the Arabs. This was a threat to the livelihoods of all those in countries dependent on foreign supplies of oil, which included the Americans because they had worked on the basis of conserving their own reserves and buying from abroad. Japan, France and Britain were not the only ones at risk; there was utter panic almost everywhere. For a few months, oil and its products were in desperately short supply, until the markets adjusted to the realisation that in fact there was plenty of oil for ages to come and that the shortage was a political artifice. By that time the damage had been done: legislators everywhere, and most wildly in the USA, turned on the

---

105 In July 1944 the self-styled United Nations Monetary and Financial Conference met at Bretton Woods, NH, to make financial arrangements for the post-war world after the expected defeat of Germany and Japan. The conference was attended by experts from 44 states or governments, and drew up a project for the International Bank for Reconstruction and Development (IBRD) to make long-term capital available to states urgently needing such foreign aid, and a project for the International Monetary Fund (IMF) to finance short-term imbalances in international payments in order to stabilise exchange rates.

motor industry and accused it of being irresponsible in promoting improvident oil consumption. Other industries and services[106] actually used more of it, but it was the car which had to bear the brunt of reducing consumption.

Suddenly it was no longer fashionable – in fact, it was sometimes deemed so anti-social as to be criminal – to drive a big car. This was another reason for Americans to feel righteous in turning from their familiar domestic giants to the abstemious and clean little Honda Civic, destined to win sales and hearts for years to come. In Europe, politically 'correct' disenchantment with the large car had grave repercussions. Citroën, needing sales to pay for the huge investment in the CX factory, found itself in serious financial trouble and was snapped up by Peugeot. Citroën had belonged to Michelin, but that brave firm which had backed the car-maker's engineering audacity for 40 years was now as lacking in confidence as all the other tyre companies: supplies of carbon black, and nearly all the synthetic polymers which had made the modern tyre so much better than the old tree-rubber variety, were derived from petroleum.

Citroën were by no means the only firm in trouble. Volkswagen would have been in trouble anyway, without any oil crisis, having been making the old Beetle for rather too long[107] and finding it hard to adapt to the manufacture of modern cars. VW's first new-generation car with front drive, water-cooled transverse engine, and some technical felicities such as a coolant heat-exchanger made of aluminium and plastics, was the 1973 Passat; it was a better car than people realised, but it was not a convincing one. The German government had to help; without such assistance, the new Golf (which reached the market in 1974) might never have been born.

It was probably sheer coincidence, but that was a year which was remarkable for the question of abortion being raised in courts and legislatures all over the place, from the USA to the USSR. They did not all reach the same conclusions about the legality and propriety of abortion, but it was odd that the issue should have arisen simultaneously in ten very different nations. Was it due to the machinations of the Women's Liberation movement, now in full swing? Was it another manifestation of that economic breakdown, requiring some new equilibration between swollen wombs and shrunken stomachs? It was a time when all manner of connections could be inferred, perhaps too often and too easily: while Britain was reeling from the oil crisis (it had already been renamed the Energy Crisis, making the connection easier to see) her miners thought it opportune to go on strike.

Calling it an energy crisis did not persuade governments to ease their pressure on car manufacturers. Simplifying the problem as politicians do when they wish to be seen to be doing something without actually doing anything worthwhile, governments everywhere latched on to the attractions of speed limits as appealing to the limited understanding of the ill-informed public. In 1973 overall speed limits were imposed in all major motoring countries. Most states of the USA accepted the 55mph blanket; in Europe the figure was generally 100 or 110 km/h, and only West Germany – conscious of the reputation that its domestic motor industry needed to maintain – bluntly refused to impose a maximum speed limit on most stretches of its Autobahn network. Before long, car buyers world-wide would come to believe the myth that only German cars were safe and reliable at high speeds.

Was this enough for either the peoples or their governments to satisfy their pent-up resentment of the motor industry? Far from it: new and frighteningly stringent regulations about fuel consumption (for example the USA's plan to have everything capable of 27.5mpg by 1985) were superimposed on the recent strictures on emissions and safety, although they were mutually contradictory.

There was a third threat, consumerism, to complicate matters even more. First the USA, then Germany and in due course other nations, discarded the age-old *caveat emptor* principle, and evolved a doctrine of absolute liability of manufacturers for the consequences of the use or even the misuse of their products. Terrified manufacturers dared not offer anything new until it had been tested so long that it was no longer new, and until so many caveats had been entered upon it that it could no longer work as originally intended.

The effect of all this interference was to create a moratorium in car design while every available engineer was put to work sorting out the existing mess. To step out of line was tantamount to suicide: never was there such a display of convergent technology as in the mid-seventies, when cars all seemed to become alike and it was very difficult to like any of them.

Those that were liked most came from Japan, which was sufficiently free from

---

106 Aviation was a good example, and something in which the USA was particularly active.

107 Much as Henry Ford had clung too long to his Model T. In 1972 it was the Beetle which at last broke the 15 million record production figure of the Ford T.

the constraints of any national tradition to be able to supply whatever people demanded. Elsewhere, national traditions took many a hard knock: even Italy caught the creeping contagion of speed limits, imposed ostensibly to save fuel but basically because it was a form of regulation which appealed to almost any government anxious to appear to be doing something. For Britain, the inflexible irrelevance of newly imposed metrication was symptomatic of her bitter subjugation to the bureaucrats of Brussels; at least there was consolation in 1975, when North Sea oil began to flow into British refineries.

It did little for the British motor industry, which in 1975 produced only 1.2 million cars after expectations of twice that many a couple of years earlier. The American industry was in just as parlous a condition, reduced to an output of 6.7 million just two years after its 9.7 million peak. Five of Chrysler's six home plants were closed down for a while, and many people argued that the company's European plants should be shut down for ever.

Times were hard for everybody. Inflation was rampant all over the world, many parts of which were still suffering from the acute famine which had run like a plague through the previous two or three years. It was not hard to see the link between poverty and hunger, between too little purchasing power and too many mouths to feed: the world population had doubled in 45 years. In the five years from 1970, it had grown by 357 million, and in a few more months it was to reach 4000 million.

About 25 million of them were working on or with cars. One in every two Americans owned a car, one in every four Britons, one in fifty Peruvians, one in five hundred Indians. Seventy years after Henry Ford had championed the cause of a 'car for the people', there was still some way to go.

CHAPTER 10

1976–85

If we cannot now end our differences, at least we can help make the world safe for diversity.

J F KENNEDY

BY THE END OF 1975, it seemed that we might be at the end of the story and that many people – especially car manufacturers – had come to the end of their hopes. The 35th and youngest president of the USA usually sounded hopeful, but the guarded optimism of the above quotation from him has a retrospective irony that bites no less in its application to the motor industry than to the political world at large – or indeed to his own life, for he said it in the year of his assassination. As we have seen, motoring in that 1963 was riding towards the crest of a popularity wave in which the diversity of cars from which to choose, and the diversity of motoring experiences that we were free to explore, were more kaleidoscopic than ever before or since.

By the second half of the 1970s, ending our differences meant something else in the motor industry, something more desperate, more sinister and cynical. While the convergence of technology and legislation was making cars more and more alike, the call was yet for less diversity.

Keenly aware of the dangers of competition from Japan and from the US-based multinationals, most members of the European motor industry believed that only by uniting could they survive. David Plastow, then head of Rolls-Royce and president of the SMM&T, said as much on the eve of the 1978 Brussels Show: by cooperation and collective development, Europe could make twice as many cars as Japan. Heading the list with an annual output of 3.8 million cars was West Germany. Almost at the other extreme was Britain, that home of diversity where small firms (including R-R) proliferated: her output was now 1.4 million, less than Italy's and scarcely more than that of Belgium – and who had heard of a Belgian brand since the days of Minerva? Yet Austins, Fords, Opels, Vauxhalls, and money, were all made there, to the tune of more than one million cars a year. As a scene for the Plastow pronouncement, Brussels was curiously appropriate.

If the place was right, the timing may have been poor. Whether or not it was public knowledge, we were already on our way back from the abyss. Most of the collaborations later to be seen as significant had already been arranged; what may yet be seen as most significant is that, whereas the European firms closed their ranks against the foreign onslaught, the Americans and some British established links with Japanese firms. If there was a possibility of conquering by assimilation, there was also a probability of survival by being assimilated. That there was hope, one way or the other, was revealed by the rich crop of new 1977 cars: a lot of them looked suspiciously similar, but if there were not many fathers there were plenty of mothers.

The astonishing thing about this period was what did not happen. All the crises, all the conceptual upsets, the soaring price of oil, the shrinking of the market and of the cars intended for it, the confinements of the battery-electric vehicle or of liquefied petroleum gas, the airbags and 50mph barrier tests and the demise of the high-performance car – all the dreadful things that had been promised us after the 1973 oil crisis somehow failed to materialise.

One car above all expressed the new optimism, the Porsche 928. Its makers were wonderfully brave about it, not only because it denied so many of their own long-standing traditions (though these will never be extinguished until the 911 is extinct) but also because it was totally new from stem to stern. That was brave enough, but the real courage of Porsche showed in the revelation of the 928 as not only an expensive car but also a big-engined one and, most of all, a fast one. Technically the car was full of interest and merit; stylistically it was again brave, inviting a return to curves in place of the rectilinear boxes that had served as car bodywork since the mid-1960s. The whole thing was a magnificent tribute to man's conviction that he should press on undaunted, leaving the moralists to pass judgement on his performance when they were good and ready[108].

Even the tyres on which the Porsche rode, tyres fatter and squatter and more plastic in feel than any we had known, were evidence of a new way of doing the things we had always done. Pirelli had originally designed the P7 – with its tight Nylon bandage surrounding and constraining the steel belts beneath the tread so that they

---

108 Moralists seldom display both these characteristics simultaneously.

could work as they should, as nearly as possible independently of the radial plies of the sidewalls – as a tyre to impart the best imaginable ride quality and road safety to large and heavy American saloons. When it was found to perform such wonders for high-performance cars as to dismiss all their previous standards of excellence, the makers of fast cars received it with joy; and the makers of tyres for lesser cars copied it, with appropriate adjustments to specification, performance, and cost, with such zeal that within a dozen years practically all tyres were made that way. Few people were aware of the details, but most people were at least vaguely aware that tyres were much less problematic than they used to be.

People at large were indeed no longer interested in the details. They merely wanted to be entertained by something new, and to be rid of the problems they associated with what was old. In 1976 Apple had produced the world's first personal computer, and all who were young in mind – or who wished to be believed so – applied themselves to mastering this unfamiliar, unimaginable, and too often unforgiving, new tool. Hardly any of them gave a thought to the fact that the underlying technology of the instrument was what had made their latest cars so unproblematic compared with those of earlier times.

In the saintly tradition that everything happens for the best, we must acknowledge that this new reliability was a by-product of the great emissions witch-hunt pursued (by the USA in particular) from the late 1960s. As the legislation developed, it came to be required that the new cars that were sold with certified low emissions (of whatever unwholesome things they were desired not to emit) should also be certified as capable of continuing as clean in their habits for not less than 50,000 miles. This meant that there had to be a phenomenal amount of pre-production testing done to ensure compliance with the new rules, making it economically more than ever necessary to employ as few power trains as possible, however many the apparently different models of cars embodying them. It also meant that many components that had been kept in use for decades or more would now have to be rejected in favour of others that were less likely to deteriorate in performance in the course of so long a mileage.

Notable among these was the mechanical contact-breaker that had been responsible for the timing of most ignition systems since Kettering devised it in the 1920s. Few car components went out of adjustment as quickly as that thing; few alternatives presented themselves as being capable of cheaply sustaining the necessary accuracy. The same applied to the alimentation of the engine: whatever the virtues of this carburettor or that, all carburettors tended to allow the engine to take what it wanted, rather than (as in the case of fuel injection apparatus) giving it what it should have.

Salvation came to both ignition and injection systems in the form of electronics. It is typical of an electronic system that, having no moving parts but being composed largely of solid-state devices, it is actually incapable of the progressive deterioration in performance associated with mechanisms. Either it works properly, or it does not work at all.

It took some years to make sure that it would always work, or failing that to devise some system of redundancies (as in aviation) so that failure is always safe because it prompts take-over by another system that has not failed. It took at least as much time to learn how to make sure that the machinery (the engine, for instance) being supported by these electronic systems would itself resist such wear and tear as might cause it to deteriorate in its sealing, its combustion, and so on. It took years to make the 50,000-miles rule effective; but when it was done, we had a new generation of cars – it would almost be fair to call it a new race of cars – of such probity as previous generations of users could scarcely imagine.

Manufacturers began to exploit their hard-won confidence in their new models by offering longer warranties, admitting longer service intervals, and occasionally even promising better trade-in prices, all of which were calculated to attract custom. This apparent confidence spread to the people, whose custom was duly forthcoming. They might have no grasp of the fine detail, but they knew that their new cars were not only cleaner (which made them feel socially at ease) but also actually better.

The German-based Green Party, which appeared to depend on the destruction of the motor industry to facilitate its eventual rise to absolute power, could not allow the motorist to feel socially at ease. Some casual observations that the German forests were looking less healthy than of yore were rapidly whipped up into an emotion-laden environmental campaign, supported by 'scientific' evidence, in which again the car was cast as culprit. Dying forest –*Waldsterben* – became a war-cry that the motor industry, especially in Germany, began to fear. Beset by calculations which showed that the trees would all have gone in ten years, the industry fought back with counter-accusations, any or all of which may have had some basis in truth. The causal contaminants, it was alleged, came wind-borne from French industry that was ever careless of what came out of its chimneys. The German forestry service had been relaxing its norms for the proper thinning and protection of the forests because tax revenues had been withheld for other purposes. As it turned out, the whole *Waldsterben* scare was a piece of political scaremongering: apart from the effects of a storm that hit southern Germany late in 1999 and killed more trees than 20 years of *Waldsterben*, the forests of Germany are as magnificent as ever.

The people remained as confused as ever, but there is always a limit to the amount of communal responsibility any individual is prepared to take. When it comes to the need for buying a car, the individual is likely to use that need to justify the desire for a car, even for a car of a certain kind. Clearly, the new cars on the market, with all their catalysts and computers and what not, were very much cleaner and more conscientious and better in every way (so we were told) than their predecessors; and that was good enough. Nobody expected them to be perfect, because nothing ever is (and if it were, nobody could afford it), but the effort had been made and now it was time to be practical and get on with life. People bought cars more happily now.

They were feeling more ready to try what was new and exciting, and the manufacturers were now able to turn their new-found electronics skills to that purpose. By the time that the film *Star Wars* had been running for a year and the first test-tube baby had been born, BMW and Mercedes-Benz were ready to offer anti-lock brakes as an admittedly costly but eminently desirable option. Actually the development of the ABS (a German acronym for Anti-Blockierung System) had been by Bosch, with an agreement that the two German car-makers should announce it simultaneously; but Mercedes-Benz callously jumped the embargo and announced theirs first, creating a fine show of righteous indignation and vows of revenge among their rivals.

Because ABS was costly, it met with some resistance. This was a pity, for among all the niceties of driving the braking skills are most difficult to acquire and impossible to perfect. Within a few years there would be cheaper systems – Honda, carefully using English for its ALB acronym denoting Anti-Lock Brakes, worked out an economical way of applying it to all four wheels of the Accord, while Ford devised a cheap system working on the front wheels of the Escort – but by then the impact had been lost and the message garbled. Ford made their system an option, costing the same as a sun-roof, and the customers usually chose the sun-roof because that was something that could be *seen*, not only by themselves but also by the Jones family next door.

Jones no longer applied technical criteria to his judgement of his neighbours' cars. He had lost touch with engineering developments during the past ten or fifteen years of frenzied evolution. He could scarcely tell an Audi Coupé from the Quattro version of it that had been introduced in 1979; but the keen motorist could, and those who tried it were amazed. The full-time four-wheel drive that could have been our inheritance from the Jensen FF a decade earlier now made it possible to deploy the unfamiliar power of a turbocharged five-cylinder engine in the Audi, and at the same time to maintain levels of grip and control at high speeds, and even on poor surfaces, such as made conventional super-sports cars faintly ridiculous.

Jointly and severally the messages about four-wheel drive and about turbocharging spread around, in all directions. Turbocharging was the simpler case: all that work on electronic engine management had dealt with the worst problems, and it remained only to decide when and how much boost to apply. The 24-hour race at Le Mans had been won by a turbocharged car for the first time in 1978 – deservedly by Renault, who had been doing so much work on the process that in 1979 they scored the first win for a turbocharged car in F1 racing. By 1982 you could even have turbocharging in the Bentley Mulsanne, though it would be 1985 before the Bentley Turbo R offered roadholding enough for you thoroughly to enjoy the extra urge.

There was indeed a brief proliferation of turbocharged cars at all levels from the sublime to the gorblimey. Some lasted better than others; some even enjoyed favour from the tax laws of certain countries such as Italy, where a blind eye was turned to forced induction. Elsewhere a more forbidding glare settled on it from the insurance companies who still held the whip hand in deciding what the motorist could or could not be allowed to afford to have. Only when the turbocharger was applied to the diesel engine (for which it was specifically intended by its Swiss inventor Büchi in 1909) was the device welcomed on all sides without reservations. From having previously been justly condemned as a noisy, smelly, dirty, heavy, intractable and underpowered menace[109] to health, road safety, and civilised refuelling, the diesel engine (nothing more than a tax-dodger in many countries) need no longer be regarded as intractable or underpowered.

The cult of four-wheel drive was slower in developing. Its domination of the rallying scene was rapid, but manufacturers loth to pay licence fees were anxious that any 4wd system in their production cars should be seen to be their own. All manner of variations on the theme, most of them makeshift part-time affairs, came on the scene under various brand names and as quickly disappeared because they were imperfect, inadequate and unwanted. There was, however, a newly popular use to which 4wd could be enduringly put.

Everybody had known about the Land Rover almost as long as they had known about the Jeep, and everybody sensible had relegated it to its proper place as a working vehicle for farmers and other honest outdoorsmen. It was therefore a brilliantly imaginative piece of thinking which prompted the Land Rover's manufacturers to produce a high-performance 4wd vehicle, powered by the 3.5-litre V8 Rover engine acquired from GM, debased for manufacture in Britain and employed in certain Rover cars. The really bright aspect was the body, which was an assertively non-utilitarian saloon of cavernous size and mildly luxurious furnishing.

Here was a new kind of sports car – a car in which the comfortably wealthy could go out into the country, as wild as it might be, to enjoy country sports, and then drive home again. They could even use it as a smart big town car. Many did. Then came others who, frustrated by the rules and restrictions of road traffic, found the idea of charging around open road-free country wonderfully liberating. What hikers and riders thought of all this was scarcely considered: here was a new way to be venturesome at the weekend.

Gradually the idea caught on. It was accelerated in the USA, where countrymen were by no means the only motorists to remain fond of the traditional blue-collar pick-up truck as a general-purpose vehicle. To put a well-furnished closed body on a 4wd version of a truck chassis was an attractive idea that was quickly pursued, notably in 1982 by the Chevrolet Blazer. Soon Nissan and Toyota were sending similar machines from Japan to join the rising flood of what became known as 'sport-utes' (sporting utility vehicles), and the most astute manufacturers were exporting them to other parts of the world where distances were considerable and roads either rough or – more often – conspicuous by their absence.

Yet it was not the rough-roaders of the world, nor even those of America, who created a suddenly swelling demand for these steroid-swollen box-cars. The swelling tide of that consumerism which had initiated the safety campaigns of the 1960s and 1970s had reached flood proportions, and polite suburbanites of acute social sensitivity and chronic personal insecurity were ready and happy to believe that all it took to keep them safely on the road and immune from damage was a big, robust, heavy demi-truck with four-wheel drive. In places where an economical lifestyle came naturally, these gross four-wheelers caused many a sad shake of the head; but in Britain and especially in the USA they caught on like wildfire. Mothers who feared for their children's welfare used these huge things for delivering children to school and collecting them each day, and for shopping trips in between. Fathers feeling braver when so well-armoured used them for bullying their way through rush-hour traffic to work in the city.

There remained, however, a large number of people who clung to the other fashionably political line of thought, which dictated a high priority for fuel economy. For these, the motor manufacturers began to display a new – and perhaps for the first time well-engineered – concern for the aerodynamic virtues. Prominent among these was Audi, whose 1982 version of the upper-middle-class family saloon set new standards in airflow management and slippery styling. Few people recognised that the contours of the new Audi 100 recalled those of the Ro80 made in 1968 by NSU, the ailing pioneer of Wankel engines whom the Audi-VW group had assimilated some years ago. Most people recognised that the smoothed surfaces and nearly flush windows of the new Audi made wonderful sense, and would be copied by most other manufacturers before long. They were right.

Then, with half the world crying economy and the other half screaming safety, France created a new kind of car which promised some of the features that both halves sought. By smoothing the contours of the old-fashioned two-box sport-ute body until the whole thing had been brought inside a single smooth volume, with a chisel nose like that of a high-speed locomotive and a rakish windscreen continuing the line of the bonnet up to the roof, the Renault Espace of 1984 finally brought structural and aerodynamic logic to bear on the shape of cars that had for ninety years been trapped within the conventions originating with the *système Panhard*.

---

109 Unlike petrol, which evaporates very quickly, diesel oil is persistent in its liquid form. When it is spilled on the filling-station forecourt, it remains where it falls, spreading in puddles which soil the shoe-soles of all who pass by and notably making slippery the soles of the driver when he gets back in his car and addresses its pedals. When it is spilled on the road, it remains there for ages, and when it eventually sinks into the pores of the tarmac it will be floated up to the surface again by the next rainfall. So long as it persists, it is the most dangerous skid-inducer of modern times, having in particular killed unknown multitudes of motorcyclists and maimed many more. Spilt diesel is indeed the most criminal of noisome emissions, but not the only one for which the engine may be blamed: there is much evidence that its exhaust fumes are strongly carcinogenic, but because early emissions legislation was aimed only at such exhaust ingredients as aggravated smog, this accusation was largely ignored. Efforts to revive it have been actively resisted not only by the engine manufacturers but also by the transport industry whose heavy goods vehicles rely on diesel to the exclusion of all else.

To match the increasing acceptance of seat harness, the interior of the Espace allowed every individual among the many passengers who could be packed in to wear an individual harness (soon to be a legal requirement in many countries for children as well as for adults), and the adaptability of the seating enabled the vehicle to be used for all manner of serious or recreational purposes. To make so much interior space available, the whole cabin was set high above all the machinery and underpinnings, and so the view of the driver was as commanding and confidence-inspiring as from a demi-truck.

Slowly at first (production was initially modest) but with quickening vigour, the idea caught the public imagination. Nobody saw that the idea was a reincarnation of that personnel-carrier of the 1950s, the Bedford Dormobile, a slab-sided sliding-doored soggy horror that began as a smart resource for lively families and ended as a scruffy transport for builders' labourers. Instead, soggy monovolumes multiplied in every market, their sales figures soaring almost as high as their centres of gravity.

Nobody bothered any more about keeping the weight low down. While ATVs and MPVs[110] toppled off many a slope or rolled over many a corner, the motor industry realised that it was on to a good thing, a means of making cars cheaper while assuring the multitudes that they were making them smaller. Making the car taller allowed its volume to be redistributed, and its length reduced, without it becoming actually smaller – but the more nearly the shape resembled a cube, the less material would be required for enclosing it, and so costs could be reduced. The customer habitually identified 'small' with 'short', so build tall and everybody will be happy. Renault were understandably quick on the scene with their little Twingo, in production by 1993, but in due course all the economy-car makers would be treading the same path.

Meanwhile a lot of interesting openings had been explored. By the early 1980s the industry had more or less caught up with the requirements made of it in the preceding dozen panic years of safety and emissions legislation, and now it was time for each to try to break out of the pack and try to establish a lead. After so long in the doldrums, 1983 was a vintage year.

It was the year in which the USA began to recover from its economic depression, well ahead of Britain where unemployment reached 3¼ million and the best-selling car was the British Leyland Metro. It was a year in which new technology made good news: the Internet opened, US President Reagan proposed his 'Star Wars' policy of developing science in space to counter threats of war and make the nuclear missile obsolete and redundant, and the compact disc made its appearance to an accompaniment of extravagant claims and reckless lies. That sort of exaggeration and deceit was customarily the province of the motor industry, but this time the car-makers could truthfully boast how well they had done.

Conscious of their duty to the taxi-drivers of this world, and jealous of the custom enjoyed by rivals who made smaller cars than theirs, Mercedes-Benz extended their range downwards with a compact C-class saloon. Conscious of their obligations to the lower-middle classes, Citroën extended their range of sophisticated saloons downwards (as distinct from tarting up their economy cars, as others might) with the BX, which brought their admired hydropneumatic suspension into a broader market-place. It also addressed a matter of growing concern, which was the cost of repairing body damage in a car that was all body: extending their principles of removable and replaceable panels, and using a lot of plastics, they enabled the owner of a BX to dismantle much of the body using only a single Philips screwdriver.

Also prominent in the 1983 line-up were two cars that would prove resoundingly successful in the still-growing world of the small hatchback. Fiat had already in 1980 made a truly small utility car which, thanks to the ingenuity of industrial designer Giorgetto Giugiaro (never better displayed than here), had an interior that was utterly original, extraordinarily practical, and uncommonly versatile; but that little Panda was very much a car for the marginal motorist. For 1983 there was a more conventional hatchback – except that it looked suspiciously tall to people who would not see an Espace for another year – that was named the Uno, was voted Car of the Year, and was to found a whole new Fiat dynasty. There was much less that was remarkable about the new Peugeot 205, except that in another year it would yield a GTi version that would be the ideal of every young fellow who thought himself a wizard at the wheel.

There were also, in that vintage year, a couple of cars from Japan that should have been paid more attention if the world had yet been smart enough. For years the

---

110 All-Terrain Vehicles and Multi-Personnel Vehicles – but we had entered the age of the acronym. The language of Japan lends itself naturally to such usage, and Japan was the home of the electronics which had come to dominate the world, so there were bound to be some side-effects.

Japanese had been doing thoughtful things like installing bolts with head uppermost so that even if the securing nut came off the bolt would stay in place; now Toyota had created an engine bay that was a model of intelligibility and accessibility, with all pipework neatly arrayed and readily identified, and with all servicing points arranged in the top stratum of the compartment. The car was the Camry, a well-finished and well-found middle-class saloon in which comfort and serenity were prioritised to good effect. Yet, for engineering of such quality and individuality as to eclipse all the others, including Citroën and Mercedes-Benz, the reasoned accolade had to go to the new coupé – unexpectedly lively and well-mannered – to which Honda allocated the Prelude name. If this were the Prelude, what should be the sequel?

CHAPTER 11

FROM 1986 . . .

The age of chivalry is gone. That of sophisters, economists, and calculators, has succeeded; and the glory of Europe is extinguished forever.

EDMUND BURKE

WRITING IN THE PREVIOUS CHAPTER OF the audacity with which Porsche launched their 928 in what might have been hostile times, I observed that many people welcomed it, leaving it to the moralists to pass their judgement when they were good and ready. Making such judgements is an unavoidable part of the interpretation of history; but the historian of the most recent years cannot be both ready and good. The perspective is too short and steep, the relationships between cause and effect too confused, just as a wood may be obscured by trees. The events have been recorded, events ranging from the rise of the Ayatollahs to the fall of DeLorean; their interpretation must wait until the pattern can be seen and the rhythm felt.

Because they fit the pulses of some long-established rhythms, much as tides mime to the moon and sun, some trends in car design can easily be identified. There are pendula which swing inexorably, if not always regularly, between one school of thought and another, between opposing poles of concern or even of obsession. Some have a very slow cycle of alternation: for a long while in the early part of the 20th century the best cars had four valves per cylinder, echoing racing practice; the same thing, if not for the same reason, began to happen again in the early 1980s. Sometimes the beat is faster: engines grow more powerful, until it becomes apparent that it is the turn of the chassis and running gear to catch up, or until an economic depression suddenly puts the emphasis on low prices and low running costs. In the decade which 1985 ended, the most obvious swing was towards a revival of interest in aerodynamics.

The arrival of the new Audi 100 in 1982 was beautifully timed to make the most of this resurgence of interest in airflow management. The cars which came after it were expected to be as good, but all were handicapped by rules that were overdue for revision or rejection. Whoever finds the best way around the legislative strictures about headlamps and bumper heights (which are relics of a self-protecting racket wheedled into effect in the 1960s by the American industry, to shackle us with mid-century tastes when we should have been making free with end-of-century technology) will come closest to realising some of our necessarily postponed ideals – always provided that the swing of some political pendulum does not interrupt our progress.

The popularity of aerodynamics may be the most obvious of recent and continuing trends, but it is not the most remarkable. The most amazing things have been happening in engine compartments, because three different cycles, of different periodicities, peaked together – just as moon and sun and planets can occasionally come into conjunction to produce freak tides. One was the quest for greater power from engines of modest size and thirst; the second was the need for better management of resources both within and without the car; and the third was a renaissance in systems engineering, something that has punctuated motor engineering

Aerodynamics studied by an aircraft manufacturer, as applied by the Bristol Aeroplane
Company to the Bristol 401 car of 1948, could be very convincing.

rather infrequently between the full electrics of the 1912 Cadillac and the full hydraulics of the 1955 Citroën.

Of these three, the first saw the brief[111] but phenomenal spread of the turbocharger, expressing a general revulsion from the sickly underpowered machinery produced by the concatenation of emissions controls and economy measures in the 1970s. The second found means of refining and controlling the performance thus revived, despite a steady decline in fuel quality and increasingly mordant economy standards. The third was realised in the application of electronics to the monitoring and regulation of all the underbonnet processes relevant to these things, at last finding worthwhile work for what had once seemed doomed to provide nothing better than pointless ignition and even more pointless dashboard calculators.

The further possibilities implicit in electronics were everywhere exciting, in such things as the regulation of active suspension, or the automatic management of the engine and the entire drive-line in response to driver demand or sensor-perceived danger. By 2000, with the hypocritically prosocial German manufacturers leading the way, it was beginning to look as if electronics, having enabled these manufacturers to create cars of such abilities as defied the competence of the average driver to exploit them, would now take over the major driving decisions from him so that the car might get along as well as it could without him. The route looks very like the one which leads from authority to tyranny . . .

Yet all these things were merely the technical effloration of the motoring times. What the world was doing was something far more frightening than what the motor industry was doing was exciting. The world was growing; and although a few of its occupants were reaching out into space, the world was growing in everything but space.

According to some scientists, it was growing warmer, and as a matter of habit they blamed this on the motor car. The terrestrial sphere is of some 268,000,000,000 cubic miles volume, beneath the surface slag of which a core of rock and metal reaches near 6000°C at its molten centre. While Earth tries to shed this heat from its surface, the sun daily pours in more – and Man thinks he can control the balance? What vanity is this? We cannot create; we cannot destroy; all we can do, as the rest of nature does on a scale to humiliate us, is to convert mass into energy or vice versa, and in the end it has to be accepted that Man and all he has made is but part of the planet, a trifling part of nature, with no rights to anything (least of all to immortality) and as readily disposable as the rest of it.

That goes for the vehicles, too, all 590 million of them, though by no means all of them cars, and scarcely any of them breathing and eating and drinking and wasting all the time as do the 6000 million people who now occupy the mere 57.7 million square miles (less than 30%) of the planet not smothered by that most amoral of regulators, the sea. It has taken less than a quarter of a century to bring that population from 4 to 6 billion, not one of whom can be criticised for wanting to have a car; but if they increase in numbers so much more rapidly than industry can build cars for them, then their majority is doomed to go carless.

They – we – shall have to find some other way, some better and more appropriate means of providing personal private transport, if much of the world is not to return to *the isolation, the lack of mobility, the lack of curiosity, and the hopelessness* of the Dark Ages from which the motor car plucked us such a little time ago. What form it will take, what materials and energies it might consume, can be no more obvious to us now than the motor car and aeroplane were obvious two hundred years ago. Meanwhile, the appetite of the motor industry can perhaps be sated by its attempts to give all the world the cars that until recently were the envied possessions of a small part of that world.

It may have been harsh economics, it may have been patronising cynicism, or it may have been a belated recognition of the simple practicality of the old hammer-and-chisel cars, that prompted many major manufacturers to offer a reach-me-down service to the less developed nations. Old Renaults had been made in Romania under licence to Dacia from 1968, by which time Hindustan was already building an ancient Studebaker and an even older Morris. In the 1980s much more was done: Hindustan began to offer its Contessa, clearly an old Vauxhall, while the compatriot Premiers were actually Dodge pensioners and old Fiat 1100 and 124 models. Old Opels were made in South Korea by Daewoo, old Mitsubishi worthies in Malaysia by Proton, old VWs in China under the Shanghai brand. In Central and South America there was less dissimulation: cars that had been retired or made redundant in Europe and the USA continued under the names of Chevrolet, Fiat, Renault, VW and others.

---

111 In its application to popular petrol-engined cars the spread of the turbocharger was decently brief; but when applied to the diesel engine (for which it had been specifically invented, back in 1909 by Büchi in Switzerland) it was found to overcome many of the constraints by which the filthy-oil engine's performance was handicapped. Most of the diesel cars that have lately prospered have done so by being turbocharged.

In South Africa Toyota did likewise, while others exploited the cheap manufacture there possible. Apart from the careless multitudes who drive in the middle of the road, much of Africa drives on the left, so it was convenient for BMW, Mercedes-Benz and others to build all right-hand-drive versions of certain models there and export them to all other right-minded countries, at prices adjusted to what each market would bear. A few of the really big manufacturers proposed what they were pleased to call 'world cars', basic and unsophisticated designs intended for cheap manufacture by low-grade labour and carefully chosen automata in factories that could be set up wherever conditions looked encouraging, and built everywhere as uniformly as possible.

Honda took a more sympathetic approach. Having made no cars at all in the first 15 years of its life after foundation in 1948, Honda had ceased to see Japan as its biggest market as early as 1977. By the end of its first half-century it was the world's eighth biggest maker of cars, and was taking the needs of the world very seriously, recognising how they varied in different parts. Starting in 1982 with the USA (where the Accord became America's best-selling car) and then Britain, Honda sought to design and manufacture in each region according to that region's needs. Further car plants were added in Turkey, Brazil and India, and then (like all the other major manufacturers) by way of joint-venture agreements Honda addressed the huge and newly inviting market in China.

Slowly but surely since 1978, when with Chairman Mao dead two years his Cultural Revolution was proclaimed at an end, China had been building its prosperity. The year 1989 was a painful one, seeing violence (the massacre in Tiananmen Square has become legendary) erupt to prevent reform turning into revolution; but in the mid-1990s China had proven itself as great a force in world economics as it was in world statistics. The rest of the world suddenly felt a profound conscientious obligation to do profitable business with China.

The liberalisation of China was less dramatic and much less sudden than what was happening further west. In 1985 Mikhail Gorbachev became leader of the Soviet Union and, recognising the acute need for Soviet socialism to be modernised, embarked on a programme of economic and political reforms. *Glasnost*, openness, was his faith, *perestroika* (restructuring) his motto, and the tidal wave of reform he set in motion engulfed him and the system he had sought to improve. In successive crises of confidence the massive edifice of the Soviet Republics began to crumble, the Soviet Bloc to fissure. On 9 November 1989 the notorious Berlin Wall was breached; by the end of 1991 the Communist Party had been declared illegal and the USSR was dissolved. Relief and astonishment, honour and opportunism, disgrace and exploitation all ran rioting round the world.

It was a time for extraordinary things. In many parts of the world, but especially in the Balkans, in central Asia, and in Africa, old-established rivalries that used to produce what we had called tribal wars now erupted in what were politically styled 'ethnic riots' but covered such areas and hurt such multitudes as would once have attracted the status of all-out wars. Millions of people were refugees, millions more destitute, millions more starving – but with 6000 million there were plenty more, and millions of them doing very well, not a few counting their millions after a dollar sign to personal fortune. Once again it was a time for the inconceivably wealthy to commission cars of prodigal specification and unbelievable expense, while others scattered their largesse among the newly profitable specialists who found and restored (over-restored, as often as not) what were sometimes mistakenly supposed to be 'collectors' cars'. Wild stories of wealth were told, alluding to Internet entrepreneurs, the Russian mafia, the narcotics trade, and all manner of lawyers, bankers, smoke-grinders and air-movers. Less obvious but less doubted was the new wealth of the leading businessmen on the Pacific Rim of Asia, where Malaysia had become the world's largest exporter of manufactured goods, and where by 1995 Hong Kong and Singapore ranked among the world's ten richest states (per capita), ahead of Britain and France.

Amidst all this, in the very years when the USSR was falling apart and the Chinese people were coming together, the major Japanese motor manufacturers all brought their skills to bear on a challenge of their own making.

This extraordinary synchronicity has been discussed elsewhere in this book, looking for examples to the invention of the calculus or of vulcanisation, to the origins of Rubik's cube or the simultaneous writings of Shakespeare, Cervantes and Montaigne. Yet what was it that prompted four Japanese manufacturers, between 1989 and 1991, to produce what they severally considered to be high-performance cars representing the then state of the art?

The cynical answer is that Toyota had just amazed the American market with its new Lexus LS400, promptly hailed as the best luxury car in the world. On the other hand, Toyota was also playing the sports-car game with its twin-turbo Supra series, some of which were fast and a few of which were fancy; but they all had flawed handling, even the last of them. It is more probable that Toyota did not see themselves, nor were seen, as competing for the peculiar distinction evidently sought by the other four of the big Japanese manufacturers. Their cars all sought, in various ways, to be not merely fast but also clever.

They all had six-cylinder engines, and all accepted the gentlemen's agreement among their compatriot manufacturers that no car would be marketed boasting more than 285bhp. Otherwise, the cars – the vivid Mitsubishi 3000GT, the venturous Nissan Skyline GT-R, the voluptuary Honda NSX, and the visionary Subaru SVX – went about things in very different ways.

We have to remind ourselves how the Japanese began. In the beginning, the Japanese motor industry was not very concerned about cars. Its main priority was building trucks and other working vehicles, and so it long remained. Only in the 1950s, when the ravages of war had been largely repaired and the departing army of occupation had created a new taste for American ways, did the Japanese begin to identify their desire for cars with a need for cars. Then, just as they had been phenomenally fast in becoming industrialised after being freed from their feudal traditions in 1868, so they now worked phenomenally fast to learn how to make cars, then how to make them good, and finally to make them better than anybody else.

Mere volume was not enough to satisfy psychological needs that were culturally ingrained. Sales in the economy-saloon market were not enough; the Japanese wanted their cars to enjoy esteem among discerning motorists. The Japanese had achieved success; they had acquired esteem. Finally they wanted something that no other motor manufacturer cherished or even understood, something that they wanted simply because they were Japanese: honour.

The time came, in the mid-1980s, when they could seek it, whether in the Canon's mouth or in the Nikon's eye, or in the pensive judgement of the Old Man whom the paternalistic Japanese traditionally fear. A decade of frenzied engineering activity, catching up with the world's new and onerous legal requirements on emissions and safety, had been brought to a pretty satisfactory conclusion by most leading manufacturers in Japan and in Europe by 1983. We have seen how Europe responded in that very year; we had to wait a little longer to see what the Japanese could really do.

Honda made a feint with the 1987 four-wheel-steered Prelude, doomed to waste its sweetness on the desert air: the world was too insensitive to appreciate the elegance of its engineering. Toyota started the real running with the Lexus LS400. What the others created in the years immediately following it did not seek, nor deign, to rival it.

None was a 'supercar' in the conventional meaning of that contemptible term, which had been conjured up by the enthusiast press in the early 1970s after they had identified, among the latest rash of high-powered motorcycles, what they called 'superbikes'. Nissan made a supercar of sorts as well, the classically constructed and most elegantly proportioned 300ZX; but it was the bloated and brutalised Skyline, full of fancy systems fighting for supremacy – over the road, each other, and the driver – which was Nissan's hypercar.

The Mitsubishi (also offered on the American market, by arrangement with Chrysler, as the Dodge Stealth) was cleverly systematised too, even to the extent of speed-related variable aerodynamics, but with typical Japanese restraint it was a gentlemanly demonstration of competence without any overt compulsion to be competitive. Both the Mitsubishi and the Nissans had 4ws systems that had been corrupted to avoid the appearance of copying Honda, but nobody saw the Subaru as copying anything: though it embodied many original ideas, it was simply a good car that was also clever and had the most modern styling of the lot.

That left the Honda NSX, sublimely superior to everything, without any drive to its front wheels, without even a turbocharger to its name. It was exquisitely worked: a whole week of running calculations on a Cray supercomputer went into perfecting the structural stiffness of its stressed-sheet aluminium hull; gossamer lattices of forged light alloys formed the most refined of all passive suspensions; the connecting rods within the intricate engine were made of titanium. There is no need, however, to explore all the car's details: its virtues are already legendary, where those of famous rivals have often proved mythical. Alas, Honda mistakenly offered it as a sports car and ruined the whole effect; what the NSX really amounted to was the world's fastest, safest, and most beautifully made luxury car. It still is.

The others, you see, had misdirected their aim. Appealing to a generation of anoraks, they merely inspired awe. The honour went to the Honda.

Disgrace was attached to many another name. Motor manufacturers everywhere, smarting at past treatment and now anxious to survive, hunted greedily for markets all over the world. Each, crazed by the need for short-term profit, fell into the trap of over-production, which can only be sustained by subordinating the technical staff to the marketing departments. Each, fearing all its rivals, was led into a shorter, faster product cycle which left no time for serious and worthy amelioration of the product. Each, having little to boast about, resorted to styling – that perpetually shameful aspect of the designer's work – to pretend merit where there was none, to sell sizzle rather than steak. It was inevitable that some should fall from grace – if 'grace' was ever the word to be associated with any of them.

As the century drew to its conclusion, so did many motor manufacturers. It was a time of collapses, mergers, take-overs, assimilations. The cars division of Rolls-Royce, saved by a sycophantic government when the parent company went bankrupt in 1971, eventually collapsed into the arms of German industry. Chrysler, reckoning that wedlock was better than deadlock, allied itself to Mercedes-Benz in a manner that implied that before long the DaimlerChrysler name would be spelled DaimlerKreisler. Oddly enough, the Daimler name itself belonged to Jaguar – but Jaguar now belongs to Ford, as does Aston Martin, and Land Rover, and Volvo, and much of Mazda, and more. General Motors has swallowed others, and made an alliance with Fiat. Rover has been ingested several times – it should have died decades before, but was successively rescued by the British government, by British Aerospace, by Honda, and by BMW – but was always regurgitated in revulsion.

Smaller firms were glad to be rescued. It took several abortive efforts before Lotus settled into Malaysian proprietorship. The once noble name of Bugatti, entrepreneurially revived in a style that offered ample mechanistic homage to le Patron but failed to echo the art and elegance which once suffused his establishment at Molsheim, finally fell into the hungry maw of the Audi-VW group. The man who fought his way to the head of that organisation, Dr Ferdinand Piëch, was related to the Porsche family and driven by an urge to outdo them; collecting names, or scalps, was as important to him as collecting revenues.

The shocking thing was that it did not seem to matter to the customers. The name was the thing, as in all things. The shoddiest of factory-made clothing, the clumsiest of footwear, was proudly worn if it had the name of some commercially cultivated fashion leader visible on it. Take any random half-dozen assorted brands of refrigerators, or washing-machines, or cookers, on display at the white-goods shop, and they would all prove to have issued from the factories and drawing-boards of just one or two manufacturers. Why then worry, if your Seat or Skoda might really be a VW?

Realities were at a discount as the 20th century approached its end; pretences were at a premium. Some of the effects were disturbing: many of the styling leads emerging from American and to a lesser extent other sources showed, with an abundance of sheer and faceted fronts surmounted by shallow-windowed turrets, a frightening affinity with the armoured crowd-control vehicles to be seen in the streets of riot-ridden towns in countries where the discontented inhabitants were in violent conflict with the authorities. Those armoured vehicles had seen earlier use in the Gulf war of 1991, a war in which some of the most advanced military technology yet devised was used alongside some that was positively ancient. We have seen in the past that war accelerated the development of technologies from which the people and the car would profit; how ironic that war should now influence styling – and fashion, inasmuch as many youths in many countries affected a form of paramilitary dress including camouflage.

A further form of *fin-de-siècle* pretentiousness was the glut of retrospective styling. It is perhaps natural for us, as the end of a definable period of time approaches, to look back at what we have lost and, supposing it to have been good because it came at a time distant enough to seem enchanting, to try to revive it. There is consolation in the observation that, after each new century has come and been accepted, we generally try to dismiss the past and launch into the exploration of a novel and possibly exciting future.

So be it. This is not a book about the future, but a book about the need for a future. Considering the past, we may censure ourselves for the ways in which we mistreated and corrupted the car; we may pity ourselves for the ways in which the motor industry and its henchmen in commerce and government misled and conned us; we may even, if we are of a finer and more forgiving disposition, recall the enormous good that has been done by and with the many and amazingly varied motor cars that we created and sustained. What we must do is to learn from the experience.

To list the cars that have mattered most in our 115 years of production would be dangerous. Emil Levassor's 1891 design for Panhard is a certainty, establishing through the *système Panhard* the basic morphology of the car so convincingly that some manufacturers and some millions of motorists still cling to it. Another certainty must be Henry Ford's 1907 Model T, a brilliantly clever device which nevertheless must be held responsible for the perpetuation of appallingly low standards in popular motoring. And then what? Perhaps the VW Beetle, the Citroën DS, and the Mini, either because they made people think or because they showed that people were not very good at thinking.

Or were the significant cars of history the ones which were failures, undeserving or otherwise? The lessons taught by the Chrysler Airflow, the Ford Edsel and the NSU Ro80 will not be forgotten in a hurry.

It is a fine subject for speculation, but the fact is that after 115 years of travelling

*The 1934 Chrysler Airflow was a good idea so badly embodied
that it brought car aerodynamics into disrepute.*

we still do not know where we are going. The future holds more certainties than the death and taxes of Benjamin Franklin's trivial list, but until we arrive at them the best we can do is to continue to travel hopefully; and a review of our motoring years reveals how much we are indebted to the car for being able to travel at all. The effect of the car upon society has been to lift what had previously been accepted as fixed conditions of human life.

One of these conditions was a servile inability of anybody but the wealthy or the desperate to uproot themselves, or to break out of the most abjectly constrained area of reasonably free movement, the radius of which for most men (and fewer women) was the distance on foot or on horseback from which one could return in a day. Such a condition was only partially imposed by the natural physical limitation of man's bipedal ability to walk, run or ride; the other part was contributed by society, in the form of curfews, feudal tenure, tribal obligations and similar boundaries to freedom.

The car changed a lot, but it did not change everything. The conditions that were imposed by nature it could progressively amend as its performance, its reliability, and its availability, progressively improved. The conditions imposed by society, being artificial, might be set aside by the coming of the motor car, only to be replaced by the further artifices of a society awakened to new strictural possibilities by the existence of the motor car.

That is why we need to examine not what the car has done to society, but what society has done to the car – an altogether sorrier tale. To begin it, let me recall again the year 1812, and the journey which illustrated a point made in the first chapter of this book. That journey was made by the Emperor Napoleon who, having sheltered the tattered remains of his army at Vilna, had to go to Paris in the most enormous haste. The distance was 1500 miles; by exercising all the authority and prerogative of an Emperor, Napoleon was able to cover it in 13 days: his average speed of 4.8mph was no better than was regularly achieved by Roman emissaries in Gaul 2000 years earlier, or Sumerians 1000 years before that. Over distances further than a man could ride in a day, this maximum rate of overland travel was a fixed condition of human life; and we have to thank that first manifestation in transport of the Industrial Revelation, the railways, for increasing that critical speed tenfold in the space of 90 years. Steam achieved that same rate of increase, ten times faster in 90 years, on the high seas, and the car made it possible on the roads; but if we were to investigate at what speed Napoleon's journey might be accomplished today, we should be shocked to find that until the collapse of the communist USSR the journey could not be made at all. A traveller was not allowed to drive his car into or out of Vilnius, which is the modern Vilna; and if he were content instead to start his trip from the nearest point to which road access is allowed, he would find that only by breaking other laws would he be able to maintain an average speed merely ten times better than Napoleon's despite the intervention of 173 years. Speed limits govern most of the roads in the Emperor's wake – speed limits that have been imposed for what prove on examination to have been political purposes. Only by risking sustained infraction of the law can the motorist hope to find in his car the emancipation that he was entitled to expect, in face of new conditions of human life fixed by an increasingly authoritarian society. There are still parts of our 6-billion-strong world where real roads are scarce (in the whole of Belize there are only four), yet where roads are abundant authority deliberately booby-traps them with speed traps and 'traffic-calming' hazards.

Critics of our political systems, and protagonists of the conspiracy theory, have observed that speed limits help to coerce the populace to remain where they are, instead of roaming around being inquisitive or simply escaping to where the grass appears to grow greener. This may be cynical, but it may also be perceptive: symptoms of paranoia, to paraphrase Mr Henry Kissinger, do not disprove evidence of persecution. There may be always a part of society anxious to take away the freedom conferred by the motor car on another part of society.

Speed limits have not come late upon the scene. As we saw earlier, the idea of these goes back at least to 1865, when Britain's notorious Locomotives on the Highway Act (better known as the Red Flag Act) earned the approval of Queen, Lords, Commons, and all righteous horse-lovers. In the Grand Duchy of Baden, limits were declared in anticipation of Karl Benz putting his first car on the road. They have proliferated ever since, all over the world; and while the consequences of disobedience ranged at various times from applause in Sicily to the death penalty in China, we have seen that the effect of such legislation upon the design of the motor car, as well as upon the utility of the motor car, has always been detrimental.

A more serious effect on car design, and therefore albeit indirectly on the vehicle's utility, has been exerted by taxation. This has especially been so in greater Europe, where taxation has traditionally been a ready expression of a world-wide tendency of men to resent what they do not understand. Other forms of restrictive legislation have likewise been almost Draconian – if they have not actually killed the car they have often stifled it – and no account of our hundred years of motoring life can be complete without (as I propose next) a look at the ways in which lawmakers have made the car a scapegoat. It will prove a study breeding such resentment as brooks no misunderstanding.

PART II

THE YOKE AND THE SPUR

CHAPTER 1

EXTORTION AND DISTORTION

Abroad, you may be a statesman; at home, you're a politician.

SIR HAROLD MACMILLAN

WITH THE SUBJECT AS EVER oppressively topical, we have elsewhere mentioned speed limits and their detrimental effect on the design and development of the motor car during all the time we have known it. Speed limits are as old as that; incomparably older is the invention of taxation, and almost as old as the invention is its abuse. It was accordingly the most natural thing in the world that, as soon as the motor car was prolific enough to look as though it would survive as a source of revenue, it was taxed.

Applied much sooner, the imposition would have killed the golden gosling. Applied much later, it would have fallen upon something that could no longer be considered merely a plaything of the rich, and the imposition would have been challenged by an outraged electorate. Applied when it was, as a price to be paid for the enjoyment of power and the privileges supposed to attend it, it had a serious effect upon car design; and it still has.

Nowhere has this been more continuously and extremely evident than in Europe. In Britain, for instance, car tax was introduced by Mr Lloyd George in 1910, according to a sliding scale based on the power that was to be inferred from measurement of the engine's piston area. This basis showed that government had some fairly astute engineers[1] among its advisers, who saw that for a given level of progress (or of volumetric efficiency – they were in effect assuming an average brake mean effective pressure for the day) it was piston area rather than piston displacement which determined the power an engine might produce; it also showed that government associated power with wealth.

The Lloyd George swinge was eventually confirmed as the Road Fund tax, the theory being that the money taken from motorists for the right to run a car upon the public roads was to be applied to the repair and building of roads. This proposition was somewhat grudgingly accepted by the few early motorists who could afford not only to keep a car but also to lay out what was then a very substantial amount of money for the privilege of using it. In 1925 the swinge, alas, became a swindle: Mr Winston Churchill, then Chancellor of the Exchequer, authorised the diversion of Road Fund moneys to other purposes, and thereafter the tax was as ordinary, as meaningless, and as unwelcome, as any other.

It was especially unwelcome in the industry, for the basis of taxation forced manufacturers to design engines with absurdly small cylinder bores (so as to minimise piston area) and correspondingly long strokes (so as to maintain a reasonable amount of torque, which is related to displacement): the British motor car quickly became a ludicrous piece of machinery, its performance and behaviour suffering sadly as a result of its mechanical deformities. When there came an urgent need to export, the British car was a commodity that nobody would want to import – and it was this hard economic fact, rather than the perfectly justified complaints of generations of motorists, which finally persuaded government to abolish the system in 1946 and substitute a flat rate of tax regardless of engine size or proportions. With what enthusiasm many manufacturers responded, endowing their cars with engines that at last had adequate breathing capacity together with sufficiently moderated rates of wear, is a matter of engineering history; it should also be a fact of social history, if ever the teachers and students of such subjects can overcome their traditional distaste for machinery.

What will also be remembered as a matter of economic history is the success of the so-called 'horsepower tax' in achieving what may secretly have been its principal object, which was the discouragement of the imported car. In 1920, 40% of all the cars on British roads were Model T Fords, which were flooding into the country at the rate of 33,000 a year. The American industry had not been hampered by the Great War in the same way as had the industries of Europe, which needed time to catch up with the progress made by their American rivals in the intervening years. The American car was thirsty, and fuel prices were soaring in Britain, in France, and

---

1 In fact those engineers deferred – that is to say, they passed the buck – to Sir Dugald Clerk FRS (1854–1932), then considered the highest British authority on the internal combustion engine. He was a pioneer of the practical two-stroke cycle and of stratified-charge combustion, and a far-sighted scientist who preferred to remain an academic than to engage in business. Eventually he reconciled the two by becoming a patent agent.

in Italy, while the stuff remained cheap in the USA. But the tax reintroduced by Sir Eric Geddes in 1921 killed the trade in American imports stone dead: even as soon as 1922 their number had dropped to only 14,000.

France in 1946, in a similar post-war situation, achieved the same end while ostensibly in pursuit of a different object. That country is one in which to profess resentment of wealth is a prerogative of a large and traditionally mean class which is not in fact as impoverished as it is at pains to appear; and so it came naturally to the left-wingers newly exercising power that income tax should be levied on a basis of *perceived* wealth. If a citizen displayed the trappings of a wealthy man (such as an ostentatious car) he was taxed as though he were indeed wealthy; if he was seen to lead a miserly penny-pinching life, he might be taxed as though he were indeed poor. If he was actually rich, and brave enough in these circumstances to reveal it, he was taxed with extra stringency to discourage him from making a spectacle of himself. For cars, there was brought in a sliding scale of taxation which progressed by tolerable and regular increments up to a level which corresponded approximately to an engine of 2.8 litres; anything larger attracted an impost $3\frac{1}{2}$ times greater!

France, which had taken the motor car to her ample bosom and nurtured it in the pioneering years – France, which had been the home of brave cars nobly bred and generously endowed, cars such as the Bugatti, Delage, Delahaye, Hotchkiss and Talbot – was once again sending its nobility to the guillotine, *les aristocrates à la lanterne*. They had beaten the world at Le Mans and on the roads to Monte Carlo before the Second World War, and since; but by the early 1950s they had all gone, unable to beat hypocrisy and envy. When the Facel Vega came later in gaudy emulation of them, it proved to base its appeal on hypocrisy and envy; it may be a sad commentary on the times that it lasted as long as ten years.

Many were the theoreticians who argued that the proper way to tax the use of the roads was to impose the duty on motor fuel, not on motor cars. The politicians, always ready to take with the left hand while taking with the right, did both. Most European countries imposed a heavy tax on fuel, a taxation[2] severe enough to be sufficient discouragement to the prospective buyer of a large and thirsty machine. Like France and others, Italy supported this measure with a sliding scale of car tax based on engine capacity, rising steeply enough to explain why Italian engines are always smaller and livelier than seems reasonable.

Italy was no less anxious than Britain to export, especially to the USA, and in 1947 the management of Fiat decided that they must make cars in the American image. Yet their chief designer Dante Giacosa – a most humane engineer whose guiding principle was economy – could not persuade their commercial director Luigi Gajal de la Chenaye that the new pseudo-American car on his drawing-boards should have an engine of decent size. Giacosa struggled against the 1.3-litre limit imposed on him, arguing that it would condemn the car to being an abominable sluggard. Gajal objected that Italian customers would jib at paying higher taxes for anything larger, and the best compromise he eventually settled on was a grudging 100cm³. The resulting Fiat 1400 was hardly one of the firm's most influential models (except that numerous bits of it found their way into early Ferraris!), but Fiat were by no means the last to learn that good export trade must be built on a healthy home market; nor was the Fiat 1400 the worst example of the nonsenses perpetrated when legislators (not to mention sales accountants) get in the way of engineers.

Britain's legislators found another method of discouraging the purchase of luxury goods after the Second World War, by imposing a purchase tax on them. Politicians here remained convinced that the car was a luxury, because they still associated the ownership of a car with class privilege and related wealth. Of course they never admitted it: instead, the postwar Chancellor of the Exchequer, Mr Hugh Dalton, proclaimed that the roads of Britain were too badly choked with cars already (something that will be remembered as a monstrous exaggeration by those of us who enjoyed the empty roads of 1946) and so purchase tax would remain for all cars sold on the home market.

Dalton's successors, notably the austerity-minded barrister Sir Stafford Cripps, kept up this discriminatory attitude against the car: when purchase tax had to make way for value-added tax as Britain strove to fall into line with the Common Market, the government devised a car tax which could be superimposed in order to keep up the pressure on any citizen who presumed to be a motorist. Denmark, which joined the EEC in the same year of 1973, taxed the car even more savagely, but at least there was no domestic industry to be pilloried in the process.

There is no doubt that these generations of politicians and civil servants (and sometimes statesmen) may have had undisclosed reasons for pretending that the car

---

2 Generally and currently it has been and is Britain which taxes fuel most heavily. In the spring of the year 2000 the average rate of taxation on all motor fuels in Britain was 72.5% higher than anywhere else in the world.

was the embodiment of vice, but it seems more likely that they actually believed it. To judge from the way they lathered up their legislation before taking a razor to the motorist's pocket, they must have believed that the motorist would stand for anything. If they were right, it is evidence of the importance of the motor car to all those millions of ordinary men who indeed did stand for all manner of harsh treatments in order to enjoy that freedom of travel which only the private car can provide.

The politicians of Britain were by no means the only ones to invest the car with a symbolic significance that it did not really have. In the 1920s we saw President Coolidge promising Americans a car in every garage, in celebration of the prosperity that would put a chicken in every cooker. In the 1930s the politicians of Germany were just as bad, albeit differently. Dr Josef Goebbels, Minister for Propaganda (nowadays we call it Public Relations) in Nazi Germany, declared at the 1938 Berlin motor show: *The 20th century is the era of the motor car. Since the National Socialist revolution, politics no longer lags behind the development of applied science. Politics shows the direction applied science is to take.*

As for that most enthusiastic of non-driving motorists, Adolf Hitler, he was full of his patronage of the Volkswagen project when he declared the show open: *The People's Car will soon be produced. It will make life pleasanter and satisfy the longing of thousands for the motor car. In time it will become the general means of transport for the German people.* According to some, the real reason for his precious KdF (*Kraft durch Freude* – strength through joy) VW was that it should ensure that the money spent by the German people should remain in Germany, but that too might be to underestimate the symbolic importance attached to the car . . .

What did *Volkswagen* mean? To translate the word as 'people's car' is altogether too facile. Dr Vilem Flusser, a specialist in linguistics and communications theory, identified three meanings for the word *volkisch*: first and most obvious is 'pertaining to the people', but a close second is 'pertaining to a specific culture'. Third is 'pertaining to a nationalist and/or racist movement', a meaning that could be found in the title of the bankrupt Munich journal that Hitler took over as party newspaper, the *Völkischer Beobachter*. It had long been devoted to anti-semitism, anti-communism, and arch-nationalism, and the Nazi party (like many other roughly contemporary groups) subscribed to the ideals of *Volk und Vaterland* to restore the self-opinion of a disparate ethnic mass in a desperate postwar mess. Thus the Volkswagen was not just a people's car, let alone just a popularly priced car; it was a car inspired by the quasi-Messianic ideas of culture and race upon which Hitler based his appeal to the

The car as symbol – Mme Louis Arpels with her Delage triumphant in the 1937
Grand Prix d'Elégance Automobile in the Bois de Boulogne.

people of Germany. No wonder that he was furious with Herr von Opel who was so tactless as to proclaim, as Hitler approached the show stand where the new little Opel P4 was displayed, *'Hier, mein Führer, ist* unser *Volkswagen!'*

Henry Ford's vision of a 'car for the people' may have done no less for the mass of Americans, who had been a mess of disparate ethnic minorities. The things jointly produced by them after their several acquisitions of citizenship were the things that struck them as American, the common uninherited heritage which bound them together by commonality of interest rather than commonality of origin or experience. The motor car of America became very much the motor car for America and by America: it was the most familiar, the most fancied and (as time would prove) the most fickle partner in the romance that was identified with America.

It is tempting to dismiss our natural suspicion that the masses of customers for the American motor industry bought what they did because they were uninformed and ignorant; although there is ample evidence that such was once the case, it is more charitable and in the long run more realistic to see the standard American car as the embodiment of all that was deemed American. It was big, it was strong, it was easy-going and docile, and at heart – despite all the pride and vanity figuring in its prinked-up fashion-conscious appearance – at heart it was almost pathetically simple.

Certainly there was a remarkable degree of standardisation running through all those many makes that once competed for favour in the USA: for sixty years they nearly all had the same track measurement of 56½ inches, not because it was the same as Britain's pioneering railways gauge but so that they could all travel in the same ruts, in the days when most American roads were made – like Adam and all good true American men – of the dust of the earth.

The cars were also very much alike in mechanical specification, and this was not only because they had to be very competitive in price to attract customers who could not otherwise distinguish their several attractions. No less important was the fact that the American customer rudely insisted on not needing to be told either how to drive or how his car was engineered: it was this attitude which forced the domestic industry to be the most conservative, the most reactionary, the most stodgy, in the world. As production engineers the Americans used to be brilliant; as design engineers they were simply not allowed to be anything of the kind. The industry rapidly fell under the sway of accountants and marketing men who insisted on the value of engineering ignorance as a tool of commerce. Whenever they had some financial manipulation to do, the first thing to be discounted was always technical innovation.

The last thing to be sacrificed was always cosmetic styling. In purely commercial terms this was sound reasoning, for the average customer could see more clearly than he could think; but it forced the car into a role for which it had never been intended, and which it could not forever sustain. Concealing its lacklustre mechanisms beneath a notably lustrous carapace of chromium ever more widespread and paint ever more wild-coloured, it became the expression of the customer's fantasies, his ambitions, and his self-deceptions.

This is the saddest thing that ever happened to the car, and we should be careful not to blame the industry for it. As I have said hitherto, the car as we know it is more a product of that part of society which demanded it than of that much smaller part which produced it. It has been defined and confined by the industry's customers, not by the industry itself; and so it stands not merely as a measure of how much people have been prepared to spend, but more as a measure of how little they have been prepared to learn.

In the end, though that end may yet be half of another century distant, those people will be seen to have hastened their own discomfiture by that negligence. In the meantime, it is the industry which suffers the consequences. By being invested with qualities and responsibilities that are actually quite alien to it, the motor car has been made to depute for sword and ploughshare, bedroom and boardroom, gin palace and gymnasium. It has proved to be only another short step, readily taken whenever society has some guilt to assuage, to treat the car as a scapegoat; and it may well be as scapegoat that the car will eventually meet its end.

CHAPTER 2

SMALL EXPECTATIONS:

THE DECADENT HISTORY OF A DECAYING IDEA

In anything at all, perfection is finally attained not when there is no longer anything to add, but when there is no longer anything to be taken away.

ANTOINE DE SAINT-EXUPÉRY,
Wind, Sand and Stars

WHAT IS MINIMALISM? THE WORD is now commonplace among musicians, as it has long been among architects; but what does it mean in the context of the car? We habitually talk about small cars, light cars, cheap cars. As often, we confuse these terms so that we use one to mean another. As always, principles lead us in one direction, practicalities in another.

In this light, how can we view the small cars of today? Either we must judge them as corrupt and having lost sight of the original objective of the small car, or we ruefully admit that today nobody makes (on a mass-market scale, in the sense of a car for the people) a truly small car. As soon as we say that, we have to remember and except the Mini. No small car was ever so true; but the Mini is not a car of today. It is, *mutatis mutandis,* a car of 1959, and only because it was in the 1960s the most passionate small car in history does it survive now. But then, what do we make of the original VW, the Beetle? We could hardly call it a small car. We should have to examine it with some care, and limit comparisons to the generally massive and generously proportioned cars of Germany at the time it emerged there, and of the USA at the time it arrived there, before realising that it was more truly a light and functionally minimalist car – and thus a notably efficient car, which was why it came to have as profound a social influence as the Mini and the Fiat 128 were to have a technical influence.

Why did we ever need a small car? Blame the horse. Horsedrawn carriages were dimensioned to suit the size, and especially the height, of the wretched animals which hauled them; the first horseless carriages accepted all current conventions of size and shape, and were therefore needlessly, uneconomically, hideously large, and in particular outrageously tall. It followed that they were unstable, uncomfortable, and sometimes uncontrollable, and that they were slower and more costly (both to buy and to run) than we might have expected of even the most primitive of petrol engines.

Much of the passion and precision invested by Ettore Bugatti in his giant-killing Type 13, le Petit Pur-Sang, could be recognised in the deceptively small Bébé that he designed for Peugeot to put into production in 1911.

Two influences improved matters. One was the early motorcycle which, being derived from the pedal bicycle, was necessarily man-sized: so were the early powered tricycles which, being a natural step along the path leading from the balancing act upon two wheels to the stability of four, encouraged the designers of what the French were pleased to call *voiturettes*. The other was the buggy or buckboard, the low and handy small-wheeler beloved of countless American sporting pony-drivers, which inspired the little 1901 Oldsmobile that became America's first series-production car.

Otherwise everybody assumed that bigger was better. Early racing was very much a power race, but Louis Renault lent it some perspective when one of his cars, running in the 'light car' class of the 1902 Paris–Vienna event, soundly trounced all the opposition. Better still was the spectacular performance of the tiny Type 13 Bugatti which in France's 1911 Grand Prix finished second in a field of giants: it was simply a stripped version of the car that had been the marketing sensation of 1910, a light but perfectly behaved and beautifully made and truly small car, weighing scarcely a third of a tonne.

The Peugeot Bébé which went into production in 1911 for a wider public was very similar; Bugatti had designed it for Peugeot, giving it a smaller engine (856cc) but embodying all the grace of *le Petit Pur-Sang*. Its proportions were exquisite, concealing its smallness, for everything except the provision for people to sit in it was scaled down to suit its size – including the control levers, the delicacy of which defied ham-fisted driving and expressed the precisely calculated sufficiency which goes to the very heart of designing a good small car.

If the Bugatti and the Peugeot together embodied better than anything else in history the idea of the perfect small car, they also marked a fork in the road to the future. To some, a small car is everything that a large car is, but reduced in scale to make it more efficient, more accessible, and – to those who feel a revulsion for grossness and excess – more palatable. Along this route came Herbert Austin's little Seven, planned (on his billiards table) to occupy no more roadspace than the motorcycle-and-sidecar combination which was all that many a working man with a small family had until then been able to afford. Further along it came the endearing Fiat Topolino of 1936, the elegant and cleverly detailed Renault 4CV of 1945, the brilliant Fiat 600 of 1955, and sundry others culminating in the Citroën ECO 2000 prototype of 1982 and such current paragons in this sense as the Honda Civic or the very different Ford Ka.

The other route was taken by those who saw the small car as utilitarian, a car that was small because that was the way to save money, not because smallness was itself a virtue. For them, small meant cheap, or low-powered, or simple, or downright basic; attempts to make it mean all these things produced in the years after the Great War a frightful shower of makeshift crudities known as cyclecars. In France they had tax-related legal status[3], as the microcars of Japan do today, but they had none of Japan's micro-engineering finesse. Those who did not reject them with derision abandoned them with revulsion.

The idea that *small* meant *cheap* stuck. Minimal performance and basic specification became acceptable, took priority: some 'small' cars were not really small at all. Manufacturers vied to make small cars that seemed big, cheating by making them narrow because in the old days of high flat floors, when passengers sat closely shoulder-to-shoulder, this showed less than lowness or shortness. By the standards of its time

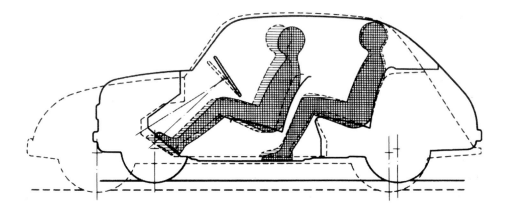

It is important to distinguish between the truly small and the merely insubstantial.
Compare here the accommodation and overall length of the Citroën 2CV (dotted
line, driver silhouette in lighter shading) with those of the Fiat 600.

even the Citroën 2CV – the most intelligent application of minimalism ever to succeed
as a car – was not really small; it was merely light and frugal, like its 5CV ancestor
(copied by Opel and others) a car for an agrarian population, not for the town.

Most of today's so-called small cars have come along this route, supposedly
offering low-cost motoring but at the price of low standards. On the way, the British
have had their Morris 8, Ford 8 and Triumph 8; the French and Germans have
suffered similarly. Today we all suffer the same international levelled-down cheap, but
not so small, cars; and for what they are, and represent, they are not even cheap.

Cost is no longer the priority. Social assumptions have taken over: no car can
be really small, because the law requires that it be designed to withstand the assault
of an errant two-ton Lincoln (so why not, logically, of a 42-ton Volvo?) rather than
to dodge it or to make room for it. All the customer asks is that it should not be as long
as the average car, because he thinks that will mean more room on the roads.

---

3 This French indulgence remains valid, although the vehicles it permits retain no resemblance
to the cyclecars of old. Drastically limited in power and in maximum speed, and almost insultingly
realistic as providing basic short-range mobility for those who might for financial, physical or
geographical reasons be otherwise stranded, they have less in common with bicycles than with
telephone kiosks.

It is a fallacy: drivers follow each other at the same distance regardless of their cars' lengths. Even at the miserable 130km/h that an ignorant and inexperienced populace now blindly accepts as the limit throughout much of Europe, the minimal two seconds gap[4] is too long for the length of the car to be significant. At that speed the difference in length between a Mini and a Carina is only 2 % of the shortest safe interval between them, and therefore imperceptible. In towns, where shortness might be a virtue, parking has become a matter of regulation-size bays which must offer enough space for our larger cars. The small car of today offers its owner no benefit beyond a feeling of being in fashion, somehow respectable by democratic standards – but democracy is merely mob rule, and the motor-industry mob know that making cars short is the way to make them cheaply[5] and so make them profitably. They also know that, in making them high to contain all that has been displaced by the foreshortening, their supposedly small cars are inevitably made less stable, less comfortable, less economical, less pleasant.

Less often than ever before are our cars used fully laden. The way to make modern cars small could therefore be to reduce the number of seats, allowing a whole new set of packaging possibilities to be exercised. Issigonis, achieving a miracle of packaging that has never been equalled, firmly believed in the need for four seats (though he foresaw modern trends towards minimal luggage) when he designed the Mini; but the 1950s, with their freedom from burdensome and irrelevant legislation, were the perfect time for anyone to undertake the task.

Anyone then tempted to do so might find ample encouragement in the economy drive triggered by the Suez fuel crisis, which caused an acute shortage of petrol throughout Europe (Britain resumed rationing, allocating only ten gallons a month to each private motorist) and showed no prospect of the situation growing easier. It was this that provided the occasion for the so-called bubble-cars which suddenly proliferated, though the type was already in existence.

In Germany and Italy, where life was as yet more austere than in Britain, distances greater, and fuel economy therefore already important, there had been new developments in car design to achieve real economies. Iso in Italy had been the first to create a so-called 'bubble-car', perhaps the nearest thing to W S Gilbert's 'protoplasmal primordial atomic globule' that the motoring world had yet seen. This Isetta – later taken up by BMW in a desperate bid to evade the disaster that was staring the firm in the face – had a 236cc two-stroke engine in its sharply tapering tail, with a full width lift-up door at the front and barely 7½ feet between the extremities.

An even earlier design, named the *Kabinenroller* and featuring tandem seating and a sliding aircraft-style canopy, was put into production by Messerschmitt in Germany; two years later another erstwhile aircraft manufacturer, Heinkel, presented a cleverly structured bubble car with an engine of only 175cc and again a full-width rising front door, and production of this in Britain was in due course undertaken by Trojan, who had their own and most peculiar history of low-powered cars.

These smooth-contoured bubble-cars (there were others, British and foreign, that were considerably more reprehensible) were actually very clever pieces of work. An aircraft manufacturer could be relied on to be ingenious and exact in structure and materials; anything so light, and yet shaped by an aircraft specialist's professionally sympathetic concern for minimising aerodynamic drag, was bound to be economical and not necessarily lacking in liveliness; anything so extraordinarily compact was likewise bound to be a revelation in ease of parking and agility in city traffic. Such things did not demand the same driving disciplines as ordinary cars. They could take an 'unfair' advantage in being able to park nose-in to the kerb, so that the occupants could open the front door and step straight on to the pavement. There were multitudes in Britain and Europe who applauded the originality and purposefulness of these novel designs, or who approved of the emancipation they promised, and who were happy to accept the compromises such elemental things demanded in exchange for the low costs of short-range motoring that they guaranteed.

The fact that their designs paid no attention to the consequences of a crash

---

4 Recognition and acceptance of this minimum safety provision is so vital to road safety that it is worth expounding here. Because the kinetic energy of a moving mass (such as a car) increases as the square of its velocity, there can be no standard safe distance at which to follow another vehicle. If, say, 45 feet were a sufficient distance at 30mph, then – assuming the same braking capability in terms of deceleration – it would have to be 180 feet at 60mph. Watch a racing car chasing another, appearing to close up on the way into a corner and to fall back on the way out, even though both cars are doing the same speed at each point on the road: in fact the time interval between them is constant. So it is on the public highway, and the safe interval at which to follow another vehicle is to be measured as a time interval. How long that time should be is a matter of how long it takes for the following driver to observe, judge, and react to whatever situation the vehicle being followed may precipitate.

5 Any packaging designer (or half-decent mathematician) can explain that it takes less material to enclose a given volume in a cubic envelope than in any more oblong shape. That is why tall cars of minimal length can be made more cheaply than long and low cars. The shape involving least material is a sphere, but it is unlikely that even the greediest of manufacturers will approach it.

merely highlighted the general disinclination of everybody, industry and customers alike, to think about the matter at all. If they were wanting in stability and roadholding (and this was not an accusation that could be levelled at them all), this was again a reflection of the low standards often displayed by conventional small cars at the time. What mattered was that these bubble-cars were tiny but habitable, economical and therefore (however briefly) socially plausible.

That was why, when Issigonis was charged by Sir Leonard Lord of Austin with the task of making a 'proper' car to challenge the bubble-cars, he felt free to make the Mini so short, so low, so wide-tracked and small-wheeled and stable and nimble and surprisingly comfortable. That, and his passion for lightness and efficiency – already demonstrated more eloquently than by anyone else (even such as Bugatti, Chapman[6], or the Italians who made jewel-like sports cars named Giaur, Stanguellini, Nardi-Danese) in his prewar Lightweight Special racer.

That passion was why Issigonis could make the BMC 1100 a more convincing and more elegant small car than any of today's bloated blighters. That insistent conviction was why he foresaw his ideal car (as he put it to me late in 1964) as a more powerful and more refined Mini, with four seats and, he grudgingly admitted, not less than 3m long. Three metres! Even Japan's microcars are longer than that – but they are like all the other modern 'small' cars, calculated for some special fiscal or other social effect, not designed for rejoicing in the truths of real motoring. Today's pseudo-small cars have all sorts of things in them, but none of the passion without which true minimalism cannot be achieved.

It is a sad confession. The small car could have changed the world. Instead, the world has changed the small car.

---

6 Chapman understood better than most the importance of lightness and therefore of smallness, demonstrating it with authority in his Lotus 3 and the faster sports/racing cars which soon followed. However, such early examples of the brand had to be approached with some caution: Chapman was a small man (he took great umbrage when Setright once said so in print!) who for some years only employed staff who were no taller than he, so the cars that he deemed habitable were not always so to others. Setright could not even get into, let alone drive, the original Lotus Europa. Later, Chapman relented to the extent of taking the very tall ex-Jaguar engineer Kimberley on to his staff, whereupon Lotus dimensions grew. Another little fellow was M. Daninos, proprietor of Facel, whose Vega was not as roomy as its apparent size indicated. At the other extreme M. Boulanger, general manager of Citroën in the late 1930s, was a lanky individual who insisted that the prototype 2CV be tall enough for him to enter without removing his hat.

CHAPTER 3

SCAPEGOAT AND IDOL

Fundamentally, all the tide of thought today, however broken up into a confusing network of channels, is setting towards the pole of Sensation.

PERCY WYNDHAM LEWIS

THE INDUSTRY NEVER FORCED OUR cars upon us; we forced them from the industry. We, the people, decided in our confused and ignorant and petty vainglorious ways what we wanted of our cars, and what we were ready to pay. Anything else, anything the industry thought we should have but that we did not particularly want, we would only accept as a free gift.

That, in essence, is how the car has been developed during a century in which so very much more might have been achieved. The car has done wonders for us, liberating us and mobilising us, showing us things and places and people we could never otherwise have seen, and giving us opportunities for making our own judgements on things for which we would otherwise have had to accept somebody else's word. What we have done for the car, on the other hand, has never had much to do with using the vehicle as an investigative tool; our main object has always been to impose ourselves, via the car, upon the world. We might use it to better our lot, but seldom to better ourselves.

In effect the car has become a shield. Very early we learned that it could proclaim all our pomp in a quasi-heraldic manner; subsequently we found that we could use it to ward off antagonists' weapons. The strange thing is that, at various times between the major wars but most noticeably since the sixties, we have been traitors to it. I believe that on those occasions we have not been turning upon the car itself, but upon the industry which makes it and which, having grown cynical about us as it discovered the hard way what unforgiving taskmasters we were, made us its slaves. Otherwise, if we stood behind our shield – our car – when we were proud of ourselves, why should we not stand behind it when we are ashamed of ourselves?

If we could accept that the car was just a tool, a piece of soulless machinery that is meant to do a fairly specific job and to be discarded when it is either worn out or supplanted by a superior tool, we would not be in thrall to it now, nor sue it on a debt that it never contracted. But consider the following description of a *limousine de voyage* built for Count Boni de Castellane, a wealthy Parisian who had made his pockets even deeper by marrying Anna, daughter of the American millionaire Jay Gould. His clothes were reckoned so elegant and stylish and rich in substance that pictures of him appear in fashion-historians' textbooks; yet he pursued the art of self-presentation further, spending some unspecified fraction of his fortune on a Pullman-bodied 40hp Panhard, the chassis of which had been extended to give a 12ft 6in wheelbase.

The coachwork of this generously dimensioned vehicle was panelled throughout in satinwood, with polished mahogany mouldings inlaid with silver. In the division between the front and rear seats were a folding table, an electric heater concealed in a polished copper frame, and a silver wash basin. This was fed with hot and cold water from two tanks hidden in the roof, the hot water being bled from the engine's cooling system. Cabinets flanking the central division held cocktail, toilet, manicure and vanity-case apparatus. The two adjustable armchairs in the rear compartment were upholstered in Rose Dubarry silk brocade, and could be transformed into a bed. The lighting for this sumptuous cabin was set in silver gilt, the metalwork on the exterior all being silver-plated copper except the door handles, which were of solid silver.

With all the inevitability that might be discovered in a Viennese operetta, the French Count had a German rival in the Baron von Eckhardstein, who felt prompted to order himself a car even more flamboyant with which, as he put it, to 'knock the feathers out of his blasted cocked hat'. The gorged reader may be spared the equally tedious and embarrassing recital of the Baron's six-wheeled De Dietrich which, like the Count's Panhard, was furnished by the Paris branch of Maple's – except to note that the rear portion of the body housed a fully equipped kitchen in which a corpulent chef named Emil prepared gourmet meals for his master *en route*. The reader will automatically understand that access to this kitchen was by a separate 'tradesmen's entrance' at the back of the car.

The same sort of thing, *mutatis mutandis,* still happens today. We have chosen to see the car as a projector of our own supposed image, so we blame it when our own reality shows through that cloud of self-propelled deception. Writing (in *On the Contrary*) about the regular solid Amurrican citizen, Mary McCarthy long ago noted that 'Stepping into his new Buick convertible he knows that he would gladly do without it, but imagines that to his neighbour, who is just backing his out of the driveway, this car is the motor of life.' And of course life has to appear to be lived, however different the dull dead truth might be. With adjustments for changes in time and location, the truth about the old Buick convertible is true still. My car has tuned suspension, extravagant wheels and tyres, and electronics which can follow Radio 3 all around the country while satellites track the course of the car all around it – so yours has to have a turbocharger and a rollover cage and white paint absolutely everywhere, while Mr Jones next door rides behind a burr walnut fascia and lamps that would fry a cyclist at 600 yards if he ever dared switch them on. In Germany the man who bought the smaller version of the late Mercedes-Benz 450SEL might have the insignia of the 6.9-litre model affixed to the tail, while the man who bought a 6.9 had them left off it. In the USA the very names of the cars have told us all we need to know: Cadillac *Eldorado Biarritz* (which calls for a 3000-mile wheelbase), Elegant Motors *898 Elegante Phaeton Brougham*, Mohs *Ostentatienne Opera Sedan*, Jeep Corporation *CJ-5 Renegade Roadster*, Oldsmobile *Cutlass Luxury Supreme Sedan*. People have done some quite dastardly things to the motor car – and then people blame it. That is people all over; in a word, society.

Our readiness to hold the car responsible for all the ills that society is heir to has never been better demonstrated than in the last 40 years. It is extremely unlikely that the US government would have lent credence and support to the environmentalists' clean air campaign, had it not been searching frantically for some issue, domestic and superficially non-political, with which to distract the American people's increasingly critical attention from the humiliations of the Vietnam war. It was the old technique, familiar to physicians and field-marshals, of administering a counter-irritant. The fuss about toxic and noisome emissions from motor cars provided a welcome opportunity to turn the people from their scrutiny of events in south-east Asia, to turn a literal smoke-screen into a metaphorical smoke-screen, to focus instead upon the unfortunates of Los Angeles and the unscrupulous of Detroit. Figures of doubtful authenticity were issued, blaming the car for emitting annually 60 million tons of carbonmonoxide, 12 million tons of hydrocarbons, 6 million tons of oxides of nitrogen, 1 million tons of sulphur dioxide, and another million tons of something described rather vaguely as 'smoke'.

In vain was it argued, as it has since been argued over the European issue of acid rain and the world-wide terror of 'greenhouse gases', that far more pollutants were vented by power stations and factories, by vegetation, by the very breath of people and animals, and by the earth itself: people were glad to turn their fury on the car manufacturers to whom they had been so long in thrall, and the government was more than pleased to encourage them.

Today there are politicians, especially in Germany, who are making themselves rich and awesome by exploiting the social plight of the relatively innocent motor car. Likewise when the smog of Los Angeles was a new spur to social activity, politicians moved in to find the easy pickings. One horse-fancier among them sought to outlaw the motor car in California. Senator Muskie put before Congress a bill requiring that exhaust emissions be 95% clean before they could be vented to atmosphere – and although that was tantamount to asking that the exhaust gas be cleaner than the air drawn into the carburettor, it sounded impressive to the ravening mob. Soon, engines were disappearing beneath a maze of supplementary plumbing which forced them to ingest their own excreta, with what dire effects upon the metabolism might scarcely be imagined. A secondary campaign by environmentalists against lead compounds, which since the mid-1920s had been among the most important and valuable (and American!) additives to gasoline, reduced engine efficiency still further, the net effect of all the associated legislation being (as later here and on mainland Europe) to make the engine grossly inefficient and shamefully wasteful of fuel. Side-effects were numerous, one of the most lamentable being the near extinction of the Wankel engine, then passing through a promising infancy. Society thus put the car back 20 years, and it may never catch up again.

People might not have been so vengeful had the ground not been prepared for them by the safety-mongers, led (as we saw in an earlier chapter) by Ralph Nader, a lawyer astute enough to recognise in the accident record of the Chevrolet Corvair an opportunity to gain notoriety and profit. His book *Unsafe at Any Speed* wildly overstated his case, whereupon the motor industry and the legislature reacted with equal violence. Although supposed to be the agents of society, the legislators completely failed to appreciate the proper function and place of the car in society: instead of prompting the manufacturers to ensure that their products were roadworthy, they forced them to make cars crashworthy.

The short-term result was a hideous enation of sacrificial structures which made cars heavy and unwieldy: the better a given model's reputation for survival in a crash, the greater seemed the probability that it would be involved in a crash. The long-term result was the legal plague of absolute product liability, which has effectively blighted developments in the motor industry and to a lesser extent in others. Yet it may be that those legislators were right; maybe they saw that most people were too proud, too lazy, and too inept, to mend their ways at the wheel, and would have accidents no matter how agile and controllable their cars became. Sir Alec Issigonis once lamented to me that when he endowed the Mini with 70% better roadholding than its contemporaries, so that its occupants should enjoy commensurately greater margins of safety, drivers no sooner realised its abilities than they began to use up all that margin.

That may be. What is certain is that, if the people at large in their cars had been sensible enough to wear the seat harness so energetically and admirably evolved in the 1960s, most of the protective measures that manufacturers were forced to embody in their cars would have been quite unnecessary. But people were too proud, or too lazy; they feared ridicule or taunts of cowardice, they spoke of interference with their freedom and violation of their assumed rights[7]; and so, since they would not be cajoled into taking care of themselves, they had to be coerced into cars in which they would be cared for whether they liked it or not. They kept their freedom to travel unbelted, though in due course that was to be rescinded in most countries; but they lost their freedom to buy light, agile, efficient and cheap cars. Then, as the cancer of speed limits spread across the world's roads, they lost their freedom to go as far as they liked in a given time. New conditions of human life were being fixed, new constraints upon freedom were being devised, cars were growing daily less attractive (though no less necessary), and society had only itself to blame.

Instead, it continued to blame the car. It did so again, most vociferously, when the oil crises – politically fomented, and entirely artificial – made all and sundry turn viciously on the motor car, holding it responsible for keeping oil starvation at bay. Once again it was in vain that the car-makers protested their innocence, pointing to the profligate consumption of oil by homes, factories, power stations, civil aviation and the armed forces. Once again the legislators, more anxious for political reasons to be seen to be doing something than to do such things as would have been more effective but less conspicuous, left the motor car to take the blame. The people, as insistently foolish as ever, blamed it too. Caught between the Scylla of emissions and the Charybdis of consumption, the wretched thing deteriorated even further.

The industry learned to be cynical and self-interested in such crises. Emission and safety legislation proved to offer means whereby to secure protection from foreign competition, a technique employed most effectively by the USA, Sweden, Japan, Germany and Australia. All these countries developed huge volumes of legislation governing the construction and use of cars – and much of it is as ill-advised as the insistence, in Britain's original Construction and Use Act of 1896, that rubber tyres (whether solid or pneumatic) must have smooth treads!

Can society's administrators, the legislators who are the agents of the people, be criticised for their follies when the people themselves are so persistently foolish? Can we not accept the car as an instrument for doing what we will, rather than as a privilege for doing what we may be permitted, rather than promoting it as a statement of our self-esteem, rather than imposing it upon others as an expression of our creeds? I do not have my refrigerator adjusted to reach deep cryogenic temperatures; you presumably do not have your washing-machine custom-painted and fur-trimmed; our neighbour Mr Jones's cooker may be larger and more elaborate than ours, but that may not be known even to Mrs Jones.

Sadly, however, man has made his car in his own supposed image – but the identification was unnecessary and the image is usually false. Worse still, having played the part of creator, man has given his creation the duty of being his god. How far distant is his discovery that it will not offer him salvation?

One of the most remarkable features of the history we have been reviewing is the motoring activity of such people as the Chinese, the Indians, the central Africans, and the like. What was remarkable was that, for a very long time, it was not a feature – and it may never have needed to be one. Such has been the pressure of legislative and other social influences on industry in the last third of a century that technological ability (as opposed to application) has waxed incredibly great. It was hoped that technology (defined by Max Frisch as *the knack of so arranging the world that we don't have to experience it*) might make the car unnecessary for those who do not yet have it. How wonderful it would have been if all those allegedly underdeveloped countries, those not yet firmly impressed by the motor car, could leapfrog this whole phase in development and proceed immediately to the next step, the next phase in communicative evolution, thus taking the lead from that part of the world still tied to its present ways!

---

7 Especially since the American Declaration of Independence, people have been incredibly presumptuous in asserting that they have rights to sundry things that they deem ideal: rights to liberty, happiness, justice, equality, fair treatment, and other ideals galore, have been tacked on to the list at various times. There is no quicker way to make oneself unpopular than to point out that it is all self-important nonsense, and that there are no such things as 'natural' rights. Duties can be imposed by society, and privileges conferred; rights are a figment of the imagination, and cannot be found either proof or sanction.

Alas, the impression made by the motor car upon such countries was, if not firm, undeniably colourful and well lit and irresistibly attractive. Just as we saw minor nations establishing major airlines equipped with the most modern aircraft, for the sake of making a good impression on the outside world, so we saw their people avid to make similar impressions on each other by flaunting the cars that, as could be seen from the evidence on display in developed countries, made their owners supermen. From there it was an easy step for the supersalesmen. Most of the major manufacturers of the world, terrified by the consequences of having built themselves a grossly superfluous capacity for production, and fearing that their existing markets would soon be sated, saw the attractions of those countries that had few cars and little or no manufacturing capacity. How tempting to fill Asia with cars almost as numerous as its inconceivably huge population – and to do the same for Africa, for South America, and for any other lesser areas that might show up on the salesmen's map of possibilities! Whether like locusts or like leeches, the major motor manufacturers have developed voracious appetites.

We must see it as one of history's typical errors of timing that technology failed to make the car unnecessary for those who did not have it. Nevertheless, at some later time technology may make the car undesirable for those of us who yet cling to it. Frisch saw all travel in that light: 'Travel is atavistic; the day will come when there will be no more traffic at all, and only newly-weds will travel.'

It should happen. The car has been throughout its life a means of communication. We have others now, means undreamed of when the car was new. They ought to supplant the car as steam displaced sail. But, on the evidence of our behaviour in the last seventy years or so, do you really think it likely that we shall let them?

CHAPTER 4

THE LIBERATOR

If all mankind, minus one, were of one opinion, and only one person were of the contrary opinion, mankind would be no more justified in silencing that one person, than he, if he had the power, would be justified in silencing mankind . . . We can never be sure that the opinion we are endeavouring to stifle is a false opinion; and if we were sure, stifling it would be an evil still.

JOHN STUART MILL

IF JOHN STUART MILL's words in his 1859 essay *On Liberty* were intended to bear upon the political and moral issues of his day, they nevertheless give us today some guidance in the conduct of what we see as the pursuit of progress. There is a serious and increasing danger that we shall be encouraged, tricked, or forced, into accepting certain losses of liberty in exchange for some vague promise of progress. There is an inference that our individual desires for liberty are somehow incompatible with the evolution of civilisation.

Did we but know our history better, we should see in it more than enough proof that liberty and civilisation cannot be traded off against each other. Rather, they are mutually complementary; and there is enough evidence, even in the history of motoring, to take a narrow but perfectly valid example, to show that the ideals of liberty have generally been realised only when some lone voice or tiny minority has rebelled against the strictures of the established, the familiar, the traditional, and most of all the conventional.

Throughout its history, the car has been a liberator, an agent of freedom. Throughout its history, the car has enabled people to break out of their constraints, to attempt something they could never previously do, to venture somewhere they could never previously go, to support ideas and trends they could never previously endorse.

As has been mentioned elsewhere in this book, Lord Clark, in his study of the art that he saw as evidence of *Civilisation,* gave us a very clear idea of the Dark Ages which went before: the things which made them so dark, he wrote, were 'the isolation, the lack of mobility, the lack of curiosity, the hopelessness'. Were these not the very things that the motor car set aside?

All cars, every one that has ever been made, share in this most noble and most humane of vocations, this conferring of freedom. Can we not identify those which

By 1949 the resurgence of the VW (shorn of its Nazi KdF prefix) was under way, with 2500 a month issuing from day and night shifts in a blitzed Brunswick factory.

played major parts, those which successively chipped away at the walls of social and economic stricture until they toppled? I believe that we can: in seven distinct stages, beginning eleven decades ago and every time involving a lone individual or a minority in the proposition of ideas never previously allowed audience, we can trace the occasions when the progress of motoring enabled yet another banner of freedom to be unfurled.

The first was in 1891, the year when we were introduced to the *système Panhard*. That pioneering Frenchman had seen the logic of arranging a car with its radiator, engine, clutch, gearbox, driveshaft and final drive to the rear axle, all in an orderly line down the centre of the chassis. From then until at least forty years later (seventy years in the USA), that logic seemed so obvious that it was never seriously challenged. Prior to the emergence of the Panhard pattern, pioneer car manufacturers tended to emulate the makers of horse-drawn carriages in their chassis and bodywork, the makers of steam engines in their propulsive machinery. It was Panhard who freed us from the assumptions of previous eras and allowed the motor car to evolve in its own way.

C'est brutal, mais ça marche! said Panhard of his own gearbox design. That would not prove good enough for the unsophisticated, and surprisingly often illiterate, American customer who sorely needed a vehicle that would allow him a greater range of autonomy (the US of A is a big place, and in much of it the population is sparse) than that afforded by a horse. Such people might have vague notions of why and when to shift gears, but seldom did they know how to do it. Rarely were they adept at maintaining finely adjusted or delicate machinery. Hardly ever could they be sure that they might rely on metalled roads: at the beginning of the century, there were only 150 miles of them in the whole of the USA. Always in the future the call would be for practicality and robustness, versatility and rock-bottom prices.

Ford addressed every one of these problems successfully in 1908 with the Model T, and with it bestowed freedom of movement and a new pattern of social communication upon a whole generation of hard-working (and often hard-living) Americans. Motoring for the people has been a freedom-seeking principle ever since there were cars, and all manner of friendly, affordable, accessible cars have been made in pursuit of the idea: the Austin 7, the Ford Y, the Morris 8, the KdF Volkswagen, and a whole series of Fiats before and after the Second World War, head the list. What they accomplished was praiseworthy, but it was always in the tracks of the car that did it first and did it most. When the Ford T first appeared, there were but 200,000 cars in the USA; by 1920 there were 9 million, and every second car coming off the production lines which made it cheaper by the year was a Model T Ford.

The epicyclic gearbox of the Ford had constant mesh in its favour, but little else. Rather more caution was needed for managing it than would now be thought desirable; but the next step in the liberation of the motorist from his shackles was not in the design of a car but in the development of a self-changing gearbox.

Originally designed as part of an early military tank, it comprised a series of epicyclic trains, and was much more complex in its mechanism and more refined in its behaviour than the Ford device. The Wilson preselector gearbox, especially when linked to the engine by a fluid coupling as in a 1930 Daimler, was the true precursor of the modern automatic transmission – without which a huge number of drivers would now be immobile. This, before all the experiments of the US industry in the late 1930s and the postwar years, was the transmission which freed us from the need for a degree of mechanical sympathy and physical coordination which would nowadays seem ludicrous.

The fact that a great number of cars are made even today without automatic transmission is due only to the deeply ingrained conservatism (call it fear of the unknown, if you prefer) ruling the fright-restrained purse-strings of the average ignorant customer. It is but a part of a whole panoply of things that the modern car retains for no better reason than that it has always had them[8] and people are happy with what is familiar. Not until 1934 was there a car which seriously (that is, addressing all commercial considerations) made an onslaught on the conventions whereby car design was trapped. At first sight, it was the absence of running-boards that made the Citroën 7A and its prompt and definitive derivative the *Onze Légère* distinctive. Then the proportions began to show: the car was wider and lower than cars in its class commonly were. A look inside showed that, despite the lowness, there was no propellor-shaft tunnel combining with the chassis to turn the floor into a semblance of an egg-crate, as was the case with low-built but otherwise conventional cars; this car did not have a chassis, either. The floor was not even encumbered by the gearlever, which instead protruded from the dashboard. This car, then the most modern and forward-looking production car in the world, had front-wheel drive.

It was not by any means the first to do so. Quite apart from the assorted sporting and racing hopefuls – Christie and Miller in the USA, Tracta in France, Alvis in England – there had been miscellaneous attempts to embody fwd in reasonably sensible touring cars such as the early Cord at one extreme and the DKW somewhere near the other. This Citroën was the first to transform fwd from a tentative idea to an authoritative statement, and with its unitary construction and other progressive features it liberated us from the strictures of the Panhard conventions which, after more than forty years, were growing noticeably stale.

Freed from that stifling pattern, we found ourselves – those of us open-minded enough to try it – with a car that was roomier, safer, more stable and economically more sensible than anything that had previously been our lot.

Turning the engine through a right angle to set it transversely athwart the nose of the car (as had been done by Christie and proposed for Fiat by Giacosa) was accomplished – together with everting the body seams, using progressive-rate rubber

---

8 The Schrader tyre valve, the familiar windscreen wiper (especially), and the spare wheel, head the list of things that should have been replaced or eradicated ages ago.

springs, and packaging the lot into a ten-feet compass of which 80% was payload space – by (Sir) Alec Issigonis in his immortal Mini. This was the second stage in the evolution of the fwd car, and a significant step in the devolution of the car for the people; but, in the context of freedom, its importance was that it succeeded in being a classless car.

Anybody could be content to be seen in one, and almost everybody was at some time or other seen in one. There was no opprobrium attached to ownership of something so humble, for its cornering ability and agility gave it a kind of superiority of its own. Indeed (as noted earlier) Issigonis lamented the way that people used up the margin that he had given them with their safety in mind, and it was a large margin: the cornering power of the Mini was equal to that of racing cars barely five years older, and 70% higher than the average touring car of the same period. If there was nothing wrong with having a Mini, there was nothing clever or difficult about it either: however unwise or otherwise the pricing policy of BMC, this was undoubtedly and

With front-wheel drive and a stressed-skin hull, the Citroën Onze Légère *presented the popular car in a new guise for 1935. Individualists were not to be denied, however, and these fashionable French couples needed an equally chic open version (complete with fold-flat windscreen) to present themselves in a style that the standard saloon would deny them.*

almost apologetically a cheap car. Rich and poor might alike justify having one.

It took only another decade for the remaining serious faults in the commonplace car to be eradicated. If the fwd car were to become the norm, the curious deficiencies in its handling had to be rendered harmless. If the transverse engine were to endure, its transmission would have to be removed from the sump and given its own place in the world – and, more importantly, its own oil. There were other problems too, all surviving from a distant and mechanically or economically more hideous age. The side-valve engine might have gone, but pushrods operating overhead valves continued to corrupt combustion chamber shape, hamper porting, and impair efficiency and durability. Bias-ply tyres might be on their way out, but radials were proving much more sensitive to out-of-roundness. Independent rear suspension might be all very well and extremely tempting, but it could introduce handling problems which as like as not would amplify the most undesirable habits of fwd cars.

All these things were ironed out by Fiat in what must still be seen, as some few of us saw it when it was new, as the most important and influential car since Ford first furnished motoring for the masses. The Fiat 128 introduced new standards in intelligible fail-safe handling; it accustomed us to the notion that an overhead-camshaft engine was perfectly acceptable and absolutely proper even in the most humble of cars; it showed how to locate a road wheel accurately centred by spigot on the hub rather than by vague bolting procedures; it pioneered the idea of passive rear-wheel steering to compensate for any spurious handling behaviour caused by suspension deflection; and it brought into fashion numerous other features, many of them minor and passing unnoticed except by the engineers of the worldwide motor industry. There is scarcely any popular car – popular in the sense of being directed to the people, for the sake of giving them individual and affordable autonomy – that does not embody the majority of the things which newly distinguished the Fiat 128 more than thirty years ago.

No single car has emerged since then to which we can point with gratitude for a major contribution to the emancipation that cars have progressively bestowed upon us. Only in one respect can we be seen to have been further liberated: freedom from the gnawing worries of unreliable machinery, treacherous electrics, despicable minor components, and deterioration of performance with age, all these freedoms we owe to the fastidious engineering and imaginative electronics of the Japanese industry.

Something else did happen, some time earlier, which gave us a new freedom of a kind, though it was one to which relatively few motorists aspired. The evidence of it was the E-type Jaguar, which in the early 1960s appeared to make possible for the first time the enjoyment of performance standards previously the jealously kept preserve of outlandishly costly and impractical machinery. The true instigator of this freedom to enjoy top-class performance at middling expense, and to provide it in a car which did not demand exceptional driving skills for normal use, was the 328 BMW from prewar Munich[9], just a few kilometres down the road from Dachau. Funny how the desire for freedom crops up in the most unexpected places: was it not out of the Dark Ages that the light of reform appeared?

---

9 The design, development and testing of the 328 were done at Munich, but the actual assembly of the cars was at the BMW factory (formerly that of Dixi) at Eisenach, where the nearest *Konzentrationslager* equivalent to Dachau was 39 miles away at Buchenwald.

PART III

THE FACE OF THE EARTH

CHAPTER 1

THE BIG CITY

'2 July 1835

'*An undulating plain, or rather a collection of little hills. Below the hills a narrow river (the Irwell), which flows slowly to the Irish sea. Two streams (the Meddlock and the Irk) wind through the uneven ground and after a thousand bends flow into the river. Three canals made by man unite their tranquil, lazy waters at the same point. On this watery land, which nature and art have contributed to keep damp, are scattered palaces and hovels. Everything in the exterior appearance of the city attests the individual powers of man; nothing the directing power of society. At every turn human liberty shows its capricious creative force. There is no trace of the slow continuous action of government.*

'*Thirty or forty factories rise on the tops of the hills I have just described. Their six stories tower up; their huge enclosures give notice from afar of the centralisation of industry. The wretched dwellings of the poor are scattered haphazard around them. Round them stretches land uncultivated but without the charm of rustic nature, and still without the amenities of a town. The soil has been taken away, scratched and torn up in a thousand places, but it is not yet covered with the habitations of men. The land is given over to industry's use. The roads which connect the still-disjointed limbs of the great city show, like the rest, every sign of hurried and unfinished work; the incidental activity of a population bent on gain, which seeks to amass gold so as to have everything else all at once, and, in the interval, mistrusts all the niceties of life. Some of these roads are paved, but most of them are full of ruts and puddles into which foot or carriage wheel sinks deep. Heaps of dung, rubble from buildings, putrid stagnant pools, are found here and there among the houses and over the bumpy pitted surfaces of the public places. No trace of surveyor's rod or spirit level. Amid this noisome labyrinth, this great sombre stretch of brickwork, from time to time one is astonished at the sight of fine stone buildings with Corinthian columns. It might be a mediaeval town with the marvels of the nineteenth century in the middle of it. But who could describe the interiors of these quarters set apart, home of vice and poverty, which surround the huge palaces of industry and clasp them in their hideous folds? On ground below the level of the river and overshadowed on every side by immense workshops, stretches marshy land which widely spaced ditches can neither drain nor cleanse. Narrow twisting roads lead down to it. They are lined with one-storey houses whose ill-fitting planks and broken windows show them up, even from a distance, as the last refuge a man might find between poverty and death. None the less, the wretched people living in them can still inspire jealousy of their fellow beings. Below some of their miserable dwellings is a row of cellars to which a sunken corridor leads. Twelve to fifteen human beings are crowded pell-mell into each of these damp repulsive holes.*

'*The foetid muddy waters, stained with a thousand colours by the factories they pass, of one of the streams I mentioned before, wander slowly round this refuge of poverty. They are nowhere kept in place by quays: houses are built haphazard on their banks. Often from the top of one of their steep banks one sees an attempt at a road opening out through the debris of earth, and the foundations of some houses or the debris of others. It is the Styx of this new Hades. Look up and all around this place and you will see the huge palaces of industry. You will hear the noise of furnaces, the whistle of steam. These vast structures keep air and light out of the human habitations which they dominate; they envelop them in perpetual fog . . .*

'*A sort of black smoke covers the city. The sun seen through it is a disc without rays. Under this half-daylight 300,000 human beings are ceaselessly at work. A thousand noises disturb this dark damp labyrinth . . .*

'*The footsteps of a busy crowd, the crunching wheels of machinery, the shriek of steam from boilers, the regular beat of the looms, the heavy rumble of carts, those are the noises from which you can never escape in the sombre half-light of these streets. You will never hear the clatter of hooves as the rich man drives back home or out on expeditions of pleasure. Never the gay shouts of people amusing themselves, or music heralding a holiday. You will never see smart folk strolling at leisure in the streets, or going out on innocent pleasure parties in the surrounding country. Crowds are ever hurrying this way and that in the Manchester streets, but their footsteps are brisk, their looks preoccupied, and their appearance sombre and harsh . . .*

'*From this foul drain the greatest stream of human industry flows out to fertilise the whole world. From this filthy sewer pure gold flows. Here humanity attains its most complete development and its most brutish; here civilisation makes its miracles, and civilised man is turned back almost into a savage.*' Alexis de Tocqueville

The English industrial landscape, 1866: the 'Black Country' around Wolverhampton.

That is the way the towns were developing in the days before the car brought people mobility and hope. Manchester – with its satellites Stockport, Salford and Oldham – was the most impressive example of urban expansion up to the middle of the 19th century; in its dependence on factory industry and its identification with the gospel of the market economy, the city demanded attention as the portent of a new age. If in truth humanity there attained 'its most complete development', perhaps it was in the Manchester Philosophical Society over which, from 1817 to 1844, presided that luminary of chemical science John Dalton. One of his pupils, a young fellow named James Prescott Joule, studied under him twice a week as a relief from working in his father's Salford brewery, and while still in his twenties announced his discovery of what we now know as the first law of thermodynamics.

The brutish aspect was much more evident to all, and the brutalising effect of the industrial city was as much feared as the replacement of manual labour by machinery among those who resisted the evolution that followed the Industrial Revelation. Friedrich Engels, closest collaborator with Karl Marx in the foundation of modern communism and co-author with him of the 1848 Communist Manifesto, was another visitor to Manchester in this period[1]; but he saw urban squalor as the product of the exploiting bourgeoisie. A different view, blaming the absence of a tradition of governmental intervention, was taken by the young French aristocrat Alexis de Tocqueville; hence his reference to 'the slow continuous action of government' in the lengthy quotation above[2].

In fact the time for such slow continuous action had passed. 'The pace of change', wrote Baudelaire, 'is faster than that of the human heart.' He was complaining of the large-scale and rapid redesign (not merely rebuilding) of Paris[3] in the 1850s and 1860s, at a time when Paris alone rivalled London as one of the world's two cities having a population exceeding 1 million. By 1900 there were 11 of them; today there are more than two dozen cities[4] housing more than 10 million each.

Rapid growth of cities is not only a 20th-century phenomenon. Manchester grew ninefold in the course of the 19th century; the population of Chicago grew sevenfold in the single decade beginning in 1845, in the course of a remarkable expansion that took it from about 30 people in 1830 to more than 3 million in 1930. By no means all of the 20th-century growth can be blamed on the car, nor indeed all

---

1 His father owned a textiles company at Barmen in Prussia, and was a partner in the Ermen & Engels cotton plant in Manchester, so it was natural for the young fellow to be sent there.

2 Taken in translation from his *Journeys to England and Ireland*.

3 The architect of this redesign, Hausmann, liked the idea of a large number of splendid avenues converging on what amounted to a large roundabout; but the sheer number of such feeder roads in many cases created problems of traffic management that have defied solution. It was left to the enterprise and vehicle-management skills of the Parisian driver to keep the traffic fluid in these circuses; visitors would be aghast at what they judged to be the rash and furious driving, just as they tend to wax critical of the local driving methods in places like Rome, Turin, or parts of London. In fact the natives are quite ordinary folk who have merely adapted their potential skills to suit the circumstances. The world is full of bad drivers who condemn all others as worse.

4 Greater by an order of magnitude than the biggest of places that we once admired as the biggest cities, these might be described as supercities, something not necessarily the same as a mere conurbation where two or more cities have flowed into each other. Caution, and a decent respect for the fading niceties of language, discourages me from doing so, and even makes me reluctant to use the word city without care. Technically, a town only qualifies as a city when it houses the seat of a bishop; the easy way to check is to look for a cathedral.

that of the 19th century on the railways: if half of the world population today is urban, only 3% of it was in 1750. It was the Industrial Revelation that caused the rush to the towns, at a time when very few people indeed had the education, the experience, the foresight, the prudence (or indeed anything much else, apart from the desire to stay alive and if possible prosper), to plan how the cities should be made tolerable, navigable, or even sanitary.

In the second half of the 19th century it was indeed the railways which packed them in. With Britain the home of the Industrial Revelation, England the birthplace of the steam railway, and London the capital of England, it was inevitable that London should be the exemplar of all that was new, encouraging, disturbing. There had already been measures taken to deal with its transport problems, once it had grown too big to be served by its river the Thames as main street (not to mention as main sewer, and as a barrier to north–south traffic). The canals had made some brave attempts, compensating in sheer mass of loads for their sluggish pace: thanks to the low friction of a barge passing through water, and to the absence of gradient, a horse could pull forty times as much along the water as it could along any half-decent road. Nevertheless the horse-drawn omnibus, pioneered very shortly earlier in Paris, came to the streets of London in the early 1820s and flourished for the remainder of the century.

It was a big business. Thomas Tilling, perhaps the most prominent of the horse-bus companies by the end of the century, could be turned to by the authorities to provide as many as 6000 horses to participate in the processions and management of state occasions such as the celebrations of Queen Victoria's Jubilee or King Edward's coronation.

There were thousands upon thousands of horses in London (the number has been estimated as high as 2 million at the turn of the centuries), not by any means all of them looked after with such care as was given to Tilling's bus-haulers, which did at least have a visit from a vet each morning. Less privileged creatures, worked pitilessly hard by collier and common haulier, by itinerant tradesman and builder's merchant, had a worse time of it; but even a bus-horse, by nature a pretty stout creature that might live a natural life of twelve or fifteen years, was worn out at five. There was no question of retirement: the horse went straight off to the knacker, and absolutely everything – meat, bones, hair and hide, hooves and entrails and all – was found a profitable use.

Only in evading the graveyard[5] did the horse's lot differ from the working man's.

The city established before the car came could not easily be adapted to the new traffic. This was the scene in Newcastle-upon-Tyne in 1880.

Likewise hard-worked and ill-nourished, surrounded by filth and beset by consequent diseases, the labourer's life was as Hobbes described it 200 years earlier: nasty, brutish, and short. While rural gentry might live to 50 or more, a mid-century Manchester labourer averaged only 17, and in 1883 the figure for a Swansea man was but 24. At the end of the century, the national average life span was 42: 'retirement' as we know it today was as rare for working men as it was for working horses.

5 Well into the 20th century the US army expected horses that died in the field to be buried by their riders, the regulation grave measuring 5ft wide by 8ft x 8ft. When the officer or NCO in charge reluctantly admitted that the ground was too rocky to dig, then disposal of the corpse by axe and fire was the rule, this duty falling upon any men who were on punitive fatigues.

The first railway to come into London was only a decade behind the horse-bus. If it did nothing to make the place healthier, it did in places make it better – simply because the lowest-grade housing was the most cheaply pulled down to make way for it. Above all, it made the place bigger, encouraging the building of expansive suburbs from which untold hordes of new immigrants from the countryside could in theory reach their work in the city centre where the trade of the Empire was focused. How realistic it was depended on which railway company was involved, and whether it served one of the more or other of the less salubrious and gentrified suburbs. Some companies accepted government's direction to provide cheap fares for working men early in the morning and in the evening, and were rewarded with new sources of potential passengers, new suburbs of mean terraced housing for the working classes in places like Edmonton and Tottenham. Others, maybe lobbying a better class of Members of Parliament (it was the House of Commons which authorised the establishment of each new line, and many members put a price on their favours and thus made a pretty penny on the side), concentrated on trains suitable for gentlemen to travel daily, and at 'respectable' hours, to their offices in the City. The suburbs they served sprouted handsome villas and elegant crescents, and many a passenger travelled by horse-drawn carriage between his home and the station.

The other major (certainly the most perceptible) thing that the railways did to London was to make it even filthier. Factory smoke and smells[6] had been fouling the air for a century already, but now the new suburbs and the fast-expanding population added immeasurably to the soot content because everybody's source of heat was the open fire burning coal, the same stuff as powered industry and every locomotive. Coal smoke blackened the air, the buildings, the faces, the linen[7] and doubtless the lungs, and the London fog (often a lurid and sulphurous greeny-yellow to justify the name 'pea-soup') became notorious world-wide.

In other parts of the world, British coal would have been envied not only as a source of commercial wealth but also as a relatively clean source of heat and power. Much of Greater Germany and much of the USA had to make do with brown coal, otherwise known as soft or bituminous coal, which was even messier. New York, a city in which not only horses might be seen working[8] in all streets but also pigs might be seen roaming in some of them as late as 1895, insisted on the use of hard black coal (what the Americans called 'anthracite', though a British collier would have been more particular in his classifications) from the Pennsylvania coalfields for all static domestic or industrial purposes. New York was therefore seen as a relatively clean city[9] at the turn of the century; but the railroads[10] were exempt from this stricture.

In any case, the web of railroads[11] was of coarser mesh in the USA; what really made the nation dirty was industry. Pittsburgh, where the steel industry consumed incredible quantities of bituminous coal, was known nationwide as 'the smoky city'. Other industrial centres, such as Chicago, Cincinnati, Cleveland and Detroit, likewise owed their soot-blackened features, their smoke-laden air and their sulphurous stench to the burning of vast quantities of soft coal. Citizens from elsewhere learned the vile nature of soft coal while travelling behind locomotives burning it: the passengers would be exposed to a relentless barrage of cinders and oily smoke seeping into the

6 The list of noisome industries (which corrupted the salubrity of most towns) to be banished to some socially insignificant area (in London's case, the south bank west of Southwark) was 200 years ago determined to include tanneries, glue factories, hospitals and lunatic asylums.

7 London's Coal Smoke Abatement Society called for a smokeless capital in March 1904. The cleanest-living deskbound gent could expect his shirt-cuffs and collar (the latter still expected to be shiny white and stiffly starched) to look grimy by early afternoon, well into the 1950s. If one were staying in town for an evening's entertainment, a fresh collar was *de rigueur*; the more costly shirts had detachable and replaceable cuffs as well – otherwise one spent the day in the office wearing oversleeves elasticated at the wrists. The author remembers walking many miles home, in late 1952, through a dense fog which not only paralysed traffic but also killed about 250 Londoners that night: it was this particular fog, lasting for four days, which brought about the Clean Air Act, which began in 1956 to enforce the use of smokeless fuel in London and other parts of England. By this time the days of the steam train were drawing to a close, with electrics and diesels taking its place. It was ironic that the tramcar, which alone might find its way through the murky streets without deviation from its proper route, had vanished from the London streets in that same 1952.

8 And dying. Many a New York child's first sight of death would be the bloated body of a horse lying in the gutter awaiting collection by the City dead-horse wagon – a long green horse-drawn (what else?) wagon with room inside for several corpses. The tailgate was lowered to form a long ramp, up which the dead horse was slowly drawn by a hand-operated winch.

9 New York City even employed a white-uniformed dung-collector on every block. These men were known as White Wings, for some elusive reason. In suburban England, the local residents were happy to collect the droppings, which made such good manure for the roses in their gardens. In major English towns, poor men made a poor living as crossing-sweepers, deferentially plying their brooms to ensure that the long-skirted (and, with luck, charitable) ladies of those days could cross the street without their ground-length hems being disgustingly fouled.

10 The Delaware, Lackawanna and Western Railroad (whose initials DLW were sometimes alleged to represent 'Delay, Linger and Wait') owned some hard-coal mines and made much advertising play of the fact that it used clean black anthracite.

11 The first in the USA was the Baltimore and Ohio in 1830. By 1860 there were 30,000 miles, rising to 193,000 in the ensuing 40 years.

carriages, especially in hot weather when the windows had to be opened as a matter of sheer survival. Hard coal made less smoke, and its cinders could be brushed off without much residual damage; but in every land where it served as fuel, where it had to be mined, processed, delivered, stored, burned, and its residues of ash and cinders disposed of, coal made a filthy, laborious and miserable mockery of civilisation.

Without the coming of the car, and its intriguing engine which encouraged us to consider all the possible alternative fuels, we might still be coal-dependent and filthy, might still be turning a blind eye to the silicosis which made miners die young, as well as to the diphtheria (carried by flies and fuelled by horse-dung) which made children die even younger. Coal would still be fuelling some electricity generating stations at the end of the 20th century, but as many as possible were converted to, or were replaced by, boilers fuelled by oil – hardly immaculate yet, but very much cleaner than the alternatives[12]. Oil had become the everyday, everywhere energy-source commodity, mainly because the internal combustion engine had found a use for it and the car had made that use substantial.

Yet what a plethora of other problems the car brought in its wake when it began to penetrate our cities!

The London traffic system is many hundreds of times more complex than anyone imagines.

This has nothing to do with influences, demonic or angelic. It's more to do with geography, and history, and architecture.

Mostly this works to people's advantage, although they'd never believe it.

London was not designed for cars. Come to that, it wasn't designed for people. It just sort of happened. This created problems, and the solutions that were implemented became the next problems, five or ten or a hundred years down the line.

Pratchett, T, & Gaiman, N: *Good Omens*, London, 1990

London was an ancient city long before the coming of the car; and there were a few others of some size which also suffered. Chicago, if not actually ancient, was already big when in 1871 it suffered a disastrous fire which destroyed its centre: proponents of a new architecture rushed to rebuild it, creating a new style (dependent on vertical rather than horizontal expansion) which was accepted as the pattern for the further evolution of the American big town.

This could never have happened without the lift, or elevator as the Americans called it. Steam power had made such ideas feasible in the early 19th century, but it took the invention (by a New Yorker, Elisha G Otis) in 1852 of much needed safety devices before, in 1857, the first passenger-carrying lift could be installed in the USA. By 1889 the now prospering Otis company could put the first successful electric lift into the Demarest Building in New York City, and by 1904 all practical limits to the height such lifts might reach had been overcome.

This was typical of the ancillary technical developments which affected not only the evolution of the car but also the evolution of the cities whose inhabitants it might serve. Modern engineering techniques were already seen in the 1870s to be far more profitable than historical precedents, and the beginnings of the new compulsion were to be found in the Monadnock Building and the Reliance Building in reborn Chicago, both of them the work of architects Burnham and Root. At the same time the even more influential Louis Sullivan established himself, doing the same sort of things in the Wainwright Building of St Louis, and the fashion was set. It was tragic that this dense heavily concentrated American pattern should have been crystallised just a few years before the car became commonplace in the USA, just too soon to allow for the openness and mobility that the car would offer.

The majority of the world's really big cities have, however, grown big since the advent of the car, and it might have been supposed that they and their new transports might have flourished together, in a kind of synergy whereby car design and manufacture and use might have been geared to architectural and economic development so that the car and the city were mutually complementary.

In most countries that did not happen, because the natural rates of development for each were differently paced and neither could be accurately forecast. The only exception was the USA, where the people had adopted the car so quickly and compulsively that it was clear to the builders that the car had to be taken into account.

'Quickly' and 'compulsively' are relative terms. The Americans may have been

---

12 Except those using nuclear power. Viewed with optimism in the postwar years when we began to see other uses than for the bomb, nuclear energy promised wonders in the 1960s – but the people at large were frightened of it, without bothering to understand it, and rabble-dependent politicians turned against it almost everywhere except in France, where it flourishes and does no perceived harm after all. From the point of view of cleanliness, however, perhaps it merely transfers the problem elsewhere: the disposal of nuclear waste is still a source of worry to many.

quicker than others, but they were not very quick. Consider the architectural models and plans of the 1930s, and it is hard to avoid the conclusion that only the Americans recognised the existence of the urban problem of vehicle management, and that even they had but the faintest clue about how to address that problem. The New York World's Fair of 1939 provided examples: the last in a series of extravagant and optimistic international exhibitions harking back to the Great Exhibition of 1851 in London, the New York show took as its motto 'Building the World of Tomorrow'. The organisers insisted on modernity in everything, and somehow contrived to present a picture of the virtues of expendability and mass consumerism in the USA. The automobile was by no means overlooked as a vital exemplar of those virtues, but what did the architects and city planners do with it? The Norman Bel Geddes *Futurama* was typical: the city of the future would by all means have clean-cut speed-oriented thoroughfares piercing it from all sides so that vehicles (notably private cars rather than public transport carriages) could flow through and to all parts as vividly and vitally as blood courses through the heart. Of means to accommodate those cars when they were parked awaiting revivification when the driver's city work was done, there was not a sign.

If the fancy modernist designers in their ivory towers did little to help, the American people on the ground saw the needs and found the means quickly enough. This was why, when summoned before the US Joint Economic Committee, some time about the beginning of the 1970s, who wanted to know how he felt about Federal aid to enable the automobile industry to make what they thought was the inevitable conversion to the manufacture of mass-transit vehicles, Henry Ford II was able to retort: *That's one problem we are not worried about. The real mass-transit system in the United States is the highway system and the automobile, which are responsible for 80% of all trips to work and all trips between cities[13], and for more than 90% of all trips within cities. The automobile business is now about 75 years old. Most of the United States has been built within that period, and the building pattern has been made possible by the unprecedented convenience, flexibility, comfort and low cost of (private) motor vehicle transportation.*

The example of the USA presents the best possible case of a society prepared to grow with its motor car, and enjoying the space in which to provide for it; none of the other nations that had tried to develop motoring could find room for the extravagant spreads of low-density building which made the typical provincial American town so suitable and easy for (and so dependent upon) the car. Those others which had the space had not made the necessary progress: the first truly Russian car was built in penny numbers in 1926; India built her first in 1946, China in 1951. Like most of the African and south-east Asian nations, newly emergent or otherwise, they were places with lots of people and with quite different priorities.

Most of those American motoring-towns were established by the simplest rule of thumb. Where two significant roads cross, a few buildings will cluster, following the age-old practices providing for law-enforcement, refuelling, and commercial hospitality; if the place thrives, more will be built along the sides of the roads approaching the intersection, in a familiar form of ribbon development. This will be followed by a period of infilling, when the areas behind the intersection will be built up, with new minor roads to provide access; and then it will be time for further ribbon development, out along the spokes of the wheel that the town's plan now resembles.

In the flatlands, in the prairies or in Texas or for that matter in the steppes of central Asia, it works a treat. The shape of the town might be influenced by the route of a river[14], or the fall of sunlight[15], but such effects are usually minor. What, though, of the several other traditional types of towns – those built along the side of a valley, or as hilltop fortresses, or around natural harbours? These – and others – present differing organisational plans, sometimes with one dominant centre for business and government, sometimes with two or even with several, and sometimes with no real centre at all.

---

13 This was already true in 1955, by which time the railroads' share in passenger transportation had dropped to 88% of the passenger-miles it had claimed in 1915. In the intervening time, thanks to the extent to which Americans were ready to buy cars and build their lives around them, travelling expanded by a factor of 12, as a result of which the railroads' share actually dropped to 5% of the total, compared with 73% in 1915.

14 London provides just such a case, growing from the intersection of the River Thames by a north–south road at the first point upstream where it could be bridged. The serpentine Thames remained its main thoroughfare for centuries – as has, more effectively because on a smaller scale, and for a lesser time, the Grand Canal in Venice. There is a wonderful and too often overlooked convenience in having a serpentine main thoroughfare, especially if it be of regular pitch and radius: nowhere in the built-up area along its banks should be more distant from it than the radius of the curve, so that feeder transport may be short-ranged, highly specialised, and economically efficient. It follows that long towns should have sine-wave motorways through their middles.

15 Public buildings (shops, cafés, banks and similar offices) generally need to be on the sunny side of the street, where customers feel happier. Industrial and private premises do not need this luxury, which may be more welcome at the back door. If a nearby hillside casts a shadow, the town's developers should take it into account.

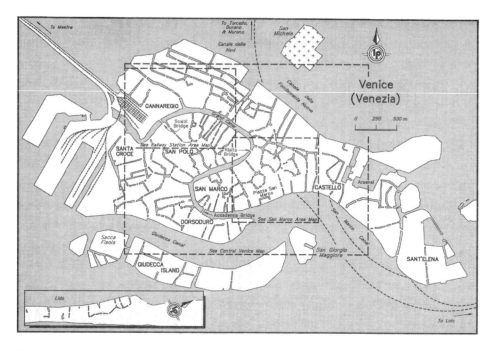

The Venetian Grand Canal was a serpentine and therefore efficient major highway through the city centre.

The provision of effective (which means economic, above all) transport from outlying residential areas to the centre or centres presents different problems in each case. The town with no real centre (typically riparian, or perhaps one that has grown along one side of a valley) tends to grow long and narrow and featureless, and internal journeys may be very long and tedious, as in Los Angeles. The big city with a really strong centre (London, Tokyo, Chicago) is like the hilltop fortress: it reaches a stage – a natural limit to further growth – where it becomes impossible to provide adequate feeder services for the people and materials (food, for example) that can only be brought into the centre, in large enough numbers and a short enough time, by a highly organised mass-transit system such as railways. The inevitable shortcomings of short-distance bus and underground systems on radial and transverse routes within the outer boundaries (if indeed such boundaries can be recognised) are minor by comparison.

The city with multiple relatively weak centres is more easily managed. Modern Copenhagen (in olden times it was a strong-centre fortress town, and if it were to be built today it would be built somewhere else) is a good example; Paris is an excellent one where, even today, traffic flows with unexpected ease most of the time, while a large number of people can live within the city confines, well within comfortable reach of their work. Apart from its deliberate multifocal design, Paris has profited from history: so long as it remained an ancient walled city, the law forbade major building in the area beyond the wall, which was reserved for military purposes. After the Second World War, when traffic was troublesome and the old military strategies were obsolete, that annular strip outside the old walls was used for an eight-lane orbital highway which, by relaxing the requirements which make genuine motorways so costly to build, could be completed with amazing speed. This, together with a wonderful *laissez-faire* attitude[16] to all road users, motorised and pedestrian alike, and reinforced during critical years by the insistence of President Pompidou that Paris must adapt herself to the car, has made it a place where one-eighth of all French people can live and work and get around using cars, trains, buses, the Métro, and their feet, with indifferent ease.

Open-minded planning could achieve something similar in many another city, even in those such as Hamburg or Hong Kong or (a place viciously hostile to the car) Amsterdam, cities where a moment's inattention will have you falling into some intrusive stretch of water. Alas, those who are disposed to be planners are, by their nature, not open-minded. They are the sort who would do everything to make you park your car where it cannot be of any use, and go on foot or by some gruesome public service to visit your city-centre bank, for instance. What would such officious people make of the 'drive-thru' banks[17] in many an American city centre?

Such people do not like speed, either; yet the one most important thing in making city transport flow freely, or indeed to make it flow at all, is to encourage it to flow rapidly. It can be done, but most city fathers are too frightened to do it. That is a pity, for amongst other things (such as in overall journey times and personal frustration, and general business inefficiency, all of which can be diminished by travelling faster) it brings about a tremendous reduction in the pollution caused by exhausts. Thanks to the car, our cities are much cleaner than they were before the car came; but we could do even better.

---

16 Let them park in the trees! After all, the modern automobile does not drip.

17 The drive-in cinema came much earlier, and did a lot for the sexual emancipation of American youth. Alas, it needs a lot of space and a kind climate.

CHAPTER 2

SOMEWHERE TO STOP

IF THE LENGTH OF A JOURNEY, be it only from one town to the next, is greater than the distance a man might travel in a day, where is he (and, if he has one, his horse/donkey/camel) to rest? Where can he find food and water, provender, social – or even sexual [18]– intercourse?

He might be an itinerant journeyman on his way to look for work, or he might be a wealthy merchant with a retinue; the problem remained.

There are still parts of the world in which, and there are still people among whom, the obligations of hospitality rank almost supreme[19] in social mores. Religious Jews aim to emulate their forefather Avraham[20], who is recorded as having asked G-d to suspend the discussion in which they were engaged because he had spotted three travellers approaching his tent and, in the circumstances (it was an exceptionally hot day), almost certainly desirous of rest and refreshment. In relatively modern times, an Arabic traveller need only proclaim himself 'a guest sent by Allah' to be welcomed because 'such a guest is always welcome': he would be cared for without question, least of all about his identity or his itinerary.

Where this kind of civilisation prevails, the weary traveller need only present himself at any house which might stand on his route. Elsewhere, the householder would expect to be paid for the materials and services provided[21]; in most countries, hospitality might only be expected at establishments where the satisfaction of travellers' needs was a professional enterprise. It might be a lonely little inn on a wild Pennine road, or a fortress-like khan on some caravan route where the mighty Oxus rolls towards the Caspian; the principles were the same.

They might not always be exercised. When the Roman Empire was at its height, it commanded a 50,000-miles network of roads that ran from Cumberland to Ethiopia, from Carthage to Byzantium – roads upon which, with military foresight and military precision, staging-posts were set at intervals (commonly 27–35 miles) corresponding with known journey speeds. Hospitality, likewise well organised, was available there, but only to travellers bearing official certification of their eligibility through office or rank.

Under this or any other regime which viewed the ordinary man as a chattel, bound to his master or to his lord or to his land by military or feudal prescription, the ordinary man was to be discouraged from travel, and those who did so might be supposed rogues or vagabonds and treated accordingly. The Dark Ages, as noted elsewhere in this volume, lasted a long time, and it took the car to free us from them.

So long as those ages remained dark, the standards of accommodation available in commonplace roadside inns and taverns remained parlous, a matter of dirt and stench and noise and vermin. Things were not necessarily much better if one could put up in a castle, where any common wayfarer could once exercise his common law right to 'fire and salt'. Far higher standards prevailed in the religious hostelries[22] to be found in some parts, but they were required to exercise their own priorities, primarily for the benefit of the poor and the clerical.

Even for them, the Dark Ages grew darker as the road systems abandoned by fallen Rome were abandoned by everybody else, and left to decay because nobody could or would undertake the responsibility for their maintenance. There was no

---

18 A load of silk often took three years to travel by pack animals from China to Europe.

19 In the Mishnah (a treatise in the Talmud, which elaborates on the social and legal implications of the divine laws embodied in the books of Moses) listing the ten forms of religious observance which ensure a partial reward in this world, as well as a full reward in the world to come, hospitality to strangers ranks fourth.

20 ברשית וירא Genesis xviii.

21 In England until about 1940, it was commonly accepted that a countryside hiker or cyclist (but not a motorist, who would be assumed to have the means to go further and fare more expensively) might reasonably expect to buy a meal or overnight accommodation at a farmhouse. Thereafter, what with wartime fear and paranoia, any such traveller might be suspected of being a spy or a German paratrooper in disguise, and the presumption of hospitality lapsed.

22 Amongst other things not to be despised (such as baths and clean bedlinen) the monasteries were often most proficient in the brewer's and vintner's arts (was it not Dom Perignon who invented champagne?) – though it was not in them but in common inns where the demon drink created problems. As noted in an English parliamentary enactment of 1604, 'The ancient, true and proper use of Inns, Ale Houses and Victualling Houses is for the Receipt, Relief and Lodging of Wayfaring People, travelling from place to place and not meant for the entertaining and harbouring of Lewd and Idle People to spend and consume their Money and Time in Lewd and Drunken Manner.'

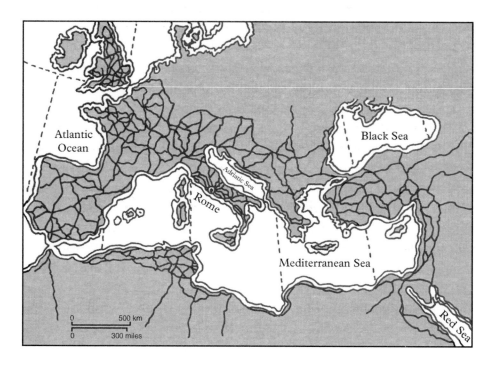

The network of Roman roads.

authority sufficiently central, no local ruler sufficiently liberal; and, as far as the defence of a territory were concerned, good roads made matters easier for the invaders as well as for the defenders. More urgently, as it must have seemed to many a petty tyrant, the deterioration of the roads would have the effect that disaffected tenants would find it harder to go off on some rampage or riot; better to keep them penned up in their hovels, unable to explore where the grass might grow greener[23].

Thus, while the peoples of the plains and of the deserts continued with their tented villages and forts, their wells and their oases, their caravan and river routes, all unchanged for centuries, the peoples of the fields and woods in Europe experienced a steady decline in travel facilities.

Thus it was not until 9 April 1657 that the first known stage coach – that is, one which accomplished its journey by stages, with horses being changed and meals taken at a suitably placed coaching inn at the end of each stage – set off on its journey, from Chester to London. At first the schedule was too optimistic: London was reached in four days, but the strain was appalling. Before long, the journey was allowed six days – and still it was made in acute discomfort, prompting Dean Swift to comment after trying it:

Next time, I do protest, sir,

I'd walk to Dublin ere I'd ride to Chester.

In winter it would be even worse, supposing that the conditions had not made the roads absolutely impassable. There was, for example, no provision against the cold. It seemed a commonplace matter-of-fact report that 'On the arrival of the Bath coach . . .it was found that two passengers had been frozen to death and that a third man was dying.' And that was in 1812, the year when Napoleon went galumphing across central Europe from Vilna to Paris.

The splendid Napoleonic roads, once established, encouraged a staging system in France that was almost a match for the English network, and to a lesser and cruder extent Germany took up the challenge too. In the USA, the ideals of the Land of the Free made travelling something that was taken for granted, and the spread of existing settlements made it even admirable. By 1783, there was a regular stage service between Boston and Hartford, soon extended to New York – 200 miles in perhaps six days.

Thus the post-house or staging house[24] or coaching inn, wherever it were and whatever it might be called, flourished: elaborate time-and-motion studies enabled teams of grooms and ostlers to effect a change of horses in miraculously short times, impeccably kept schedules made arrivals precisely timed, with food and other facilities ready; and if overnight stops were commonly a scratchy business of uncomfortable bedding and discomfiting bedmates (not by any means all of them human), at least

---

23 It may be asserted as a fairly general rule that where, on the other side of the fence, the grass appears greener, it is so as to hide the mud.

24 There was a further requirement for places to have extra horses available for helping to pull a coach up some severe hill. These establishments, which might be found at the bottom of a bad hill anywhere, in the country or in town, were not affected by the economies of the staging system; they survived as long as there was horse-drawn transport. Probably only twenty years separated the functions of the appropriately named Wagon and Horses inn, where supernumerary horses were kept at the ready at the bottom of Surbiton Hill in Surrey, from those of the Cooper Car Company, manufacturers of racing cars, just beyond the top of the hill.

St Pancras Hotel and the adjacent railway station, one of London's main termini, painted by John O'Connor (1830–1889). Forty years later Pissarro painted the same subject.

it made the early morning's return to the miseries of the coach interior less intimidating a contrast.

By this time, however, the railways were beginning to exert their influence. As the railways spread, so the stage-coaches failed, and the inns that once thrived on the business the coaches brought them could only survive as places of resort and entertainment for the local residents. Now every town of substance acquired its railway hotel, adjacent to the station, and in the capitals and other major cities where the lines had their termini grew great hotels of palatial size and splendour.

Luxurious hotels were appearing elsewhere, too, principally in the spa towns that had sprung up into favour when the discovery of the supposed benefits of taking the waters attracted the well-to-do to what were, in Belgium and Switzerland and England and later in Germany and the USA, the first holiday resorts. These were palatial indeed, resorts for the wealthy – but not only the wealthy, for they were obliged to take with them at least the core of their private retinue of servants, who would be lodged in meaner rooms, either in the attic or in the basement according to the whim of the architects. The notion of providing a full staff of servants to care for the guests seems not to have occurred to anybody until the invention of the first modern hotel, the Tremont in Boston, Massachusetts, which opened in 1829.

None of these establishments could have endured without the service provided by the railways. Such was their location – within comfortable reach, by foot or by carriage[25], of the first-class end of the railway platform – that the coming of the motor car at first did nothing to disturb their *modus operandi* or their success. The growing thousands of European motorists who took to the roads each Sunday, as the 1920s gave birth to the 1930s, went out for the day, not for longer.

It was notably in the USA, a land that was huge and where journeys must often be long, that things were different. Here was a nation that had established itself by travelling, that had developed itself by travelling, that would refresh itself and take a new start in life every so often by travelling some more. Here was a nation that had learnt, more quickly and more decisively than any other, that it was the automobile which made all things possible, all points accessible. In a tradition that was essentially hardy and practical, the practice of the pioneers was to make do with tents for any necessary overnight stop *en route* to some distant business appointment; but on the most frequented routes a few minor entrepreneurs built cabins (not necessarily log cabins, but something better than mere huts) that could be let by the night to passing trade. They were usually in isolated places, so staffing was minimal and plumbing sometimes less than that; but it was enough for starting an idea that was, being intended purely for the use of the motoring public, an essentially American one.

Groups of individual tourist cabins appeared along routes such as US Highway 66, and business travellers began to rely on them. One such establishment, on Route 101 at San Luis Obispo, 80 miles from the city of Santa Barbara in Western California, was set up in 1924 with an electric sign .OTEL, while the first letter flashed alternately H and M. This was the first use of the word Motel, and the proprietor (one James Vail) called his place the Motel Inn.

---

25 In London, which enjoyed at least ten major termini and a whole constellation of first-class hotels, it was natural that a new style of public-service carriage should ply for hire in the streets of the capital. It was designed to be drawn by one horse, and to contain four passengers and a good deal of luggage.

The word was self-explanatory and the idea prospered. By mid-century, motel cabins were no longer built separately: a string of rooms, all under one roof and each with an adjoining car-parking space, became the efficient and economical norm for a motel. One arrived and departed with minimal fuss – but one left with an empty feeling, since there were no facilities for feeding the guests. The provision of early-morning coffee seemed, when at last it came, a tremendous advance.

As always, it is the first step which starts a progress. Soon there would be breakfast. Before long, the motel might be a place for holidaying as well as a place on the way to business; but holidaying is at best a seasonal business, so proprietors began to add facilities for conventions. Today the business-wise motel[26] is to be found, close to major roads, on the outskirts of towns both major and minor, not only in the USA but also in all other countries which can be described as motorised.

The great railway hotels are moribund. The great holiday hotels have mostly had their day. The well-sited roadhouses, originating in the 1930s and designed to be places of resort and entertainment not only for the local residents but also (and preferably) for those well-heeled enough to drive a car and take it ten or a hundred miles in confident expectation of an evening's relaxation and stimulation, are flourishing. So are the sporting hotels, for the private car has given townspeople access to country pursuits, has enabled them to go to golf courses, horseriding centres, ski slopes, shooting ranges, flying clubs, boating marinas, mountaineering bases and many other such establishments which could never have prospered and would probably not even have been created were it not for the private car which made it all feasible.

There are even people who will drive to some place where they will proceed to enjoy a walk . . .

---

26 It does not so describe itself, for the word motel has a taint of low-class cheapness about it. Nor, for similar reasons, would it admit to being a commercial hotel, as the old railways hotels catering for commercial travellers once did. It usually calls itself a 'luxury hotel and conference centre', and sometimes that is a truthful description. Sometimes (Do you have to walk miles in the rain to reach your spot in the hotel car park? Will a man, the parking valet, be sent to fetch your car to the door?) you might wonder . . .

PART IV

THE TURN OF THE WHEEL:

REVOLUTIONS IN TECHNOLOGY

CHAPTER 1

THE NATURE OF REVOLUTION

At last men came to set me free; I ask'd not why, and reck'd not where;
It was at length the same to me . . .

BYRON

ON 14 JULY 1789, A French mob stormed the Bastille. The scene has been depicted in paintings and drawings galore, for art has always been the dupe of propaganda; you and I, and many a Frenchman of that period, might well prefer that witty Fragonard painting, *The Storming of the Citadel*, but popular feeling insisted that the Bastille job represented some kind of universal emancipation. In fact, when the rioters broke open that grim-faced Parisian prison, all they found inside was seven old men who were frankly irritated by this disturbance of their peace and orderly quiet.

That did not matter; the act was political, not practical – and because of it and its consequences, we are subjected to a more than Chopinesque deluge of Revolutionary Studies in every imaginable medium. So why not in this one, too?

What had the French Revolution to do with cars? Not a great deal, except that in its wake the French, trying like mad to be revolutionary (even if it only meant being different) in anything and everything, instituted not only the mischievous metric system but also the cackhanded and ungallant practice of driving on the right.

Indirectly, though, that revolution had all manner of influences because, with the insistent superiority that the French have always assumed, the French has been seen as the model of all revolutions. A Russian, while stifling his embarrassment that what he knows as the October Revolution actually took place in November, might resent it. An American, if only he realised (as few Americans do) that the American Revolution actually preceded it, might be downright derogatory. Not even the English ignore it, though we have had more than enough of our own revolutions in earlier times, and smugly assume seniority because of that priority. In fact, our choice of epithets for the Glorious Revolution and the Bloodless Revolution says a lot about our notions of what is either noble or humanitarian.

It was the confusion of those two ideals which made the late 1780s so trigger-happy. Rousseau proclaimed that 'Man was born free and is everywhere in chains':

and now we are shackled by entirely unreasonable speed limits. Burns declared that 'A man's a man for a' that': and now every pimpled youth and yellowing pensioner believes himself the rightful proprietor of a hot hatchback. Most seditious of all, the English poet Mordaunt made this drive-now-pay-later appeal to the shackled human spirit:

> *Throughout the sensual world proclaim*
> *One crowded hour of glorious life*
> *Is worth an age without a name.*

It was this suspicion, that we were all missing something, which prompted the American revolutionaries to ratify as a self-evident truth the notion that man was entitled to the pursuit of happiness – which is all very well provided that he is absolutely sure of having identified his quarry, and does not go off chasing a wild goose only to discover that it was a red herring.

The revolutions which have punctuated the age of motoring, the age that has occupied half the time that has elapsed since the French Revolution began, have often begun similarly with the espousal of some ideal and then sunk into an adultery of conventions. Some of those revolutions have been technical, some of them social, but hardly any of them achieved the object that had been identified by whoever initiated them.

We have had enough revolutions in history to know by now that all revolutions are like that. When Brutus and his fellow conspirators plunged knives into Julius Caesar and Rome into chaos, they surely did not do so with the intention of leaving matters worse in the end than they had been before; but that was, in the long run, all they achieved. And what about all those revolutions which swept Europe in 1848, the Year of Revolutions, when to cock a snook at authority was the height of fashion and to cock a pistol at officialdom was the height of ambition?

In the long run, perhaps all the good they did was to remind us that the only revolutions from which man has learned to mend his ways have been those that were quelled. Probably the best example of this is the first, the prototype 3300 years ago of all modern revolutions, the challenge to authority that was led in the Sinaitic wilderness by Korach. Multitudes died because of this wealthy man's ambition, but a man's a man for a' that; it was, we may usefully note, his wife who incited him to rebellion.

It was Lancia's mother, shaken in the accident which followed a spring fracture while he was driving, who inspired him to pursue the notional ideals of independent suspension which were to lead him to create one of the most revolutionary of cars, the prototype Lambda – which became more and more corrupt, less and less revolutionary, with every passing year of production. In the end, it was almost ordinary. Revolutions tend to be like that, too.

If its motion be not arrested early, what happens when the cycle of revolution runs its course? The French example is in fact a good one, though it takes a bit of following – if only because, despite the scores of recorded names that glimmer like receding stars against the black namelessness of the mob, there were no truly great men to inspire it and to signpost it. The French, who began by overthrowing the king, ended up with an emperor; having discovered their royalty bankrupt a couple of years before they rioted, they once again allowed their bankers ownership of the royal debt within a couple of years after they quieted; when it was all over, the people were neither much more nor much less self-seeking and independent than before it started.

A cycle of revolution, it seems, comprises five typical phases, though with considerable scope for overlap among the first three. Tactical muddle, ideological confusion, opportunistic brutality, and a disorderly aftermath, lead finally and ironically either to diversion or reversion, when someone emerges who is strong enough to exploit the situation by applying the countervailing measures which are needed to restore some kind of stability. He may be new, he may be different, but he proves no less a tyrant than the one originally overthrown. The modern European model of a front-wheel-drive saloon, with its engine out ahead of its front wheels, is just as imbalanced as the earlier European model of a rear-drive saloon with its engine hung behind the back wheels.

The French descended all too quickly from a debate of views to a debauch of violence. Revolutionary progress was measured by the succession of the Great Fear, the September Massacres, the Reign of Terror – nothing clear enough in its motives to succeed, nothing well enough organised to last. It is from such material and moral chaos that great men (we may forever debate whether they are good men) emerge; in France the turnabout occurred after six years of this turmoil, the same time that it took to progress from the first Model T Ford to the first pressed-steel Dodge, from the Daimler fluid-flywheel preselector transmission to the Oldsmobile automatic, from the launching of the first *Dreadnought* to the sinking of the *Titanic*.

After half a dozen populist years of blood and vindictiveness, a counter-revolution of royalist supporters took a turn at violence. They were turned off very

The true instigator of the rear-engined revolution in racing cars was not the 1934 Auto-Union nor even the 1924 Benz. Neither of those was entirely convincing; this Cooper 500 was, because in and around 1950 it demonstrated possibilities that nothing else offered.

smartly by a young artillery officer who, commenting on the narcoleptic speed of 'a whiff of grapeshot', gave his name (he was, as it happens, of partially Scottish descent) as Napoleon Bonaparte. Soon he was promoted to a general and sent to Italy, whose treasures he looted on such a scale as to redeem France from insolvency; it was his success as a revenue agent, rather than as a soldier, which marked him out as the general who would become head of state. In 1799 he was appointed Consul of France, after which the French were kept much too busy to be revolutionary. Is it too fanciful to see the Lotus 18 as Chapman's 'whiff of grapeshot', even though the real instigator of the rear-engined F1 revolution was Cooper?

Chapman's ability to make his rivals run around in circles does not prove him to have been a true revolutionary; he wanted to stay ahead of the game, but not necessarily to change the nature of the game itself. There was more of the zealous missionary, less of the Warren Street spiv, about Jim Hall; but the superiority of his Chaparrals inspired more resentment than revolution.

Perhaps nobody apart from Louis Renault resented André Citroën, and surely nobody of any real consequence (you may deduce for yourselves whom I thus exclude) resented Sir Alec Issigonis; yet whether these were separate revolutionaries, or parties to the same movement, or merely agents in the longer process of evolution, is questionable.

It was, I suppose, inevitable that the word 'evolution' should raise its niggard head; but it helps us remember that many a profound change is not at all revolutionary. Many revisions are merely mechanistic, and I always insist that what is so glibly glorified as the Industrial Revolution was in fact a Revelation, literally an exponential process of exploration, discovery, and emancipation – a Realisation, if you will, and undoubtedly something which furnished the means of revolution, but not in itself revolutionary, as was, say, the Economic Revolution of the Roman Empire. What to make of China's Cultural Revolution, which shared 1967 with the appearance of the Wankel engine in Mazda and NSU cars (not to mention the Cosworth-Ford DFV engine in the F1 Lotus), is beyond conjecture: it cannot be a proper subject for these pages, for cars and culture have nothing in common.

Cars and revolution? A very different matter, and not only because Lenin drove a Rolls-Royce whereas Hitler, for all his enthusiasm, could not drive. I hope to show how the fervour and the fuddlement, the fanaticism and the factiousness and sometimes the futility of revolution have characterised the changes that motoring has undergone.

Revolution, you see, is like any other turnaround, like a clock-hand, like a spinning wheel: when it has turned full circle, it is back where it started.

CHAPTER 2

ForWarD

THE RUSSIAN REVOLUTION TOOK AGES to get started; the Cultural Revolution took even longer to be finished. Is it possible that, because they took so long, they cannot last? Is the same true of those motoring revolutions that took ages to take effect?

In the ideal revolution, the overthrow of the *ancien régime* and the vesting of authority in the newly revolutionary idealists ought to take place quickly; subversion should come like salvation, in the blink of an eye. It does not often work like that, anything so brief usually proving to have been nothing more than a mere revolt; and it certainly did not work like that in the case of the French Revolution, which so many have so mistakenly been led to believe was the quintessential revolution.

It is generally reckoned to have started in 1789; but between fits and starts it was a long time coming into effect, and a long time dying. It was hopelessly incomplete in 1792, when Rouget de L'Isle responded to the request by the Mayor of Strasbourg for a patriotic song, and composed the *Marseillaise*; and it was hearing that bloodthirsty and uncivilised incitement to violence, in the streets of Paris amidst the revolutionary echoes of 1830, that inspired Hector Berlioz to elevate it to the status of a choral and symphonic hymn. The thing to note is that in all verses except one, he writes the exhortation *Marchez!* Only in the verse sung by the massed choir representing the People is the word *Marchons!* The masses are always the cannon-fodder, the slaves, the dupes.

Motoring revolutions are no different. They take a long time to get going, even longer to peter out; and, when they are finished, the only people to have profited are the merchant bankers. Take front-wheel drive, for example: why do you think it so good that almost every major manufacturer foists it on you? If it is so good, why did we not have it sooner? Would it have occurred to you that the first production example, enjoying considerable popularity for a while (for reasons that were, as usual, irrelevant), appeared as early as 1900? More unlikely still, would you have associated it with Porsche?

Cugnot's steam-driven tricycle of 1770 was probably the first front-wheel-drive automobile, and the fact that it crashed into a wall on its first trial ought to have put people off the idea for ever. Alas, they persisted in thinking of the motor car as a horseless carriage, and so they were always tempted to put the horse before the cart – an arrangement only justified by the numerous natural shortcomings of the horse, ranging from its incorrigible idiocy[1] to its lack of periscopic vision.

Panhard and Levassor sought to break away from those conventions when in 1889 they exploited the dismissal of the horse and introduced the *système Panhard*. This simple and logical arrangement of components recognised the necessity of front-wheel steering (carriage design had convinced everybody about that) and derived from that the need for the rear wheels to be driven. The rest was obvious: if the radiator were to be at the front of the car to enjoy a strong draught of air as the car proceeded, then the engine ought to be close behind it so as to simplify the connections between the two. Between the engine and the rear axle there had to be, in turn, a clutch and a gearbox and a propellor shaft. Thus the driver could sit amidships with a decent view over the engine, he and his passengers were given some protection from the headwind by the engine enclosure, and all the machinery could be assembled between (or on a platform above) the two parallel girder beams of what became the conventional chassis.

Thus was set the pattern for nearly all the cars in the world for the next 60 years, and for a large proportion of them (especially those made in the New World, whose major revolution was older than the French) even to the present day. It made estimable sense – but only if one accepted the propriety of the internal combustion engine and mechanical transmission.

There were staunch objectors who did not. These dissidents (ignoring the diehard steam addicts) were impassioned by the thought of using electricity wherever possible; and amongst them were the Austrian firm of Lohner. Formerly coachbuilders, they had taken to making petrol-driven cars in the 1890s, but their

---

1 Hippophiles may protest, but in vain. No creature that is fool enough to allow me to sit on its back is sensible enough to be trusted with carrying me.

enthusiasm for electricity tempted them to hire a youngster who was crazy about it, the son of a tinsmith named Porsche. He devised a system of electric motors (whether fed by batteries or from a petrol-engined dynamo was irrelevant, but in time Lohner did both) incorporated in the hubs of the front wheels. Thus front-wheel drive was achieved with an ease that the mechanical engineers of the day were unable to emulate.

It worked as well as could be expected, but did not last commercially because such cars were more costly to run than simple petrol-engined ones. Electricity is, after all, nothing more than a mode of energy transmission, not a form of energy in itself, and although it is a wonderfully flexible transmission it is also grievously inefficient. Porsche cashed in on it eventually, in the Great War of 1914–1918, when the suitability of his so-called *Mixte* transmission for army gun-carriages and the like made him successful enough to appear clever.

Before then, a clever mechanical engineer (who was to have much more influence on Second World War tank design, with his T34 for Russia, than Porsche with his Tiger 1 for Germany) tried in the USA to make front-wheel drive work mechanically. Walter Christie saw sense in having the engine's crankshaft revolve in the same plane as the wheels: it eliminated costly and consumptive right-angle drives in the transmission, and it made the car less troubled by gyroscopic and torque reactions when the engine was accelerated or slowed.

He took the idea too far: his 1907 GP racer had only the most rudimentary transmission. Christie relied on the flexibility of an exceedingly large engine (at 19.9 litres, his was the biggest Grand Prix engine of all time), but the car was barely controllable.

All mechanically driven front wheels created problems of controllability for decades to come. A variety of front-wheel-drive motorcycles at the turn of the century served notice of the difficulties, but by the 1920s front drive attracted experimenters in sporting cars such as the Tracta and Alvis, and even in racing cars – especially in the USA, where the De Dion axle was brilliantly adapted by Miller to serve the front wheels of his Indianapolis racers.

Later in the 1920s, Harry Miller met E L Cord, president of Auburn. From that meeting sprang the front-drive Cord car, a machine which caught all the attention but dropped all the chances. The significant technical feature of the Cord was a new constant-velocity universal joint for the driveshafts, permitting greater angular displacement of the wheels; earlier front-drive cars had awfully large turning circles.

The universal joint was the source of most difficulties. It had almost always been the Hooke joint (still to be found in the propshafts of front-engined rear-drive cars), the output speed of which varies cyclically according to the angle of deflection. Complex double joints and others were developed by the Frenchman J A Grégoire, progenitor of the Tracta – not to be confused with the American B F Gregory, whose front-drive designs inspired Miller – and it was mainly Grégoire's persistence which made front drive eventually a commercial as well as a technical success in France in the mid-1930s. Germany might lay claim to similar success with the little DKW two-stroke, at its best a very pretty little sportabout; but that claim is exaggerated, and the real achiever was the 1934 Citroën *Onze Légère* (known in England as the Light 15), which remained in production and in great demand until the mid-1950s. Early specimens needed a greasing of the driveshafts every 500 miles (or was it kilometres?), but the major mechanical problems were overcome and the Citroën rightly flourished.

Rightly, but for the wrong reasons. The truth was that its unitary hull made it lower, lighter, and stiffer than conventional saloons; its wide track, long wheelbase, and minimal overhangs, made it stable; and its low power made it insensitive to mid-corner throttlings.

People ascribed all its virtues to front-wheel drive, but perhaps only in one way did it help. A front-drive car is naturally nose-heavy; add to this the debasement of the front tyres' cornering power by the camber changes induced by the independent suspension which was a natural corollary of front-wheel drive; add the further debasement caused by the sheer load on the tyres, which in those days were skinny affairs running much closer to their limits than today – and the result was a pronounced understeer that the unskilled driver, and especially the fast unskilled driver, found very forgiving.

Very few engineers in the motor industry, and nobody outside it, knew much of the new science of roadholding and handling. Miller reckoned that his front-drive racer was no faster in a straight line than the traditional types, but that skidding in corners was less. Speedway expert Barney Oldfield had told the SAE in 1926 that, with the foot on the throttle, such a car would go where it was pointed, whereas with the foot off the throttle it would not go where it was pointed – an Indianapolis-speed simplification that most people found it hard to swallow.

Nor were they impressed by suggestions that a front-drive touring car could be cheaper than the orthodox variety. The rear-engined car, pioneered by Rumpler,

Benz, and brilliant Ledwinka, must be cheaper: it too dispensed with the propellor shaft, but it needed no complex transmission elements. Swinging half-axles were easy to contrive, and on the rough and steeply cambered roads of the Tatra and other middle-European mountains they worked surprisingly well. Where there was more grip, they were dastardly; but nobody knew why Porsche's suspension arrangements were so treacherous – least of all Porsche himself. As often happens in cases of conceptual larceny, he corrupted the ideas he stole from Ledwinka; but such was the confidence reposed in him that everyone was sure that his KdF *Volkswagen* and Auto-Union *P-Wagen* must be all right, however much their antics were all wrong.

It only needed a rethink of suspension design and tyre equipment to make the rear-engined car all that was claimed for it (though when speeds rose higher it would need aerodynamic aid too), and in the early 1960s it looked as though, after repeated and sometimes disastrous failures by Renault, Hillman might have done it with their sweet and stable Imp. Sadly, it was too heavy and too badly let down by minor faults; and so the front-drive Mini, which (thanks to the availability of Rzeppa's innovative constant-velocity joint) had beaten it to the market-place by a couple of years but had not yet taken hold, was suddenly seen as the exemplar of the right way to go.

Stable if not sweet, the Mini echoed the Light 15 in having its wheels widely separated, one at each extreme corner of a body roomier than one had any right to expect. It was actually a triumph of packaging: others had designed front-drive cars with transverse engines, but it was Issigonis who managed to get almost everything out of the way of the occupants.

The Mini was seen, however, as the triumph of front-wheel drive. Few people outside France had come to terms with the wondrous Citroën DS of 1955, which alone of all cars was designed in every last little respect to make front-wheel drive and suspension and aerodynamics and payload capacity all mutually complementary. Renault made a success of the R16 because it was clever and modern, not because it had front-wheel drive. The elemental little Mini made a more emotive appeal: this was the rabble-rouser that brought about the revolution.

In the eyes of the people, the Mini was the giant-slayer that had come to save them from Goliath and Galaxie; and its suave sibling the BMC 1100 won the hearts and bottoms of all those sedentary souls whose only idea of sedition was to seek a redbrick runabout, an alternative to Oxford and Cambridge[2]. Yet it was only a British revolution; in European terms it was barely a revolt.

Fiat could see what was wrong with the manifesto, and how to rewrite it. With one of the most admirable engines of all time, with a separate gearbox that did not chew up the viscosity-index improvers (long-chain polymers which were vital additives) in the engine oil, with new refinements of wheels and suspension complementing the latest in tyres, and a new understanding of what was wanted and how to achieve it, they made the 128. That was the car in which all the serious flaws of previous front-drive cars were eliminated, in which all the standards met by conventional small saloons were exceeded, and in which all the major manufacturers of the world would in due course find their inspiration.

By this time all the serious faults of the VW Beetle had also been eradicated. It was now a good car; but it could no longer stay in fashion. Before long, VW of all people were making cars in the image of the Fiat 128 – and the world concluded that if VW, of all people, had abandoned its traditions and switched ends, this must be the right way to go.

What happened? Was the world duped, or did it remain happy under its post-revolutionary regime? What happened was that the tyre manufacturers had to learn fast how to cope with the overweening demands of overloaded, overpowered, overbraked and overheated front wheels. Those at the rear were merely followers to keep the tail of the car at a reasonable distance from the ground, but nobody had the courage[3] to market a front-drive car with extra-wide front tyres and skinny rears, even though this was deemed acceptable for a rear-engined car of similarly evil imbalance.

Look at a drawing of the mechanical elements in any substantial front-drive car of today, and you will see such a massing of componentry in the extreme nose as would suffer awful vilification if it were instead grouped in the tail. The modern front-drive car is merely an old rear-engined car being driven backwards, and its inherent limitations are just as strict, even though they are different.

Is it any wonder that Audi and then a flood of others found it desirable to redistribute the weights and loadings, to share the work among all four tyres? Is it any wonder that four-wheel-drivers win all the rough stuff, that rear-wheel-drivers win all

---

2 Does the younger reader need to be told that these Oxbridge names were given to contemporary rear-drive Morris and Austin cars of parlous quality and dubious manners?

3 Apart from Citroën, early examples of whose exceptional DS had tyres of narrower section at the rear than at the front.

the races, and that having an engine in front but driving the rear wheels is still considered optimal by those who demand the best – whether at or from Rolls-Royce and Bristol, Daimler-Benz and BMW, or Jaguar and Lexus?

Maybe the wheel will soon come full circle. Maybe the people will soon tire of being tossed between extremes, and allow themselves to be led upon the middle way. Is it any wonder that the Honda S2000 has been hailed by perceptive drivers as a new paragon of roadworthiness, considering that its distribution of masses (within the wheelbase, so that – as in the Bristol – the polar moments of inertia in yaw and in pitch do not grow excessive) is very similar to what Panhard and Levassor arranged in the centenary year of the French Revolution, when the car was still young?

CHAPTER 3

THE CAN . . . OF WORMS?

THE FRENCH REVOLUTION CREATED AT least as many difficulties as it sought to redress. The problems it addressed were essentially internal; the attention it invited was uncomfortably international, and within half a dozen years France was busy fighting the armies of England, Prussia, Austria, Spain and Sardinia. The French won plenty of battles, but they lost a lot of lives, and by no means all of them on the battlefield. Scurvy and other diseases of malnutrition were rife in the armed forces, and the five-man Directoire offered a prize of 12,000 francs to the patriot who would devise some means of preserving and packing food so that soldiers and sailors could rely on it.

Fourteen years passed before Nicolas Appert proved himself that patriot. He had been a chef, pickler, confectioner, preserver, brewer, winemaker and distiller in his time; and for 14 years he had been very patient, methodically experimenting with an idea that had been ventilated by an Italian naturalist, Lazzaro Spallanzani, back in 1756. For reasons yet to be understood by the Frenchman Louis Pasteur, refined by the Englishman Sir Humphry Davy, and given innovative industrial effect by the American (!) Isaac Solomon, food hygienically packed in an hermetically sealed container and correctly heated would then last for years without deterioration, either in palatability or in nutritional value.

Appert had been using clumsy glass jars with wired and waxed cork stoppers when he published his findings (and collected his francs) in 1810; but in that same year, Peter Durand in England had taken out a patent on the use of iron and tin for making 'canisters' (a Greek word for the reed baskets used by the English for storing tea, coffee, spices and fruits) for food preserving. John Hall and Bryan Donkin of the Dartford Iron Works took it up, spotting a good outlet for their tin-coated sheet iron[4]. The Duke of Wellington (not for nothing was he called 'the Iron Duke'!) encouraged them, and by 1818 they were delivering large quantities of canned food to the

Admiralty Victualling Depot. A year later, the method reached America, and there it began its spectacular growth as one of the major industries of world economy.

Within a century of Appert's award, everything imaginable could be bought in tin boxes: biscuits and ointments, cigarettes and manicure sets, gunpowder and gramophone needles. In another decade, pressed tin had become the stuff of toys for children, teatrays for their parents, and billycans for Matilda. It was more probably tin-plated mild steel than tin-dipped iron sheet, but the main thing was that it was a cheap, positively common, downright lower-orders material. People would not want to think of such trashy stuff being used in their motor cars.

It was already happening, though, because more and more people wanted more and more cars more and more cheaply – especially in the USA, where in 1920 there were 9 million cars on the roads. It was in America, where book-keepers and salesmen first abbreviated the word 'canister' to 'can', that engineers led the world in developing techniques for designing and pressing sheet metal in forms that gave it uncanny strength and stiffness. They showed that it could perform sterner tasks than keeping food in and bacteria out; it could replace wood and cast iron, it could challenge wrought steel, it could provide a lighter, cheaper, better alternative to traditional engineering materials and technologies.

It was in America, in the Delaware of 1870, that Edward Gowan Budd was born. In '88 he began to study engineering in Philadelphia, and by '99 he was working in the pressed-steel industry, doing things for the railroads that had helped to build America. There were pressed-steel hubs for rolling stock, and there were pressed steel

---

4 There were some early problems with cans that were lead-lined, or even too generously soldered. The trouble was identified with lead poisoning, something about which today's agitators get very agitated, usually without noticing that most piped domestic supplies of drinking water were, from Roman times to the latter half of the 20th century, delivered through lead pipes. Lead figured in pressed-steel bodies, too, until well into the 1970s or even, among smaller manufacturers, for another decade: ripples, dents and unsightly seams in the newly assembled body-in-white were leaded by skilled men who melted lead from a stick of it into the hollow of the blemish and then filed it smooth before it went to the painters. Their employers knew, by that time, that it was unhealthy work, and ensured that these men worked short shifts and drank plenty of milk. Many jobs carried similar risks: certain workers in the railway shops and heavy industry wore aprons in the capacious front pocket of which they carried an oil-soaked cloth for wiping down exposed steel. The state of their trousers defies imagination, but they regularly contracted cancer of the scrotum.

bodies for carriages, thousands of them for the Pullman Company in particular. They were lighter, they survived crashes better, and they were much less of a fire risk than the timber-bodied railroad cars they replaced; and on the strength of this demonstrable superiority, Budd sold the concept of pressed steel bodywork panels for the motor car to Emil Nelson, then chief engineer of Hupp.

That was in 1909. Three years later, frustrated by the reluctance of his employers to exploit the situation which his vision had created, Budd set up his own company and began preaching revolution to all who would listen. One of them was the brilliant Czech engineer Ledwinka, of Tatra fame, and there are those who say that these two together sold the first all-steel car bodies. It may not be true, for several American vehicle manufacturers were investigating the notion at about that time; but Budd was certainly the first to supply all-steel bodies in volume when, having already sold examples to General Motors, Studebaker, Willys and Oakland, he took an order from Dodge for 70,000 bodies in 1916, to be followed by 99,000 the following year.

These were all of the open tourer type, each composed of about 1200 separate pressings; but the possibilities inherent in the system were so appealing to the fast-growing American industry that by 1917 Budd had developed an all-steel fully enclosed four-door saloon body. Dodge put it on the market in 1919, their production rate soaring so steeply that by 1923 they had sold a million cars.

Those bodies still sat on old-fashioned chassis frames – themselves pressings – but Budd could see further than that. In 1924 he began a long-lasting collaboration with another revolutionary genius, André Citroën, and their ideas were focused on the perfectly heretical notion of the car as structurally neat and simple and sturdy as a tin can. It meant distributing stresses (and, if they were unavoidable, strains) throughout the sheet area, making the roof and the floor and the rest do more useful work than merely excluding the weather. It meant a lighter, lower car with plenty of multiple curvatures in its shape, and it meant a serious shock for the establishment, for it meant the elimination of the traditional chassis – which in turn implied that the traditional propshaft would somehow have to be moved out of the way. By 1930 Budd had the prototype ready, with all-steel body and front-wheel drive; and it was this that Citroën developed to become the famous *Onze Légère* of 1934, destined to become one of the best-loved and longest-lived cars in Europe.

One of the most admired and longest respected was the Lancia Lambda, a car which was the expression of so many new ideas as to be more iconoclastic than revolutionary. Vincenzo Lancia modelled his prototype on principles he had seen embodied in ships' hulls, and if the car had gone into production like that – a stressed-skin hull, more advanced than anything before it except the 1905 Renault racer built for the Gordon Bennett event – it would have been twice as marvellous. Instead, the Lambda which went on sale in 1922 simply had chassis side-members of deep swaged pressed steel, which was merely an advance on the integration of crude chassis and cruder panels riveted by Lagonda in their dismal 11.1hp tourer of 1913. Later Lambdas reverted to ordinary separate chassis: Lancia was a brave driver, but he could not fight customers who wanted coachbuilt bodies. That needed the gambler's courage of an André Citroën.

Not all Budd's clients were as brave as Citroën, but so long as they played a straight bat (Louis Renault was a notable exception, and Budd hit him hard where it hurt, in a German law-court) they were treated generously. He had licensees in Austria, Czechoslovakia, France, Germany, Italy, Poland, Sweden, all of them growing under his fairly undemanding tutelage. In Britain his major client was Lord Nuffield who, as William Morris, had visited the Budd factories in 1925. They were impressive, covering more than 3 million square feet; Morris returned to England with something more modest in mind, setting up the Pressed Steel Company in Cowley with half the finance coming from Budd. Neither Morris nor his customers were prepared to dispense with the good old chassis; but something identifiable as a chassis frame was integrated with the body, and Morris sales in 1929 exceeded 63,000. That was identical to the world total production in 1903; but in 1929 the American motor industry kept 600 of Budd's presses at work, and just one of his factories consumed a thousand tons of steel strip daily . . .

The consequences of revolution are always diverse. Any major breakthrough in design entrains a wake of technological spin-offs, from space Sputniks back to Crécy cannon. In Budd's case, the failure of contemporary welding techniques to meet his demands encouraged rapid evolution in arc welding, while the drumming of unsupported metal panels prompted the development of acoustic deadening compounds. The elimination of wood from the car structure led to new kinds of upholstery, in turn encouraging growth and invention in the spring clip industry; and because upholstering could now be postponed until after the body was built, the absence of wood also allowed new high-temperature paint-baking techniques to be introduced, with a resulting increase in the quality of finish achieved and a colossal improvement in its durability.

Stamped by American presses out of steel sheet in Italy, the flanks of Fiats.

The revolution changed people's lives in far-reaching ways. Only with the introduction of the pressed-steel body did it become feasible to mass-produce a fully enclosed design; only when saloon cars thus became commonplace did specialised heavyweight motoring clothing disappear, and only then did the interior heater become both feasible and desirable. Once there was no longer any need to dress up warmly before going out, people began to resent the need to dress up warmly at all; in temperate climates (as distinct from regions where the winter is always severe) domestic central heating did not precede but followed the car heater. Thereafter the clothing trade had its own revolution: trade in hats and overcoats faded, waistcoats followed heavy underwear into oblivion, and fashion began to follow form and function in all manner of sometimes stimulating and sometimes depressing ways.

They were ways that could never previously have been explored; and the motor industry is still exploring new routes today. Preserving and packing food in glass jars grew very much more popular in the USA (whom everybody else always follows, at a respectful or awed distance) during the Second World War, because Japan overran the major sources of tin. Even now, tin remains unexpectedly costly, almost a semi-precious metal, and the motor industry has painfully determined that galvanic corrosion is best kept at bay by cathodic protection, so the best and most durable steel body panels are now zinc-clad. It took longer for the further implications of the stressed-sheet hull to be realised, for they depended on the further growth of the market. Only when production quantities were truly vast could the possibilities of automated production be thoroughly exploited. I remember visiting the Vauxhall works at Luton when I was still a schoolboy, very soon after the end of the Second World War: when all the body panels had been assembled on a jig, somebody blew a whistle and out ran a horde of little men wearing rubber-soled plimsolls and wielding rubber-headed hammers as they ran all over and around the car, swiping and clouting here and there to adjust a fit or correct a clearance before it went to the finishing welders.

Go to one of the leading factories today, and the men look bigger, doubtless due to a better diet, but there are very few of them indeed, and they are supervisors, not sweating Stakhanovites. Machines are more accurate, more reliable, more consistent and more productive than men, they eat less and sleep hardly at all. But where have all the workers gone? Where are all the men whom those machines have so effectively supplanted?

They are well preserved, well heated. You will find them stored in long motionless rows out on the roads, each one sealed in his own gorgeously enamelled uniform modern version of the archetypal tin box.

CHAPTER 4

THE POPULAR FRONT

THERE IS A LEY LINE, AS well as an historical connection, linking Eton College with Stowe School. On its royal way, it continues beyond the younger school, passing the ancient site which gives a name to Abbey Curve on the Silverstone circuit; and it was clearly intended by the Great Architect and Surveyor that in the fullness of time (that is to say, in July 1989) the good and the faithful should be able with unerring ease to progress from the 18th International Trombone Workshop – which by the very nature of things would be at Eton College – to the British Grand Prix which was to be contested a few days later at the racing circuit just over the fence from Stowe. Between the two events, there should clearly be no distraction.

In some futile pretence that they were not finally overthrown 174 years earlier on the playing fields of the older school, the rascally French created a diversion during those very days of precious pilgrimage. On 14 July, 52 million French and far too many other people celebrated the storming of the Bastille and all the associated horrors of the Revolution.

As every motoring enthusiast realises, the whole frightful affair was an affront to the freedom which was once etymologically identified with France; and, as any philologist can confirm, it explains why France has never produced a true people's car. The 2CV Citroën was not such a thing: it was conceptually and emphatically a rural car, not an urban car, and was accordingly no more than a peasants' car.

It was at the other end of her social scale that Royal France found her leaders, her adventurers, her makers of waves and of empire. Every common factory hand in General Motors is fully aware of the patrician origins of his employer, can specify the officer-and-gentleman origins of Antoine de la Mothe *Cadillac* and recognise the even more knightly name of Robert Chevalier, Seigneur de *la Salle*. But Revolutionary France, resentfully dismissive of the evident shortcomings of her *sans-culottes*, denied the upper classes their freedom to lead. Freedom, literally and metaphorically, had gone west.

It was a pre-Revolutionary Frenchman who, before the *Mayflower* had left old Plymouth for New Plymouth, had been the first foreigner to set foot on the land of Michigan. It was another, his title eventually to be blazoned on the bonnet of GM's handsome La Salle, who first sailed the Great Lakes. What then of Cadillac? While the empire of the Great Mogul was disintegrating after the death of Aurungzeb, Cadillac was serving a four-year term as Governor of Louisiana, having some years earlier (when Prussia was proclaiming Frederick I its first king) established Fort Pontchartrain and thus founded Detroit.

For some years it was to remain little more than a fur-trading port, and Ransom Eli Olds would not have thought to set up his car factory there had he not met a man

The Biggest Automobile Plant in the World – the Ford factory at Highland Park, Detroit – discharges a shift of workers one afternoon in 1924. Hordes of them queue for trolleybuses.

named Smith. The encounter took place on the platform of Detroit station, and Olds' chat turned to a discussion of his plans and problems. Smith was a copper-miner, and he offered there and then to finance Olds provided that he stayed in Detroit.

The factory was operational in 1900, but the cars that his partners wanted him to make did little for the success of Oldsmobile. Like most other American cars then, they were too big and too stately for their time and place. In the whole of the USA there were only about 150 miles of properly surfaced roads, and Olds realised that something light and unpretentious was needed. He built a little buggy-like prototype which he reckoned could be built for $300 and sold for $650, but his partners dismissed it contemptuously: cars had to reflect the wealth of the rich who bought them, and what idiot would expect the common working man to buy a car?

It was a working man who settled the question when the factory burned down in 1901. Time-keeper James Brady, realising that the little buggy was light enough to be manhandled, pushed it out of the blazing building: the curved-dash prototype was the only thing saved.

It was therefore the only means of salvation. Local contractors – Leland, the Dodge brothers, Everitt and the Briscoe kids – could make the components, Olds could assemble them, and tester Roy Chaplin (who drove one across Canada from Detroit to New York) proved that he could sell them. By 1906, production had reached 6500 a year.

America had the beginnings of its Motor City, and its first mass-production car. Brady became Mayor of Detroit, and Chaplin became US Secretary of Commerce.

The Oldsmobile was not revolutionary, however, merely opportunist. Its coeval Mercédès was technically the revolutionary, introducing all manner of engineering niceties that have since been deemed necessities. It was made in small numbers, for in those days only the rich[5] could aspire to such refinement; the idea of making cars to sell in large numbers to the poor could not prosper in a Europe where a 19th-century pox of revolutions had done little or nothing to make prosperity a fortune to be shared. That revolution could only happen in the Land of the Free.

The man who made it happen was one with the courage to give up the land. Henry Ford had been born back in 1863, into a farming family which urged him to stay on the farm and have some land of his own. Imbued with all the curiosity and daring of an America enjoying the freedom of the period after the Civil War (which, in its thinking, was far more revolutionary than the American Revolution), Henry preferred to seek that peculiarly American freedom to work whatever miracles might result from ingenuity, industry, or luck. At 27 he went to work for Edison in Detroit; at 30, he made an engine; at 33, he made a car.

It was crude, but Ford had inherited that American farmer's mentality which dictated satisfaction with anything that worked and kept on working, no matter how badly. He sold that first car to a friend who is believed to have remained a friend; Henry received $200 for it, and promptly built another. Soon all his friends were encouraging him to set up in business.

Thus was born the Detroit Automobile company. It died young, for the public was not ready, even if the car was. Henry, now 38, gambled on motor racing as a means of making a name; he was reasonably successful, and after a couple of tentative moves into and out of the registry of companies, he formed the Ford Motor Company. As the market grew lively, he prospered; and his vision began to run ahead of the unremarkable cars he was making, to contemplate what others had not yet had the imagination to see – the revolutionary effect of an affordable car upon the common man.

Henry began to be seen as an uncommon man. His challenge to the Selden patents made him a popular hero; his arrogation of all engineering and business decisions made him a boardroom ogre; William Durant of Buick, engaged in the creation of General Motors, made him a take-over offer but could not find the $8 million that Ford asked; and in the end it was farm-boy Henry's sympathetic attention to the needs of the poor man that made factory-mogul Ford rich.

It was in 1908, a year before Lloyd George set before the people of Britain what he was pleased to call the 'People's Budget', that Henry set before the Land of the Free what he saw as a car for the people. Crude, simplistic, ramshackle, minimal, it was nevertheless brilliant in its expression of what only Henry had initially been able to comprehend. He was not a genius, not an intellectual, not really an engineer nor even an humanitarian; but he was supremely shrewd, and just as his suspicion or contempt for others prompted him to go to extremes of centralisation in his control of every aspect of his business, so did his nature encourage him to exploit all the gifts he brought to bear: the vision of a car for the people, the sense of what that car should be, the ability to create it, and the courage to produce it.

---

5 The first of these cars was sold to Baron Henri de Rothschild.

So profound was the effect of the Model T Ford upon America, so much did it change the nature of the nation, influence its architecture and its clothing, its industrial development, its economic prosperity, its art, its music, its social structure, its housing, its health and wealth and arrogant insularity, that Henry Ford who was responsible for it all must be seen as the most effective revolutionary ever to make a motor.

Adolf Hitler was also an effective revolutionary, but he can only be credited with a part-share in the creation of the VolksWagen. Ferdinand Porsche, his partner, was no revolutionary; he just kept thinking, despite firm and steady repression by his directors at Daimler (both in Germany and in Austria), that there must eventually be a good market for cars for the common herd. When in due course the Führer put the idea to him, Porsche had his design principles ready, but in reality Hitler was employing him, not his ideas – which were not altogether his anyway. In effect, he was just one of the crowd that Hitler, the plausible therapist who had treated Germany's injured pride and inspired it to seek *Kraft durch Freude* (strength through joy), had enthused as workers in his revolution.

What was different about the KdF Volkswagen was that it was not merely a people's car, but *the* people's car. The Volk of VW was not just any folk, but the Volk of the *Völkerwanderung,* of the *Völkischer Beobachter* and the *Völkerschaft,* the *Herrenvolk*. Only after the *Volksführer* had met his end in a Berlin bunker did his pet project, shorn of its KdF badge, go from strength to strength through joy, as people the world over (not least in America) rejoiced to discover that motoring did not have to remain what it had so long been. In breaking down the prejudices of the American motoring public, the VW was as influential as anything or anybody, and thus one of the most revolutionary of cars.

Much more iconoclastic in concept was the Issigonis Mini, which did as much as the Model T and the VW to revolutionise motoring society – not least, from the political revolutionary's standpoint, in being the first classless car.

It was not just that it was small, for Herbert Austin's unforgettable Seven was small. The Austin Seven was designed to occupy no more road space than the typical motorcycle-and-sidecar combination which, in the early 1920s, was the limit of the working-class Englishman's vehicular ambitions. A proper car in miniature, it killed off the cyclecar movement, and it stimulated copyists and licensees all around the world, east from America to Japan. But it was just an ordinary car made small, with all the attendant penalties of being made cheap.

Even that cheapness did not automatically qualify it as a car for the people. In 1926 4.7 million people in the UK had an annual income of more than £130. Of these, 3.94 million were dismissed by the SMM&T as potential car owners because their annual income was less than £450. To enjoy more than £2000 pa was the privilege (or due, in some cases) of only 87,700 people, who might be seen as likely to own more than one car each. That left 672,300 likely customers for the same number of cars. Now it can be seen that the SMM&T was hopelessly supercilious in its estimation of the car-buyers' equivalent of the poverty line, taking no account at all of the second-hand market. It can also be seen that there was some justification for the apparently disproportionate number of upper- and upper-middle-class cars offered on the British market (and likewise in Germany, for doubtless similar statistical reasons). Nor did the SMM&T take into account the social implications of car ownership, according to which no factory hand (whatever his income) below the rank of foreman would have dreamed of going to work in a car, though a motorcycle was admissible.

So the Austin Seven was not automatically a motor for the multitudes. There were eventually 290,000 made, but that took from 1922 until 1939. Of that period, the years from 1929 to 1935 were the leanest and most straitened in the 20th century-history of the British working man, and that is something for which neither the car nor its designer may be held responsible.

The Mini, which came in a time of prosperity (when the fuel crisis which inspired it was over) and which was to succeed in being a socially classless car, was different. It was small, and it was cheap, but it was the first car to have its constituent parts so arranged that the major part of its total volume was useful space to be occupied by the people who would buy and enjoy it. The transverse engine, front-wheel drive, rubber suspension and so forth had all been done before, in something or other; but where had you ever seen body seams everted so as to make more clear room inside? The Mini was four-fifths living-room, and only one-fifth engine-room; Issigonis had given priority to people.

That, too, was revolutionary. The compacted front-drive saloon has come a long way since 1959, and much of the overlay has masked the brilliance of the original. The accretions have been nothing more than the accumulation of post-revolutionary looting and plunder; no amount of *savoir faire*, or *verismo*, or (do you have an ear for echo?) *Vorsprung durch Technik*, can conceal the original Graeco-British inspiration for the turnaround in popular cars.

It has been literally turnaround, which is to say revolutionary; and it has been gyratory in another sense, for it is not only the engine which has been repolarised. No longer necessarily aligned north–south, it now commonly runs from west to east; and so does the entire industry. Some lines may be perpetual, but what a lot of the rest are being redrawn!

CHAPTER 5

RE-INVENTING THE WHEEL

KARL MARX HIMSELF EXPRESSED THE OPINION that Russia was not ready for Marxist revolution, but something of the sort nevertheless occurred. After the Fascist revolution in Italy and the coming to power of Benito Mussolini in 1922 (which coincided with the toppling by Fiat of the French supremacy in motor racing), it was likewise held by experts that such a thing could not happen in Germany because that nation was too highly developed to be amenable to it; but we all know that the experts were once again wrong. What then of Switzerland, jammed between Italy and Germany, with France blocking any escape to the west and the alien horrors of Prague and (which is even further east, though one seldom realises it) Vienna dissuading any attempt to go east?

Although the French Revolution had a profound effect upon the internal affairs of Switzerland, that smugly comfortable little country never had a real revolution of its own. The nearest it came was in 1847 (the year before most European nations underwent a revolution of some sort), but the Swiss were too highly organised to let it happen. Today they are even more highly organised, not to say richer, and the possibility seems even more remote. That makes it all the more enjoyable that, in the year which saw the 200th anniversary of the French Revolution, it should have been Switzerland – a country with virtually no motor industry – which bore the seed of a revolution in motoring design.

Marc Birkigt, who was responsible for the second half of the Hispano-Suiza name, was no revolutionary. Neither was Louis Chevrolet. Perhaps Michael May was; but the real radical, the fellow who in 1989 put a very hollow-gutted cat among the pigeons, is that freethinking and happy-go-lucky chap whose creative styling always brings a touch of healthy irreverence to the Geneva Salon. In that year, Franco Sbarro redefined the wheel.

It was about time, for the wheel had been with us for about five thousand years.

It was also singularly appropriate, for the wheel – like the cylinder, the poppet valve, the bullet, the dinner plate, and many other adjuncts of civilisation – is formally a body of revolution.

It is also, as we have hitherto known it, frightfully ill adapted to the tasks it is expected to perform. This cannot be blamed on the original inventor, however, because the probable truth is that the wheel was never invented. The use of a roller to support and mobilise a heavy load to be moved a considerable distance was a natural enlargement by Pensive Man of his experience when losing his footing on smooth gravel. What the unknown Sumerian artificer usually credited with the invention actually invented was the axle. It did more good than harm at the time. It enabled loads to be horsedrawn at much greater speeds than could be sustained by teams of men shoving rollers underneath the load platform; but it brought with it a combination of material abuse and mechanical distress that has been needlessly inherited by the modern high-performance motor vehicle – which, quite honestly, needs something better.

The supposition that an axle is necessary led to the further supposition that a hub and its associated bearings were essential parts of the wheel. Few cars still have axles today, but the hub has remained a supposed necessity. From that supposition derive all the horrors of wheels as we know them today.

Even as we knew them yesterday, wheels were poor things. Right up to the 20th century[6], wheels had been made of wood. It is a nasty, tricky, treacherous substance, truly fit only for making trees or lining cigar boxes, and if made into a wheel it will shrink, split, crack, and generally come apart at all the joints. Shrinking an iron tyre on to its periphery proved some sort of palliative, so long as you knew how much shrinkage to allow: the rule of the wheelwright's thumb was that the length of the iron band should be three times the diameter of the wheel plus one thickness of the iron band. Even thus compressed in defiance of pi, the wooden wheel still needed much maintenance[7].

---

6 Ultra-conservative Mercedes-Benz continued to fit wooden wheels to their Mannheim model until production ceased in 1939.

7 See footnote 9.

Next came the wire-spoked wheel, exploiting the fact that steel is much stronger in tension than in compression: all the loads to which the wheel is subjected are taken in tension by a large number of steel wire spokes. These have no resistance to bending stresses, and so they must be laced in a complex pattern criss-crossing in all three planes. Building such a wheel light enough, round enough, free of lateral distortion and concentrically true-running, was a slow task demanding much skill and seldom perfected.

The so-called 'artillery' wheel, with its hollow-cast spokes, was actually better than this, but was viewed with disdain by the enthusiasts who fondly supposed that the wire wheel must be superior because it was used for racing cars, as began to happen in about 1905 and was generally the case from about 1912 to about 1960. As with most deductions from racing practice, this was fallacious. In any case, the motor industry was more concerned with costs than with other issues, and by the 1930s was wedded to the pressed-steel disc wheel. Such things can be quite efficient, being reasonably light, reasonably stiff, and reasonably resistant to accidental damage. In dimensional accuracy they often fall far short of propriety, however, and they are not without other weaknesses.

They are subjected to frightful stresses. Close to the hub, they are severely loaded in the nave area around the fixing studs or bolts; in the disc portion, any flat area acts as a collector and concentrator of lateral loads; at the junction of disc and rim, the bending loads are dreadful. The rim itself goes through a cycle of tension and compression in each revolution which does no good at all to its fatigue life, but that is another issue which will only be addressed when[8] the tyre and the rim cease to be separate entities.

Meanwhile, the wheel is the focus of fashion as well as of forces, and untutored eyes have led it hopelessly astray. Many of today's fashionable designs – cast, or in rare and costly instances forged, in a more or less suitable aluminium alloy – are functionally quite abominable, set about with numerous stress-raisers and corrupted by loading materials in tension when they ought to be in compression, or more occasionally vice versa. There are wheels with tangential spokes, so disposed that when fitted to one side of the car those spokes are in tension under braking, while the same wheels fitted to the other side are in compression – and they cannot both be right. There are wheels which are held to their hubs by a number of studs which does not correspond to the number of spokes, nor to any multiple thereof, and which therefore suffer severe maldistribution of stresses in their vicinity. As a further and notable example of metallurgy subjected to the abuses of fashion, consider those cast wheels which imitate the pattern of wire spokes: at every junction where the spoke-lines cross, there is a sudden sectional variation which invites differential cooling rates of the molten metal in the mould. The resulting embrittlement can be disastrous: little more than twenty years ago, one such wheel fitted to BMW motorcycles was often known to fracture completely at every one of these junctions.

The fact that such failures are rare nowadays merely proves that all such wheels are made with a surplus of material, so as to keep stress levels relatively low. They are therefore substantially heavier than they ought to be, making utter nonsense of the fashion for light-alloy wheels.

It is a rare thing to see a really good wheel design. Amongst conventional pressed-steel types, those of Bristol and Alfa Romeo used in the 1950s to be better than the rest; amongst the more unusual, some (but not all) of the forged light-alloy wheels used in racing by Jaguar and Porsche were good, and the Minilite cast-Elektron wheel (which did so much to inspire us, and could have done so much to educate us, thirty years ago) was very good. In mass production, though, the only place to see an utterly pure and thoroughly engineered wheel of modest cost was on a DS or 2CV Citroën.

Despite these, we need something better; and as is usually the case when a problem can be avoided rather than faced, nothing is even better than something. When there is nothing there, neither can there be malfunction. When there are no spokes to break, no naves to tear, and no discs to crack, there is also no unsprung mass to confuse suspension and impair roadholding: nothing is, because of this extremely important consideration, very much better than something, for nothing is lighter than nothing.

Nor is that the sum of the virtues of vacuity. When there is nothing there, no impediment is presented to suspension and steering joints – and the arms or other member through which they act – being brought as close as possible to the rim itself. That is an achievement of great importance, for it is tantamount to bringing the joints as close as possible to the contact patch between tyre and road. Thus there is the

---

8 As Setright has been fervently hoping for about thirty-five years . . .

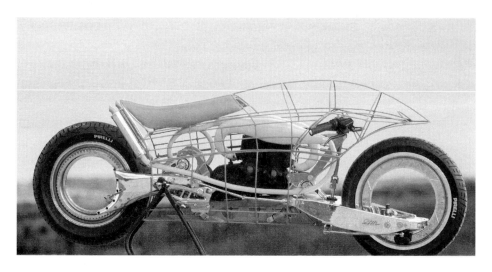

When hub and axle are eliminated, as Franco Sbarro succeeded in doing in
1989 (for cars as well as motorcycles), the wheel comes into its own.

shortest possible distance between the point at which all the vehicle's dynamic forces act and the point through which they are transmitted and controlled.

The extreme case is that of the motorcycle which, with conventional front forks, has to transmit through a steering head (itself containing a pair of bearings only about six inches apart) forces which originate at the tyre/road interface some three feet distant. The flutter and distortions allowed by this miserably weak construction can often be felt, can sometimes be seen, but are always threatening.

Almost as bad is the old-style kingpin attached to the stub-axle of a car wheel: the separation of the steering bearings is even less, and their distance from the road still badly disproportionate. The wide separation of steering bearings by a MacPherson or Cordiano strut, or in those exemplary double-wishbone suspensions to be found in the best Honda and Daimler-Benz designs, is very much better; but still we are left with ridiculously tiny hub bearings (there is no room for anything bigger, except in a proper Citroën – look into your CX, and rejoice!) trying to brace themselves against the levering loads imparted by forces generated at road level.

Early wire wheels, built like those of bicycles, could be seen to develop their own slip angles (additional to those of the tyres) when subjected to lateral loads. Wooden wheels, unless kept well-watered[9] to maintain engorgement of their fibres for a tight fit at every joint, did the same; and, albeit on a much smaller and invisible scale, it is sure that our little stub-axle hub bearings do the same.

Franco Sbarro has eliminated all that. He has not re-invented the wheel; he has disinvented the axle. It has gone, and so therefore has the hub. What he has logically done is to enlarge the bearing until its outer race is integral with the wheelrim.

Others of us have wanted to do that, from time to time, especially in the quest for a better motorcycle steering system. We have been put off by the bearings industry, perhaps, as I was when I sought advice from SKF. Sbarro likewise found that firm inert, but unlike the rest of us who took 'No' for an answer, he treated it as an invitation to further enquiry, and eventually found that the bearings he wanted could be made (by at least two other firms) without the existing art having to be enlarged. They are ball bearings, not rollers, with each ball making contact at four points and only one ball at a time doing any real work; their velocities are much higher than in a little hub, but the loadings are much lower, so friction is no greater but accuracy is much greater.

Everything else flows from this. Suspension and steering joints, being attached directly to the inner race of the bearing, are barely clear of the rim and so are separated from the true point of action and reaction only by the depth of the tyre – for the time being, an irreducible minimum.

Unsprung mass is reduced by a very large and exceptionally welcome percentage; and this alone, even if the wheel offered no other advantages, would be enough to make it a valuable asset to any motorcycle, racing car, or indeed any other kind of cars in which the ratio of unsprung to sprung masses is threatened either by the heaviness of the wheels or by the lightness of the rest of the car.

Braking is, like suspension and steering, as immediate and positive as it can be. As has been done in a few other instances, the disc is located (by floating mounts) on the inside of the rim, and is gripped by an internal caliper carried by the inner bearing

---

9 The far-ranging motorist cannot always depend on a source of water conveniently to hand, let alone a handy hose for applying it, wherever he stops for rest and replenishment. It was for this that the Friend of Man was trained to cock his leg at everything resembling a wheel (beginning with what he was taught to think was an axle tree); today's dog, providing unwanted laving of today's metal wheels, is merely exercising his hyperdeveloped kidneys in conditioned response to an urge bred in him through 2500 generations.

race adjacent to the bottom suspension joint. Such 'inverted' disc brakes have been proved efficient, because of their greater effective radius, time and again: they first appeared on the last prototype HRG in the early 1950s, in a design by Palmer that originated in aviation, and they have most recently showed up in the Audi V8. In between, they have varied in complexity from the intricacy of Honda to the simplicity of Wal Philips – on motorcycles in both cases. Sbarro simply saw their suitability for his wheel, and made the most of it – without giving the assembly enough rotational inertia to make it more of a gyroscopic problem than existed previously.

Driving the wheel may demand more ingenuity than braking it. Sbarro's motorcycle designs lent themselves naturally to chain drive, while his cars were a little let down by driveshafts that terminated outboard as vast spun steel trumpets. There could have been better methods adopted.

But who can predict the outcome of a revolution when it is only just beginning? A few designers and manufacturers expressed considerable interest; others found themselves unable to cope with the shattering of their icons. More still merely had a good laugh, amid much shuttering of Nikons, and went away from Sbarro's Geneva stand thoroughly bemused. Those who reported on the invention generally failed to explain it; those who read their reports generally dismissed it.

There are no revolutions more pathetic than those which the people see no need to follow. Must it always be, as in this sad case, that the car world must submit to what Marx (or Blanqui, or whoever really said it first) called 'the dictatorship of the proletariat'?

CHAPTER 6

INCONSTANT MESH

IT IS A TRIBUTE TO the increasing power of communications that, despite revolutions having occurred throughout history, a large proportion of the world's population thinks that *the* revolution was the French, which began in 1789; and that the remainder probably considers that *the* revolution was the Russian, which became a reality in 1917.

What things happened in that bloody year! Henry Ford opened his River Rouge factory, to reach new heights of mass-production technology in the dissemination of his Model T. He was doubtless encouraged by President Woodrow Wilson who, in the previous year, took the unprecedented step of providing federal funds for road-making. America was growing keen on the automobile: Pike's Peak hillclimb was inaugurated in 1916, a year that Europe remembered for the battle of the Somme. Now it was 1917, and the Russians had removed themselves from the Great War so that they could get on with their revolution, which would in time shed even more blood; and not until much later in the year would the USA obligingly enter the struggle.

Meanwhile, the principal combatants in what was theoretically a world war concentrated their men, their mines, and everything except their minds, upon the sanguinary cockpit that was Passchendaele.

Here was the start of another revolution; for a revolution is a procedure resulting from men swearing 'Never again!' Of all the most horrifying examples of carnage in the last century, or even the last millennium, putrefying Passchendaele must rank among the two or three most repulsive. Much and many were cut down – including, as John Masters noted, 'the centuries-old, slow-matured trust between classes; a social structure that accepted the good intention even where the deed was unworthy or foolish; a friendly Britain. The privates and the generals of 1917 had alike grown up in a world where to question was to doubt, and to doubt was to undermine this basic strength, which had given Britain growth and some change without revolution.'

Britain had in fact had a revolution, exactly a hundred years before the bloodthirsty French, in 1689; but because of that 'basic strength' it was a bloodless revolution which brought the Dutch institution of William and Mary to reign over us.

One cannot imagine the Dutch being revolutionary; yet, forty years on from Passchendaele and River Rouge, a bright-eyed little inventor by the name of Hubertus van Doorne was working on something that ought to have changed (and beautified) the face of motoring. The Variomatic transmission, steplessly adjusted within wide limits by automatic reference to engine speed, load, torque, and throttle position, brought the ideal hyperbola of tractive effort within the repertoire of an ordinary car.

The use of flexible belts over adjustable pulleys was all that most people saw, but that might have been found in the Bedelia back in 1911, along with many other friction drives that, like the grievously inefficient and impossibly noisy hydrostatics beloved of a later generation of inventors, were doomed to fail. The DAF system was different from all of them, not only because it was mechanically efficient but more because, thanks to the ingenuity of its control system, it was functionally efficient.

It survives today in a modernised form, in little Fiats and lesser Fords, in superior form in sundry Nissans, and in its most refined form in a Honda Civic; but as yet it must be deemed a failure because people will not bother to understand it, let alone to accept or demand it. Have people forgotten what 1917 taught, the need to question both act and motivation and to have no reverence for specious authority? People are still tyrannised by the establishment; they still revere the hand-operated stepped-ratio gearbox, despite the fact that it is even more ancient than the screenwiper and very nearly as primitive. People are still slaves to money; they are taught to prefer the manual 'box, because an adequate one is cheap to make, whereas an adequate automatic would cost more than any manufacturer would want to spend.

Henry Ford would have had people think differently; and for some time he did. Following a similar device in his 1906 Model N, his 1908 Model T incorporated a two-speed-and-reverse gearbox based on a simple epicyclic gearset. Its teeth were always enmeshed, and the selection of one or other combination of the gearwheels could be contrived by simple friction clutches or brakes needing no skill to operate.

It was a shrewd blow on behalf of the simple would-be driver against the self-appointed elite who knew how to change gear in a conventional car. It was not easy, in those days, for people brought up in the Horse Age with no education in mechanics. The requisite skills did not come naturally, and were seldom well taught; thousands, and then millions, of new motorists who had not acquired those skills, or could not, or through plain cussed pride would not, were neverthless enabled by Ford to become motorists, mobile at last and free to explore a world vaster than the horse had permitted them to see.

Promising an even wider view (thanks to another and greater revolution), Alcock and Brown had flown the Atlantic before Ford's rival General Motors set themselves to devise some sort of automatic transmission. They toyed with electricity (as Porsche had once done) for three years before dismissing it; they pursued a steel-roller affair, analogous to the later Hayes and Perbury failures, before Alfred Sloan saw that it would be a loser and nipped it in the bud. By the time that they had put synchromesh (a high-tech elaboration of the old sporting car's clutch stop) into the Cadillac, twenty years had produced millions of Ford drivers who had never known how to handle a gearlever and simultaneously coordinate two pedals. Synchromesh spread rapidly, Vauxhall and Rolls-Royce being among the quickest to adopt it, and at long last the inept could aspire to something other than a Ford.

Some skill was still needed, for it was not until the late 1950s that synchromesh found its way into bottom gear. The inept, when forced to a crawl on a steep hill, simply stopped and restarted, while the adepts sneered and swore at them for their inability to double-declutch into bottom gear. A mere mechanical skill had become a shibboleth, and it still is: people feel obliged to drive three-pedal cars to prove themselves members of an elite, though the skills nowadays required are absurdly trivial. Are act and motivation never to be questioned?

By 1930 there was no need for skill. Daimler in England had adopted the Wilson[10] preselector gearbox and the Föttinger fluid coupling, a combination which was the precursor of most of today's automatics. The box housed a series of epicyclic geartrains, each engaged by a friction brake; the driver selected whatever gear he wanted next, cocking the mechanism by moving a lever along a notched quadrant; when he judged the time opportune, a kick at the clutch pedal triggered the appropriate brake band and the gear was captured.

For a racing ERA or Talbot, that was enough; the brake band for bottom gear served in lieu of a clutch for moving away from the start. For a sporting Riley saloon or some such, a centrifugal friction clutch allowed the engine to idle in gear. Touring cars such as the Daimler and the Armstrong Siddeley had a 'Fluid Flywheel' (an inspired trade description of the fluid coupling) interposed between engine and gearbox, to cushion each gearshift and ensure ineffable smoothness of take-off from rest.

Herman Föttinger had devised his fluid coupling at the beginning of the century. Exquisitely smooth in operation, it always yielded a torque output equal to the torque input, so it needed to associate with a gearbox having as many ratios as one served by a conventional clutch. He also invented the torque-converter coupling, which (at some cost in efficiency) gave some internal multiplication of torque over part of the speed range and could therefore work satisfactorily with a smaller number of gears; but he insisted that it would be unsuitable for cars. He was still insisting in 1930, when Commendatore Salerni (later Count Teremala) made it work.

Elsewhere, motor manufacturers paid attention to the possibilities of the epicyclic geartrain. It had not been a new idea even when Ford introduced it, but it took time to understand it. It did not take long for Sturmey-Archer to see that their two-speed hub for pedal cycles could be elaborated into a three-speeder, but decades passed before it was spotted that the system could easily provide four ratios, and more decades before someone detected the presence of a fifth. The motor industry, always anxious to prune costs, took the opposite direction: making do with three ratios, rather less than perfectly spaced, allowed them to manage with far fewer gears than whirled within the four-speed Wilson.

The alternative way of exploiting a cheaper geartrain was to accept a less suitable set of four forward ratios – though sometimes they could all be made available in reverse as well, as was also true of the heavy eight-speed Maybach semi-automatic 'box encumbering some 3-litre Lagondas. Thus came from France in the early 1930s the elegant electromagnetically operated Cotal 'box, to remain in limited production for about twenty years.

In the USA, where big and lazy engines (deliberately contrived to minimise the need for shifting gears) made three-speed gearboxes the norm, General Motors worked on a combination of a similarly simple geartrain with a fluid coupling. America could have had it in the same year as they had independent front suspension, but America was still suffering from the Depression which followed the Wall Street Crash, and the first development was a semi-automatic epicyclic gearbox combined

---

10 Major W G Wilson made his name as a transmission engineer through his work on the British tanks of the Great War, but his association with the epicyclic gearbox dates back to 1898 when he made it for the Wilson-Pilcher car.

with a conventional clutch for starting and stopping, in the 1937 Buick and 1937–8 Oldsmobile. GM buses of the same year had the fluid coupling, however, and by 1939, when the economy had taken a turn for the brighter, car buyers had their own New Deal: GM's fully automatic Hydra-Matic transmission was announced, for the 1940 Oldsmobile and the 1941 Cadillac.

Forced to compete, Chrysler had come up with a rudimentary split-range semi-automatic Fluid Drive in 1938, while in Britain and France prewar efforts were directed towards automating the shift procedure of the conventional synchromesh gearbox, with uniformly dire results.

The Second World War interrupted such nonsenses in Europe; but when it became truly a world war (that is, when Japan and America joined in), it actually encouraged the development of automatic transmissions by the American motor industry. Tanks were the problem, traditionally difficult to steer and easy to stall, whereupon they became stationary targets. GM were summoned to provide a solution, and their heavy-duty Hydra-Matic did the trick. As military vehicles grew ever larger and heavier, GM worked out a torque-converter coupling which allowed a 'hot shift' for sustained power, and fears of stalling were finally allayed.

One of the minor follies of Passchendaele had been 'useless tanks bogged in the slime'; but, after the Great War, had we not sworn 'Never again'? In the Second World War, the most sickening atrocities were committed well away from the battlefields . . . and when the war was over, GM knew just what their cars should have. The Buick Dynaflow of 1948 and the Chevrolet Powerglide for 1950 had the new torque-converter drive, and by 1962 a good 74% of all passenger cars sold in the USA had automatic transmissions.

Something more suitable for the weeny wailing engines of European cars was being developed in Britain, where Australian inventor Howard Hobbs worked hard for a dozen years on his Mechamatic before installing it in a number of door-to-door delivery vans and his son's racing Lotus Elite. Young David entered 18 races in 1960, and won 15; at the Nürburgring in '61 all the other Elite drivers ganged up and insisted that his car be transferred from the GT to the 1600cc sports class – which he won, as well as beating all the other Elites.

It was a brilliant four-speed automatic gearbox based on one compound epicyclic gearset controlled by two plate clutches and three disc brakes, all hydraulically operated. Fully automatic when required, it also allowed positive selection of any gear, full-engine braking, and overspeeding protection. In weight and size it was comparable with manual transmissions; it was ideal for small engines.

Only Borgward had the courage to use it, and Borgward was not to endure. Ford tried it, Volvo and Lancia and Fiat tried it, but they all took the coward's way out. When practically anything could be sold to a car-hungry populace, it was easier to sell three-pedal cars than to tool up for something new. Even in America, the old do-it-yourself gearbox made a stand: the gearlever became a status symbol. The car with 'four on the floor' had a Man at the wheel, and only an elderly woman would drive some rubber-band contraption called a Daffodil.

Salesmen learned what lies to tell about each kind of transmission, and if they judged their customers correctly the latter were only too happy to believe them. Only the increasing density of city traffic prompted doubtful, if not questioning, men to insist on two-pedal cars; and they were not questioning enough to recognise the virtues of the synchromesh and converter-coupling compromise offered by NSU, Citroën and, for a short while, Porsche.

Only in the USA, where thousands of marginal motorists grew to love the new little Honda Civic, did anyone appreciate the possibility that a two-pedal car might leave the decisions to the driver while relieving him of the physical work and excusing him for lack of skill. Today's Hondas have a developed version of the original Hondamatic. There is a converter coupling driving a layshaft gearbox, but in place of the conventional synchromesh is a multiplate clutch to engage each pair of constant-mesh gears, with no limit to the number of ratios even though conventions (and lack of space, if the gearbox is to occupy the same amount of it as a synchromesh one would) currently dictate that there should be four.

And still people choose to trample a clutch pedal, to heave a lever around, to waste time with every shift and waste energy through being too often in the wrong gear.

It was the fuel crisis of 1973 that did most of the harm. Automatics and their engines need to be perfectly matched to each other, and when it suddenly became socially urgent to reduce fuel consumption, it was prudent to enfeeble the engine and foster the four- (or better still five-) on-the-floor. If the emergence of first-class automatics was not permanently prevented, it was at least put back twenty years by the Iranian revolution.

As is usually the case when a revolution is complete, we are back again at the beginning, with everyone wondering how, if ever, we might get rid of this awful contraption about which Panhard was so apologetic more than a hundred years ago.

All the revolutionary ideas of a century of transmission development have been chewed up and swallowed, much as Pierre Vergniaud commented on the French affair a century before Panhard: 'There was reason to fear that, like Saturn, the Revolution might devour each of its children in turn.' It happened in France, it happened in Russia, it happened in Coventry and in Detroit; but in Saturn's case, you will remember, his appetite was eventually cheated, and when his son Jupiter grew up he led a revolution against his father. Hub van Doorne's brainchild has grown up with fair promise: its lineal successor, using complex and costly steel belts in compression rather than rubberised-fabric belts in tension, has successfully handled the output of a Formula 1 engine, enabling the Williams car so equipped to lap the Silverstone GP circuit two whole seconds (an enormous margin in racing terms) faster than an otherwise similar car using a conventional gearbox. The racing rulemakers promptly banned it as soon as they heard about it, but there is hope yet, as there is for the promising Torotrak, likewise the lineal successor to the old Hayes-Perbury ideas.

CHAPTER 7

TYRES AND TIMING

THE REVOLUTIONARY PROCESS CANNOT LONG abide in one place. Almost always, the spark of one movement's zealot finds tinder elsewhere. It is as though revolution were a generative force which, once it has set gestation going somewhere, must immediately seek another union if it is to survive.

Thus, no appreciable time elapsed between Sir Isaac Newton inventing the calculus (the first giant step for modern mathematics) three hundred years ago in England, and Baron Gottfried Wilhelm von Leibnitz doing the same thing in Germany. Just as independent of each other, but likewise brought to conception by the same roving revolutionary idea (14 years earlier, the world population had just reached 4000 million, so there were plenty of possibilities), were the Hungarian architect Erno Rubik and the Japanese ironfounder Terutoshi Ishige, whose mathematical puzzle-cubes were much the same in time and in motions.

It was accordingly to be expected that when a Connecticut tinker named Charles Goodyear achieved the vulcanisation of rubber in 1839, the same would be done in England by Hancock (who gave the process its name) and in Germany by Ludersdorf. In this case, however, the embryo was as revolutionary as the seed: the tyre industry was waiting to be born – but when an intelligent young Scot named Thomson invented the pneumatic tyre in 1845, it proved to be premature.

The arrival of the motor car was all it took to induce birth. The centenary of the French Revolution was the year in which the *système Panhard* brought logic to the morphology of the car, so that what had been a tentative series of experiments could at last become a convincing programme of production. In that same 1889, the bicycling world was astonished by the performance of one William Hume, pedalling to three devastating victories in the Queen's College Sports at Belfast. John Boyd Dunlop had reinvented the pneumatic tyre.

Looking back at the ensuing 100 years, it is possible to resolve all the changes and developments in the car tyre – upon which many of the changes and developments in the car itself have depended – into two parallel but not synchronous processes. One was revolutionary in its suddenness, the structural change which brought us the modern radial-ply tyre. The other was more like a revolutionary movement in its subversiveness, the chemical change which freed us from the shackles of natural materials.

Chemists had been trying to synthesise rubber since the middle of the 19th century, most successfully in England. For some purposes, their isoprenes might have been good enough, but not for tyres. It is always a mistake for man to try to emulate nature: there is always some concealed feature of the natural material which eludes perception (and would doubtless defy imitation) by mere scientists. It is much better for man to do his own thing, to be original and creative, to produce materials which are deliberately different and unnatural. In the early years of the 20th century, this course was being pursued in Germany, with some modest success during the Great War.

Remote from the sources of natural rubber and by no means master of the seas, Germany had every incentive to explore the possibilities of synthetics. By 1936 (a good year for revolution, as Franco was proving in Spain) what might be called the ParaBellum industry (the *si vis pacem* bit was open to doubt) had an SBR or styrene butadiene rubber in production. They called it Buna (Bu was obviously butadiene; less obviously, Na – *Natrium* to the German chemist, or sodium – was the raw material from which styrene came); but everybody else called it *ersatz*, artificial. To the man in the street, 'artificial' was synonymous with 'inferior'.

Did he but know it, the 'art' or 'artificial' silk which he deemed a cheap and nasty textiles substitute for real silk was poised (under its proper French name Rayon) to replace natural cotton in the tyre carcass, because it was better. So was SBR better than natural rubber in many ways, though overheating was a problem.

The heat build-up was caused by internal friction or hysteresis in the material. It was lazy rubber, not bouncy; and this proved to be the secret of better grip – very much better on wet roads – and a quieter ride. With war imminent, Britain and Canada collaborated with the USA for its production in serious quantities – even though the major American tyre-makers (except Firestone, who went for SBR) had chosen hard-wearing polybutadiene to supplement or supplant natural rubber, despite its abysmal wet grip.

Nobody drove very fast for very long in the Second World War, during which

The stretchable beads of early tyres were trapped in the turned-over edges of the rim, and could be held by security bolts inserted at intervals around the wheel.

precious supplies of natural rubber were reserved for aircraft tyres. When the war was over, it was soon followed by a new generation of cars sustaining[11] significantly higher speeds on the new motorways. Despite improved carcasses of super-Rayon, or even the cool-running DuPont Nylon which had been new as recently as 1939, SBR gave problems. Dunlop's attempt to exploit it was a disaster; but old-established Avon, while pioneering this high-mu synthetic rubber in motorcycle tyres, hit on a clever method of capping a cool-running natural-rubber car tyre with an SBR tread. It put them on top of the high-performance tyre world for the last few years of bias-ply dominance.

The years of the bias-ply tyre were numbered, for already the radial-ply tyre had come into being. The concept had been patented, quite brilliantly, by the head of an even older-established British tyre company, India, which had an enviable record of technical innovation. Even as late as the early 1960s, when India was finally swallowed up by Dunlop, the chief designer was considered one of the very cleverest tyre-compound chemists in the industry; but in 1914, the boss was Christian H Gray who, with his assistant Thomas Sloper, invented the radial-ply tyre, wire-cord belts and all.

It was one of the tragic consequences of other events in 1914 that no attempt was made to produce the new tyre, for it would have been a vast improvement on the woven-canvas carcasses of the day. Bicycle tyres had enjoyed a weftless construction since 1893, when India first made them before setting up J F Palmer with an independent company; his 1892 patent was valid in the USA, but not in England where David Moseley of Manchester had a prior claim dated 1888. Bicycle tyres also had wired edges, invented in Tottenham by Welch, from 1890. But did cars profit from all this?

They did not. The patent system once again proved more likely to hinder than to foster progress: the patents were strongly held, and the motor industry was not inclined to pay royalties. Car tyres shambled on with beaded edges (invented by an American working in Scotland – William E Bartlett filed his patent just 36 days after Welch) and with self-destructive casings made of woven stuff not unlike the Gent's Yacht Sailcloth[12] used by Dunlop in his original tyres. It took a quarter of a century for them to catch up, during which time the finest car tyres in the world were the Palmer Cord Aero and those made in the USA under Palmer licence by Dr (of medicine) B F Goodrich[13].

Ingenious and good things were also being done by Pirelli, today ranking with Continental as the oldest surviving European companies in the industry. As well as unwoven fabric and a wide steel bead, early Pirelli tyres pioneered the use of carbon black to multiply manifold the strength and durability of tyre rubber. The first black tyre on the market was a 1907 Pirelli, but the same idea had occurred simultaneously and independently in England, and by about 1919 the traditional white or creamy colour of tyres had changed to black almost everywhere. A lot of people were wearing black, too . . .

Whenever it rained, a lot of people wore macintoshes. It was a connection by marriage between the MacIntosh and Michelin familes that led the intelligent and artistic André Michelin to look into rubber; in 1895 he was the first to fit pneumatic tyres to a car. In 1929, he slept badly on the night train from Paris to Cannes . . .

Next day, Michelin began to investigate the possibilities of running trains on

---

11 They reached higher speeds pretty promptly; sustaining them depended on the introduction of newer and better bearing materials and lubricating oils. Prior to this evolutionary development, sustained high speeds on the prewar German express roads had been a problem: Bentley had to warn their customers not to overdo it, and the high overdrive ratio at the top of the Bentley 4¼-litre gearbox in the late 1930s was intended specifically to alleviate the problem.

12 A fine canvas in which warp and weft threads were equal.

13 The initials BF do not in this case signify what they are commonly held to represent – that is, the Bookmaker's Friend. Long before he was doctored, Goodrich had been named after Benjamin Franklin. His company was the first in the USA to produce a car tyre, and was also first to create the rubber-wound golf ball.

rubber tyres. To take the enormous loads, their rail tyres soon had steel wire carcasses, the benefits of which were before long applied to truck tyres. Car tyre developments were going in another interesting direction: the Michelin Pilote[14] of 1937 was the first low-profile (80-series) tyre, and the first to be designed for use on a wide (70% or more of the section width) rim. Developed during a revolutionary year (1936 saw not only Franco in revolt in Spain, but also King Edward VIII off the throne in England, not to mention the remilitarisation of the Rhineland and the publication of the General Theory of economist John Maynard Keynes), the Pilote provided the last of the elements to be brought together to make the tyre that Gray and Sloper had devised.

The man who saw what to do had never heard of Gray and Sloper. He was a clerk in the export sales department of Michelin, Marius Mignol by name, and he had overcome one of the frustrations of his job by inventing a special slide rule. One day Edouard Michelin spotted it, recognised the genius of the man, and had him promptly transferred to the product experimental department. It is a good firm that can do such a thing.

Mignol found his new companions worrying how to make separate measurements of frictional losses in the tread and sidewalls of a tyre. Make a tyre without sidewalls, he suggested; just run a few hoops of wire from bead to bead to support the tread, and measure the losses in what you have left.

The result was amazing: evidently most of the losses had come from the sidewall plies. Now, though, the tyre had no directional stiffness at all; if only it were not so floppy, they might be on to something good. So put some sort of stabilising belt under the tread, said Mignol.

The experimental tyre was now even more amazing. It developed exceptionally high cornering power and low rolling resistance, and it ran even cooler than the first unbelted test tyre. Development work pursued variations in materials and measurements, especially in the sidewalls, but by June 1946 Michelin were ready to patent the radial-ply tyre. It was a revolutionary year, after all: Greece was in turmoil, the Bank of England and the mines were nationalised in Britain, Perón came to power in Argentina, and Italy became a republic.

Whatever the politicians of the nation felt, the severest shock in Italy was doubtless suffered by Pirelli when Michelin's patent application was published. Pirelli had been working on radial-ply tyres themselves – not with steel, which was not part of their traditions, but with advanced fabric constructions which were. Careful to avoid any hint of infringement, Pirelli worked on for another five years before patenting their Cintura.

Most other tyre-makers were apathetic, and many were the blunders made by those who tried their hands at radials. Least enthusiastic were the Americans, who had most to lose: Goodyear, most hostile of all, sought quite positively to defer or if possible to prevent the more widespread adoption of the radial, because of the enormous investment in replacement machinery that would be required if the monstrous American factory were to change its product.

All such attempts were doomed. The belted bias-ply tyre was a short-lived failure; so were the fibreglass belt, and the contour-moulded bias-ply tyre[15] that had been so conspicuously successful in Grand Prix racing in the latter 1960s. All the time it was becoming increasingly evident that the days of the bias-ply car tyre were drawing to a close: Michelin were the first to stop making it, Pirelli were second, only a year behind.

It was also becoming evident that though these two companies were streets ahead of everybody else, neither of them was entirely right. Pirelli sidewall construction was superior, as were the resulting handling characteristics; Michelin's steel belt was superior, as were the resulting roadholding and ride. Michelin uniformity was unequalled, but on the other hand they were not strong on compounding: it was long after the war that they took their first steps into synthetic rubber manufacture, which they bodged so badly that they had to start again in the 1960s, and even today the majority of their tyres are formulated for wear rather than grip. Pirelli chemistry has always been outstanding, but the Italian firm's major contribution (which would allow their compounders more freedom) was yet to come, in a year which saw some revolutionary happenings of very mixed character.

The Isle of Wight Pop Festival was one of them. Despite or because of it, the age of majority in Britain was lowered to 18. Elsewhere, things of greater moment were happening: the Troubles broke out in Ulster, and men stepped out on to the Moon. It was 1969, the Year of the Nylon Bandage.

The Pirelli CN36 was the first production tyre to embody it. A band of

14 To be distinguished by all means from the current Pilot range.
15 The inspiration for this came from a Firestone corn-harvester tyre built many years earlier.

circumferential Nylon cords, heat-treated to develop a strong tensile force, tightly constrained a two-ply steel belt which in turn girdled a high-performance Rayon radial-ply carcass. The bandage prevented the belt from doing anything other than what it was wanted to do; and with the sidewalls thus freed from the burden of supporting the belt in the performance of its duties, they could be designed to function more purely as sidewalls should.

At last it was possible for each part of the tyre to be made properly for its specific function, and for the appropriate polymers (and, in due course, new cord materials such as Kevlar) to be used in each of the regions where specialised requirements could now be isolated and satisfied. At last it was possible for the radial-ply tyre to assume the proportions in which it worked best, with very wide tread and very shallow sidewalls supported by very wide rims. Just as it had taken 55 years for China to go from republican reconstitution in 1912 to Cultural Revolution, so it had taken 55 years for the radial-ply tyre to go from full statement of principle in 1914 to full realisation of principle.

Nowadays, everyone makes radial-ply tyres like that, and our cars could not otherwise be the marvels that they are.

There are still revolutions to come, especially such profound structural revolutions as exemplified by the Pirelli triangular tyre, killed by the oil crisis which emerged from revolutions in the Middle East, or the Continental everted tyre which was all set for a full-ballyhoo launch as a production item at the Geneva Show in the late 1980s. Just days before the Salon opened, the attention of the car manufacturer involved was drawn to a new and probably much better proposition by another tyre manufacturer. Collapse, as Mr Punch used to say, of Interested Party. Sometimes, as I observed of the Korach affair when introducing this section of my book, the most informative revolutions are those which fail.

Of all the relevant revolutions to come, perhaps none is more overdue than the revision of the wheelrim. Ever since the beadwire and the well-base rim were successfully imposed on the industry, there have been attempts to dislodge both – the Pirelli triangular tyre was one such, the Michelin TRX another – but all such attempts have been forcefully suppressed by an industry more concerned to sell what it can already make than to make something better. Only some of these attempts have been associated with efforts to provide a tyre capable of running safely after deflation, and of these the most recent, and the most likely to succeed, is the Michelin PAX, in which an entirely novel articulation of the bead area allows the tyre's sidewalls to be firmly anchored in a rim which, despite being shallower than any before, steadfastly refuses to allow a deflated tyre to roll off it. The addition of a springy annular cushion inside, between the beads, provides all the necessary further resistance to run-flat injury; and the contours and curvatures of the sidewalls and the carcass elements make the tyre a better tyre than normal when it is running inflated as a normal tyre would.

However, not even mighty Michelin could conquer the suspicions of the motor industry drawn up in hostile array to question the commercial safety of invoking a new pattern of wheel rim, and committing themselves to one tyre manufacturer where normally they would rely on multiple sourcing to keep prices competitive. Michelin has accordingly formed an alliance with Pirelli to strengthen the cause – an alliance so potentially powerful that the old strangleholds may yet be broken, the PAX tyre could be accepted by the motor industry, and a new era would dawn. A century after Michelin was announcing *nunc est bibendum!* there is every possibility of this new Latin alliance proclaiming *PAX VOBISCUM!*

CHAPTER 8

FEAR OF FLYING

SOMETHING FAR MORE REVOLUTIONARY THAN the political shenanigans of the French in 1789 took place six years earlier.

It also took place in France: in November 1783, Pilâtre de Rozier and the Marquis d'Arlandes made mankind's first flight in an untethered aircraft – a hot-air Montgolfier balloon.

A few days later their consultant, the noted physicist Professor J A C Charles, made the first flight in a free hydrogen balloon, accompanied by one of the brothers Robert whose work as chemists had been crucial to the success of ballooning.

They had succeeded in dissolving rubber. What had that to do with technological revolution? Previously, the materials of airbags or gasbags made for balloons were either too heavy or too porous; thin silk rubberised by the Robert process was light enough and impermeable enough to hold hydrogen.

The very idea of buoyant flight seemed essentially French; being based on a principle stated by Archimedes, it appealed particularly to those who put their faith in the Age of Reason. Hindsight shows them to have been on the wrong track (even the Americans took their last military airships out of service in 1961), but while the idea remained popular it prompted Zeppelin and his assistants[16] to carry out some of the most important and fundamental research into aerodynamic drag. This took place at the end of the 19th century, the first Zeppelin airship being launched in 1900.

Meanwhile, the motor car had been created, and its rapidly developing engine gave promise of power units suitable for aircraft propulsion. This was enormously encouraging to those sterner-minded thinkers and tinkers who were working out the problems of kinetic flight, which relied upon inducing airflow over a wing. Here the principle had been stated a century earlier (1687) by Sir Isaac Newton, whose laws of motion were then translated into aviation terms (1809) by the brilliant and far-sighted Sir George Cayley.

His first full-size glider flew in 1809; forty years later, his gliders were man-carriers. In 1890, Ader's *Eole* was the first piloted aeroplane to leave the ground by its own power, and by 1903 the Wright Brothers had established the reality of powered kinetic flight, truly free flight. The real revolution was at last in full swing.

It is a sorry comment on the insularity of man's thinking that the two sides, the proponents of buoyant and of kinetic flight, would not pool their efforts. It was not until 1955 that the ML Aviation Company flew their Utility, the first aeroplane with inflatable fabric wings.

In that same year, two more brothers did something rather revolutionary with a wing. The Swiss brothers May put one, upside down, on a Porsche Spyder. They reckoned that it would improve the car's cornering power, a valuable asset in the Alpine pass-storming sprints that they entered; but the competition stewards could not understand it, and therefore forbade them to use it.

Nobody forbade the use by Mercedes-Benz of an airbrake on their sports-racing cars at Le Mans in 1955. Nobody but Mille Miglia winner Stirling Moss, who tried the idea, and engineer Rudolf Uhlenhaut who had the idea, realised that the huge panel rising from the tail of their Le Mans car developed aerodynamic forces which included a downward component allowing corners to be taken faster.

The last time (and the first) that Mercedes-Benz had won the Le Mans event had been in 1952. During practice they tried out an airbrake on the roof of one of their 300SL team cars; it was even more like an inverted wing, and Uhlenhaut doubtless thought hard about it thereafter – but it was not used in the race, for the 300SL was quite revolutionary enough as it was. He was not the first to try the principle, though; that distinction belonged to another German, Fritz von Opel.

In 1927 – the year of the first Mille Miglia, the year of the first sound film, the year when Lindbergh made the first solo flight across the North Atlantic and the Marchese di Pinedo made the first flight of any kind across the South Atlantic – von Opel gave the first demonstration of a rocket-propelled car. He did 127mph, and he was uncomfortably aware that even if all four wheels left the ground the propulsion would continue. Fear of flying (entirely justifiable, for the car would then have gone

---

16 The leader of these investigators was named Klemperer.

even faster, completely out of control) prompted him to build a pair of wings on to the side of the body. They were large, they had considerable camber, and their function was to develop lift as wings do in kinetic flight – but, since they were given negative incidence, to develop it in a downward direction, thus keeping the car's tyres firmly in contact with the ground.

The brilliant aerodynamicist Jaray would have appreciated the idea. He knew about the problems of lift generated by aerodynamic bodies; but nobody in the motor industry took much notice of what he knew. They simply adapted his designs, allowing stylists to corrupt them: many of the so-called 'streamlined' cars of the 1930s doubtless would have developed less drag when going backwards, as was certainly true of the much-vaunted (but not much-bought) Chrysler Airflow. Most of the people in the motor industry were pretty pigeon-brained, and they duly posted the Opel wing idea in the pigeon-hole for rocket-propelled cars, should such things ever come into fashion.

When the idea resurfaced, it was connected with a bird much more reluctant than the pigeon to get airborne. The chaparral or road-runner is a bird that relies on its legs to get it out of trouble; and Chaparral is what that intelligent Texan revolutionary Jim Hall called his own sports-racing cars.

The generality of high-performance cars had meanwhile, though progressing through a series of stylistic triumphs, degenerated into an aerodynamic disaster. Those with any pretensions to 'streamlining' (including especially the occasional faired-in Grand Prix Maserati, Gordini, or Cooper) were inclined to get airborne at high speed; on fast circuits such as Reims there were places where their front tyres barely touched the road[17].

The extremely clever work done in France by Panhard and by Deutsch & Bonnet, and in England by Bristol and by Frank Costin, enjoyed very little appreciation and no emulation. Only Jaguar, who relied on ex-Bristol aerodynamicist Malcolm Sayer to maintain their competitiveness, received any praise. Few laymen knew any more about Sayer's antidotes to lift than they did about Costin's use of reversed camber (as exemplified in the Lockheed Constellation), but they all thought the D-type Jaguar beautiful.

So it was; and by 1950s standards it was fast. A decade later, Group 7 sports-racing two-seaters were often stylish and pseudo-aerodynamic, but they had prodigiously powerful American engines and were very fast. Lola and McLaren took most of the laurels in the CanAm races and inspired most of the copyists, but the most significant contribution to the series was made by Chaparral, an ostensibly tiny firm headed by a couple of oil-wealthy Texans named Hap Sharp and Jim Hall, and aided by an exceptionally competent glassfibre constructor named Andy Green. In fact the organisation was a front for General Motors, but that does not detract from the brilliance of Hall. The second-series Chaparrals were full of revolutionary ideas, advanced and unorthodox, and some of them were aerodynamic innovations or developments that were to lever the world.

The spoiler at the lip of the tail was not new; it had appeared on a Ferrari in 1961 at the instigation of another American driver, Ritchie Ginther. The Chaparral was probably the pioneer of spoilers at or beneath the nose of the car, though, something so effective that they have since spread to even the most mundane of family saloons.

Hall stormed motoring's Bastille in 1966. What a year of upset that was! It saw the Little Red Book of Chairman Mao, and a snide red rag of a book *(Unsafe at Any Speed)* by Ralph Nader. It saw Ford win at Le Mans for the first time, and the first Hovercraft go into service off the coast of England. It saw the first wide-grooved hand-cut rain tyres in use at the Nürburgring, where Chaparral exploited them to win the 1000km race. Hall had always worked very closely with Firestone, who that year imposed the wide low-profile tyre on racing; and he knew that the latest tyres generated higher cornering power if imposed upon by greater downforce than was applied by the mass of the car. He saw that an inverted wing or airfoil could develop an aerodynamically induced downforce with the least penalty in weight or drag: the aviation industry had been working since the beginning, since the Wright Brothers confected a rudimentary wind-tunnel out of an old starch box, to make wings efficient by minimising drag in relation to lift and weight. The first successful application of the idea was to the Chaparral 2E which appeared at Bridgehampton in September

---

17 The problem was not limited to racing cars. The 3-litre Marcos coupé of the 1970s suffered it at its top speed of 130mph; but when the Ford engine was replaced by a Volvo one which needed a bigger radiator, the necessary accommodation was found (without spoiling the looks of the shapely bonnet) by letting the bottom of it protrude beneath the car. Fortuitously it acted as a subternasal dam, correcting the balance of airflow over and under the car and thus eliminating (or at least reducing to manageable magnitude) the problem of front-end lift.

1966; so advanced was Hall's thinking that it was not copied for another two years, when it began to appear in Formula 1 racing.

The airfoil proliferated rapidly; so did complications. There were adjustable wings, variable-incidence wings, wings with dihedral, wings at the back and at the front, some of them attached to the body of the car, some to the suspension. Some did not remain attached, and some very nasty accidents ensued. Early in the 1969 season, the rules were changed: in future, only a relatively small wing, mounted low and fixed directly to the sprung mass of the car, would be permitted, together with nasal airfoils of even more restricted size.

Quickly clipped though it was, the wing had already checked another incipient revolution. It arrived just in time to nip four-wheel drive in the bud. Noting the prowess of Ferguson Formula racers (not to mention the Jensen FF tourer), several manufacturers thought to try four-wheel drive in F1 cars. Cosworth, Lotus, Matra and McLaren all had a go – but in the utterly artificial circumstances of F1 racing, with unlimited tyres and unrealistic ground clearance on unnaturally smooth surfaces, as much tractive and braking grip as could be endured was available even from 1969 wings at racing speeds. Another decade would have to go by before the Audi Quattro and its rallying derivatives demonstrated what 4WD could do at ordinary speeds and on any surface. Meanwhile, Jim Hall must have been musing on the other things that had happened in 1966 . . .

What he did was to reverse the principle of the Hovercraft, and with it he shook the entire CanAm establishment out of their not particularly effulgent wits. His Chaparral 2J was a car whose entire plan area, save only the front wheel arches, was skirted to create a plenum chamber underneath it, from which air was sucked out by a pair of fans driven by a separate small two-stroke snowmobile engine of 45bhp. If the skirted area measured no more than 5ft by 10ft, a depression of a mere thirtieth of an atmosphere (0.47 lb/in^2) would induce a downforce amounting to 1.5 tons.

Making its debut with fastest lap at Watkins Glen in July 1970, the 2J was for the rest of the season consistently the fastest car in CanAm racing. It was promptly dubbed 'the sucker car' – and, acting on the notorious American principle of never giving a sucker an even break, the other competitors raised every imaginable objection to it. They complained about the auxiliary engine, and about the cloud of dust spread rearward by those extractor fans; but the most telling complaint, given strong emphasis by the erstwhile lawyer who ran the McLaren team in the USA, was that the car's fans and skirts contravened the earlier ban on moving aerodynamic surfaces.

It was not the first time that a motor racing clique had taken steps to forestall progress that might have upset their established order. Revolutionary things might be happening in America, such as the founding of the Women's Liberation movement, but the good ol' boys of motor racing had no wish to be disturbed. In December 1970 the FIA ruled the Chaparral system illegal; and in 1983, when I last spoke to him, Jim Hall still felt too bitter to be able to discuss the affair.

Far more resilient a revolutionary was Colin Chapman, who brought the quick-thinking ruthlessness of a kerbside car trader to bear against every new set of inhibitory regulations the establishment could erect in defence of the Old Order. In 1978 he once again took a smart step out of the morass of arguments that had been raging about aerodynamic aids and appendages – and so his chosen driver, Mario Andretti, whose biorhythmic patterns matched as perfectly as possible the racing calendar that year, became World Champion at the wheel of a Lotus that appeared impossible to challenge.

Chapman no longer relied upon airfoils to generate downforce from above; the Lotus 78 was pulled down by a suction induced beneath it, not mechanically but by the motion of the car through the air. As much as possible of the underside of the car was shaped to form a venturi passage through which a large mass of air was guided from front to rear, with the road itself forming one wall of the venturi and skirts on the car to seal its edges. The faster the car went, the stronger the suction beneath it: with its tyres loaded so heavily (and yet weightlessly) the Lotus could outcorner and outbrake anything with mere wings.

The lawyers had a go at the apparatus as soon as they decently could, and now racing cars manage on a regulated combination of limited wings and unskirted venturis. They are not to be dismissed as entirely irrelevant, though; the Celebrated Man in the Street, for whom all revolutions are supposed to be waged and for whom they always prove to have been poor investments, still believes that what is good for racing cars must be good for his car.

To some extent (T C Mits, the Celebrated Man&c, has always been paid some sort of dividend in every revolution) he is right. When politico-religious revolutions in the oil-bearing Middle East left the motorised world to contemplate a fuel shortage of crisis proportions, the motor industry at last felt safe in deploying the aerodynamic knowledge it had so long been accumulating. The years after 1973 saw an increasing proliferation of cars, in all categories, dominated in design by the desire to diminish drag.

By the time most of them were ready, the oil crisis was no longer a reality, and T C Mits was not all that concerned about fuel consumption. He was not at all unhappy, either, to discover that the refinement of body contours and elongation of gearing that promised economy could as easily produce higher speeds. Not at all put out by the discovery that T C Mits was enthusiastic enough in principle to want to drive fast, even though the laws everywhere cramped his style, the industry responded by giving him more power while maintaining the low drag.

Everything happens for the best. It was known that aerodynamic lift cannot be generated kinetically without some drag; and so the industry's efforts to minimise the latter resulted in a valuable reduction of the former. Minimal drag presupposed zero lift.

Since ordinary road cars had hitherto developed positive lift of quite alarming intensity at high speeds, it followed that the new generation of faster and more slippery cars was also more stable, more steerable, more stoppable, more safe. The principle that Fiat had applied in designing the (mechanically) revolutionary 1922–3 GP cars (the first racers to enjoy wind-tunnel analysis, which amongst other things determined the shape under the tail) was now working to common advantage in fun cars and business cars.

It was as much as could be hoped. Not everybody got it right, and many a car that started out in life clean and smooth grew aerodynamic appendages, bibs and spoilers and fences and wings, that corrected errant airflow and were made styling features although they were actually confessions of failure. Positive downforce, inducing drag and consuming power, is counterproductive however it be generated.

When the method involves the wing or the venturi, it only works at high speeds (the downforce increases as the square of the airspeed) and only in clear air, as many a racing driver has found to his dismay when the turbulence behind a competitor has suddenly robbed his wings of their efficacy. The suction car, sharing with the venturi the need for boundary fencing if it is to work efficiently, cannot hope to seal itself against roads as uneven as roads ordinarily are; and in any case it is hard to imagine a modern urban society tolerating clouds of dust and air being blown back, or up or indeed in any direction, by a streetful of unbagged Hoovers. The sucker car, alas for its own good and ours, was just too revolutionary.

One can overdo it, as large numbers of ardent Chinese youngsters (especially T C Mits, the Chinese Man in Tiananmen Square) more recently and painfully had to learn. The most effective revolutions, those from which the people at large profit most and suffer least, are those which are conducted slowly and almost surreptitiously. The French had no good excuse for their bloody rioting: a contemporary of Newton had told them, in a voice of classical French clarity and good sense, that *Patience et longueur de temps font plus que force ni que rage*. La Fontaine wrote that, for us all to bear in mind, a hundred years before the balloon went up.

CHAPTER 9

FLUID POWER

NEVER MIND WHEN YOU READ THIS. What matters is that I am writing it on *le quatorze Juillet,* the anniversary of the storming of the Bastille and a day on which, while millions of French lose themselves in an orgy of uncritical self-congratulation, they and we should be mourning the passing of an age of Reason that has been disturbed, of Enlightenment obscured, of Proportion toppled, of Nobility martyred and of Society unbalanced – all for the sake of Bigotry unequalled. The music crashing out of my Isobariks[18] as I write is the bloodthirsty march *Ça ira!* which accompanied the aristocrats of France to the guillotine; but the joke is on those damnable revolutionaries. *Ça ira* became in 1793, by order of the Duke of York, the official regimental quick march of the West Yorkshire Regiment.

To turn the adversary's own assets against him is a trick even older than Jacob's wrestling. In the days when bands accompanied the troops into battle, playing one of the other side's tunes might allow a detachment to infiltrate the enemy's lines; *Ça ira* was used with such success as to acquire the status of a military honour. Perhaps it was corroborative evidence of the Reverend Rowland Hill's suspicion that the Devil had all the good tunes; perhaps it served the French right, for they were and still are given to playing other people's tunes. For all their pride, they still emulate the Americans whom they profess to despise, just as in their revolution they were aping the Americans.

They took their ideas of hydraulics in cars from the Americans. More truthfully, the Americans rammed the idea down their throats, when Duesenberg came to take the 1921 French Grand Prix from Ballot: before the French car failed for other reasons, its mechanically operated brakes were visibly less effective than the hydraulically operated brakes of the American car.

Forty years later, when the new-fangled computers were promising a revolution in artificial intelligence, the latest translating computer was set to work on a Russian technical text and rendered the equivalent of 'hydraulic ram' as 'water goat' – which proved how artificial some kinds of intelligence can be, and what havoc can be wrought by revolutions. It also served to remind us what the word 'hydraulic' really means, and to justify the fact that the working fluid in the braking system of that Duesenberg was plain water.

It demanded the most scrupulous design and machining of the complicated joints in the system, the circuitry of which passed through the kingpins to reach the brakes on the steered front wheels. It also assumed that the car would never be run in wintry conditions; but the fundamental premise was that four-wheel brakes had arrived and were here to stay.

Mechanical braking systems involved a lot of friction in the operating linkages, and a lot of difficulty in achieving balanced braking of all four wheels. To the better engineers of those days (there were some good ones around then) it was perfectly apparent that an hydraulic system would eradicate most of the system friction, while the equality of pressure throughout an hydraulic circuit guaranteed an equilibrium that could never be approached by mechanical means.

Fiat, which had most of the very best engineers at that time, used hydraulic brakes in their 1914 Grand Prix car, which was not powerful or fast enough to make much of a mark but was in most other respects an advanced and notably well-balanced design. Bugatti, an expatriate Italian not averse to copying Americans, tried the idea in his 1921 Type 28 racer, feeding water to the front brakes but retaining mechanical operation at the rear and thus missing the point. His joints were as finicky and expensive as the others, but it would not take designers long to come up with simpler and more practical alternatives, as soon as they were persuaded of the need.

The practical problem was a chemical one: it was the quest for a fluid suitable for low-temperature use which initially delayed the adoption of hydraulics. Simplified circuitry required flexible seals, but the traditional leather could not be worked with sufficient accuracy. Natural rubber reacted very badly to such fluids as had been proposed as alternatives to water.

---

18 In my experience, the only loudspeakers that do not sound like loudspeakers. They were made by Linn, but not any longer.

Hydraulic brakes were a feature of the very advanced Chrysler 70 of 1924.

Nothing daunted, Duesenberg put the straight-eight Model A on the market in 1921 with water as the brake fluid for summer use, recommending the addition of some primitive antifreeze in winter. The only familiar ones were alcohol and glycerine, neither of which was kind to natural rubber; mineral oils were worse, and if vegetable oils were safe chemically they had dangerous tendencies to turn sticky and form gum.

A variety of blends was quickly developed, now that manufacturers were keen to profit from the advantages promised by hydraulics. The pioneer was a Scot named Malcolm Loughead, most of whose work was done in the USA. Whether in splendid isolation or embarrassed insularity, the indigenes could not easily pronounce his name, let alone spell it; so, although he kept it for personal purposes, the name of the business became Lockheed (the aircraft corporation is related) and very soon it was almost synonymous with hydraulic brakes.

By 1924 such brakes were incorporated in what was then perhaps the best mass-produced car in the world, the new Chrysler 70. In the same year, England had them in the 12hp Bean, which was nothing of the kind. A more important English challenge to Lockheed's patents came in 1926 from Wakefield (later Castrol Ltd) with a patent for a mixture of castor oils and alcohols, which came into regular use and remained so until the 1939 advent of the Second World War.

During and after that war, the petrochemical industries of Britain and Germany did wonders. Based on the ethylene glycol which had become familiar as an engine coolant additive, glycol esters and polyglycols became available. The former served as diluents, the latter as lubricants – though they never matched the exceptional properties of specially prepared castor oil and often needed additives to improve lubricity.

During this same period, new seal materials also became available, synthetic 'rubbers' which could be matched to the properties of the chosen fluid so that they would swell just enough to ensure a good seal, but not so much as to impair operation. The only snag was that these new fluids, unlike the prewar ones, were strongly hygroscopic: enormous pains had to be taken in later years to overcome the high-temperature treachery of fluids contaminated by atmospheric water[19]. But there was no going back: in Britain, which was fairly typical, no new car had mechanical brakes at the front after 1949, nor at the rear after 1952. Soon after that, the disc brake invaded the scene, and the heat problem became so intense that it had to be seriously addressed.

Meanwhile, another revolution had taken place in America, when in 1951 Chrysler introduced power steering. The need had first been identified in France in the very early years of city-to-city racing, when tired drivers sometimes failed to muster the strength to haul on the wheel of a heavy understeering car on its way into a tight corner. Private cars were often worse, but the big ones were usually driven by professionals who were hired for their strength as much as for their skills, since a lot of muscle was needed to start their engines 'on the handle'. As owners began to do

---

19 The phenomenon known as 'brake fade' had previously been caused by shortcomings in brake design and friction materials, but now it was also induced by boiling of the brake fluid. For many years the industry's standard test procedure involved an aggressive descent of the Grossglockner Pass in the Austrian Alps.

their own driving (the rule rather than the exception in republican America), steering was made lighter by making it lower-geared and thus increasing the leverage ratio.

Steering took a turn for the worse when independent suspension came on the scene. Imperfect geometry produced wheelfight, countered not only by steering dampers but also by even lower gearing which was by its nature more irreversible. The disappearance of the beam front axle invited relocation of the engine further forward, so there was more weight on the front wheels; the associated multiplicity of joints in the steering linkage introduced new sources of friction. For every one of these ills, lower-geared, slower-geared steering was the easy cure.

In surprisingly few years, the quality of steering was grievously debased. Experienced drivers were appalled, but they were few in number; the mass-producers sought volume sales among the inexperienced. Knowing no better, this new generation of drivers found it comforting that their inept treatment of the steering wheel should be cushioned by the system's insensitivity. Rolls-Royce called it 'the sneeze factor', trailing haplessly as they did – and as everybody else did – in the wake of the American industry.

In America, cars were growing heavier, tyres fatter, cities more congested, and parking more and more tiresome. It was naturally there that some form of servo assistance for the steering became an evident need; and it was properly Chrysler, then the most conscientious engineers of the Big Three, who did it first. It was also inevitable that no thought should be given to making the steering anything but lighter, since the characteristics of good steering had been long forgotten; so the servo system was quite simple, and the results quite awful.

The more fastidious manufacturers turned for help to the aviation industry, which had been forced to develop fully powered controls for transonic flight and had encountered the same problems of control feel or feedback. Within a decade, the finest car systems offered assistance related to the force applied at the steering wheel, rather than to its movement, with the best work of the 1960s being done by Aston Martin, Bristol, Daimler-Benz and Jaguar, in various conjunctions with such specialist firms as ZF of Friedrichshafen (for which the F originally stood) and Adwest of Coventry.

More recently remarkable has been the spread of servo steering down into smaller and lighter cars, prompted by the wholesale adoption of front-wheel drive with negative-offset steering and strut suspension. These in combination usually dictate that some two-thirds of the nose-heavy car's laden weight must be jacked up, sometimes by as much as an inch, when the steering is turned from full lock to the straight-ahead position. This can make parking very hard work, which is why so many quite light modern cars have such low-geared steering; power assistance provides a complete and very welcome remedy.

It was France which put front-wheel drive on the map; and it has been left to France to pursue the uses of pressurised hydraulics to ends beyond the vision or ambition of less capricious lands. Probably the first car to have powered steering of acceptable quality was the 1955 Citroën DS, a car in which engine-powered high-pressure hydraulics also operated the suspension, the brakes, and originally the clutch and gearbox, while even attending to the needs of wheel-changing.

With a little more imagination the system could also have worked the windows, locked the doors, adjusted the seats, and clamped loose luggage in the boot; as it was, nobody could accuse the DS of being unimaginative. On the contrary, nearly everybody other than the French themselves (to most of whom it appeared perfectly logical) accused it of being revolutionary.

Once again, it was the uniformity of pressure throughout an hydraulic circuit which commended the use of what were in effect liquid pushrods to refine ideas about interconnected suspension that had been verified mechanically in the little 2CV. Having an engine-powered supply of liquid at very high pressure (controlled by a different kind of working fluid, gaseous nitrogen sealed in a variable-displacement sphere like those used for the actual springing of the car) enabled those liquid pushrods to be varied in length, even while the car was in motion. This made it possible for the ride height to be kept constant or deliberately varied, with manifold other tricks for special occasions or circumstances.

Given the provision of such a wonderful power source, virtually frictionless and amenable to the most sensitive and precise control, it made sense to use it for the brakes and for the steering. Both were exceptionally good by contemporary standards, but neither was like any other car's, a feature which made the DS anathema to the conservative.

They had even more to get apoplectic about in 1970. Just imagine: a year after the Concorde, fastest and most beautiful of Bristols, had taken to the air in defiance of kinetic heating, pressure gradients, trim changes and all the control and other problems associated with sustained flight at 60,000ft and Mach 2, the fuddies and the duddies were shaken with dismay by the very thought of the Citroën SM having fully powered steering with entirely artificial feel. It was simple, really: the basic accumulator pressure powered the steering, but pitted against it was the output of a secondary pump driven by the transmission so that its output was proportional to the road speed of the car. At parking speeds, it offered no resistance; at 110mph there was enough to cancel assistance.

With some modifications, the SM system was carried on into the CX. By a marvel of production engineering, hydraulic cylinders and pistons for this car were made so accurately that seals could be omitted entirely, stalled flow of the liquid in the faint gap between the parts providing sufficient blockage, with utter reliability and the irreducible minimum of friction. Only with a ring-main circuit such as the Citroën's could such an idea work, recirculating the faint dribbles of leakage past the pistons.

With further changes, notably in the behaviour of the suspension in roll and the automatic electronic sensing of incipient requirements, the system was carried on into the consequent XM; and if only there were some way of anticipating 'the random brick in the road', we should today be enjoying true active suspension, for which (as Lotus and Citroën and others have demonstrated) hydraulics furnish all the power and accuracy and speed of response that could be desired.

A strange thing, though: none of the firms whose cars incorporate some form of powered hydraulics (and there are now plenty of them, for it is a desirable adjunct of anti-lock braking systems as well as of self-levelling suspension) has ever bothered to furnish the same assistance for the driver's clutch foot as his brake foot and his steering hands enjoy. Only once, when Maserati were in the hands of (if not exactly in cahoots with) Citroën, did they go one better than Citroën themselves and provide a powered clutch as well as all the rest in the splendid original version of the muscular Khamsin.

For that matter, nobody has yet had the nerve to do away with all the mechanical gubbins of steering and do the whole job hydraulically. Power is still deemed 'assistance', something superimposed on existing and excessively antiquated mechanical steering systems that resemble something out of a pioneer steamship. Drivers happily rely on the liquid pushrod to stop the car; why can it not be trusted to steer it? The mechanism is merely a slave element nowadays; it has been omitted from some agricultural tractors, and from some Citroën dream-cars; but what would the customers, the People, in whom all judgement and power have been invested by successive revolutions, have to say about so rational a thing being done in a production car?

No doubt but ye are the people, and wisdom will die with you – the biting sarcasm of Job always comes back most mordant to the memory when the after-effects of revolution have to be considered. Recently I saw in a Parisian news-vendor's stall a magazine pointing out that, more than two centuries after the revolution, France was still not much good at providing either liberty, equality, or fraternity to the Africans, Armenians, Jews, Indians, Orientals and other minorities who would like to live as or among Frenchmen. Car buyers and sellers are much the same: a lifetime after Fiat and Duesenberg initiated hydraulics in the car, half a lifetime after they became universal, there are still opportunities being denied. Some revolutions take a long time; the fighting may continue.

The amazing inconsistency of the motoring public may be illustrated well enough by their complete indifference to the use of electricity, as opposed to hydraulics, to steer their cars. An electrically powered steering rack first did production-car service in the automatic-transmission version of the original Honda NSX, but that was a car so replete with sensational refinements that very few critics got so far as to examine the steering. The next step was for an electrically powered rack – devoid of any but electrical and (through the controlling black box) electronic connections to the driver's steering wheel – to direct the rear wheels of the Honda Prelude, the four-wheel steering of which was so far beyond the comprehension of the public that, fantastically good though it was, the publicists were forced eventually to ignore it.

Since then, electrically aided steering (always, lamentably, of only the two front wheels) has emerged in a number of little economy cars, and the People – convinced, in what they believe to be the Computer Age, that everything electronic (and preferably digital) must be better than anything and everything else – are beginning to show signs of accepting the idea of 'steering by wire', an expression meaning that the steering mechanism of ordinary cars might be as innocent of mechanical connections to the steering wheel as are the rear wheels of a post-1991 4WS Honda.

In vain the proponents of hydraulics might complain that their systems could be just as remote and sensitive. In vain might Citroën remind us that its magnificent Activa prototype featured purely hydraulic four-wheel steering, without mechanical connection, as long ago as 1988, at a time when the production Honda Prelude 4WS system was still a conventionally mechanical system with hydraulic servo.

Mark you, there was a time – nearly thirty years earlier – when computer pioneers and other control freaks thought that the way to achieve almost everything might be pneumatic . . .

CHAPTER 10

COMPUTER CONTROL

The most effective revolutions, those from which the people at large profit most and suffer least, are those which are conducted slowly and almost surreptitiously.

WHO SAID THAT? I DID, in an earlier chapter. Now I should like to amplify it: such revolutions are most effective when they embody changes that are beyond the comprehension and beneath the notice of the people, and the revolution may be deemed successful when those people, finally recognising the extent and the inevitability of the changes and the improbability of ever really understanding them, first embrace them as a fashion and then worship them as a fetish.

It has not happened often in the evolution of the car. Wholesale changes in materials for spark-plug insulators and brake linings have been made from time to time, and minor revolutions have followed the introductions of the self-tapping screw and the baulk-ring synchromesh without anybody getting shot or even angry. That is the way to do it, though; the best revolutions are quiet.

Somebody (I have tactfully forgotten who) recently made a public-relations film entitled *The Quiet Revolution*; but not even that idea was revolutionary. Back in the early 1960s, the electrical giant AEI made the most beautiful industrial film I have ever seen, and they called it *The Quiet Revolution*. Their own film unit, led by a masterly Russian photographer, created this lyrical documentary about the harnessing of water power from the Himalayan snows to bring electricity to the towns and villages, to the factories and the cottage industries, of northern India. Musically and pictorially it was a dream of a film; but I still wonder if they gave the right title to the right work. You see, AEI also produced at that time an instructional film explaining the making and uses of semi-conductors and transistors.

They appeared new then, forty years ago. It was a thrilling time for invention and discovery, for portentous revelation and potential revolution. In a seven-year cycle of exceptional creative excitement, beginning with the publication of Galbraith's *The Affluent Society*, new wonders sprang up on all sides. Rear-engined cars took over the Grands Prix; we had the Variomatic transmission from DAF, Hovercraft prototypes from Sir John Cockroft, and four-wheel drive from Ferguson; Russia landed the first rocket on the Moon and launched the first man into orbit; NSU introduced the Wankel engine, Courrèges and Mary Quant introduced the mini-skirt – and not for nothing was it dubbed the Mini. All these things were intelligible; but the novelty that beggared the imagination was the new-fangled electronic computer.

Computers themselves were not new. The Cambridge mathematician Babbage had conceived his first mathematical machine, the Difference Engine, as early as 1812, though nobody could engineer it for another 90 years. In the USA, a statistician named Hollerith was faced with a vast unsorted jumble of facts from the 1880 census, and invented the punched-card machine, borrowing ideas that Jacquard had embodied in his weaving looms a century earlier. In the 20th century, electrical and

Dr J W Mauchly in his ENIAC computer, 1946.

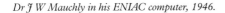

mechanical engineering had advanced enough to make statistical machinery that was accurate and fast, inspired by men like Bush of MIT, Stibitz of Bell Telephones, and my father, may he rest in peace. Good solid stuff, all of it; but it took the pressures of war to prompt the creation of an electronic computer. Britain, where Cambridge graduates Turing and Welchman led a growing team of cryptoanalysts urgently seeking means for transcribing coded German telecommunications, was first in 1943 with the successful computer named Colossus. In the USA Mauchly's ENIAC was completed at the University of Pennsylvania in 1946. These devices were amazing, they were big, and they were hot, because they were built with ordinary radio 'tubes' or valves – and so were they all, until the advent of the Swinging Sixties and a cheap solid-state switch even smaller and destined to be even more devastating than the micro-skirt.

The galloping miniaturisation that followed the development of the micro-processor happened just long enough ago to be generally forgotten, but in the early sixties we were waiting for it to happen. People were still arguing about the relative merits of punched cards and punched paper tape, ferrite-core memories and magnetic tape. Fluidic switching promised to make the pneumatic computer even faster than the early electronic variety, prompting Weber to build a bright pneumatic brain for masterminding the inspection of their elegant and intricate carburettors; but miniaturisation killed all this speculation. The step from the transistor switch to the microchip, as colossal a step as Industrial Man had taken since the coming of steam, was taken very quickly. A decade after IBM delivered their STRETCH computer to the Atomic Energy Authority (who rented it for $300,000 a month, a lot of money in 1961) one could buy a computer small enough to hold in one hand. Another five years, and one could buy it cheaply.

This meant that such a device could be incorporated in a car. Before the decade was finished, BMW had done just that – but it was nothing more than a toy looking for a serious job of work to do. Meanwhile, the transistor switch had found one, and amidst a noisily incoherent babble about 'electronic ignition' the outworn, outdated, outrageously erratic Kettering contact-breaker found its days numbered.

That was the period when 'electronic' was the new buzz-word. It should have connoted a system embodying at least one solid-state device, but T C Mits and Joe Q Public, neither of whom cared a hoot about technicalities, would as happily use the word to describe any small electrical gadget. To the Celebrated Man in the Street, a transistor was just that – a small electrical gadget – and therefore of no more consequence than the multitude of others that had quietly revolutionised the telephone, the radio, the office and the factory without anybody being much the wiser. Electricity was not something you normally saw; you could not hold a lump of it in your hand to examine it. Better ignore it, then, and leave it to the specialists who understood such things. At least it was likely to be clean and quiet and not need house-training . . .

Seldom had the industry had it so easy. Probably not since the arrival of nitrocellulose paint had any significant change been so little opposed. Internal opposition from the cost accountants was as much a problem as usual when something is new and not yet cheap; but soon there was a panic about clean air, and another about fuel consumption, and laws that required proof of 50,000 miles without adjustments or degradation of emissions. In the circumstances, the costs could be passed on to the customer as the price of social necessity (otherwise known as respectability) even if it proved necessary to transistorise everything downstream from the petrol tank.

So the Black Box became fashionable. Nobody knew what was inside it; we were not supposed to know, we could never hope to understand, and we really should not worry. It was a Black Box, and we had better accept it, mysteries and all.

We did.

We even went out of our way to buy black boxes for the cars we already had. Ignition systems galore were marketed by newly sprouted little firms almost as numerous. Some systems were excellent, many were rubbish, and more than a few customers were mystified when their nice new electronic ignitions proved to play havoc with their fancy electronic rev-counters.

Meanwhile the industry was busy learning how to do things properly. An awareness grew of the dangers of radio-frequency interference playing havoc with in-car apparatus, dangers considerable enough to prompt conscientious testing methods for ensuring that each individual car would be safe from electronic assault when negotiating streets flanked by unknown ambuscades of fluorescent lights, microwave ovens, pirate radio stations or what not.

Electronic ignition did even greater wonders for reliability than it did for performance. Electronic injection, the obvious antidote to much of the most worrying legislation, took longer: Bendix were probably the first to try it, but they did not persevere. Mechanical systems seemed so appealing, and had been around so long (the first Wright Flyer had fuel injection, in 1903), that it was bound to be a slow business proving that Messrs Lucas, Tecalemit, Kugelfischer et al. were wrong. Using air-metering ideas propounded by Tecalemit's associate Mr Jackson, Bosch proved it; and then they had the wit to go on and combine injection and ignition systems in one utterly masterly black box.

You could have it in a BMW in the late 1970s; more to the point, you could have it in a VW. The Scirocco/Golf GTi with digitally stabilised idling at one end of the tachometer scale, a safe non-damaging rev-limiter at the other end, and imperturbable efficiency everywhere between, was sweeter and crisper and cleaner and quicker than anything else in its class or some considerable height above it.

T C Mits did not argue. Joe Q Public took longer, unable to shake off his inborn conviction that if he were stubborn enough he could get something half as good for a quarter of the price. What he got was single-point injection, not quite as ghastly as our electronic carburettors but no less likely to disappear in a few years – or, with luck, even fewer.

It was a fortuitous combination of happenings which urged the next step. The remorseless march of emissions legislation made monitoring of the exhaust, and prompt adjustment of ignition timing or mixture if not both, a necessity for some markets. The fashionable rise of the turbocharger made knock-sensing as valuable a necessity for performance as it was for emissions control; without it, the turbocharged engine was doomed to have a low geometrical compression ratio and therefore to be unacceptably dull and thirsty in part-throttle operation. Electronics could cope with all this, and did.

Thus I was prompted to reconsider something I had written in or about 1973. If the good Lord had meant man to fly at high altitudes, I commented in a study of supercharging, He would have made the atmosphere of constant density. Pursuing that argument through a maze which led to Witzky's stratified-charge engine (a revolution still waiting to happen), I concluded that, if G-d had meant engines to be turbocharged, He might at least have shown us the way to computerise variable injection and ignition timing.

He did; and what happened? The first fruits were garnered in the improbable world of motor racing, where social necessities were imposed on competitors for the sake of respectability. It was a sign of the times that fuel consumption, second only to emissions in the popular motorist's green-hazed conscience, should (for a few seasons in the 1980s) be made a crucial factor in Formula 1. We may be glad that the work done in both fields has been complementary; the electronics industry should be proud.

Control systems now display extraordinary efficacy. They can be sensitive not only to such familiar factors as speeds, loads, manifold pressures and engine temperatures, but also to transients of defiant brevity such as incipient knock, and to ambients of hitherto unsuspected importance such as fuel temperature.

Such systems have made the F1 racing engine a thing of remarkable fuel efficiency as well as formidable power; they have made the production engine capable of feats (such as burning 'impossibly' lean mixtures) which make it practically more useful and socially – if not factually – less undesirable than ever before.

Given the potential inside the black box, much more can now be done. Electronics are trusted now, having proved better able than we ourselves are to supervise our braking and damping, our steering and air conditioning, our tuning of radio or engine. Electronics will therefore be entrusted with management of the entire transmission: starting with wheelspin control already, the process will end with thoroughly, sensibly, impeccably, steplessly, and incomparably automatic ratio selection and engagement; and not before time.

After that, there will be other jobs to be done, perhaps better, certainly differently. And all because we did not argue when the transistorised car followed in the popular wake of the transistorised radio.

Nasty things can happen when we argue from false premises. We argued against compulsory use of seat belts, back in those generally salutary sixties; so it was judged necessary by the Legislators (whose premises are almost always false) to enforce standards of crash-resistant construction which made the car heavy, thirsty, and frighteningly ungainly. It took a long time for the industry to correct these faults while continuing to meet the standards, and it made certain unscrupulously mealy-mouthed advertisers an ill-deserved fortune while T C Mits and JQP were conned into believing them.

It reminds me of something else that happened in that stupendous seven-year cycle. John F Kennedy was elected president of the USA, and was assassinated – but not before he had pointed out one of the truths of revolution, that the people who resist gentle progressive change are the people who bear the responsibility for the violent change which becomes its substitute.

CHAPTER 11

THE AIR INSIDE

WITHIN EIGHTEEN MONTHS OF THE launch, in 1964, of the Ford Mustang in the USA, the Ford Motor Company – having already sold half a million of the thing, mostly the lower-priced, lower-powered six-cylinder version – recognised that Joe Q Public was as ready as ever to gratify any appetite that he could be persuaded to believe he had. Accordingly the company's British arm prepared and in 1969 offered to T C Mits a long-bonneted closed coupé, its sporting pretensions cloaking an assembly of Cortina-based components, named Capri; and the offer was made to appear as though it were Ford's response to demand, the Capri being advertised as 'the car you always wanted'.

British and European motorists were entirely happy to believe the slogan, and the Capri was a great and lasting success. It was, however, by no means the first example of that golden rule of merchandising which states that demand is best established by making potential customers yearn for something that they had not previously realised they wanted. That rule was effective even before the coming of the Industrial Revelation promoted mass selling, a century before Ford's assembly line exemplified mass production. It had indeed been demonstrated with great effect by a young man who was born in 1784.

He was Frederic Tudor, the fourth son of an upper-crust Bostonian who was George Washington's Judge Advocate General. The lad's three brothers were sent to Harvard, and doubtless (since those who have the fortune to go there are seldom given to doubt) graduated to the status of regular solid citizens. Young Frederic, however, was not given to the idea of studious monotony; he wanted to get on, to get up and go. While yet only 13, he got up and went from school; presumably not short of capital behind him, nor of the persuasive art that would enable him to have access to it, he became a merchant.

That was not enough. It is not given to revolutionaries to recognise the concept or expression of 'enough'; young Frederic now set himself up as an inventor. He had numerous ideas, all of them so positively preposterous and so negatively profitable that, one day when his notions were under review, one of his brothers admitted to some surprise that Frederic had not tried to break up the ice on the Boston ponds and ship it to the tropics.

The logic of this enchanted the youngest of the Tudors. Selling snowballs to Esquimaux might be the popular example of commercial folly, but selling them to Hottentots . . . ! As a start, he shipped 130 tons of ice to Martinique. It melted in six weeks.

Any of the major European architects could have told him that ice needs insulation. The typical great country house[20] of the aristocrat living a luxurious life in a temperate climate usually had buried in its grounds an ice house, in which the winter's ice (from the garden's ornamental water features, if no natural source were at hand) was stored to serve the summer needs of larder and pantry. Underground storage helped keep it cool, but insulation of various sorts was used too.

Frederic investigated the practical possibilities of insulants in endless variety, eventually settling on a commodity that was always cheaply available in the age before iron: sawdust. With that problem solved, he next set about rationalising the packaging of the product: he wanted ice-blocks of uniform size. A friend created an ice cutter in the form of a sled with two parallel runners of saw-toothed iron: drawn by horse across the frozen ponds, it did the trick.

Within fifteen years, the business was big. Tudor had obtained title to the New England ponds, and had acquired monopoly rights to the building of ice houses in Charleston, New Orleans and Havana. His own fleet was shipping ice, thousands of tons of it, to the West Indies, to Europe, even to India and Persia[21].

---

20 This was the first desideratum of such a person, as was made clear in a famous listing by G K Chesterton:

I wish I had three hundred thousand pounds
Invested in some strong security;
A midland country house, with formal grounds,
A town house, and a house beside the sea . . .

21 The story so far is the American story. In Russia, at the same time as Tudor was developing his trade, a Jewish family (later, on their travels west, to take the name Bielefeld) made themselves rich by cutting ice in the gripping winter of the deep interior, wrapping the blocks in sacking, and floating them downriver to the big resort towns of the wealthy on the sunbathed coast of the Black Sea.

His customers were delighted with it – but they were not entirely sure what to do with it. Tudor's first response was to take a sea tour, convincing bemused customers that a hospital without ice was little more than a plague-foundry, that the ancient sages' advice against putting chilled food into a warm tummy was based on ignorance of the salutary virtues of iced drinks and ice cream. Then, having ensured that the rich and fashionable would continue as exemplary customers, he set about cheapening his service – simpler ice houses, price reductions for bulk orders, undercutting his competitors, and so on – so that the mass of people might affordably indulge in refinements previously the preserve of the wealthy. What had

been a luxury became (as the car was to become, after being first a curiosity and then a luxury) a necessity.

The need for it became more intense as the cities grew and had to be fed. The regular visit of the iceman made it possible, for the urban housewife whose husband's providence extended to the installation of an ice-box in the kitchen, to store and serve foodstuffs (notably meat and dairy products) that would otherwise perish faster than they could be bought in the sweat-spattered streets of a summer city. But then the growing cities – not only the industrial cities which would in due course make cars and componentry, but also the commercial cities which would sell them and fund them – needed their own scaled-up cold-storage services to the warehouses and the retail outlets. As the machine age flourished, so flourished the science of thermodynamics and the technology of refrigeration; and the big cities flourished with them, as they could never have flourished without them. The great food factories, the railroad cars which supplied them, the ships which ferried meat from Argentina or New Zealand to Britain, or eventually fished off Cape Province for Spain or in the Pacific for Russia, all depended on refrigeration.

Chilling food and other things was welcome enough, but chilling the very air was a more difficult matter. Yet there were industries that needed it if they were to keep pace with the development of an increasingly urban civilisation. Crude fans had moved the air in ships and in mines for some time before improvements in know-how allowed the same to be done for the Johns Hopkins hospital; that was a start, but textiles mills, colour-printing works, chemical factories and other industries – tobacco, for instance – all called for control of air temperature and humidity. It was an American named Willis Carrier who in 1906 first hit on an effective method, soon proved in industry. By 1922 Carrier's 'man-made weather' had been adapted to the needs of a theatre in California, by 1928 to an office building in Texas; but then the Great Depression struck, and then the war, and it was 1949 before the United Nations Building in New York spearheaded further developments. In the 1950s little air-conditioning units became available (even as retro-fits, to be found in places as implausible as the venerable Algonquin Hotel in Manhattan) for domestic service, and it seemed as though life need never be the same again.

If it seemed that all these developments were taking place in parallel with the development of the motor car, that was reasonable: the process of using mechanical energy to effect a heat-change, which lay at the heart of refrigeration and air-conditioning, was the exact reverse of the process of using heat to produce mechanical energy, which was the essence of the internal combustion engine[22].

Common to both processes was that device known as a heat exchanger, more familiar to motorists as the misnamed 'radiator'. The water which circulated around the cylinders of early car engines was inefficiently cooled by passing through gilled tubes exposed to the air, but in 1901 Daimler's new Mercédès pioneered the more efficient 'honeycomb' heat exchanger which passed far more air close to much less water; in the 1930s came the modern film-block version which was far better still. So why were such devices so slow to be adapted for controlling the conditions inside the body of the car, where the passengers froze or sweltered according to the season?

Quite simply, most early cars were open-bodied, and any such system (though it could have been devised within the competence of the times) would have been doomed to waste its sweetness on the desert air. Only when the new techniques involving pressed steel[23] began to make the closed car an affordable and attractive proposition did the question arise; but by then the motor industry was addressing customers who were painfully price-conscious and could not have countenanced the extra cost of even a simple interior-heating system such as might have been installed with a heat-exchanger through which engine coolant might be circulated[24]. People simply assumed, and accepted, that they would have to manage in their cars as they managed in their homes, by manipulating windows and shutters.

The need was real enough. Quite apart from temperature effects, the mere process of living results in readily perceptible and eventually objectionable physical and chemical changes in the atmosphere. Some of the oxygen in the air is converted to carbon dioxide. Moisture, heat, and airborne organic matter (the last usually perceived as odour) are liberated. In addition to these tributes to any human (or other animal) presence, the interior of a car might in those days[25] yield airborne traces of varnishes, paints, leather, upholstery materials, and seepages of fuel or lubricants from the engine compartment, fuel and oil tanks, and exhaust fumes sucked back into the car after discharge from the engine. Even in civilised domestic conditions, where one might expect an airspace of more than 200 ft^3 per person, it takes 5 ft^3 of fresh air a minute to keep the impression of stale air at bay. In a closed car, conditions are much worse.

By the 1970s, there were already a few cars capable of effecting a complete change of air inside the body twice a minute. By studying the aerodynamics of the bodywork so as to determine in what high-pressure zone fresh air should be admitted[26], and into what low-pressure zone vitiated air should be discharged[27], and by supplementing this velocity-induced flow with a fan-induced through draught at low speeds or when stationary, engineers had made the interior a much more pleasant place to inhabit; and those same studies had shown where and in what direction the engine exhaust should be discharged if turbulent backdraughts were not to bring its smoke and smells back inside the car.

In the early days of the closed car there was no such science. Each car was a matter for practical experiment, opening some windows and closing others, noting which wound up and down and which were hinged like flaps. If the occupants were robust enough to generate visible clouds of tobacco smoke, it would be helpful in visualising the flow; other guides (and inhibitors) were draughts and noise. Even in bitterly cold weather, it was essential to have at least one window open: many supposed this to be necessary so that the driver could make the hand signals that were then conventional, and it was true that this explained why the chosen window was usually that adjacent to the driver[28], but in fact the opening was needed to prevent exhaled moisture condensing as an obscuring mist on the chilled surfaces of the

---

22 It was not incidental that the most inspiring teacher, at the Technische Hochschule in Munich, of the brilliant student named Rudolf Diesel was one of the great authorities on refrigeration.

23 See Part 4 Chapter 3.

24 Renault, who into the 1920s strenuously resisted the example of Panhard and kept the 'radiator' between the engine and the passengers, could divert some of the hot vitiated air from the radiator into the cabin; but in time even Renault capitulated and adopted the Panhard system.

25 By the 1970s one of the worst offenders was the whole family of thermoplastics, used on a large scale for upholstery and cabin trim. The plasticisers in it would leach out when it was hot, and condense again on the windows, gradually dirtying and darkening them. The smell was less than pleasant. Industry had to work hard to diminish the problem.

26 The leader in this scientific enquiry was the aerodynamicist Dr Kamm, working like several other specialists (especially in Germany) on drag-reduction. His most famous and influential work was done on an experimental BMW body in the late 1930s.

27 Often by some devious route through the luggage boot or at the rear edge of a door. Windows had ceased to play a part in cabin-air control.

28 The Park Ward-bodied Lagonda M45 saloon of 1935 had a quick-action lever for the driver's window: bash it forward and the pane dropped as though from the gallows, haul it back and it rose heavily. All other doors had conventional window-winders.

29 This could be a particular hazard at high altitudes. On a good sporting open car the windscreen could be folded flat, entirely out of the way, ensuring the best possible vision at the cost of a frozen face.

window glass. In particularly humid weather and in fog[29], as well as to obtain a refreshing draught on really hot days, most windscreens could be opened – usually a couple of inches, sometimes much more – at the bottom, the framed glass being hinged at the top and clamped in its chosen place by wing nuts or knurled knobs.

Inevitably, it was as cold inside the car as outside; so people dressed as though for the outside, in overcoats and scarves, hats and gloves, all supplemented with rugs and muffs and even hot-water bottles. In some cars there were little flaps in the front footwells or elsewhere on the front bulkhead, admitting warm air from the engine compartment into the passenger compartment, but all too often that warmed air reeked of hot oil or of petrol leaking from ill-fitting unions or a defective carburettor. In other cars the air (and its accompanying stinks) found its way in through chinks in the toe-board or bulkhead, and had to be tolerated whether one liked it or not.

Hot weather was more easily managed. The ventilation offered by open windows could often be improved through small vent flaps or scoops through which fresh air from outside could be led into the sides of the front footwells. Sometimes these flaps could be operated from inside the car; sometimes one had to get out to set them; and many a time they would fail to stay as they were set and gradually or suddenly close themselves again. It was some consolation if they remained sealed in the cold season.

The coming of the interior heater was slow (for cars with air-cooled engines it was even slower), but it was inevitable. In the 1930s it was a commonplace optional extra in American cars, and in only twenty years it enjoyed the same status in Britain. By the end of the 1950s it was pretty well a standard part of the everyday car's apparatus, with all the side-effects on clothing and domestic heating noted elsewhere in this book. And maybe it was some kind of compensation for Britain's notorious backwardness in accepting and preparing for the vagaries of climate that saw Britain the home in 1963 of a fundamental rethink about the workings of the heater.

It had been an unsatisfactory device, awkward to control and unpredictable in effect. Air passed through a film-block heat exchanger, picking up heat from engine coolant that was being pumped through by way of a by-pass pipe in the water-cooling circuit. You want more heat? Open further the turncock which valves the flow of hot water. You want less? Turn the valve the other way. How far? Search me. How long will it take? Nobody can even guess.

It was absurd, and suddenly in 1963 Ford of Britain had enabled us to see clearly how absurd it was. The new Cortina had a new heating and ventilation system, and most minds were turned to it by the novel appearance of some 'eyeball' ventilators set into the fascia panel. Some of them were there only for controlling the input of fresh unheated ambient air, rammed into the car by its speed and sucked out again by its wake. The others were fed air from the heater – but now the temperature control was instant, and could be exercised with accuracy because the effect could be sensed immediately. All Ford had done was to delete the water valve, leaving the flow of hot water at constant full bore; but now, by mixing air from the heater matrix with air that had by-passed it, and by varying the proportions of the mix, the chilled or superheated driver could by fingering a single lever draw from those eyeballs an immediate fix. The world had become a better place – though it took a few years for all other manufacturers to copy.

It was also becoming a better place because the clumsy old dynamo of *Dreadnought* days was being rapidly supplanted by the alternator, proven in America to generate more electricity at idling speed than the dynamo, and to go on generating even more as its speed rose beyond the dynamo's inherent limitations. Now it was feasible for a car to use electricity more freely, the world could become a place that was better still, more clearly visible. It was not just a matter of better headlamps, it was also a matter of mist-clearance.

In luxury cars first (Rolls-Royce offered it in 1948), and soon in any car that we might call well-equipped, the rear window had printed on or even in its glass a heating element which, fed with lusty current, would warm the surface enough to dispel the moisture condensed on it when a breathing driver first clambered into a cold car. No longer did the morning begin with a long wait for the heater to divine the engine's calorific output at a distance[30], while the hapless driver (dressed for a warmed car, and cursing the need to stand about in the chilly air with the doors open) sought to clear the fogged windows with a cloth, with paper tissues, with a discarded wiper blade, and always with a curse for the rash folk who set out immediately and

---

30 In really cold climes, the drill was different. Coming home in the dark evening of an electrically lit winter's day in Lapland, where only the dull black of the trees hinted which grey was sky and which was snow, the motorist garaged his car and took out its battery, to keep it warm indoors for the morning start. In those miserable latitudes, where the temperature may be around -40° (C or F, it makes no difference), the power of the battery drops faster than the mercury of the thermometer. Some cars (as in Canada and elsewhere) have petrol-burning auxiliary heaters, run for half an hour or so to get the car safely warm, its battery alive and its lubricants uncongealed, before starting.

impatiently with no more view of the road than they could wipe by hand from behind the wheel.

It took a good many years before the same electrical heating could be applied, by wires so fine as to cheat the eye, to the windscreen – still a rare thing, although first fitted to a small Ford. It took almost as many years for the external mirrors of some cars to be electrically heated. But what took longest of all was for the motorist outside the southern states of the USA to appreciate that proper air-conditioning nipped in the bud all the processes of condensation inside the car.

Nash in the USA did very well out of advertising that their new 1938 car had air-conditioning. By our understanding of the term, Nash were telling a fib – all they offered was really a better-than-average heating and ventilation system – and the first to make the real thing available were Packard in 1941. Everyone assumed that the sole purpose of air-conditioning in a car was to keep the interior cool when the outside world was panting hot, and the majority reckoned that the considerable cost of the extra equipment was not going to be justified in the northern states.

Everyone, as usual, was wrong. The process of chilling the air also dehumidified it. That cold dry air could then, if appropriate to the weather, be reheated by conventional means before passing it into the cabin; but it would remain dry. The windows would remain clear. If you doubted it, all you had to do was to switch off the air-conditioning – and be ready to hit the brake pedal as the windows suddenly clouded[31].

Public acceptance of this demonstration of basic physics was slow and resentful, fed by a suspicion that if air-conditioning were really necessary we should all have had it long ago and it would by now be much cheaper. The well-heeled and the well-educated took to it in the 1990s; the rest, as had happened in the USA twenty years earlier, glared in resentment at the car going by with all its windows closed on a searing hot day, its serene and soberly jacketed occupants clearly showing off. But those well-dressed people were just as glad of their modern apparatus in the dead of winter, and understood better than most when Honda, announcing in 1998 that they were to build a new small economy car for the needful millions of China and adjacent Asiatic fastnesses, explained that air conditioning would be a standard part of the specification. It was no longer a luxury; it had been recognised as a necessity.

---

31 Worse could happen. Setright once contrived a fall of snow inside a parked Rolls-Royce on a wet night.

CHAPTER 12

FOUR-WHEEL EQUALITY

From each according to abilities; to each according to needs.

KARL MARX

MODERN TIMES, WHICH WERE UNDOUBTEDLY upon us by 1800, may have begun in 1776. It makes no difference whether you consider the reason for this to be the proclamation in that year of America's Declaration of Independence, or the working establishment of the partnership formed with Matthew Boulton a year earlier which enabled James Watt to make and sell the world's first practical steam engines. Either of these happenings would suffice alone to found an epoch; but in fact they should be seen together, for the Declaration was merely a statement of intent, and it was steam which unified America by making possible communications over distances ten times greater (and therefore over an area a hundred times greater) than could be administered by a central government relying upon the horse.

Nevertheless, early motor manufacturers – while misguidedly taking many of their engine and transmission notions from steam practice – continued to derive their ideas of chassis construction from horse-drawn carriages. That was why, for a long time, they failed to understand what the pneumatic tyre did and could do. To them, it was merely a device for cushioning the ride, a supplementary suspension element. The incredibly inept steering and braking provisions of early cars were due to the fact that before their time it had been the horse which (duly encouraged by tongue and whip, though only the latter found its way into the Highway Code) steered, did some of the braking, and provided all the traction.

That was why some pioneers argued in favour of front-wheel drive that it was natural for the horse to go before the cart. Had the wretched animal been given periscopic vision, it might with advantage have been put behind; but the early cars were made by a process of adaptation, not by origination.

The crude friction-block brakes of the horse-drawn carriage were applied to its rear wheels, because that was easier than putting them on the pivoted front axle which turned with the traces strapped to the horse. Precisely the same argument was advanced for rear-wheel brakes on early cars, and usage became so crippling a convention that the motor-racing fraternity bitterly opposed four-wheel brakes until 1914, when Delage, Fiat, Peugeot (most significantly) and Piccard Pictet adopted them. The example had been set by Isotta Fraschini a year earlier, and the same firm's touring cars had them as early as 1909. At the other extreme Rolls-Royce fought against the idea until 1923.

The difficulties involved in making four-wheel brakes work satisfactorily have been reviewed already in this book, when I explained how they were only decently resolved by the use of hydraulics – though Vauxhall devised a clever system of pneumatically powered brakes for their very advanced 1922 TT racer[32]. Yet there was still a reluctance to make the front tyres do the braking work that they could (that is, the majority of it) even a decade later: cars boasting four-wheel brakes (with a little red triangle on the tail to warn following traffic!) had little front brakes and big back brakes.

The front tyres, people said, were for steering; the back ones were for making the car go, and so they must be the ones for making it stop. The notion that all four tyres had a share in the steering was only beginning to dawn upon a few enquiring engineers, led by Maurice Olley (first at Rolls-Royce and then at Cadillac), some time between Lindbergh making his solo flight across the Atlantic, in 1927, and America building a record 4.5 million cars in a year, in 1929. The almighty crash which followed had nothing to do with brakes or steering . . .

It was the Wall Street Crash, and it shattered capitalistic society. Economic disaster and mass unemployment were hardly the background for America to build her 50-millionth car, as happened in 1931; far from having any capital to spend, too many people had not even any income.

What Karl Marx might have thought of this is beyond conjecture, but presumably the author of *Das Kapital* would not have recommended giving cars to those who needed them and taking the payments from whoever had any money. He

---

32 Voisin was even cleverer. He used the rotation of each wheel to drive a pneumatic compressor which energised the brake when it was applied. Thus the braking force was proportional to the speed, and as the wheel slowed to a standstill (whether because the car was doing the same, or because the tyre had lost adhesion) braking assistance was nullified. Voisin's system provided anti-lock characteristics decades before they were sought.

had advanced his 'From each . . . To each . . .' principle in 1875, 27 years after his Communist Manifesto (and 15 years before he denied being a Marxist!), but he was besotted with his naïve idea of the class struggle. Not being an Englishman or an Indian, Dr Marx was unable to appreciate the nature of, and the distribution of responsibilities within, a society structured according to class, sharing instead the belief common in other and vulgar countries that it had something to do with wealth.

What some of those vulgarians did (and, to their credit, they saw that it was better than continuing to fight in the Great War) was to initiate the greatest revolution of what we have defined as modern times, the Russian Revolution. Ironically, while the lower classes provided the mechanics of it, the Revolution was engineered by the intelligentsia of the middle classes, who were meant to pool their abilities and needs with the peasants. As sometimes happens when matters are left to engineers, things went wrong, and as a result one of the world's biggest and potentially greatest nations was effectively taken out of scientific and technical circulation for longer than it could afford.

Meanwhile the capitalist nations continued to make war, to make progress, and to make money. America in particular amassed enormous wealth, although it was not until the late 1930s that any serious attempt was made to improve its distribution. Serving (if that be the word) as 'the arsenal for Europe' in the Great War was what made the USA rich enough to enjoy millions of cars, and to do it even better next time around. It is salutary to remember that while the British forces in the Second World War made extensive use of the Bedford truck, the German forces made similar use of the Opel truck, and the profits from both firms continued to be paid to General Motors in the USA even after Pearl Harbor.

A year or so before that assault brought the USA into the war (though nothing ever brought the war into the USA), the Arsenal created a car of sorts that was destined to give more drivers a better idea of the advantages of allowing tyres to share duties than any other before or since. The Jeep astonished everybody with its abilities, not least those who drove it.

Had its potential been developed, four-wheel drive might by now be commonplace. Instead, the very components that it might have protected were developed to make it appear an unnecessarily expensive contrivance. When the Ferguson four-wheel-drive system of the 1960s was built into a 1.5-litre GP car, and later into a 2-litre sports-racing car, it proved unbeatable in the wet; but at the same time the tyre manufacturers were introducing new wares which, exploiting new polymers and new modes of construction which allowed more generous tread areas and more responsive carcasses, could better cope with the increased performance of the latest racing cars.

A few years later, when another brief flirtation with 4wd saw Cosworth, Lotus, Matra and McLaren stymied by the reluctance of leading drivers to waste time experimenting with novelties, wings arrived to provide artificial loadings for newer and even wider tyres that could then take and transmit all the urge of the latest engines.

As for the use by Jensen of the Ferguson 4wd system in their 1968 FF, it was their own caution which killed it. Playing safe, they also offered a 2wd version, the Interceptor, which looked so nearly identical (and exceedingly handsome, at that) that the image-builders lusting after a Jensen saw no virtue in spending extra thousands of pounds for the one which behaved well, when the much cheaper (and in behaviour much nastier) Interceptor looked just the same, just as good.

The tragedy of the Jensen was doubled, because with the FF system came anti-lock braking as well as 4wd; and with the FF they both went. It would be almost a decade before either returned; when they did, it was in circumstances that proved Dr Marx wrong yet again. Discussing Hegel's proposition that all great events and personalities in history reappear in some guise or another, he added: 'The first time as tragedy, the second as farce.' Well, the Jensen may have been tragic, but the Audi Quattro was anything but farcical.

Audi achieved a miracle with that car: they actually made us think. They showed that since all four tyres supported the car, steered the car, and braked the car, a properly even distribution of stresses demanded that they should also share the work of propelling it. Moreover, they showed that because of the non-linear characteristics of tyres, the energy absorbed by four tyres each doing a quarter of the total work was less than was consumed by two tyres each doing a half, and (in a consumption-conscious society, as ours then was) that this slightly enhanced efficiency finally justified the cost and weight of the extra transmission elements, even if the greatly enhanced performance and safety might not appeal to everyone.

Incidental to all this was the fact that the system had to be partially disabled for anti-lock braking to work. Curiously, this made people much more conscious of the importance of lock-inhibitors than they had been, even though BMW and Daimler-Benz had been giving it plenty of emphasis.

What they all missed was something that was only spotted by another nation, which had lately been making more progress and more money than any other. In

Japan it was revealed by Mazda in 1983 that they were toying with the idea of four-wheel steering, electronically controlled so as to increase understeer and stability at high speeds and oversteer and agility at low speeds. Honda, who had revealed in 1980 their work on anti-lock systems costing far less than the German ones, said nothing about what I had thought a promising idea; but in 1987 they demonstrated their 4ws method, in which the steering of the rear tyres in additive or subtractive modes was made dependent on the degree of steer-angle input by the driver, and in which speed as such was quite irrelevant.

Not even the Audi Quattro, nor even the Jeep, came as such a dazzling revelation of truths to which, though they were now blatantly obvious, we had all been blind. Obviously, all four tyres on any car share the work of steering the car; obviously, active steering of all four will produce more direct and immediate and accurate results, free of spurious yaw and roll effects, than the conventional method of active steering at the front and passive steering at the rear which introduces a couple of phases of delay and confusion (and therefore of potential danger) in any steering manoeuvre; obviously, it should be possible with totally active steering to modulate the responses of the car so that it always feels consistent (perhaps preferably, but not necessarily, neutral) regardless of speed or lateral acceleration.

Obviously, it is only when this is achieved that the front and rear tyres can be reckoned to take fair shares of steering duty; equally obviously, the Honda method – which is unique in achieving this – is the right method, or at the very least the best and only satisfactory method so far.

So far? Revolutions take time; they need precursors, just as Russia had a bit of a revolution in 1907 before the big one in 1917. Pietro Amati in Italy built a really neat 4ws prototype in 1927; F W Dixon and A P R Rolt (the latter forever associated with FF Developments, except by those who recall him as a distinguished racing driver) attempted a similar chassis a decade later. Mazda clearly came closer to what was wanted, but stopped thinking just a shade too soon.

Some people only started thinking after they realised how astonishingly effective the Honda system is. When it was announced, every other manufacturer on the planet pronounced it rubbish, with a conviction so empty that babes yet unborn may hear its echoes and laugh. Within a year, many of those manufacturers were privately admitting that they were working on it, and some were even advancing ideas that they thought might improve upon it. That is quite all right: if revolutions have precursors, they should also leave(*pace* Marx) legacies. The Prelude should have a sequel.

It will only be acceptable if the improvements are real. Much more probable, I fear, is that four-wheel steering will suffer the same corruption as has four-wheel drive. How many rival manufacturers, obliged to match Audi in the market-place without conceding anything to Audi in respect or in royalties, have brought out patent-dodging alternative methods of insinuating four-wheel drive into otherwise ordinary cars? How many of those competing systems do not give full-time drive to all four tyres, but instead leave two of them doing all the work most of the time, merely summoning useful effort from all the additional machinery to divert some traction to the other two tyres when the first two can no longer cope? How many?

Too many. If the same thing happens to corrupt four-wheel steering, the motoring world will once again be confused by marketing men, misled by avarice, and deprived of something wonderful, just as happened with the Jensen.

On the other hand, it is possible that something better will emerge, just as there are now better full-time 4wd systems than the one in the original Quattro. It is this possibility which encourages me to reconsider my view of the greatest revolution of modern times; for it occurs to me that time may show it to have been the wave of permissiveness which washed so many nations in the late 1960s.

Grundies and groanies may treat 'permissiveness' as automatically deplorable; but what does the word say – except that, whilst I am indubitably right, you (despite maintaining views quite contrary to mine) may also be equally right? Should that idea strike you as revolutionary (and I can think of only one society that has long treated it as axiomatic), consider whether *tolerant* or *dogmatic* better fits your notion of civilisation. Or would you rather whip a horse?

PART V

PERSONAL EFFECTS

CHAPTER 1

MAKING A START

IT IS AS TRUE TODAY as it was in the dawn of motoring: driving calls for skills that can be acquired and for aptitudes that must be innate. The cultivation of either may disguise some lack of the other, but can never wholly compensate for it. Those people who, confident in the superiority of their reasoning or perception, insist on the innate equality of all people may sometimes be reduced to impotent protest by the evident inability of some people to drive as well as others; the fact that such failures often strenuously deny their ineptitudes makes the problem no easier to resolve, but a problem it remains. As the cartoonist Fougasse observed in *Punch* half a century ago, no man – however modestly dismissive of his abilities as a scholar or an athlete, however frankly he might admit to being a duffer at golf, a goof at tennis, a flop at the piano or even a failure with the ladies – will admit to being anything but excellent as a driver.

The motor industry knows better. Recognising the commercial truth that if cars are to be sold to more people they must be made manageable by more people, the industry has for more than a hundred years devoted much energy to making driving an easier task. In the course of that century we might observe several distinct tendencies: one is to reduce the amount of physical effort demanded of the driver, a second is to reduce the need for practised coordination of different activities, a third is to eliminate any non-linear response to the operation of a given control, and a fourth (most recently) is an attempt to protect the driver from the consequences of his own injudicious actions by systems intervening to modulate his control inputs. Overall there is a fifth, which is to relieve the driver from any need to understand the workings of the apparatus in his charge.

It was perhaps rash of the pioneer car-makers to assume that the owner would be so enthusiastic about the possibilities of the new motoring that he would avidly study everything pertinent to his machinery, would master the niceties of mixture control and ignition advance and the mechanical conversion of crankshaft torque to tractive effort. The assumption was rash even in the pursuit of the further assumption that the owner would employ a professional driver, for if that owner were himself technically ignorant he would be unable to assess the suitability of the servant he put in charge of his vehicle.

All too often the new owner, assured that his novel vehicle was (as indeed it sometimes looked) merely a horseless carriage, assumed that his coachman would be able to undertake these new duties – one of the most rash of all assumptions. Quite frequently the main criterion applied in the choice of a chauffeur would be his physical strength, in view of the effort visibly required for starting the engine.

It could be a daunting process. Even when cylinders were few, they were large; even when fuels were so poor or so variable that compression ratios were low, it still took a lot of weight or of muscular exertion to turn the crankshaft by means of the handle supplied (sometimes as a separate tool, and sometimes as a permanent fixture semi-permanently disengaged by a hold-off spring) smartly enough for the piston to draw in a supply of air/fuel mixture and compress it for ignition. Slow in their motions and erratic in their convulsions, primitive engines needed large and heavy flywheels to smoothen their rotations; but the very inertia that they supplied to ease the task of keeping the starting handle swinging made the swing harder work to initiate.

All the time there was the dreaded hazard of the backfire. If the ignition were (as in the early Daimlers) by hot tube – which had first to have its burner primed and lit and sustained, however wet and windy the weather, until the platinum tube was incandescent – there was no telling at what point ignition of the charge in the cylinder might occur. If the ignition were electrical, the point might be known; but if there were no means for retarding it so that the spark happened after the piston had reached and passed the highest point in its compression stroke, then premature ignition[1] might cause combustion violent enough to reverse the direction of the engine's rotation. This reversal of the crankshaft carried the starting handle with it; and it was not unknown for that kickback to carry the man manipulating the handle with it. More

---

1 Very early engines were slow-running and it never occurred to their makers that the spark should ever occur before the end of the compression stroke. Even so, the presence of some local hot-spot (most commonly a deposit of carbon) within the cylinder might be enough to induce premature ignition.

often than flinging him in the air it simply broke his thumb, and for decades instruction manuals carefully recommended that the thumb be not opposed to the fingers but should instead be laid over the handle. This precaution was not always enough: the inept man starting a violent engine might still suffer a broken wrist or forearm.

It was at least as likely that nothing would happen at all. If the engine did not want to start, one might swing the handle for half an hour and achieve nothing. Many early engines had hopelessly erratic mixture provision, often relying on the surface evaporation of the early very light and highly volatile petrol[2] pooled in the body of the carburettor. As a further handicap, early engines had 'automatic' inlet valves, innocent of mechanical actuation but held closed by a very light spring: the partial vacuum induced in the cylinder by the piston moving downwards during its induction stroke caused atmospheric pressure to lift this lightly sprung valve allowing fresh mixture to flood in. Swing the handle too slowly and the valve might never open enough.

So there often had to be another chore before starting: priming cocks – little taps atop each cylinder – would have to be unscrewed and a presciently judged modicum of petrol poured in before the cocks were screwed tightly closed again, leaving enough neat petrol in each cylinder to provide a rich vapour that could readily be ignited – though not so wet that it moistened the spark-plug points, in which event the engine still would not start. Once the engine fired, there was a good chance that it would keep running[3].

One way or another, starting drills could become very complex rituals. By about 1910 it took a veritable Briareus to manage the procedure: using the variety of handles, levers, ratchets, screws, valves and sight-glasses provided, one might have to check the presence of fuel in the tank, pump up air-pressure within it[4] to deliver fuel to the carburettor, open the main fuel tap, adjust the hand throttle, retard the ignition, engage any half-compression device such as had become popular in big engines, adjust the rich-mixture control or alternatively make use of priming cocks, turn on the main oil-supply tap beneath the tank of lubricant, adjust any drip-feeds downstream of that tap, check that the handbrake was engaged and the gearlever in neutral position, and finally switch on the ignition circuit. Then one might address the starting handle.

It all made work for the working man to do. If the driver were not a working man, he might be irritated by it all, and especially by the last item on the list. Let him buy a car of good quality, well made by meticulous engineers, and he might find that if there were any vestiges of warmth and of petrol vapour remaining in his engine after the last time it was used, he could simply 'start on the switch': a flick of the ignition advance/retard lever would produce a spark (or in the case of trembler-coil ignition systems a stream of sparks) in one cylinder, igniting the residue of unburnt mixture trapped there when the ignition was last turned off.

It might work. It often did; but it was not entirely dependable. This might be profoundly worrying to the Czar of All the Russias who, as we saw in an earlier chapter, was most at risk of assassination when mounted in his car and waiting to depart. It was at least irritating to the lesser owner of a lesser car, and when in 1914 Cadillac made electrical starting apparatus a standard provision, it was recognised that a new and significant step had been taken towards the popularisation of motoring. In the early years after the Great War, when there would be more ladies and fewer chauffeurs doing the driving, such provisions rapidly became universal.

One might have supposed that, as a consequence, the starting handle would then have disappeared. It did not. We are a mean, suspicious and grudging people, and when beset by the novel and unfamiliar (which by its nature cannot yet have proved itself trustworthy) we cling, as might a shipwrecked mariner cling to a raft, in desperation to what we know. We gladly bought our cars with batteries and electric starters and dynamos and the most modern ignition systems and carburettors, but we insisted on retaining our starting handles[5].

---

2 It was because of these ill-controlled evaporative carburettors (sometimes incorporating some sort of wick to increase the evaporative surface) that motor fuel was required to be so light and volatile. It was most unfortunate that the stuff sometimes called 'petrol' was also carelessly or pompously (there was a lot of pomposity around in those days) referred to as 'motor spirit': the unwitting and inexpert might then purchase some apothecary's white 'spirit' which was very much less volatile and quite unsuitable.

3 Not everybody knows the old maxim 'Never start anything you cannot stop'. Apart from the Morgan 3-wheeler and the Type 59 Bugatti (both of which mysteriously provided for insertion of the starting handle on the right flank of the car) and a sprinkling of rear-engined cars which understandably invited insertion of the thing from behind, cars commonly located their starting handles right in front, centrally between the wheels. Quite a lot of people have been run over by their own cars immediately after starting; for reasons connected with its unique transmission, most of these cars were Model T Fords.

4 Petrol pumps, whether mechanical or electrical, were rare in the early days. Cheap cars managed, until well into the 1950s, with gravity feed.

5 The same would happen when run-flat or puncture-proof tyres became available. He was rare and valorous who would venture out without a spare wheel and tyre.

We were right. Our batteries (we should properly have called them accumulators, but we were always careless of technical propriety) were untrustworthy, leaking and boiling and suffering grave abasement of the voltage when cold. Our dynamos (which only charged at their full rate when the car itself was charging at top speed, but proffered little when the engine ran slowly through the murk or the blizzard) were not always up to the task of replenishing the batteries as quickly as our headlamps and starters could deplete them.

So the clever driver adopted a battery-saving drill for the first cold start of the day. First he would open the bonnet and tickle the carburettor(s) – which meant depressing the little button on top of the float chamber, forcing the float down and thus partially flooding the instrument with fuel, to serve much the same purpose as the priming-cocks of an earlier era[6]. Then he would set the choke or rich-mixture control, make sure that the gearbox was in neutral and that the ignition was switched off, and then give the engine a couple of turns of the starting handle. This would break down the initial 'stiction'[7] of chilled oil in the bearings and with luck induce a charge of rich mixture in the cylinders. Finally, with the ignition suitably retarded (if there were manual means of doing so) and the ignition switched on, he elected either to give the starting handle a smart upward pull or, if nervous of backfire and possible injury, would then apply the starter motor to what should now be an easier task.

In the 1920s and 1930s there was a further sophistry. In emulation of aero-engine practice, large and high-quality engines had two spark plugs per cylinder, served by two separate ignition systems. In cars, as distinct from aircraft, it became normal for one system to embody the conventional battery-and-coil apparatus for engendering sparks, while the other relied on the magneto[8], which generated its own electricity and needed no battery. The coil gave its best sparks at low rates; the magneto gave increasingly stronger sparks as the engine turned faster. Some people used the coil for starting and switched over to the magneto when the engine was warm; others left both switched on all the time, to which some engines responded well while others objected but faintly.

European cars began to lose their starting handles in the 1950s: as fuel quality improved, compression ratios increased to exploit it, and engines became literally too hard to handle. This had happened already in the USA, not only because fuel there had not suffered wartime degradation but also because the typically large American engine (especially if it were a V8) offered far too much resistance to being turned by hand. In a land where women drivers were much more numerous than elsewhere, the starting handle was intolerable. Yet, if the engines of the USA were big, so were the cars they propelled: there was everything to be said for really big batteries and really powerful starter motors.

There was less to be said in favour of the dynamo generators that were expected to sustain such systems. Structurally indisposed to turning at high speeds and electrically inefficient when doing so (in other words, they consumed considerable power in being driven), they were nevertheless poor in output at low speeds. As was only to be expected, it was the USA which came up with something better: the alternator, which generated AC current far more efficiently than the dynamo created DC, gave a respectable charge at virtually all speeds, could be spun twice as fast as the average engine, and weighed less than half as much as the equivalent dynamo. It began to make its mark in the USA in the 1950s, spread to Europe in the 1960s, and became pretty well universal in the 1970s.

With it, battery flattening became far less common. Now it was possible to equip a car with much more electrical apparatus: the electrically heated rear window allowed the driver a mist-free view behind, a plethora of lights (more powerful in the 1960s as the new quartz-iodine or 'halogen' lamps replaced the old incandescent tungsten-filament type) improved depth and detail perception of the view ahead. Radio and tape players, with more abundant and sometimes better loudspeakers, progressed from being optional extras to being basic expectations. So did cigarette lighters, though the salesman buttering up a customer always called them cigar lighters. Electrically powered windows first appeared in one of the notorious Docker Daimlers, before the days of alternators, but now they began to spread. For Scandinavian cars there were electrically heated seats, as there were for domestic cars marketed in the northern states of the USA; for the southern states, air conditioning was the thing, electrically fanned.

6 Some costly cars offered the driver a priming pump to be operated from his seat. Best known was the Kigass equipment, also to be found in some aircraft: pushing the pump knob caused neat petrol to be squirted into the inlet manifold.

7 Static friction. The word was coined in the aviation industry.

8 The original magneto invented by Simms in 1897 produced only a low-tension spark. A year later Boudeville came up with a high-tension instrument which was inherently far more suitable, and this was developed rapidly by Bosch.

Alternatives to the electric horn (which uses a lot of current, though seldom for long) disappeared, though there had once been elegant alternatives powered by hand or by engine inlet vacuum[9]. The same applied to windscreen wipers, and a good thing too: vacuum-operated wipers slowed down as the throttle was opened, the engine speed rose, and inlet manifold depression was weakened. The faster you went, the less you could see. Electrically powered windscreen washers followed, and electrical fuel pumps paved the way for the electronically controlled injection systems to come – not to mention all the gubbins in black boxes that would eventually follow. And it was only with that eventual coming – of electronically controlled fuel injection and ignition with full compensations and adjustments for temperature, fuel quality, barometric pressure, and the colour of the driver's eyes – that starting at last became as carefree[10] as it always should have been.

---

9 Until the 1950s, it was socially imperative that a horn have a 'good tone', and upper-class cars made a feature of wind-tone horns which were often conspicuously displayed at the front of the car, looking like baby chromium-plated trumpets. In the 1960s came an Italian-led fashion for shrill pneumatic trumpets supplied from a tiny electrically motored air compressor, which needed to be protected under the bonnet. After that, as people grew more sensitive to noise (or more ready to object to the sound of any noise caused by somebody else) all 'horns' degenerated into miserable little electric buzzers, resembling most drivers in having no identifiable tone at all.

10 And we, inevitably, became careless – to the point where we had to be protected from our own dim-witted ineptitude, with safety interlocks to prevent the engine being started if the transmission were not in neutral. Some even disallow a start unless the clutch pedal (if any) be depressed; some tried to require seat harness to be fastened first, but (in some countries, at least) the customers decided that this was going too far.

CHAPTER 2

CHANGING GEARS IN CHANGING TIMES

SO MUCH (as we have noted in the previous chapter) for persuading the engine to work. Now to make the car move. In the early days, this – like so many of the driver's tasks – could be quite hard work. It was emphatically not patronising to suggest that it was not a lady's work: even though they might be born healthy, by the time they were adults ladies[11] had been constrained by diet, upbringing, cloistering and clothing – especially by corseting – to enjoy little strength and less stamina. Fainting was almost expected of them; they were very different from the bigger, stronger and altogether more robust women of today. Admittedly there were some Edwardian ladies who not only went as well as men in the hunting field but also flourished on the hockey field or on the ski slopes; but for these activities, and possibly for bicycling, they were generally excused their stays, provided that they resumed normal whalebone-bound femininity promptly afterwards. Admittedly also there were working women who were not handicapped by the usages of the fashionable world, but they were rarely in a position of such prosperity that a car might be accessible to them. In the beginnings of the 20th century very few of them drove at all, and most of that few drove only the smaller machines available, or perhaps the little electric cars that were popular for a while in some towns such as New York.

In the larger cars, considerable leg power might be needed to operate the clutch pedal – or considerable weight, for most cars had fixed seating, at dining-chair height above the floor, and their pedals were therefore necessarily not far ahead of the heelboard. Indeed, quite a lot of very early cars had pedals resembling those of a piano. Others had huge things rising from beneath the toe-board but just as badly placed: ergonomics was an unknown science.

Once the clutch had been freed (and there was much confusion about the language of clutch operation: many were the blunders caused by misunderstanding what was meant by the clutch being 'in' or 'out', the terms being applied either to the pedal or to the mechanism itself without clear distinction) one had to pause for a few seconds for the gearbox internals to lose their inertia before engaging bottom gear with a waggle or a heave of the gearlever. Only then could the handbrake be released and the left leg eased at the clutch pedal to effect a smooth progression away from standstill.

It might as readily cause the engine to stall, or effect a start of neck-snapping jerkiness. Some early clutches were gentle enough, if frequently serviced – their leather friction surfaces needed much care – but many (notably the scroll variety) were abrupt and unforgiving. It is hardly surprising that, even disregarding the difficulties of gearlever manipulation and engine control, changing gear was something that most drivers preferred to avoid as much as possible.

In some modern languages the expression is 'shifting' gears, not 'changing' them. One understands; one sympathises; but the origin of the 'changing' is that in the earliest days we were not referring to gears at all: we spoke of changing *speeds*.

Indeed some of the earliest cars had no gearboxes, but relied on an adaptation of the flat belts and fast-and-loose pulleys used in factories for driving the spindles of machine tools at various speeds. It was a similar source, equally well known to the mechanical engineer, that provided a twin-shaft arrangement of fixed and sliding gears (rather like the 'back gearing' of a lathe, that best known of all machine tools) to constitute the gearbox which Panhard promoted so successfully that for some time it was an industry standard.

In Panhard's time, engines were very inflexible. Throttles in primitive carburettors were sometimes useless except for stopping the engine, automatic inlet valves allowed very little speed variation, and only by advancing or retarding the ignition, using the small lever conventionally ratcheting in a quadrant attached to the steering column either above or below the wheel, could the driver exercise much control over the rate at which the engine ran. With the engine so nearly a constant-speed device, the only way to vary the speed of the car was to change from one of the possible combinations of gears contained in the gearbox to another. That was how the expression 'change speed' became current, and is why we still speak of 'a four-*speed* gearbox' when 'a four-*ratio* gearbox' might be thought more accurate.

---

11 *I have defined Ladies,* wrote Gwen Raverat, *as people who did not do things themselves.*

For at least a decade, the gearbox with three or four speeds was operated by a lever sliding along a quadrant. One had to change speeds progressively, moving from one to the next in orderly sequence, with little lacunae or 'neutrals' between each of the positions where one or other sets of sliding gears had been brought into mesh. In 1901 Maybach introduced the gate change in his epoch-marking Mercédès, allowing any one of the four forward speeds to be selected from the one neutral position. Since this new car, so marvellous in comparison with any earlier Daimler, also had a decent carburettor and mechanically operated inlet valves to make it more flexible, we might more readily talk of changing gears; but we still preferred not to do so, for the internals of the gearbox were essentially the same as before and all the difficulties of coaxing the teeth of rotating cogs to fall into mesh with each other remained daunting to many drivers.

Double-clutching was the trick which made gear-shifting a civilised procedure. Double-declutching, we usually called it, because it involved two dabs at the clutch pedal. The first removed the load from the gears currently in mesh, allowing the gearlever to be pulled into the neutral position. Releasing the clutch pedal now puts the engine in touch with the gearbox innards again, and the driver can use the accelerator pedal[12] to alter the rate of rotation of the driven gear pinion so that it is likely, in his judgement, to correspond to that of the pinion he wishes to engage. The second disengagement of the clutch should allow the gearlever then to be pushed into the appropriate slot, whereupon the clutch pedal is released again and normal communications between the engine and the wheels resumed. If the driver's judgement and control were perfect, there would be no sound from the gearbox, nor much resistance to the final movement of the gearlever; if he had erred a little, he would have felt more resistance and all around would have heard the frightful screech of gearteeth out of synchronism but nevertheless attempting mutual invasion; and if the driver had erred greatly, the noise would be even worse and the resistance to engagement absolute, the gearlever unable to move out of neutral. It was fortunate that the old engines were slow running and had hefty flywheels so that they were slow to respond to the accelerator, giving the driver time to sense what he was doing.

Skilled drivers earned praise for their silent changes of speed. Sporting drivers, keen to speed the process, learned merely to slip the clutch a trifle, especially in the first phase of the procedure, so that a downward change could be effected very swiftly and smoothly with the accelerator held well down as soon as the first gear had been vacated. For a quick upward change, the makers of sports and racing cars began to

336

offer what was known as a clutch stop, a friction brake brought into action by forcing the clutch pedal to the bottom of its travel (a limit that would have otherwise to be avoided) when the freely spinning clutch disk would be abruptly slowed. It needed precise timing and resolute operation of the controls, but it enabled the next set of gears to be brought into mesh almost instantly. Stamp the pedal and snatch the lever, both at once, and there you were.

This was a skill rarely exercised and a refinement seldom made available. Not until the racing cars of the era immediately before the Great War, and the sporting cars of the decade after it, did the gearchanging habits of the motorist noticeably change. The cause of this was the evolution of engines, following the example of the undeservedly successful racers designed by Henry for Peugeot, which breathed much better at high revolutions, and were much more pusillanimous at low revolutions, than their predecessors. In cars designed according to these tenets, the performance at which the peak-power figures hinted could only be realised by keeping the crankshaft (now less burdened by flywheel inertia) turning at high rates, and this dictated free use of a gearbox with much closer ratios than before.

An entirely new style of driving had to be cultivated. In 1908, the internal ratios of a Grand Prix racer by Fiat were typical of those to be found in any gentlemanly touring car of the time, almost perfectly evenly spaced in increments of a little more than $1\frac{1}{2}$ to 1 so that the ratios were 1:1, 1.53:1, 2.38:1 and 3.68:1. The driver, be he racing professional or touring gentleman, would progress methodically through these until top gear was reached, and would not expect to abandon top gear until the time came to stop, unless he encountered a particularly steep hill. The engine aided and abetted him: described as having 'good back-up torque', such engines pulled most strongly at low speeds simply because their constricted breathing caused progressive strangulation as they turned faster.

---

12 This action is imperative for a downshift, but if one is attempting to slow down at the same time, the need for one's right foot to be engaged on the brake pedal is a source of potential confusion. Resolving it was much easier when the accelerator pedal was set low between the others – that is, to the left of the brake pedal. It was then much easier than it is now, with the accelerator pedal on the extreme right, to press with the ball of the foot upon the brake while jabbing at the accelerator pedal with the heel, which was the gist of what became known as the 'heel-and-toe' process. Central accelerator pedals disappeared from racing cars slowly in the 1950s; they had vanished from road cars by 1940.

Engines of this strongly supportive nature, imbued with a character more akin to the drayhorse than to the racehorse, continued to meet the needs of the large luxury car in Europe, and also the needs of practically every American car, until well into the second half of the 20th century. Constrained by the influence of the horsepower tax (which in effect was a tax on valve area) in Britain, the humdrum English middle-class tourer likewise suffered high-speed asthma but could pull well from cruelly low speeds in top gear; and the humdrum English middle-class driver, often frightened to change gear, exploited it cruelly.

More enterprising drivers sought cars of more sporting character, of the type derived from Henry's 1912 GP Peugeot, in which the internal ratios of the gearbox were 1:1, 1.13:1, 1.52:1 and 2.04:1 – very much closer, so that although the car might not be electrifying in its acceleration from standstill, once it was well under way it could be kept pressed well up to the bit by frequent recourse to the gearlever so as to keep the engine spinning in the top of its speed range where it was at its peppiest.

This was the new way to secure really high performance, and the makers of sporting cars duly followed Henry's lead. The early 3-litre Bentley, before it was detuned and castrated for the carriage trade, could be had with gearbox ratios of 1:1, 1.3:1, 1.6:1 and 2.6:1, and Bentley's salesmen used to astonish potential customers by driving it at a steady 60mph while slipping freely from one gear to another of the uppermost three. Most customers in the 1920s had never done 60mph at all, let alone in second gear!

Taking note of the unquestionable fact that most cars offered a much easier shift into top gear than into any other, transmission engineers developed the 'constant-mesh' gearbox in which all the gearwheels were permanently in mesh but those on the output shaft were carried on bearings which left them free to rotate idly. The appropriate gearwheel could then be locked to the shaft by a dog-clutch (a wheel having coarse gearteeth on its face rather than on its edge) as had usually been the practice with top gear in earlier 'boxes. This development took time and was done in easy, affordable stages, which began with the advertisement of 'silent third' and progressed down through the gears until they were all similar – although it took decades before the sliding-pinion bottom gear was finally ousted, and it is still with us in the reverse gear[13] of many manual boxes.

With the constant-mesh gearbox, changes were much sweeter, and the need for synchronising by the double-declutching procedure less exacting; indeed it was possible, given muscular speed and strength, to snatch the lever from one position to the next without any pause at all, as competition drivers did. Other drivers were happy enough that, with all gears always enmeshed, it was possible to give them helically cut teeth which were very much quieter than the old straight-cut spurs. A well-made gearbox of this type, especially if it had close ratios in the old Henry fashion, could be sheer bliss to operate.

Following rapidly on the heels of the constant-mesh gearbox came synchromesh. It was evident to transmission engineers that the new construction allowed for the interpolation of a miniature device analogous to the old clutch-stop, serving instead as a friction clutch to synchronise the dog-clutches before they were brought into engagement. From this reasoning sprang the invention of synchromesh, introduced by General Motors in the 1928 Cadillac.

With this mechanical refinement, driving became less of an art: however desirable the finesse of double-declutching might remain in the interests of smoothness and of skid-prevention on icy roads, that daunting procedure could be dismissed from the repertoire. Declutch, throw the gearlever knob in the appropriate direction, and engage the clutch again. Whatever you did (if anything) with the accelerator in that interval would not matter: it took only a little pressure on the gearlever to overcome the slight resistance of the synchromesh mechanism doing its work, and then you were in the desired gear. It was as easy as that, and soon it was spreading like wildfire – better, indeed, than wildfire, for it spread across the oceans surrounding America without faltering.

Within America its arrival could scarcely have been better timed. During the maturing of an entire generation of Americans, a substantial proportion of American drivers had chosen to avoid the hazards and responsibilities and embarrassments of gearchanging, by confining their driving to the Ford Model T whose two-speed epicyclic gearbox had all its teeth always in mesh and demanded only familiarity, not skill (and feet, not hands), to control it. Rival makes had to rely on engines that were big, lazy, but astonishingly flexible, so that their drivers should not need to shift gears. In 1928, when synchromesh appeared on the American scene, the Ford Model T had

---

13 First – in 1964 – to offer synchromesh for reverse gear was Lamborghini, who reckoned that he (like his wealthy customers, for whom time was money) had better things to do with his time than wait for the gearbox internals to consume their inertia and slow to a stop before the reverse gears could be coaxed into mesh.

been out of production a year and a considerable number of motorists felt betrayed; the appearance of synchromesh on the American scene must have seemed providential.

Across the oceans it was no less welcome, for in the British and European economies the large and lazy engine was too thirsty for the pockets and pump prices commonly involved. Synchromesh first graced the shifts between the top two ratios, seldom extending to bottom gear until well into the 1950s; but it was between the uppermost ratios that most of the work was done, a fact mirrored in the geographical influences to be detected in the ratios themselves. For instance Italy, a country of many hills and some long flat roads, used to go in for three quite closely spaced low ratios and a remote high top gear.

Germany, with everything from Alps to *Autobahnen*, favoured a very low bottom gear and a very high top, but with the intermediate ratios evenly and perforce very widely spaced. This arrangement produced quite respectable acceleration figures in cars that were conventionally heavily built to withstand the rough roads that used to be prevalent in Germany; but it also required that the engine be taken to its peak in each gear before an upward shift if acceleration were to be sustained, and that careful timing had to be strictly observed even if it meant making a shift in the middle of a potentially hazardous overtaking manoeuvre. It was another aspect of the German tendency to follow strict rules and leave nothing to chance, whatever the cost.

The English used, as we have seen, to be congenital top-gear staggerers, but had no mountains worthy of the name, few very fast roads, and because of the density of population rather a lot of traffic; so their top gear was rather low, the next was close to it because that was the only other gear in frequent use and an easy change was demanded; and any others were calculated to serve the unlikely eventuality that the driver would dare to attempt one of the more famous hills such as Porlock, Sutton Bank or Wrynose[14]. Indeed only the skilled and intrepid would attempt a shift into an unsynchronised bottom gear on such a gradient; the more timid preferred, however much it might dismay the infuriated drivers baulked behind, to come to a complete stop, apply the handbrake, engage bottom gear and with all imaginable difficulties start off again up the hill.

A few firms provided a freewheel mechanism in the drive line, which allowed the car to coast down long gentle hills[15] with the engine idling but the car in gear ready for prompt reapplication of power. The only ones to persevere with this for any considerable time were Rover, Saab, and Bristol (with different reasons in each case) but it was a welcome side-effect that this freewheel enabled a swift clutchless gearchange to be effected simply by releasing the accelerator pedal and moving the lever to the appropriate slot[16]. Eventually gearbox designers overcame their problems in providing synchromesh on bottom gear, and freewheels disappeared.

Synchromesh itself was greatly improved and refined in the years after the Second World War, when an unprecedented number of new motorists took to the roads of the world. Different designs provided different degrees of feel, and different amounts of resistance; some were unbeatable however fast you moved the lever, some were unbeatable because that movement would be blocked until the time was right, and some could be overridden by a hasty hand and produce nasty noises.

The best of them allowed a sensitive driver to effect a silent and utterly smooth gearchange without using the clutch, employing a method known to some drivers of unsynchronised gearboxes in earlier years. The technique for an upward shift was to apply light finger pressure to the gearlever in the desired direction of movement, release the accelerator pedal, and pause very briefly in neutral for the engine to slow a little; when everything was rotating at the correct rates, the fingers could sense the diminution in resistance and the lever practically fell into place. For a downward shift the procedure was varied by accelerating the engine as soon as the lever moved out of the slot being vacated. The whole business was governed by one simple and philosophically unassailable proposition: if you are doing everything else perfectly, why should you need to use the clutch pedal?

The next stage in the evolution of driving methods involved growing accustomed to a variety of 'overdrive' mechanisms that provided an extra high top gear. The earliest of these had appeared before the Second World War as alternative gearsets in the rear axles of some American cars; most of those which flourished in

---

14 For the benefit of bicycling tourists, there used to be published in Britain a guide to the hills that might be encountered, listing their lengths and gradients. The timid motorist sometimes availed himself of this guidance to avoid the roads that might prove too steep for him.

15 Long and steep hills would bring the danger of brake fade when the brakes were used continuously to prevent the car speeding out of control. In the Rover system, at least, the freewheel could be locked; in the case of the Saab, the engine involved was a two-stroke and therefore gave no significant braking on the overrun anyway.

16 In Bristol cars from type 400 to type 406 the freewheel was built into the unsynchronised bottom gear.

the 1950s involved epicyclic gears tacked on to the back of the gearbox and engaged by electrohydraulic means. They flourished because it was a quick way of providing a fifth gear while continuing to use a four-speed gearbox already established in production; by the 1960s most manufacturers had got around to creating five-speed gearboxes, and the costly overdrive disappeared.

The fifth gear became desirable because there were now plenty of roads where high speeds could be reached, or fairly high speeds could be sustained economically in a ratio too high for anything but cruising at less than full power. In the 1990s six-speed gearboxes began to appear, sometimes for the same reasons (except that top speeds were even higher), sometimes to provide closer ratios to suit super-sports engines that had been developed to have extremely peaky characteristics.

Many racing gearboxes muster no more ratios than six; but racing gearboxes boast extremely close ratios, and racing engines have little or no flywheel inertia. Furthermore, racing gearshifts have to be very quick indeed if precious time is not to be wasted, as it always is in a conventional stepped-ratio manual gearbox; and racing drivers are expected to display reasonable aptitude, so obstructive time-consuming synchromesh[17] is out of the question. Given that pressures on his mental concentration are increasingly intense (the modern racing driver is, after all, primarily an athlete rather than an intellectual) it was to be expected that the driver's gearshift management should eventually be automated for him when the computerised systems of the car were up to the task. At various times and in various categories according to the vacillation of the regulations controlling the sport, this was done completely or partially, leaving the driver to demand an upward or downward shift by means of buttons on the steering wheel or paddle-shaped triggers behind it; the actual work was done by servo mechanisms (usually hydraulic) controlled by the same electronic devices which monitored the road speed and adjusted the engine speed during the extremely brief fraction[18] of a second taken for the operation.

This, whatever the regulatory bodies thought, was as it should be; but it was the height of impertinence for the manufacturers of road cars with ponderous clutches, heavy flywheels, and wide-ratio synchromesh gearboxes, to profess to offer in ordinary if pretentious family saloons and cosmetic two-seaters an automated gearchange of similar prowess. The automated gearshift in a conventional gearbox was an idea that had been tried often before: there were four commercial attempts between 1904 and 1908, by the Sturtevant Brothers in the USA, by Leander Megy and by Johabert Maugras in France, and by Captain F W Stanley[19], youngest son of the Earl of Derby, in England. Like later attempts, they came to nothing. The same fate lay in store for numerous assorted attempts to automate the clutch, leaving the driver to move the gearlever. None of these things was ever subtle enough to be as good as a skilled driver, nor to avoid giving occasional offence even to a poor driver. None, despite what modern control systems can accomplish, yet is – though some may be given credit for lightening the driver's load much of the time and being capable of being overridden by the driver whenever he chooses.

As far as private cars on the public highway are concerned, racing practice is irrelevant. As far as the astute customer for such cars is concerned, flagrantly inept imitations of racing practice are blatant trickery. By now, the intelligent and studious driver knows that a good modern automatic transmission – something that we can consider to have become established in basically definitive form by 1955, when the Chrysler TorqueFlite transmission first graced the Chrysler Imperial car, and something that has been improved immensely since – is far more useful. The sad thing is that very, very few users of automatic transmissions have the faintest idea of how to exploit them, and very few of the remainder have the faintest desire to learn.

Thus it is clear that the automatic transmission has just as parlous a future as the old limb-operated clutch and cogbox. Enthusiastic motorists have been telling us for a hundred years that they believe in changing gear themselves and know how to do it; and throughout that time it has been evident to the informed listener that of all these enthusiasts[20] few really do know how, fewer know why, scarcely any knows when – and practically all are too proud to be taught.

If the automatic transmission is to suffer in the same way, then it must be

---

17 Probably the only true Grand Prix car to possess synchromesh was the W196 Mercedes-Benz of 1954–5. Any contribution by the gearbox to this machine's overwhelming success was less attributable to its synchromesh than to its possession of five forward ratios at a time when – in spite of the convincing 5-speed examples set by Mercedes-Benz in 1938–9 and by Delage in 1927 – its rivals had only four.

18 Less than one-tenth.

19 This ingenious young aristocrat did it for a bet, wagering that in six months he could do better than the Sturtevants had done. In the event he took nine months and did far better than the Sturtevants.

20 *It is unfortunate, considering that enthusiasm moves the world,* wrote Mr A J Balfour in 1918, *that so few enthusiasts can be trusted to speak the truth.* Perhaps the enthusiast is not to be blamed, for what fosters his enthusiasm may be his inability to see the truth.

replaced by something even better, which must surely be some form of steplessly variable transmission. This again is something that has been attempted throughout motoring history, right back to the efforts of Spaulding in 1897 and Fouillaron in 1900. There have been valiant efforts involving friction rollers, or variable-pulley belt drives, or toroidal drives, or hydrostatic pumps and motors. Buick engineers wanted to do it in 1944 but were stifled by their seniors in General Motors. DAF did it delightfully in small cars from 1958. Evolved versions have been given scant attention: in the mid-1990s a steplessly variable transmission was installed experimentally in a Williams F1 racing car, and in the hands of driver Coulthard it lapped the Grand Prix circuit at Silverstone two seconds faster than the same car fitted with the standard gearbox, one of the most modern of its kind. By prevailing standards this was an *enormous* improvement – but when word of it got out, the regulatory authorities had it and all other fully automatic transmissions banned. In the advancement of technology, racing can be remarkably counter-productive.

The situation begs some great leap forwards, or even sideways, into a different approach to the whole problem. The imminence of the fuel cell as the propulsive means of the future car suggests that gearchanging is something we might as well stop worrying about, since we may not have to do it much longer.

CHAPTER 3

WHAT TO WEAR

LIKE THE HORSEDRAWN CARRIAGES FROM which they had the great misfortune to be derived, the earliest motor cars were usually open-bodied. Those who ventured out in them assumed that, apart from the change in motive power, nothing would or should change. Much of the fallacy in that assumption was exposed even before the cars began to display their ability to travel faster than horse-drawn carriages; when that began to happen, people discovered the effect of wind chill, and motoring clothing became specialised.

Rugs were not enough, although they were not dispensed with for many years. They had the advantage of keeping the nether parts of the passengers protected, and the further advantage of being discarded when one dismounted so that one was not overburdened by heavy weather-protection; but they were something of a hazard for the driver, getting in the way of his feet and of the numerous pedals and levers that sprouted beneath and around them.

The coat was the thing. In all but the kindest of climates people habitually wore heavy clothing when travelling, but the motoring coat became a wonderfully weighty matter. It had to contend not only with the cold, the wind, and the rain, but also with whatever muck and rubbish was thrown up from the surface of the road.

As early as 1892, touring by motor car became a fact established in the records when Hippolyte Panhard, 23 years old but accompanied by his uncle Georges, drove by attractively gastronomic stages from Paris to Nice. He had trouble with his car on the return journey, but what was more significant was that some of the roads over which he travelled had not been resurfaced since the days of Louis XIV[21].

By the time of the motor car, the roads of France and of Britain were the best in the world, but they were still fairly foul. Their surface was usually dust, except in wet weather when it was mud, and it was liberally plastered with the dung of horses and occasionally (especially on the approaches to market towns) of driven herds of cattle or sheep. Flung up by hooves and wheels alike, this mess – more or less pulverised according to the weather – clouded the air and those who passed through it. The worst might be intercepted by the dashboard[22], but the rest had to be kept by coats and hats, by veils and goggles, by gloves and by gauntlets, from rendering driver and passengers unpresentable.

Those who had experience of them knew that furs were the best insulators. In the more central parts of Europe motorists wore particularly shaggy furs or fleeces, which were all too easily soiled and only with difficulty cleansed. Elsewhere the fur was worn as a lining to a coat of reasonably smooth (and therefore more easily brushed or sponged clean) but heavy woollen cloth. Gabardines, which rely on the tightness of their twill weave to exploit the surface tension of raindrops and thus keep the rain out, proved unsatisfactory when the rain bombarded them[23] at motoring speeds, but any cloth had to be closely woven if it were to be suitably protective. Sometimes the outer surface of the motoring coat would be of some proofed material such as Macintosh, the rubberised cotton or other stuff developed by Charles MacIntosh[24], a pharmacist who started a rubber factory in Scotland in 1823. Sometimes the motorist would prefer to don an extra layer of waterproofs when the rain was heavy, and otherwise rely on a fur-lined leather coat which was the most windproof.

---

21 Wretched reader! Did you not know that the sun of Louis Quatorze, *le roi soleil*, set when he kicked the bucket in 1715?

22 The dashboard was originally the board in front of the driver's feet, where it would stop dirt from being dashed or spattered up onto his clothing. The spats worn by gentlemen over their shoes and ankles were originally called *spatterdashes*, since they served a similar purpose, though they were retained for warmth until well into the 1930s. When cars developed not only mudguards but also bonnets to house the frontal engine, the dashboard (which had accumulated a number of instrument gauges and minor controls) was raised to the driver's chest level, but retained its name.

23 For reasons mostly to do with aerodynamics, the maximum velocity of a raindrop in still air is only about 18mph (even French rain is limited to about 29 km/h), but the velocity of the wind must be added to that when considering the speed of the raindrop's impact.

24 He had a niece, Elizabeth Pugh-Barker, who married a French cavalry officer named Edouard Daubrée who was the business partner of the father-in-law of James Michelin, and thus created an interest in rubber for Michelin's sons André and (more particularly) Edouard to exploit. Though it contain many people, ours is a small world.

Whatever the material, the coat would be long enough to reach the ankles and fully skirted to provide ample wrapover. Fastened to the neck, it would be topped off by whatever hat the gentleman in question might judge proper: the peaked caps affected by the student fraternities of German universities were popular in Europe, but frowned upon by polite English society. The ladies, not unexpectedly, found occasion to seek out an amazing variety of headgear, but generally found it practical to surmount it with a gauze veil, tied becomingly beneath the chin.

Some ladies, anxious to preserve a complexion that did not really belong outdoors, would adopt a kid-lined full-face mask of leather. They and others might keep their eyes protected from the dust by a talc or mica visor incorporated in the veil; others, like their menfolk, adopted goggles. Early cartoons, posters, and anti-motoring propaganda, made much of the anonymity offered by these goggles to present their ferocious and faceless wearers as devilish unworldly fiends terrorising the highway – an allegation that was not often true, but often enough.

The dust and the clothing styles of the period combined to create a need for car bodies designed to suit the circumstances. The voluminous skirts then worn by ladies made it impossible for the wearer to climb over the greasy side-chains which were a feature of the transmission of most large cars in the early years: entry was accordingly made by ascending steps at the rear of the car to a small door between the rear seats. If a folding canvas top were to be incorporated, as began to be demanded when weather conditions made a roof more than a mere indulgence, this necessitated a most elaborate hood, large enough for its rails to arch over the doorway. Practical experiment soon showed that if the hood, when folded down as it usually would be, were inclined at a steep angle, it would create behind it a region of low-pressure turbulence in which the clouds of dust sent up by the car's wheels would be concentrated rather than flowing in a backdraught into the interior of the car.

This primordial tail-wing or spoiler was one of the features of the body style named in 1904 after the King of Belgium for whom it was first created. The King, who was very keen indeed on large and very fast motor cars, discussed his needs one day with the head designer, M Charles Ferrand, of Rothschild & Fils, the coachbuilding firm which was one of the minor enterprises of the banking family's French branch.

The discussion took place in the apartment of His Majesty's Parisian mistress, and ranged over a number of matters. The first was the provision of a long step (which in due course we called the running-board) filling the space between the front and rear mudguards on each flank of the car, upon which a ladylike passenger could mount before entering the car through a side door. The next was the King's desire for a rather *rococo* style with three-dimensional curvature of the surfaces, and with panels rather larger than in the past so as to reduce the visual clutter of multiple joints. The idea was for a progressive rising of the bodywork from a relatively low and impressively long bonnet to a very high and curvaceous tail, behind which the hood when folded would project at an angle of about 40 degrees from the horizontal to give full effect to its aerodynamic function. All these and other ideas were discussed with the attentive collaboration of His Majesty's lady friend, who finally settled a debate about seating: drawing together a couple of heavily buttoned upholstered corner seats that were part of her apartment's furniture, she bade M Ferrand copy them.

Chain drive to the rear wheels rapidly disappeared as the much cleaner and more self-contained system of propellor shaft and live rear axle, pioneered by Renault, took over. With it came a corresponding preference for the side-entry body with running-boards and a higher-sided and more generous enclosure of the passengers, culminating soon in fully enclosed saloon bodies – though these presented problems in wet-weather visibility, making it necessary for the driver (usually an employed chauffeur) to sit in a separate compartment open to the elements. Suitably uniformed, gauntleted and gaitered, he could be left to suffer those elements as part of the hazards of his calling.

For the passengers within, motoring was becoming less and less rigorous. More complete protection from the elements, even in an open car, was only part of the reason for this; a more important contribution was made by the widespread resurfacing of roads in Britain, Europe, and the USA: by 1930 dust had ceased to be the major problem that it had been. Motoring clothing could now be much simpler; as a result, it could also be much cheaper, which was of great importance to the new generation of working-class and lower- middle-class motorists upon whom the motor industry depended for the further success of their enterprises.

For the average man in a reasonably temperate climate, there was no real need for anything more elaborate than a good hefty overcoat (the belted Ulster, in a heavy Crombie cloth, was generally reckoned ideal) supplemented by a scarf, warmly lined leather gloves, and some kind of hat. Even when driving an open car, little more would be thought necessary: the gloves might have to be gauntlets to prevent rain and wind going up the sleeves, but speeds were seldom enough to dislodge even a Trilby, let alone a peaked cloth cap. The popularity of the cloche hat among mid-century ladies

The passengers' compartment could be enclosed, as in the Renault 45 of this 1912 Gamy print, before it was safe to do the same for the driver.

may even have had something to do with its stability in a motor-induced breeze.

Warmth was still a problem in any but the sunniest climes. People were still used to dressing up when venturing out, and the car – still without proper heating until mid-century – made no difference to that need. Pioneer motorists' passengers had charcoal-heated footwarmers beneath their rugs, and all the tricks of portable and pocketable heat learned on the grousemoors or the battlefield were employed to supplement the handmuffs up above. Later and less privileged travellers kept the rugs and made do with hot water bottles and thick socks.

The footwear that had to accommodate one or two pairs of heavy knitted socks had in turn to be accommodated. Not every manufacturer bothered; but General Motors, remembering the hard-living homesteaders who made up so large a section of their earlier customers, instructed their design engineers that the driving pedals must be separated widely enough for operation by a pair of gum-booted[25] feet. This standing order applied in all branches of the firm, in all countries, and was still operative in the 1970s. It may be in the GM rulebook yet.

When heaters did at last become part and parcel of the normal car – first as optional extras, then progressively through the 1950s as standard equipment – the need to dress up like a deep-sea diver before getting into the car could be dismissed. This was a revelation, nowhere more astonishing than in Britain, a nation that had always resisted the installation of proper domestic central heating because the weather was never cold enough for long enough for it to seem economically worthwhile. While mainland Europe and the northern states of the USA had long taken what the latter called 'steam heat' for granted, Britain persisted in its miserable open fireplaces burning coal, the heat from which mostly went up the chimney. The Clean Air legislation of the 1950s, designed to alleviate the smog that was the curse of winter Britain, made coal-burning in open grates a thing of the past, and substitute fuels seemed to have little to commend them. The nonsensical situation – it was no longer necessary to dress up to go out in the car, so why should one have to dress up when returning home? – finally goaded the people into some action, and in the late 1950s and early 1960s the British, celebrating their first wave of prosperity in decades, rushed to have domestic central heating installed.

The elimination of one absurdity encouraged the elimination of what many people considered another. In the 1960s people at large rebelled against formal clothing. The heated car had destroyed the market for heavy underwear, for overcoats and hats, for gloves and waistcoats. Perhaps over-reacting, or else giving expression to some other presumably social need that can be debated and deplored (or, just possibly, applauded) in many a place other than this, people likewise rejected the suit, the necktie, the tailored shirt, the creased trouserleg, the polished shoes. The people were simply not going to wear uniform any longer – so they all resorted to T-shirts, farmer's trousers of blue denim, and wildly elaborated sports plimsolls known as 'trainers', in which they all appeared more uniform than they ever had.

There was another influence on clothing. Beginning in the early 1960s, the need to wear a safety harness when in a moving car began to be earnestly addressed. It took

---

25 We like to call these things Wellington boots, but we should not. The boots and half-boots made for the Iron Duke (Field Marshal Arthur Wellesley, first Duke of Wellington, d.1852) were of highly polished leather, and utterly different in style.

a long time to make its wearing compulsory, even longer to persuade some motorists to comply with the regulations, but seat belts soon became an intrinsic part of every car, and they soon proved to put an unsightly shine on certain clothing fabrics (especially worsteds) where they rubbed on the shoulders. Even to find the fastening for the harness, underneath the skirts of a jacket or topcoat, could be awkward: it was another reason to abjure the clothing conventions of the past.

More lightly dressed than ever before, people needed seats that fitted more closely. Travelling with correspondingly less luggage than ever before, their holiday needs could be satisfied with smaller luggage coffers – especially when they started to enjoy their new-found prosperity by flying abroad for their holidays, in which their cars played no part.

Car manufacturers noted these developments with pleasure, and began to act on them; but not for long. By the 1980s, the majority of people in the industrially advanced countries, whose developing cultures most encouraged atheism or agnosticism, had begun to shrug off their various levels of religious hypocrisy and behave like the heathens they really were. While numerous religious cults flourished to emulate or supply an alternative to the minorities who were showing themselves more determinedly religious than ever, huge international movements (starting with a form of consumerism that made a fetish of health) encouraged the idolatry of the human body, seeking a lifestyle so healthy and so prolonged that they appeared to be in pursuit of immortality.

To this end, sporting activities and all manner of exercise regimens were undertaken by all manner of unlikely people, all over the world, and where once the motor manufacturer had only to consider whether his customers might want to carry golf clubs, now it was imperative that they should be able to carry with them all the impedimenta of cycling, footballing, skating, surfing, mountaineering, and winter sports that somehow never ceased to dream up alternatives to traditional skis. The car had to find room for everything – and reducing or eliminating the ashtrays, because smoking had become politically incorrect, was not enough to solve the problem.

Quite simply – and, thanks to the car, quite quickly – life had changed. In 1949 Mr Rodney Walkerley, the sports editor of *The Motor*, had replied to an enquiry from someone who wondered what was the correct wear for attending a motor race: 'anything', he wrote, 'so long as it is well cut'. Fifty years later, that advice would not be understood – but nobody would dream of asking for it, the only question being whose advertising to display across one's chest or back.

CHAPTER 4

SPORT

ON MONDAY 24 JULY 1894, Baron Theodor von Liebig must have been a very happy young man. The newspapers would have reached the tiny village of Gondorf, clustered around the castle which was his mother's home, gazing out over the Mosel river; and he might have been forgiven a derisory chuckle as he read that in Paris, two days earlier, 21 assorted cars had assembled to undertake a reliability trial on the 126km road to Rouen, and that 17 of them had actually managed to reach the finish. Promoted by a newspaper, *Le Petit Journal,* the trial was to be hailed as the first motor sporting event of all time, a triumphant demonstration of these new motor cars' potential for door-to-door diminution of life's losses of time and chance.

Wie kläglich! Wie armselig! 126 paltry kilometres! Just as that motley French assembly was stuttering out of the Porte Maillot, the Baron's Benz was puttering along the river road from Boppard through Koblenz to Gondorf, on the last lazy 40km-leg of a proper journey, one that had started 939km away in distant Bohemia. *Wie viele?* 126? A woman had done almost as well, as far back as 1888. While her handsome and heroic husband Karl was asleep after toiling almost to breaking-point over his newly created car, staunch Frau Benz had got up in the dead of night, taken their two children, and gone off to prove that she could drive it herself. She had met a few problems – she cleared a clogged pipe with a hatpin – but valiant Bertha Benz, who had supported Karl almost to exhaustion and close to penury, drove the Benz all the way from Mannheim to her home town Pforzheim – and that had been 100km, some of them hilly.

Baron von Liebig had not shirked hills. His was a true door-to-door journey, far more eloquent of what the car could and would do for us than any futile sporting trial which started across a line in a Paris square and finished across another line in Rouen High Street. That way of doing things was fit only for buses; the Baron arrived at his mother's front door, having started just a week earlier at his own front door.

The Baron's house is still there, looking much the same as it did then, prominent on a bend in hilly Jablonsky Street, in the town of Liberec in Czech Republic: but, after half a century of communist rule and a few more years of confusion, the big house is no longer a private home, but provides office quarters for a textiles institute.

The change is more notional than real. Young Theodor von Liebig was a textiles magnate, and so were his forefathers before him. Grandfather Johann, founder of the family firm, had already expanded it considerably when, sometime in the first third of the century, he had invented a blend of wool and cotton that seems to have been what England came to know as Viyella. A new factory was set up to produce it, and he prospered even more. His ennobled son, Theodor Franz von Liebig, spread the firm wider still, not only in northern Bohemia but also elsewhere in the Austro-Hungarian empire; Czechoslovakia did not yet exist, and the Germans knew the town which is Liberec as Reichenberg. So it was not at all unseemly that Freiherr von Liebig should court the daughter of the Clemens family, respectable and rich bankers. On 15 August 1871 he married her, and ten months later – to the day – their son Theodor Johann was born.

When the lad was barely 18 his father died, and suddenly the young man was in charge of 14 factories and a substantial family fortune. If five younger sisters had not made him so already, he now became a serious, methodical and decisive young man, with the good grasp of technical subjects essential to somebody in the textiles industry where mechanical engineering was at that time relatively advanced. Like many thoughtful young men of the time, he made it his business to take an interest in developing technologies, and the motor cars that had been introduced a few years earlier by Benz and by Daimler had fired his enthusiasm. One day he read a report in the periodical *Fliegende Blätter* that he found convincing, and on 31 October 1893 he paid a visit to Karl Benz in Mannheim. A brief drive around the flower beds in Benz's garden, and in a quarter of an hour he had paid a substantial deposit and gone.

At that time there were only two motor vehicles – a Serpollet steamer and a Benz tricycle – in the whole of the Austro-Hungarian empire. In December the Emperor Franz Joseph had a third within his domain, when a Benz Viktoria (production number 76) arrived at Reichenberg by train from Mannheim. It was attended by one of the factory mechanics, master locksmith Johannes Thum, whose job was to set the car up and teach the new owner to handle it. If there was only one pedal, there were six or seven hand levers . . . Most of them were linked to the 3hp engine of the Benz Viktoria, an engine which allowed it to average 20kmh on the seventh day of the Baron's trip. Overall he managed 13.6, but his route was a tough one, albeit meticulously planned. He and a friend, a young medical student named Franz Stransky, spent months preparing their scheme, devising a route which dipped south so that they could visit the Benz works in Mannheim. The Baron wrote to the manufacturer to tell him what they had in mind, and poor worried Benz answered by return that he could not guarantee the car for such a long and arduous journey.

What must driving have been like in those days? Was the constant cough and chirrup of the engine, with one huge 2.9-litre cylinder and an exposed crankshaft and flywheel, drowned by the creaks and rattles of the springs and bodywork as the rutted and bumpy road passed beneath? The Benz was more advanced than many later cars in having a fairly flexible engine, but the transmission relied on fast-and-loose pulleys like those of a contemporary flat-belt lathe instead of having a clutch and gearbox. Benz had patented a form of Ackermann steering, after the principles of Lankensperger; but he had done little or nothing about brakes. Engine cooling was rudimentary, electrical insulation unreliable. Could such a contraption hold together?

Undeterred, they set off at dawn on 16 July, heading north to the border post at Zittau where they passed into Saxony, and then on to Bautzen, a solid little town centred on a castle that would look very serious indeed but for its display of just about every kind of spire, turret, tower and minaret that its fanciful architects could devise. Here and in the countryside the roads are sometimes still cobbled, as they must have been then. It was all hilly going, over the ridges of the Erzgebirge hills where silver, tin and brown coal have been mined since time immemorial. Turning parallel to the ridge, the Baron headed west through Dresden – but there is precious little original left of that, and what there is can be distinguished, even from the distance of the passing Autobahn, by having been burnt ineradicably black, more than half a century ago.

The police would not let him stay in Dresden; the crowds that the car attracted were so big as to be a problem. Presumably Wilsdorf, through which he passed next, is the same place as the Wilsdruff of today. After 14 hours' driving he reached Waldheim and called it a day, with 196km behind him. The next day was shorter and possibly trickier, with only 112km passing beneath the Viktoria's big wooden wheels and slender solid rubber tyres in nine hours, and the night was spent in Eisenberg.

Tuesday was straighter and flatter, on a road that threaded along a series of towns that were doubtless smaller but perhaps as busy then as they are now. Jena was the home of Zeiss optics, and of textiles specialists whom the Baron would have known. Weimar, the administrative capital of Thuringia and the intellectual centre of Germany, had been the home of Goethe and Schiller, Bach and Liszt, the Cranachs and Nietzsche. In recent years it has been polished and painted and gilded as an expensive and artsy focus for rich tourists, but however brightly the sun shines there is no escaping the shadow of the hill behind the town: there are still people in Weimar who cry when they remember the screams that reached them from Buchenwald.

The road, straight and flat past poppy-strewn cornfields punctuated by the odd half-timbered barn or gold-tipped church steeple, goes on through Erfurt, and so did the Baron, for once again the police feared the crowds and would not let him linger. On it goes through ancient Gotha, famous for publishing, and 90 years ago a place that made redoubtable aircraft. In a field nearby stands still a solitary hut, its roof monogrammed and dated, which looks as though it might have survived from the airfield buildings, but the Baron came earlier, and pressed on to Eisenach.

When he arrived, he was refused hospitality by an innkeeper who feared a petrol explosion. I am surprised that he relied on inns; with his banking connections, could he not have arranged to stay with the Rothschilds who were first in time and rank among the influential families who once gave this lovely town its impetus? It is still a lovely town, as rich in old buildings and in art nouveau as Liberec is, its people equally delightful. Overlooking it is Luther's sinister old Wartburg fortress, after which an unfortunate car was named; but other cars also issued from this town, the little Trabants which are still to be seen, and the Dixi, BMW and EMW of perhaps more precious memory.

From here the Baron's route became tougher. Down through Fulda and Offenbach to Frankfurt and Darmstadt would bring him to Mannheim, but it was 282km, and the two friends pressed on through the night to arrive at the Viktoria's birthplace after 26 hours' driving. The fountainhead of the German motor industry, Mannheim is a grey and uninviting place today, dominated by the Daimler-Benz symbol and wrestling with the serpentine traffic that comes from its own loins. When von Liebig and Stransky arrived, it was already a big and busy place.

Karl Benz was amazed and delighted. Work stopped, the entire factory staff (about 50 men) was called out into the courtyard to set up some tables, a barrel of beer was rolled out, and he made a speech as emotional as it was solemn.

I had not dared to hope . . . True, we are only at the beginning; but
the highway has already been conquered. No less than seven
hundred kilometres have been covered by the Benz Viktoria on

this occasion; seven thousand – no, a hundred thousand – will be added to that!

Driving on to Bad Kreuznach (still delightful), Bingen and Boppard on Friday, and finally to Schloss Liebig at Gondorf, the Viktoria added 214km to its tally. The castle is still there, looking just as it did a hundred years ago, but now housing a commercial collection of fine art and antiques. Looking at the lawns, the generous windows, the stables, one can imagine what a comfortable haven it had been; for von Liebig and Stransky, a few days' rest seemed in order. Afterwards, they drove to Reims and back, and then spent a week of August driving home to Reichenberg, bringing the total that summer to 2500km.

It was the outbound trip which was the real adventure. Who knew what might await them, doing what nobody had ever done? It was a tribute to the patient brain-cudgelling of Benz in the years when he worked out how best to design a motor car, to the traditional excellence of Benz workmanship (before the firms amalgamated in 1926, Benz quality was superior to Daimler), and to the careful preparation by von Liebig and Stransky, that the car gave as little trouble as it did. The carburettor flooded, the petrol tank sprang a leak, the spark plug (was it the first to have an annular electrode?) gave trouble, there was a faulty contact in the ignition system, the odd loose nut and a loose wheel wedge; that was about all. By the standards of the 1890s, the Benz was astonishingly reliable. Nor was it inordinate in its thirst for petrol, whether (which is not clear) it used 140 or 175 litres for the journey; but its evaporative cooling system had a frantic thirst for water, and poor Stransky (it seems to have been his job) visited wells, brooks and streams for a total of 1500 litres.

These were not the only difficulties. There were frightened horses to be calmed; there were sleeping drunkards to be lifted from the road. There were curious crowds, suspicious police, hostile innkeepers. There was even the young lady of Hünfeld who was embarrassingly keen to be abducted . . .

The following year, Theodor and Franz took a different route and reached Gondorf in four days. Distance was no longer a problem; the next matter to be addressed was speed. The individual epic journey, as these young men unwittingly demonstrated, was not enough to capture the imagination of the public, nor likely to linger in the memory of any but the participants.

There would be epic journeys to come. There would be some drivers who, whether out of commercial interest or a desire for glory or even out of sheer curiosity, would embark on forays embracing whole continents, across America or around

Australia[26]. There would be others who, resenting the established reputation of the railways, raced some crack express train from the Côte d'Azur to Calais or from Sydney to Perth. Even the 1907 trip from Peking to Paris, staged as a race by the newspaper *Le Matin*, emerged as merely an epic 60-day journey, if only because the victorious Prince Borghese was so magnanimous to rivals stricken by the misfortunes that his Itala survived that they might never have finished at all without his sympathetic assistance.

Epic journeys did not capture the imagination of the public, limited as that imagination has always been – almost as limited as its memory, which cast off these briefly publicised demonstrations with the same bored indifference as attended all other nine-day wonders. The public wanted to see rivals in contention; had it not been for the single-tracked limitations of the railway, they would have been glad to see locomotives racing. As it was, they continued to race horses; and why not cars?

That 79-mile reliability trial from Paris to Rouen in 1894 merely proved the feasibility of it. For the following year there was to be a real race, over a distance that even von Liebig would have thought epic, 732 miles from Paris to Bordeaux and back. To quieten protests about the perils of speed, the major award was reserved for four-seaters, which were obviously practical vehicles; but two-seaters, though they were deemed deliberate devotion to speed at all costs (an ideal to which the prim proprietors of the event dared not admit), were admitted nevertheless.

It is strange, this enduring popular conception of the sports car as being essentially a two-seater. In the early days of some of the most notable sports-car races, such as the Tourist Trophy and the 24h event at Le Mans, the regulations (anxious to emphasise that the object was to develop the touring car) prescribed four-seaters, carrying ballast to represent the weight of passengers. The cleverer entrants saw that the ballast could be carried much lower (usually as weights bolted underneath the chassis) than the passengers could, bringing the centre of mass nearer the ground and thus enhancing the stability of the car. Even so, by the end of the 1920s the two-seater had asserted its right to participate, and thereafter nearly all the nicest cars to drive were two-seaters.

---

26 It was no sports car, but a Citroën 5CV, which in 1925 first circumnavigated Australia. It took five months. A couple of young men with a Harley-Davidson motorcycle and a sidecar halved that time in 1929.

This contribution of motoring sport must not be overlooked: it prompted the manufacture of some sports cars that in their respective times were the most gratifying and satisfying machines that the keen driver could experience. By their contemporary standards the best sports cars had the best steering, the best gearshifts, the best roadholding and handling, and the best brakes, of anything on the market. Probably not a quarter of those who bought them could drive well enough to appreciate them fully; but if the others did no more than enjoy the association with them, they did enough to ensure that sports cars remained popular in the market-place and therefore remained available to those who could really derive an emotional, physical and intellectual uplift from driving them.

The sports car seldom appeared to offer anything relevant to the needs of the motoring populace at large, but in fact it made a major contribution to the satisfaction of the driving masses. It did this by establishing the highest norms of behaviour possible according to the state of the art; and it was by the gradual adoption of these norms by succeeding levels of ordinary production cars that cars more generally became better behaved. When the young enthusiast with a two-seater became the mature paterfamilias with a touring car seating four or five, it sickened him to find that it was so mediocre to drive, and he sought something better. In due course, his demands (if repeated often enough and backed by money enough) became effective.

It is beyond Setright's scope to judge what were the nicest cars to drive in the era before the Great War. In the 1920s they were undoubtedly cars of sporting blood: above all the Bugatti T35, but also the 3-litre Bentley in the form in which it did so well at Le Mans, and later in the decade the six-cylinder 1500 and then 1750 Alfa Romeo, together perhaps with the chain-drive Frazer Nash. In the 1930s the successors of the Bugatti and Alfa Romeo remained peerless, but the best Aston Martins also seemed good until the BMW 328 came into the picture and ordained new standards. After the Second World War, with manufacturers everywhere making everything imaginable for a booming market, the picture was one of confusion, and of a lack of discrimination between the cars that were really sporting cars for the people (at various times the MG TC, the Fiat X1/9, the Mazda MX-5), the cars that with some serious work on them could be competitive (various Healeys, the Fiat 124, the Ferrari Dino 246, some of the later Chevrolet Corvettes), and the cars that were best left to the professionals and best kept off the public highway.

Whatever their degrees of sportiness, all these kinds of sports cars drew their virtues from what sport had shown was possible. That was what sport taught; it invented practically nothing, seriously developed very little, but it taught us what could be done and enabled us, if we had any such hankering, to do it. Just occasionally, though, somebody in the industry would create a car that was utterly beautiful to drive, but a car that had no place in the sporting arena and should never be subjected to the indignities of competition by any owner of decent feelings: from the Pegaso and six-cylinder Bristols of the 1950s to the Honda NSX of the 1990s there has always been something to deny the trivial sports car its ultimate authority.

In 1895, however the officials of the Paris–Bordeaux race might pontificate, nothing and nobody could be thought authoritative. There was not yet much consensus about anything to do with the motor car, least of all about its future. All it could do was to set about making history. At the end of history's first real motor race, we caught some glimpse of how we would see and judge matters in the future. Recorded as fastest four-seater, and therefore the major prizewinner, was a Peugeot which finished third, in a matter of 60 hours – but what everybody remembered was the outright winner, a two-seater Panhard averaging 15mph to complete the round trip in just over two wearying days and wicklit nights. Historians still argue whether the driver, Levassor, supped on soup or champagne at his hasty Bordeaux turnabout; none will concede nor even consider that he might have taken both, though none could deny that he must have needed both. So much for historians . . .

As for history, it now came thick and fast. The city-to-city race was a perfect demonstration of the motor car's potential for door-to-door diminution of life's losses of time and chance. The burgeoning French motor industry saw every justification for creating purpose-built racing cars, for inviting the public to enjoy the spectacle, for whipping up every enthusiasm that might be turned to custom. While America mustered just two starters and one finisher (the little Duryea, still in the prototype stage after two years as the nation's first horseless buggy) in a frostbitten race from Chicago to Evanston, France looked on 1895 as an entrée to a perpetual feast of speed.

Time and chance worked their ways upon that menu, as each demonstration was diminished in perfection by losses of life. The years 1896 to 1903 saw a succession of scandalously dangerous road races, usually from Paris to another city, each more ambitious, more ruthlessly realistic, more callously indifferent to consequences, than the last. France was not big enough for the visionaries of that age: after racing to Marseilles, they raced to Amsterdam, to Berlin, to Vienna, and finally (though they did not know with what deathly finality) they set out for Madrid . . .

These races were undoubtedly great, as they were undoubtedly visionary. The hazards were horrific, the drivers heroic, the cars gigantic. Thundering like duns at a poet's door, skipping like the stones they flung across the rutted roads, these spider-wheeled chariots were usually big, often heavy, invariably ill-balanced and frequently ill-mannered, intractable inchoate triumphs of audacity over perspicacity. Men were still learning how to make cars go well, having barely discovered how to make them go at all; but men were learning very fast.

Painfully, and at frightful cost, they learned their most grim lesson on that road to Madrid, in the race from Paris which became known as the Race of Death. Strongly supported by 179 entries, and publicised up to the hilt, it drew 100,000 Parisians to see the cars start (one by one, against the clock) from Versailles, and they

Here outside Bordeaux the dreadful 1903 race from Paris to Madrid was stopped, and Louis Renault – fastest in the Lightweight class, and second overall – learns that his brother Marcel has crashed and died.

thronged the roads all the way to the end of the first stage at Bordeaux. They thronged unchecked, undisciplined, untutored in the dangers they approached, unable to conceive the speeds that the cars would reach. They filled the narrow round-crowned roads, parting only reluctantly at the last moment to let a speeding car pass; but they were not always quick enough. Stray children, stray dogs, oxen, the clouds of dust raised by the cars, all added to the drivers' confusion. Competitors and spectators alike were killed, their mangled remains sometimes discovered only after the blinding dust-clouds had settled. Gabriel, the fastest man to get through to Bordeaux, admitted that he sometimes had to steer his huge Mors by the poplar-tops that alone were visible to show which way the road went.

The race was stopped. All motor racing might have been stopped; but the sport was already diversifying, and it was the newer kinds of competitions which saved it. The sprints and hillclimbs at Nice were examples of events growing in popularity: the first European hillclimb, a club outing in 1899, was a full-blooded speed event by 1902. The Alps were there for storming, and in Britain there will hillside bridle paths which offered a shorter but subtler challenge: one such, begun at Shelsley Walsh in 1905, retains the longest continuous history of all sporting events. Americans from 1916 would rise to the 14,000 ft challenge of Pike's Peak, approached by 12½ miles of dirt road winding into the clouds.

Climbing crude paths was a test of reliability in the early days; speed itself hardly mattered. Britain's Thousand Miles Trial of 1900 was meant to prove the practicality of the touring car, as was the original Tour de France; by 1905 the car's practicality could be taken for granted, and trials became speed-oriented handicaps for cars that were only nominally tourers. The Herkomer and Prinz Heinrich events, staged in the Austrian Alps first with the participation and secondly with the patronage of His Royal Highness, shared with the Isle of Man Tourist Trophy the early development of the sports car; combined with contemporary efforts to organise a winter convergence upon Monte Carlo, they also nurtured what would become rallying.

It was all very deliberate, very earnest, very well-intentioned; but what the people wanted was, like Gibbon's ancient Romans, circuses. There was no substitute for the real pure racing car, for sheer undiluted speed. If the world's fastest cars could no longer be raced from city to city, let them be raced on some sort of closed circuit where the public could be better controlled, and more effectively charged for spectating. Perhaps the cars would then prove even faster.

That is what happened. The great races remained road races, but were now –

The most evocative motor-racing photograph ever published? Felice Nazzaro
flings his winning Fiat through Sottano during the 1907 Targa Florio.

beginning with the 1903 race for the Gordon Bennett Trophy – conducted on road circuits that were closed for the event (an indulgence refused by English law, but tolerated in most other countries), usually conforming to a roughly triangular plan that left town by a major road, turned across country to the next major road radiating from that same town, and thereby returned to the starting point. A lap might in the early days cover well over thirty miles, but the spectators would have many opportunities to see the competitors, for the early races would be spread over two days: the first Grand Prix de l'Automobile Club de France, in 1906, thus covered 770 miles, and for many years afterwards the normal distance was 500.

The Renault which won that 1906 event weighed about a ton and was timed at 92.4mph under the impulsion of its 12-litre engine. It was fairly typical of the cars which would dominate racing for the next few years, during which Fiat proved the most consistently competent. The roads remaining rough, the springing of the cars remained of necessity soft; but, with no brakes before and little more than sprockets behind (where the brakes were at the chassis end of the driving chains), their axles were relatively light, and these substantial cars rode and handled beautifully, cornering as fast as anything built in the next twenty years.

That they were daunting to drive was due to the inordinate length of the races. Drivers who had been obliged to help their mechanics hack off punctured tyres and lever on new ones, who had been perched aloft and unprotected in a windblast thick with stone chips like bullets and raindrops like needles, grew too fatigued to heave the wheel into a turn or to haul on the brakes as hard as they must.

Truth to tell, after a few hours the spectators were not excited any longer. Few of them were drivers, after all, few of them educated enough to take an intelligent interest in the variety of engineering features paraded before them as the fruits of competition. Few of those sweaty pedestrians, their suits stiff and shiny with ingrained dirt, their skirts as grimy as the brooms they emulated, their smell rivalling the hot oil wafted in the wake of each passing car, could appreciate the skills of cornering or the perils of braking. Only in the waistcoat pockets of the well-heeled would there be a watch to monitor the relative positions of drivers who had started at 90-second intervals. What these people wanted to see, once the novelty of actually seeing cars had worn off, was real fast intelligible massed-start races.

Because in Britain racing on the public highway was forbidden, it was in Britain that the first purpose-built track was built to provide just this sort of spectacular racing. The high-speed track at Brooklands, the famous 'concrete saucer' – a masterpiece of high-speed earthmoving and concreting by the army officer who designed it and the labouring men and horses who built it – allowed the very fastest cars to sustain top speed all around its bankings. Even the very dullest spectators could understand it – could at least understand the scratch races, if not the handicap events.

The Europeans, who considered that cars were meant to be driven on real roads at whatever speeds those roads might allow, despised the artificiality of the oval track. France and Italy, and others to a lesser extent according to their sizes and fortunes, jealously preserved the tradition of road-racing, not only in the succession of Grand Prix races for the cream of purpose-built single-seaters[27] (a succession which grew from the annual French event in the early years to the fortnightly travelling circus of today) but also in sports-car events, most remarkably the Targa Florio in Sicily and

---

27 The driver had to travel alone after 1925, but prior to that a riding mechanic was variously optional or mandatory.

the Mille Miglia in Italy, most lastingly in the 24-hour race at Le Mans in France.

The Americans, across whose vast land the intricacies of road-racing seemed irrelevant, took a hint from Brooklands and built a more compact and more symmetrical Indianapolis. By 1911 they too had settled on 500 miles as a proper length for what has survived as the oldest original race.

It may be that these venues, and these types of races, reflected the ignorance of motor engineering and the appetites for sensation of the various nations. It may be that the people, the viewing and puzzling and paying public, can properly be blamed for the progressive change in character that has in a century transformed motoring sport. It may be; but there is ample evidence to suggest that what the idealists see as the corruption of the sport, and what the sensationalists do not even wish to consider as the denial of its true purpose, was embarrassingly evident as a commercial and/or nationalistic undermining of the sporting spirit from the very earliest days, and detectable as early as that 1903 Gordon Bennett event for which the German team was sabotaged by arson.

There is, perhaps unfortunately, very little justification for the popular argument that motor sport is responsible for spurring the invention or development of technologies from which in due course the production car and ultimately the public will profit. In fact the urgencies of the motor sporting calendar do not allow the proper development of the technological novelties that, usually bred in aviation or communications or weapons science, do sometimes become available. Many a promising idea has been ruined or dismissed by racing engineers in too much of a hurry to do a thorough job. The dispassionate observer will also dismiss as half-baked pie-in-the-sky the belief that there is something ennobling, instructive, intoxicating, in driving a good car on a challenging road, faster than anyone else. To enjoy doing so, even to attempt to do so, is mere vanity, when all that should matter is that one does it as well as one personally can, without reference to how well or how fast (the two terms are not always synonymous) anyone else may do it[28]. Yet men have always behaved like this; long before the motor car gave them another way to demonstrate their prowess, they raced each other on foot, across water, or on the fleet and gullible back of camel or horse. Can we then deduce that motor racing is just a contest between men?

There was a steward at the 1962 Grand Prix de Bruxelles who stated quite categorically that it was a race for machines, not for men. On the other hand there were drivers who in 1972 complained vociferously that the differences between one

GP car and another at that time were such as to make the differences between one driver and another quite insignificant. More recently, as races have been constrained more and more into the confines of compact arenas the better to televise them to a world-wide audience hungry for the tough-guy sensationalism of athletes engaged in constant close-quarter battling, the regulating bodies have developed racing rules which seek to make all the cars as nearly equal as can be managed, the better to ensure close racing from start to finish.

Yet, if the race were for machines, who would take the credit for those which are victorious? Pride of ownership, pride of creation, pride of association, these are the essentially human things that impel men to blazon their cars' names on their clothes and on their trophies.

Does that make motor sport commercial? It always was; but seldom has it been only commercial. At various times it has been in the grip of nationalism, patriotism, communism, eclecticism, vandalism and once or twice of mysticism. We have seen a race rigged at Tripoli by drivers who had banded together to profit from an associated state lottery; we have seen a race wrecked at Indianapolis by dishonest abuse of the cautionary light-signals; we have seen a race turned topsy-turvy at Hockenheim by the intervention of an aggrieved member of the public; and we have seen too many races made distasteful by the bitterness of mutual enmity between a couple of leading drivers.

Corruption is not a modern disease. At the very first Grand Prix race in 1906 (it was, as we have seen, a two-day affair) the cars had to be guarded overnight by the three noble stewards who were the only members of the organising body who were free from commercial interests and could therefore be trusted. Sabotage was a constant worry in those distant days, when the surreptitious notching of an exposed copper oil-pipe could ensure fatigue failure of the metal in a race that lasted for several vibratory hours. It is still a worry today, though the techniques might rely on a burst of microwaves rather than a Swiss file. Yet we called the activity a sport then, as we call it a sport now; and a sport it has always been, no less than athletics or cricket, horse-racing or boar-hunting. The driver who deliberately baulks his challenger today

---

28 'So I can ride a superbike around a circuit faster than anybody else on this planet. Big Deal! It doesn't make me a better person. There's probably half a dozen things you can do better than me. That doesn't make you a better person either.' Carl Fogarty, racing motorcyclist, 2000.

is applauded, where forty years ago he would have been severely reprimanded, and eighty years ago it would never have occurred to him to do it; but in the 1920s races were won by minutes, in the 1960s by seconds, and today by mere fractions – if not by infractions.

The dead heat nevertheless remains an oddity, usually reserved for triumphant team-members who have managed to gather together to swamp the finishing-line after a long sports-car race at Le Mans or Daytona. Yet there was a spate of such things in 1961, when the Dutch, French and Solitude Grands Prix all ended with a display of that bitter strife bred by almost precisely equal combinations of car and driver. As Francis Bacon observed rather earlier, 'There is little friendship in the world, and least of all between equals.'

There have been stranger finishes than those. There was the winning spinning driver who crossed the line backwards and was sent back down the road to do it again properly. There was another who took the chequered flag upside-down – a position which later made rally-driver Carlsson legendary, so often did he adopt it while setting his little Saab to ski the snows of the Scandinavian rallies. Scarcely had he become famous than all rally drivers began to make a fetish of driving sideways, something that racing drivers had stopped doing years earlier.

The skills and judgement developed by the greatest drivers are marvellous to ponder, but not always wondrous to behold. The smooth precise man who never wastes an inch nor ever makes an error is assumed by the crowd to have a better car; they take more pleasure in the man who teeters on a perpetual seesaw of slide and counterslide. Thus, popular appreciation of drivers is often coloured by their entertainment value. The modern man submerged in scientific marvels which allow him no scope for fancy wheelplay makes his appeal to the grandstands and the cameras by a display of aggression. He makes the same impression as the mighty man of valour ninety or a hundred years ago, practically standing up to the steering wheel the better to wrestle with it. In the intervening decades, armplay was what folk loved to see.

They loved Nuvolari, dancing in his cockpit; and Moss, tweaking his wheel all the way; and Rosemeyer, scything through corners that others took only in snippets. But they never took much notice of slender Cagno, deft and delicate in his handling of Fiat and Itala giants in the days of racing's genesis; or of restrained Caracciola, secure on rainswept roads while slower men went sliding into the scenery. They paid scant attention to meticulous Prost, until he suddenly stood before them as a champion. They could not help but admire Jim Clark, visibly faster than all about him, but only the tyre technicians knew how incredibly balanced was his use of all four corners of the car, to a degree not even approached by any of his contemporaries.

It remains futile to attempt any verdict on who was the best. It may be unimaginable that anybody should deny Fangio a place in any shortlist, but who is to make the penstroke which denies a place to Brooks or Bordino, Varzi or Wimille, Alberto Ascari or Michael Schumacher? And what does he know, be he a racing man, of the virtuosity of the rally men, especially of Makinen and Mikkola? And how does one rate the special gifts of those whose reckonings are in the splinters of seconds whittled from a Worcestershire hill or chipped from some Alpine cleavage by the likes of Mays or Mitter? Or how class those whose care of car, and stomach for speed, must be cultivated throughout the nightlong daylong devilry and drudgery of Le Mans or Spa, those whose names are as long honoured as Barnato, Gendebien, Bell, Ickx?

Finally who, uncomfortable as he might be in his presumed duty, would be so brave, so stern, so moralistic, or so priggish, as to strike out all those who took drugs to help them and who may indeed (and who can tell?) have been helped by them? Some certainly did: usually it was to enhance their powers of endurance, not only in long-distance races but also and perhaps more so in some of the newly strenuous rallies which, emerging early in the 1960s, continued non-stop for days and nights on end. That decade was notable for widespread and popular experimentation with drugs of many kinds: some had been prescribed in earlier times for medical purposes, others seemed to be devised then and there for social purposes. People from top to bottom of society essayed these artificial aids, and likewise people from the top rungs of motoring sport to grass-roots level. It did not happen only in the 1960s: it was known earlier, and has presumably continued since, though presumably at a reduced level because medical inspection and intervention are now a sterner threat to the competitor, and because most events are of shorter duration albeit of heightened intensity.

If nothing else, the use of and supposed need for drugs proved that the competition was between people, not between cars. Men and women[29] galore and

---

29 Yes, there have been some notable women: Mme Junek (racing in the 1920s) and Mlle Mouton (rallying in the 1980s) spring first to mind.

multicoloured make the mosaic that pictures motoring as a sport. They did not have to win championships to be memorable: scores and hundreds of names are notable, thousands necessary for the Byzantine patterning of events crowding the calendar ever more thickly each year. From France and America they spread first to Germany and England, to Italy and Austria, to Russia and Spain and all of Europe. When the Great War had redrawn the boundaries of nations and extended the domain of the internal combustion engine (staff cars were raced across Egypt then, and record-breakers across Australia), all the world came to know the sport which motoring was. When the Second World War had redistributed the wealth of the nations, when the Vietnam war had redistributed much of the guilt, and when the anticipation of a space war had revolutionised communications, all the world seemed to need such sport as motoring could provide. By 1975 the world population numbered 4 billion people; now it is 6 billion, and not a single soul among them is out of the range of a satellite beaming the news of the latest soul-stirring, tyre-burning, rabble-rousing episode in some motor-sporting championship or other. Everybody seems to be watching, and if (as has happened) victory goes to a Brazilian man in an English car with American tyres and a Japanese engine, so much the better.

The sport has suffered more than enough nationalism. Doubtless, like many an –ism, it served its purpose at the time, reviving the morale of the downcast, raising the standards of the repressed, and occasionally spitting in the eye of the overweening. France was unquestionably the leader, until Italy in 1907, and Germany soon after, stepped in to challenge her. It looked like being France again after the Great War, at a time when Germany was considered inadmissible, but in 1922 Mussolini came to power in Italy and adopted as a major part of his foreign policy the reduction of French influence. Was it coincidence that from 1922 Italy dominated motor racing until Hitler had settled into power a dozen years later, when his brand of National Socialism used motor racing as an advertising medium to impress the world?

Nothing like that ever happened again. Perhaps the sport of motoring was never so sporting as in the two decades after the fall of Hitler. It was sheer human spirit that made Italy top dog for the first of those decades, and dogged enthusiasm that made Britain supreme for the second. Then it was the turn of the French, with a new generation of keenly schooled drivers, enough to supply all the leading teams until the present era, when everything from the oil companies to the television subtitles is truly international.

The USA could so easily have swamped them all. Only sympathy for the splendour and simplicity of American isolation can explain why it did not; but the Land of the Free is well enough represented, in the list of the truly great and influential car-makers of racing history, by the most freethinking of them all, the Chaparral. Goodness knows there have been cars by the hundreds to cement that mosaic of drivers by the thousands; but the names that have significantly altered the course of racing history and had a lasting influence on its engineering have been few indeed. Peugeot, Fiat, Mercedes-Benz, Cooper, Lotus and Chaparral are those names, in chronological order; and if others favoured by enthusiasts or deified by idolators be examined, they will be seen only as arch exponents of established principles, or entrenched defenders of established interests.

The name of Porsche might grudgingly be added in recognition of the special case for the sports car. The competition development of the touring car for rallying might beg for the honouring of Citroën, Mini, Lancia and Audi. Yet already we are beginning to make excuses, and there should be no excuses.

None of them should need any excuses. To the sport-minded they were all marvellous, all beautiful, the successful and the failures alike. We may be able to see a beautiful integrity in the uncompromising and dauntingly competent stance of today's cars, wide and low and sticky with rubber, clean and complex as a surgical theatre, a blare in the ears and a blur in the eyes and a fireproofed gauntlet flung in the face of relevance. So was there a beautiful intensity in the tiny cigar-bodied single-seaters of the early 1960s, their waxing tyres strangely remote on fragile suspensions summoning an image of water boatmen, those slender insects which go skimming the surface with oars that seem barely to touch the water's meniscus. Their tiny jewelled engines sang a pure high strain, a clear clarion with six scales and a tiny polished wood-tipped gearswitch to pluck each in turn from the coils of exhaust pipes ecstatic in their mating.

What cataracts came spouting from the trumpets of the generation earlier! What variety there was – unthinkable today – as V8 engine vied with straight eight, fat four with slim six, and as much argument raged about the right structure for a chassis or the right shape for a body as about the right angle of an engine. Most noble rage of all, though, was surely in the last days of the supercharger, when cars coughed like lions and bellowed like dragons, when their very sound seared like venom and their smell scoured the heavens, and the little giants that were men sat bolt upright in them to sight their long bonnets along each sliding secant and spur their sizzling tyres through each drifting tangent. How the photographers loved to catch them head-on in their four-wheel drifts, how the public thrilled to watch them in profile on their full-swill razzle, glorious in detonating defeat and uproarious in explosive victory!

What men or gods are these? might a motoring Keats marvel. What pursuit more mad than found further back, in the vintage years, with senses not yet sated? Were not those machines beautiful, in their proportions as in their promise? When superchargers were new and springs were stiff, when engines twisted in the torture of their own heat and drivers blistered behind them, when the very pores of the cars opened with the anguished hours to lard the lean earth with their oily sweat, was it not bliss to be a spectator? And very heaven to be a competitor, making music with a forged gearlever that begged to be used, while making peace with a fractious clutch that begged to be left alone? Making constant corrections, even along the straights, with a steering wheel that kicked you for your pains – and making whoopee afterwards with fashionable friends who loved you for your valour?

Beyond them, before them, loomed the giants. They were not as heavy as they looked – nothing short of a railway locomotive could be as heavy as some of them looked – nor as clumsy; but because they were so large, and because their engines turned so slowly, they were often faster than they looked and much faster than they sounded. Like all the giants of history, from the Anakim of Genesis to the Normans of the 13th century, they were soon cut down, but while they held sway they were magnificent. Sculptors were inspired by them, painters bemused by them; the Manifesto of Modern Art proclaimed the racing car the new ideal of naked beauty. The future may never present another past like it.

Yet the beauty of motoring sport was always only skin deep, and always the worms of avarice, of commerce and politics and conquest for the sake of personal or national or other notional vanity, were busy beneath that alluring complexion. It was not sabotage that killed off the series of races for the Gordon Bennett Trophy, but the boycott imposed by the French, who resented the rules which prevented France from being more strongly represented than the other nations. Instead they instituted an annual event for the Grand Prix de l'Automobile Club de France; but when, shortly before the onset of the Great War, the 1914 event at Lyons was won by Mercédès, the crowd (who had hoped for a victory by their hero 'Gorgeous Georges' Boillot in a Peugeot) watched sullen and silent as the fast, finely trained and faultlessly disciplined German team finished first, second, and third. Two years later, fighter pilot Georges Boillot was killed in the air over Germany. After another two years, it was made clear that German participation in postwar motor racing would not be countenanced.

If it was nationalism which strongly influenced the conduct of major events in the early 1920s and late 1930s, it was business that intruded more openly year by year from the 1950s. In 1957 the oil companies which had admittedly been putting a lot of money into motoring sport (doubtless for reasons having little to do with charity or altruism) brought pressure to bear on the regulatory body to alter the rules of Grand Prix racing. From 1958 it was to be fuelled only by what was euphemistically called 'pump petrol', an expression which allowed a good deal of cheating before the rules were tightened even further. The cars, hitherto fed clever and complex potions (of which methanol formed a major proportion, but with adequate measures of acetone, ether, nitro-benzene, and similarly exciting stimulants), were now intrinsically slower; but it was argued that races were too long for the sustained interest of the lay spectators, so race distances were shortened, fuel loads thereby lightened, and the cars were thus apparently as fast as ever.

In the 1960s the spread of television made the advertising industry take much more interest in motor racing. Soon the rules against carrying advertising matter (rules that had never prevailed in the USA, needless to say) were relaxed to allow small decals to be stuck onto the bodywork. Next, 'sponsors' were allowed the display of a plain rectangle, of regulated size, bearing their name before the ever more inquisitive cameras. By the end of that decade, clever little Colin Chapman of Lotus had found out that the convention of cars in international events being painted in national colours (a practice instigated during the old Gordon Bennett days) did not amount to a legal requirement: instead of the traditional British Racing Green (it was strictly Parsons' Napier Green, the colour of the car which won the 1902 event) the Lotus F1 car now appeared in the livery of a Player's cigarette packet, and soon every contestant became a mobile advertising hoarding.

Bereft of their identities, the cars began to enjoy less and less interest. Often their makers' names were submerged in a froth of fulsome titles blurbing the names of their 'sponsors'. At the same time, the drivers were enjoying more and more attention, as had been happening progressively since the introduction of the World Championships in 1950. It was much easier for the spectating enthusiast to follow the fortunes of a man than to stay in touch with the intricacies of a machine; it was very much easier for the sports editors of newspapers and magazines, of radio and television. By 1980 the details of the competing cars mattered as little to most followers of the sport as did the details of a golfer's putter, a sprinter's spikes, a batsman's box. The details which attracted attention concerned a driver's athletic training, his business flair, his diet, his sex life, and above all (as was becoming the case with most of the new godlings that the people chose to worship) his wealth.

Everything that happened to Grand Prix racing happened also to sports-car racing, to rallying, to hillclimbing and sprinting and to the specialised forms of competition (oval-track racing, for instance) cultivated in countries such as the USA which had their own particular traditions to be traduced. The effect was always most noticed at the top, but there was always an effect to be detected all the way down to the grass-roots participants in minor events at the bottom of the pyramid. There are still many thousands of them, and they are generally younger now because the physical burdens of competition driving are more severe than ever before: the forces experienced when cornering or braking a modern racing car are six times more violent than in 1950, for instance.

There may be many thousands of them, but they are not the ones who matter to the organisers of the sport, the men who arrange the venues and the advertising and above all the television contracts. The people who matter to them are not even the louts who flock to the grandstands and spectator enclosures at each track for a major event, and who threaten to become as intemperate and possibly violent as their counterparts in other highly publicity-dependent sports. The people who matter most are the ones who make F1 racing the most popular spectator sport of all, the ones who goggle at their television screens and watch the advertisements and buy the beers and the burgers, the watches and the computers, the holiday packages and the investment packages, that are so lavishly promoted. Sometimes, admittedly, just sometimes, the advertisements are for cars.

CHAPTER 5

ARTS AND FASHIONS

'This is life!' said I to myself. It seemed to me that I'd never known the height of physical pleasure until I'd driven in a motor-car. It was better than dancing on a perfect floor with a perfect partner to pluperfect music; better than eating when you're awfully hungry; better than holding out your hands to a fire when they're numb with cold; better than a bath after a hot, dusty railway journey. I can't give it higher praise, can I?

C N & A M WILLIAMSON, *The Lightning Conductor*

IN OCTOBER 1902 THERE WAS published what was possibly the first motoring novel. Within 23 months it was in its seventh edition. The Williamsons, husband and wife, had a winner.

Their formula was successfully repeated, several times in the next few years. By 1906 the Williamsons could confidently confirm the high social tone of their books by dedicating *The Car of Destiny* (which involved the young King of Spain, above which level social tone could hardly expect to climb) to 'a dear and valued friend, the Dowager Lady Dalrymple of North Berwick'. In their stories the hero and heroine were always well bred (and fortuitously well endowed with the world's goods, to which in the real world the well-bred do not always have access), chauffeurs and other servants either rascals or saints, the middle-class interlopers variously dependable or given to sharp practice.

Apart from the romantic theme of each story, there was a travelogue taking in the most tasteful sights of the chosen country (in *The Lightning Conductor* the main scene was France), and there was a surprisingly realistic account of what motoring was like in those days on those roads. Daily maintenance, running repairs, finding fuel, skirting hazards, all the problems of early motoring – including the dust, the weather, and the occasional antipathy of other road users – were recounted frankly, and in sound but not excessive technical detail. Whatever might be the merits of the story, or indeed of its setting, the account given of motoring was honest – and, as can be seen from the quotation, unswervingly enthusiastic.

That enthusiasm could also be found, though it was less fancifully applied to the page, in the work of such a man of letters as Rudyard Kipling. He never drove himself, but (perhaps because he was an engineer manqué, schooled in his travels on the Indian railways and particularly keen on ship construction) he was tremendously keen on cars. Frustrated by his early problems with a steam car, he came to be very appreciative indeed of the virtues of the early Lanchester, which showed that he had his head screwed on properly. In later life he settled for a Hooper-bodied Rolls-Royce Phantom.

A generation later, the escapist reader yearning for romance and fortune in the variously difficult era following the Great War could still enjoy the latest manifestations of motoring, coloured by the current modes of fashionable society, in such novels as those now written by Dornford Yates. Because of that war, the world of high society was a different place: Yates dismissed the daily discipline of motor management, and only the random mishap discoloured the sky-blue purity of motoring as the well-heeled knew it. The romance was of a different tone, possibly sliding off into a detective story, a spy story, or a comedy of manners, but always it revealed the author's prejudices and jingoism – his uncomprehending dislike of Jews, his comprehensive dislike of Germans, and his ineradicable conviction that there was and could be no car on any road fit to hold a candle to the Rolls-Royce.

His works, too, sold very successfully, until there came another war to change the world and challenge its assumptions even more, and to give its survivors an appetite for a different kind of escapist stories. In the Cold War which followed the Second World War, Ian Fleming now flourished glamour and espionage in place of elegance and etiquette: his hero James Bond now made free use of the car as one of the tools of his trade (and, from time to time, of his trifling). His foes used cars more seriously but no less as a matter of course, and his readers loved it because this was the time when much of the world was at the height of its love affair with the car. It was just a pity that Fleming used to get his motoring technicalities wrong; he used to make mistakes about guns, too.

One would never expect a traditional American, schooled 'to ride, shoot straight, and tell the truth' as many a traditional American was, to make that kind of mistakes. When Ernest Hemingway deigned to mention cars at all, it was as likely to be a whimsical piece of social comment. When John Steinbeck allows himself to become involved, however, he does what nearly all Americans nearly always did: he takes the vehicle for granted. What he writes is about the land, and what he writes about that is really about the people. There are a lot of Charlies in *Travels with Charley*.

Truths are often sad, and the sad truth about the car is that it was generally thought too prosaic even for prose. For poetry, it was almost unthinkable. The world of literary criticism is very nearly as precious and pretentious as that Other World of art criticism, and poets are inordinately sensitive to it. Just occasionally we find a poet good enough or brave enough to go it alone: Louis MacNeice would quite often reveal an enthusiasm for motoring, perhaps best revealed in

Take corners on two wheels, until you go so fast

That you can clutch a fringe or two of the windy past [30]

while laureate John Betjeman had no compunction in accurately placing Rover, Austin, and Hillman in their social levels in *A Subaltern's Love-song*, or Lagonda, Hupmobile, and Delage in *Indoor Games near Newbury*.

Maybe the place to seek high-flown language is not in poetry but in politics. Maybe, since the word of a politician is even less to be trusted than that of an enthusiast, we should look in the politics of art. At a time when the exploits of the big blasting Fiats in brassbound Italian Racing Red had recently captured the admiration of all Italy and much of motor-minded Europe, the Futurist Manifesto harangued us to abandon alike the classical pediment and the romantic impediment from our appreciation of art, and to substitute the forms and motions and implications of the machine, the new man-made god. Marinetti, author of the manifesto, propounded a new ideal of naked beauty: it was the racing car, with its huge blood-red bonnet from which came, fat and serpentine in polished copper, an exhaust pipe which breathed fire and shrapnel.

In the end the motor car never really made it as an artist's model, doubtless because the advertising industry (which employed what we were pleased to disdain as 'commercial artists') gave us so much of it, in forms variously didactic, dramatic, or erotic. If machinery figured in *ars gratia artis*, it was the machinery of heavy industry and colossal architecture, the machinery that was not so highly advanced[31] that it did not demand the devoted wage-earning slavery of Stakhanovite Man wielding his sledgehammer or spanner in a sweat of communist world-rebuilding fervour. Usually in the form of vast murals, this kind of paintings, not Fabergé eggs, was fine art in post-revolutionary Russia; strangely, it was also popular in capitalist America and fascist Italy.

No established school of art can ever accommodate the new ways of thinking and the new ways of living which follow each other in the mud-stirred wake of technological progress. Neither revolt nor revolution amongst the practitioners of an established art can ever successfully appoint a new subject-matter to the establishment. What is needed is an entirely new art form. What the car found, to picture its motions and mechanisms and meanings and menace, was the cinema.

Children of the same epoch, the offspring of the same union between science and industry, fostered by the same capitalist ambitions and populist aspirations, the car and the cinema grew up in each other's arms. The mighty racing car, taking a fast bend in a long powerslide as it successfully raced the train in D W Griffith's *Intolerance*, was welcomed to the then silver screen as a new icon ready for worship. More humbly, Ford's immortal but by no means impregnable Tin Lizzie was the butt of hours of slapstick comedy which successfully entertained millions. The cheap jalopy pictured lending a tortured practicality to the life of the humble homesteader was, no less than the burnished phaeton of the Beverly Hills socialite, an illustration – and no less art than any ink-and-paper illustration by Doré or Beardsley, Dürer or Heath Robinson – giving expression to something we began to describe as the 'standard of living'.

To that extent it was realistic, as has been much that we have called art; but as long as the cinema restricted itself to the monochrome picture, there was always somewhere to be found a hint or more of the surrealism newly pervading graphic art elsewhere. Machines and motor cars might have notable parts in Chaplin's *Modern Times*, in Cocteau's *Orphée*, in René Clair's *A Nous la Liberté*, but what mattered was their fanciful treatment: in the Cocteau film, Death rode in a Rolls-Royce, and her outriders straddled big American v-twin Indian[32] motorcycles very like those of the New York Police Department.

When monochrome composition gave way to technicolor[33] riot, the car's role

30 From *Sunday Morning*. Read also *An Eclogue for Christmas*.

31 It is a sad commentary on the shortcomings of the artist as commentator that most artists never came nearer than the furnace and the forge to representing machinery. The massive scale and the lurid lighting of these much earlier representatives of the industrial age were presumably easier for the paint-dauber, the charcoal-wielder, and other approximative myopics of the art world, to recapture in two dimensions. I doubt if any self-professed artist, let alone the painters recognised as such by society, ever even tried to understand or to translate the meticulous spirit, the informing propriety, or the unforgiving accuracy, suffusing the milling machine or the centre lathe.

32 After all these years I concede that they may have been Harley-Davidsons, but I remember them as Indians. Both were pretty deadly.

33 James Clerk Maxwell created the first colour photograph in 1861, but it was not until 1935 that Kodak could begin marketing colour ciné film. The process developed by the Technicolor [*sic*] Corporation was rather different, but the Man in the Street was ever careless of technicalities (observe his careless abuse of the word *electronic* from the 1960s) and it was common to describe all the colour films which began to dominate the cinema as the 1940s gave way to the 1950s as *technicolour*.

in the cinema descended to that of the bit-player, or more commonly one of the crowd – as it was in Hollywood life. There were exceptions: Herbie, the magical VW Beetle, was a star of sorts, as was James Bond's Aston Martin in *Goldfinger*. More often, the hero and/or villain drove carefully tuned and adapted lookalike versions of popular American models in some crucial chase episode – an idea carried to its limits in the team of three Mini Cooper S bullion-snatchers which were perhaps the real heroes of the 1969 film *The Italian Job*. Since then the car chase, replete with crashes and miraculous avoidances and stunts that need a lot of rehearsal (and a lot of replacement cars, as well as quite a few replacement stunt drivers), has become a sickening cliché of the screen, ever more noisy and violent as the typical viewer grows likewise.

If we must recoil in eventual disgust from the role of the car in modern popular art – a situation not eased by the contributions of the advertising industry, where fantasy and irrelevance have grown beyond anything that might have been imagined by the pioneering copywriter who hammered out his *'Somewhere West of Laramie . . .'* advert for the Jordan Playboy in the early 1920s and earned undying fame among other advertising copywriters – we might yet enquire how art was applied to the car.

The truth appears to be that it hardly ever happened. There were a few sports-racing BMWs that were offered by the manufacturers to noteworthy artists of the 1970s as mobile canvases to be adorned before they took the field at Le Mans and other venues, but the artists seem to have been daunted by the challenge and they achieved nothing of note. Far less inhibited were the youthful artists and art students who were invited by Citroën to do what they would to the appearance of the 2CV, by that same decade identified as the car for exuberant but shallow-pocketed youths anxious to make their marks.

The results were amusing, but the whole thing was dismissed by everyone as a *jeu d'esprit* not reproducible elsewhere. The trouble with art is that it evolves very slowly, whereas the marketing of the car demands that changes be made quickly and frequently. Accordingly, what we have seen applied to the car has not been art itself, but fashions in art – and even they, ephemera though they are, do not change in synchronism with the marketing pressures perceived by car-makers.

Some artistic fashions have come from other disciplines to infect the car with notable effect. Some of the first were applied to the styling of the interior, most readily in early examples of the closed car, where furniture and fittings might echo the tastes and materials (especially the fancy woods) popularised by the Art Nouveau movement at the turn of the 19th–20th centuries. This most pervasive style could most readily be seen in the proliferation of poster art featuring the car at about this time.

A contemporary development in car design was the isolation of the radiator (in those days a necessarily prominent structural feature at the front of the car, one which had to be exposed to view as it had to be exposed to airflow) as the ideal thing to be styled so as to identify the car. In quite a short time the radiators of Rolls-Royce, Ford, Delaunay-Belleville, Vauxhall (including the tapered flutings on the bonnet behind the radiator), Coventry-Daimler, and a few others culminating in Bugatti, became very well known, and most others could be dismissed as derivatives even though the minor differences were quite enough for the keen motor-noter to identify rival brands.

This was not enough for some people; they wanted to add more, to enhance the distinction, and several sculptors (the French seemed to be best at it) produced suitable miniatures. By 1910 Rolls-Royce were quite perturbed by the motley collection of mascots that owners were tacking on to their cars, and decided to furnish their own official mascot – something that had been done for the Vulcan car as early as 1903. A successful English sculptor, Charles Sykes, was commissioned to fashion something suitably dignified and decent but not thereby the less delightful, and he created what has since been known around the world as the R-R emblem. Its true title was *The Spirit of Ecstasy*, but the common folk knew it better as 'The Silver Lady' – which was often true prior to 1914, when nickel plating took over from silver plating. Chromium plating was overlaid[34] in the 1920s, persisting until the lost-wax process of investment casting was sufficiently developed in the latter 1950s for R-R to make the thing in stainless steel.

Other mascots proliferated after the Great War. Many were mere commercial tack-on things, as tacky as things can come, but there were jewels among the trash, especially the frosted glass castings made by Lalique[35]. The first of these were

---

34 Chromium plating is porous, and will soon be pocked by rust unless it has been applied over a substrate of nickel plating, which is impermeable. When nickel was in short supply in the years after the Second World War, it often had to be omitted; the results were soon seen to be deplorable.

35 René Jules Lalique was getting on a bit by this time, having been born in 1860. Originally a jeweller by trade, he later discovered the artistic properties of glass at the same time as his close American contemporary Louis Comfort Tiffany. These two together pretty well defined what glass could do in the environment of Art Nouveau, and their respective factories prospered accordingly.

commissioned by Citroën, but Lalique soon saw what a market he had and he made the most of it.

The important mascots, however, were those which became officially associated with particular brands of cars, and the art therefore was often subjugated to the commercial imagery. Most elegant of exceptions was the flying stork of Hispano-Suiza, created by the French sculptor F Bazin to surmount the radiator of the Hispano-Suiza from 1919. The stork had previously nothing to do with motoring, but already had effected an important liaison with the noble name of Hispano-Suiza, supplier of one of the most distinguished aero-engines of the Great War. This engine[36] was used without exception by the SPAD aircraft which served the most famous fighter group of the Service Aéronautique Français during that conflict. It was the Groupe de Combat No 12, renowned for the quality of the several aces who flew in it, including Fonck and Guynemer[37], and it was known as *les Cigognes*, the aircraft carrying on their flanks the badge of a flying stork in profile. It was this badge which Bazin recreated in three dimensions for use as a radiator mascot on Hispano-Suiza cars; copies were occasionally supplied for other purposes, but usually it was only those specimens intended specifically for use on the cars that the artist signed.

By the time that the new H6 Hispano-Suiza had made its 1919 debut at the Paris Salon and been recognised by connoisseurs as the rightful holder of the title of Best Car in the World to which Rolls-Royce were still clinging so petulantly, the cursive elegance and luxuriant finish of Art Nouveau trappings were beginning to fade in their appeal. The new fashion in applied art was for clean unadorned functionalism, as most persuasively propounded by Germany's new Bauhaus under the leadership of Walter Gropius.

The motor industry was still too young to have a proper understanding of what the functions of most car components really were, and could not reconcile itself to the new fashion at all. Instead it created a fashion of its own, a fashion for high-class engines to appear as nearly as possible architecturally monolithic, with no accretions or ancillaries to spoil the smoothness of the exterior. What horrors this imposed on the inlet and exhaust manifolds, the coolant conduits, and other necessities mercilessly buried alive within the confines of the enamelled slab that the high-class engine pretended to be, can only be supposed an affront to the engineers of the time.

Then, in 1925, came the Paris Exposition des Arts Décoratifs – not so much an exposition as an explosion of jazz-age imaginative freedom to exploit formal and tactile qualities inherited from all manner of previous disciplines and new discoveries.

From the title of the exhibition we took the name *Art Déco*, and the wave of hedonism sweeping the western world in the 1920s (among those who could afford it, we should add) found applications for it everywhere, the car being no exception. Art Déco was versatile, refreshing, erotic, indulgent, wildly sensual or coolly elegant. It flourished in the contours of car bodies, in the mouldings that highlighted them and the painted coachlines that graced them, in the applied metalwork of headlamp brackets or engine-bay ventilators, in the furniture and fittings of the cabin interior, in the full expanse of a fascia panel or in the fine detail of a bracket on that panel carrying a tiny crystal vase to sustain a little posy of flowers to grace the interior of a formal coupé body. Art Déco was suddenly everywhere, from patrician Panhard to plebeian Peugeot, perhaps never more flamboyantly than in the implausibly advanced Bucciali nor more tastefully than in the road cars built and bodied by Bugatti.

The Wall Street Crash of 1929 and its aftermath, a world-wide economic recession, denied any continuity for the cultivation of the decorative and applied arts, in the car or elsewhere. Yet business had to continue and to prosper if we were not all to be left to rot; marketing people had to find ways of continuing to sell, manufacturing people to find ways to make what the marketeers could sell. In the USA General Motors had already begun to apply, though not yet with any formal internal ruling on the matter, the idea of the annual model change – essentially a styling change, an amendment or a facelift, that might add nothing of value to the car that endured unchanged beneath the skin, but could add seriously to its value as a marketing proposition to encourage continuing sales.

Such accelerated change of appearance created a tempo of fashion that not even the fashion industry could match. Styling ideas came and went in dizzying succession: there was a wave of tightly contoured turret-topped coupés in America in the 1930s, accompanied by ripples of interest there and elsewhere in faired headlamps, tall

---

36 It was a light-alloy V8 of about 200hp, and the first to feature an overhead camshaft and fully enclosed valvegear above each bank of cylinders. To help the war effort, it was made in England and America, too; interestingly, only the examples made in the Hispano-Suiza factory proved reliable for long periods, whereas all others, especially those made in England, had much shorter working lives between overhauls.

37 Capitaine René P Fonck was the most successful fighter pilot of any combatant nation in the Great War. Among Frenchmen, second only to him was Capitaine Georges M L J Guynemer.

*Fashions as they were: 1934 –
tailored lady, crisp attendant,
handsome Mercedes-Benz
500K, and the clever lighting of
photographer Zoltan Glass.*

narrow noses, tiny rear windows, tubular-framed seats, partially or wholly enclosed spare wheels. There was also, underlying the ripples and the waves, a swell; and it came from the work of the great industrial designers for other industries.

Streamlining was the catchword. Serious efforts had been made in the 1920s (and, on a more limited scale, before) to determine the best shapes calculated to penetrate the air with the least possible resistance; but the practical realisation of these shapes was handicapped by engineering objections and by the indifference of the marketplace. Chrysler tried to popularise functional streamlining with the Airflow model of 1934, but failed almost catastrophically. True streamlining would have to wait for decades before it could be designed into a production car; but, influenced by the latest aircraft in particular, and to some extent by the latest express locomotives, the public liked the *idea* of streamlining, and the acute industrial designer exploited this enthusiasm. Perhaps the most acute was Raymond Loewy, whose Coldspot refrigerator of 1932 was an overwhelming success in the USA. All earlier refrigerators had been frankly rectilinear descendants of the primitive ice-box, but here was one which was curvaceous, organic, streamlined.

Humans are curved, not box-shaped; maybe that was the deep-down reason for the popularity of the streamlined style. At any rate it flourished, producing shapes for kettles, toasters, locomotives, cinema organs, cars . . . And not even in the cars was there any real concern for efficacy of airflow-management: streamlining was meant to appeal to the eye alone. It was not functional streamlining; it was aesthetic streamlining.

The 1936 Lincoln Zephyr, though of no perceptible engineering merit, was a masterpiece of aesthetic streamlining, and its resounding commercial success – in dramatic contrast to the fate of the Chrysler Airflow – left stylists in no doubt where their future might lie. Because it allowed and even encouraged the drawing of fantastic lines and the sculpting of fantastic shapes, streamlining was the perfect aid to the annual model change, permitting the stylist to produce something just a little more fantastic in each succeeding year. By 1937 Harley Earl, the big and brash boss of the GM styling department, devised a new tool for assessing the acceptability of such fantasies: the 'dream car' would be a styling exercise to be shown to the public, whose reactions could be interpreted as a guide to future designs for production.

This was the era in which the USA removed the car from the influence of contemporary art, and instead made the car acutely susceptible to the changes in fashion that the American industry deliberately and methodically dictated. The European industry could not possibly keep pace (not all of it wanted to, American tastes being viewed in some quarters with grave misgivings) and seldom tried, although some feeble imitations of American features occasionally appeared, usually too late and looking too laboured.

The fantasising had to stop when the Second World War brought us all face to face with realities that might never have been imagined. It also brought us visions of machines (military aircraft, in particular) that seemed, if only by association with the young heroes who tempted death in them, imbued with a glamour all their own. Nowhere was this more true than in the USA, a nation which came to the war but to which the war never came: when the war was over, Americans would be offered cars which made a point of styling features inherited and adapted from the warplanes that had become familiar through every newspaper and newsreel.

The fashion was promptly for tailfins, and for lavishly glazed canopies with

It is the house and the happy couple that set the tone of luxury and prosperity in this 1949 advertisement, but it is the new Buick Roadmaster (with four Venti-Ports to each flank) which is supposed to do so.

curved screens, for rounded contours imitating the monocoque construction of aircraft, and for airscoops generously chromed for emphasis – and for distraction from the truth that they were dummies leading nowhere. There was also a brief fashion for aircraft-inspired vents and outlets, best remembered as the infamous portholes on the flanks of the 1949 Buick. Named Venti-Ports, they were supposed to recall the exhaust stubs of fighter planes, and were originally fitted with hoses whereby heat might be conducted out of the engine-bay; but the principal of a California high school complained that some of his male students used the ports of his Buick as urinals, and halfway through the first year of production the ports were sealed off to survive only as styling excrescences.

Very soon the styling cues imported from wartime aircraft made way for others plucked from more modern and more glamorous aircraft, the jets. Swept-back tailfins of vast dimensions soared above tail lights doing their best to look like jet exhausts; and because jet-fighter pilots sat well forward in the fuselage, ahead of the engine, the windscreen of the American car moved forward and the tail, housing a luggage compartment of increasing area and decreasing depth, was elongated almost beyond belief and certainly beyond the limits of easy manoeuvring.

Europe despaired of the Americans at this point, and would no longer be led by them. The offerings of the American industry were to grow ever more preposterous throughout the 1950s, and the worst that European designers could do was no worse. In the 1960s all that was to change, and America snapped out of its bluster, suddenly to produce a generation of cars that came as a complete surprise, cars that were clean and pure in their shapes and which bore themselves with that easy elegance that generous dimensions facilitate.

It was too late. Let the Americans appreciate what they had, by all means; but Europe had found new fashion leaders, and had found them at home. Until the early 1960s Germany was a dead duck, with only the mid-1950s 300SL Mercedes-Benz and BMW 507 to relieve the hideous monotony of artless, passionless domestic saloons and the grimly functional ubiquity of the VW Beetle. France had seen all its claims to style and grace fail before the onslaught of a vicious levelling-down at the instigation of a strongly communistic fiscal system. England was building cars in profusion, but in a cacophonous jumble of unrelated styles[38] that could never have been described as fashionable and bore very little relationship to art, however they might qualify as contemporary[39].

In car styling as in much else, the fashion centre of Europe was in Italy, more or less equally divided between Milan and Turin. The fashion houses – in some cases they had grown to be vehicle manufacturers for modest runs of cars designed for such clients as Peugeot – had coachbuilding backgrounds, and a traditional facility for

---

38 At one extreme Frank Feeley was still doing his elegant best for Aston Martin and Lagonda, and Dudley Hobbs was maintaining his blend of sobriety and aerodynamic efficiency to confirm the supreme quality of the individual and idiosyncratic Bristol. At the other extreme were the sickly confections – this was, remember, the ice-cream heyday of whitewall tyres – of the Rootes Group (Hillman, Humber, Singer and Sunbeam), while Austin and Morris and the rest of the cheap end made little attempt to set or to follow fashions until the Mini (from which styling was conspicuous by its absence) emerged in 1959.

39 *Contemporary* was a buzzword widely and uncritically used by the English in the context of design at this time. To be seen in Woolworth stores were cardboard plates printed with the ancient and long popular Chinese design known as 'willow pattern'; perhaps because it was in bald cobalt blue and white, it was labelled 'contemporary' in the hope that the word would sell them as it sold most things. The most truly contemporary design was a reflection of the sudden burgeoning of television in the British home: everything from ashtrays to kitchen sinks took on the shape of the bulging barrel-distorted rectangle that was familiar as the television screen, and this fashion spread into the car in the shaping of instrument dials, badges, and even steering wheels.

AUTOMOBILE CLUB DI MILANO
GRANDE CONCORSO INTERNAZIONALE DI TURISMO
Oltre Lire 40.000 di Premi
13 MAGGIO GYMKHANA AUTOMOBILISTICA L. 5000 a Premi

DeDion Bouton

1 HOMME ACTIF EN VAUT 10
S'IL A UNE QUADRILETTE
Peugeot

EXPOSICIÓN REGIONAL VALENCIANA
GRANDES FIESTAS
AUTOMOVILISTAS = Premios 10000 pesetas
y objetos de arte
GINKAMAS 8ª
KILOMETRO „LANCE"

designs based on production cars of modest origin. They had sculptural flair, and often a sporting spirit, and they made many mistakes, but every so often they did something so right that it would influence the motoring world for years to come. They were the likes of Bertone, Pinin Farina, Ghia, Touring, Viotti and Zagato, and any one of these names served as a byword and a pass among all nations.

If Italy called the tune in the 1950s, it must be admitted that Britain and Germany perked up their ideas a bit in the subsequent decade. It was not through any increased aesthetic sensibility (neither nation was strong on aesthetics) but a by-product of the increasing fervour with which all Europe began to follow motoring sport. The enthusiasm had always been there in Italy, but it was in England in the 1950s that motor racing erupted on an unprecedented scale, to continue its growth and keenness for decades to come, and to infect all Europe (and much of America) with an enduring passion not only for racing but also for rallying and other forms of competition.

Traditional open-wheeled single-seaters remained a law (or at least a lore) unto themselves, but the two-seater sports car or the gran turismo coupé that fared well in the sporting arena proved to be very influential in the market-place. Such features as light-alloy wheels, low-profile tyres, aerodynamic appendages that might only be expected to work on the Mulsanne Straight, lighting arrays that might only be expected to be serviceable in the Scandinavian forests, and all the bucket seats and alloy-framed steering wheels and associated gewgaws, were showered generously on the meanest of family cars, while the real sporting models (especially the wedge-shaped ones of the early 1970s) exerted a profound influence on basic shapes.

Sometimes the influence was less direct. The GT40 with which Ford sought to impress their name upon sports-car endurance racing was a tough-looking American version of the sort of Ferraris that Ford wanted to beat, and the later Mk 2 version did actually succeed in winning the 24-hour race at Le Mans in 1966. Although it was actually derived from a Lola built in England by Eric Broadley, the Ford GT40 profited from the immense publicity given it to become in the early 1960s the new model of what the race-bred road car should resemble, and in 1966 Lamborghini shocked the Genève Salon by showing his new Miura, a car which appeared to be precisely what a rich man's roadgoing GT40 should be like, and one which threatened to undermine every established principle in the traditionalist's book. What made the Miura look even more striking was its colour, one that had surely never been seen on a car before, even at a motor show: tantalisingly poised somewhere between yellow and orange, it became in the next few years the most compellingly fashionable colour – first for sporting cars, eventually for everything – ever to take over the motoring scene, in varying interpretations from Positano Yellow to that sunburnt orange which distinguishes western Texas.

The Miura had a further and more lasting influence on fashion. Cleverly offsetting that extraordinarily positive colour was the ultimate in negativity, matt black: it was applied to everything – window surrounds and wiper arms, mirrors and grilles, louvres and lamp-rims – that might conventionally be polished or plated. Again the industry at large was keen to copy: it took time to find black coatings that would stay matt and not chip or flake off, but in the end it would be a useful production economy. The public was not at all indignant about the cheapening of their cars, where there had once been costly chromium or stainless steel, because the public had been told that non-reflective black was safer in that it did not cause dazzle.

And so it went on, the eternally double-crossing pendulum of perfidious fashion swinging with predictable duplicity. After the all-black car came a passion for cars that were all white. More recently, a sudden taste for pale wood floors (there had to come a time when wall-to-wall carpeting would be deemed dowdy) and pale metal furniture and fittings, in domestic interiors and in restaurants and office buildings, was carried over into the interiors of cars for the surfacing of controls, handles, fascia panels and the like, while their exterior paintwork was chosen from a bewildering variety of metallic silvers all offering the pretence of aluminium body panelling. There was plenty of fake carbon-fibre in the interior trim, too, as blatantly unconvincing as the fake woodwork that had been happily accepted by the multitudes for half a century.

Artifice has become entirely acceptable in that time, but of art there has been precious little. What we are left with is fashion; but, as Coco Chanel (who must be recognised as an authority) told us years ago, *fashion is what goes out of fashion.*

TIMESCALE

WSR = world speed record; LSR = land speed record; italics in motoring column indicates a production car as distinct from a prototype or a racer

POLITICS AND ECONOMICS	LIFE AND ART	YEAR	MOTORING
Napoleonic wars begin	Bolton & Watt steam-engine patents expire Volta: electric pile	**1800**	
		1801	Trevithick steam carriage
	First steam tug (*Charlotte Dundas*) at work on R Clyde	1802	
	Eli Whitney (USA) proves interchangeability of machined parts Trevithick steam locomotive	1804	
	Maudslay: precision screw-cutting lathe	1810	
Napoleon retreats from Moscow, journeys Vilna–Paris	Beethoven: symphonies nos. 7 & 8	1812	
Napoleonic wars end		1815	
		1824	Brown: car with coal-gas engine
	Goodyear et al.: vulcanisation of rubber Nasmyth: steam hammer	1839	
		1846	Thomson: pneumatic tyre
revolutions in many European countries		1848	
	Otis passenger lift allows tall buildings	1857	
American Civil War		1861	
		1862	Lenoir: car with coal-gas engine
American Civil War ends; industrial development accelerates		1865	
	Nobel: dynamite	1866	
Japan: abolition of feudal system starts industrial development		1868	
		1870	Markus: car with petrol engine
		1877	Selden patent
		1886	Hammel *Benz* Daimler motorcycle
		1887	*Daimler*
	London: first electric railway	1890	
Sino-Japanese War Dreyfus trial Czar Nicholas succeeds to Russian throne	Aubrey Beardsley: *The Yellow Book*	1894	Paris–Rouen trial
Jameson Raid	Trial of Oscar Wilde	1895	*Duryea*

POLITICS AND ECONOMICS	LIFE AND ART	YEAR	MOTORING
Cubans revolt against Spain	Cézanne: first show		Michelin: first pneumatic car tyres *Lanchester*
Klondike gold rush	Alfred Jarry: *Ubu Roi*	1896	*système Panhard*
	Queen Victoria's diamond jubilee	1897	Nice speed week
Fashoda crisis	Ebenezer Howard: *Garden Cities*	1898	*Renault* shaft drive
Boer War	Havelock Ellis: The Psychology of Sex	1899	100km/h exceeded by Jenatzy electric record-breaker
Boxer Rebellion	Zeppelin no.1 flies Max Planck: quantum theory Freud: *The Interpretation of Dreams*	**1900**	
British create first concentration camps in South Africa	 Queen Victoria dies; Edward VII succeeds Marconi wireless signal England–Newfoundland Picasso: first exhibition	1901	 *Mercédès* *Oldsmobile* curved dash
Anglo-Japanese Treaty Boer War ends		1902	
Lenin founds Bolshevik Party in London	Mrs Pankhurst starts Suffragettes Wright Brothers: powered manned controlled flight	1903	
Entente Cordiale Russo-Japanese War		1904	
Foundation of Sinn Fein	Einstein: special theory of relativity Richard Strauss: *Salome*	1905	first motor buses in London
	first *Dreadnought* launched San Francisco earthquake	1906	*Rolls-Royce 40/50* Grand Prix racing initiated
Anglo-Russian convention financial crisis in USA, Japan, Germany, Italy	Ziegfield Follies	1907	Brooklands track *Cadillac* standardisation test
	Hoover vacuum cleaner	1908	*Ford model T*
	Blériot flies English Channel Diaghilev: *Ballets Russes* Pathé produces first newsreel Marinetti: Futurist Manifesto	1909	Indianapolis track
Union of South Africa Mexican Revolution	Zeppelin: first passenger air service B Russell & A N Whitehead: *Principia Mathematica*	1910	Monte Carlo Rally
Agadir crisis Italy invades Libya	Amundsen at South Pole Libya: first use of aircraft in war	1911	Indianapolis 500
Balkan crisis	*Titanic* sinks; iceberg survives Ravel: *Daphnis et Chloé*	1912	*Cadillac* electric starter *Peugeot Bébé*

POLITICS AND ECONOMICS	LIFE AND ART	YEAR	MOTORING
			Ford introduces line assembly
Wilson becomes president of USA	Niels Bohr	1913	Pittsburgh: first drive-in filling station
Income tax legalised in USA	Stravinsky: *The Rite of Spring*		
Panama Canal opens		1914	*Cadillac V8*
The Great War			*Dodge* pressed steel body
Italy joins Allies in Great War	D W Griffith: *The Birth of a Nation*	1915	
	Einstein: general theory of relativity		
		1916	Woodrow Wilson provides Federal funds for roadbuilding
			Hudson Super Six
			Packard Twin Six
USA enters Great War	Diaghilev/Cocteau/Satie/	1917	Ford opens River Rouge factory
	Massine/Picasso: *Parade*		
Russian Revolution			
Great War ends	world-wide influenza epidemic (–1919)	1918	
League of Nations	USA exports jazz and prohibits liquor	1919	*Citroën Model A*
			Hispano-Suiza H6B
	Gropius: Bauhaus established		*Fiat 501*
Palestine mandate	Le Corbusier: *Villa Savoie*	1920	*Duesenberg Model A*
world-wide economic crisis	acute unemployment	1921	*Rumpler Tropfwagen*
new economic policy in USSR	Berg: *Wozzeck*		
Mussolini assumes power in Italy	Joyce: *Ulysses*	1922	Fiat sets dominant new engineering fashions in GP cars
	Walton/Sitwell: *Façade*		*Austin Seven*
runaway inflation in Germany		1923	Fiat introduces supercharger in GP cars
			Tatra 11
	Gershwin: *Rhapsody in Blue*	1924	*Lancia Lambda*
			Chrysler
			Delage GL
			Milan–Como motorway
	Barnack/Leitz: Leica 35mm camera	1925	
general strike in UK	Lawrence: *Seven Pillars of Wisdom*	1926	'Cannonball' Baker drives truck across USA in six days
	Goddard: liquid-fuel rocket		
Stalin assumes supreme power in USSR	first 'talking' film	1927	LSR: 203 mph (Segrave)
	Lindbergh: first solo flight across Atlantic		*Bentley* scores first of four successive wins at Le Mans

POLITICS AND ECONOMICS	LIFE AND ART	YEAR	MOTORING
	Heisenberg: uncertainty principle		Mille Miglia
Chiang Kai-shek president in China	Disney: first Mickey Mouse cartoon	1928	*Cadillac*: synchromesh
	Brecht/Weill: *Die dreigroschener Oper*		car radio
			Duesenberg Model J
			Miller scores first of nine
			successive wins in
			Indianapolis 500
Wall Street Crash	Hemingway: *A Farewell to Arms*	1929	USA builds record 4.5
			million cars
			Motorola car radio
			Chevrolet International Six
world-wide economic disaster	Buñuel/Dalí: *L'Age d'Or*	1930	*Daimler*: 'fluid flywheel'
			with preselector gearbox
	Marlene Dietrich: *The Blue Angel*		Alfa Romeo scores first of
			six successive wins in
			Targa Florio
			Cadillac V16
Japan invades Manchuria	mass unemployment, severe inflation	1931	USA builds 50-millionth
			car
Spain becomes a republic	WSR: 407mph (Stainforth,		*DKW* front-wheel drive
	Supermarine S6B)		
Germany relieved of reparation payments	Huxley: *Brave New World*	1932	LSR: 254mph
			(Campbell)
	Walton: *Belshazzar's Feast*		*Ford V8*
FD Roosevelt becomes US president,		1933	
launches New Deal	end of Prohibition in USA		drive-in cinema, New
			Jersey
Hitler assumes power in Germany	first German concentration camp,		Rolls-Royce produces
	Dachau		new Bentley
		1934	Auto Union & Mercedes-
			Benz begin Nazi
			domination of GsP
	WSR: 440mph (Agello, Macchi-		*Citroën 'traction'*
	Castoldi MC72)		*Tatra 77*
			Bugatti T57
Italy invades Abyssinia	Tizard/Watson Watt: radar for Britain	1935	first Autobahn,
			Frankfurt–Darmstadt
Britain begins rearmament	Gershwin: *Porgy and Bess*		first parking meter,
			Oklahoma
			first pedestrian-priority
			crossings, London
			LSR: 301mph
			(Campbell)
			on salt lake in Utah
			Fiat 1500
			Cord 810

POLITICS AND ECONOMICS	LIFE AND ART	YEAR	MOTORING
Spanish Civil War	J M Keynes: *General Theory of Employment, Interest & Money* Marconi/EMI: regular high-definition television, Britain	1936	*BMW 328* *Peugeot 402*
Japan invades China		1937	*Oldsmobile*: automatic transmission *Fiat 508C Balilla 1100* *Lancia Aprilia*
Munich conference dismembers Czechoslovakia Anschluss: Germany annexes Austria		1938	*Chrysler*: fluid drive Citroën 2CV prototype Caracciola (Mercedes-Benz) reaches 268mph on Autobahn
Second World War begins	Joyce: *Finnegan's Wake* WSR: 469mph (Wendel, Messerschmitt)	1939	*VW*
Italy enters war	Disney: *Fantasia* plutonium produced penicillin (discovered 1928) made effective	1940	sealed-beam headlamps, USA Pennsylvania Turnpike *Willys Jeep*
war includes USSR, Japan and USA		1941	*Packard*: air conditioning
	Germany: V2 rocket USA: first electronic computer	1944	
end of war	atom bomb Orwell: *Animal Farm* Biró: ball-point pen	1945	
		1946	*Panhard Dyna* *Renault 4CV*
independence of India Marshall Plan	Yeager flies faster than sound Dior: New Look	1947	*Bristol 400* *Ferrari 125/166* *Cisitalia* *Standard Vanguard* *Kaiser* *Peugeot 203* catseyes on British roads
Berlin blockade State of Israel created prosperity in USA	transistor invented Henry Moore austerity in Europe	1948	*Daimler*: electric windows Goodrich: tubeless tyres *Morris Minor* *Studebaker Champion* (styled by Loewy)
NATO China becomes communist People's Republic	Orwell: *1984*	1949	*Jaguar XK120* *VW* *Citroën 2CV*

POLITICS AND ECONOMICS	LIFE AND ART	YEAR	MOTORING
Korean war (–1953) Malayan guerilla war	Jackson Pollock USA: McCarthy inquisitions (–1954) credit card (Diners' Club)	1950	*Porsche 356* disk brakes on V16 BRM GP car
	London: Festival of Britain, nb Royal Festival Hall (Matthew)	1951	*Chrysler Hemi* *Ford Consul/Zephyr:* McPherson strut front suspension *Goliath:* fuel injection *Pegaso*
Egypt: nationalist revolution	DH Comet in service	1952	experimental disk-braked Jaguar wins 12-hour race at Reims
	Beckett: *Waiting for Godot* hydrogen bomb		*Mercedes-Benz 300SL* rise of Japanese motorcycles
USSR: Khruschev takes power on death of Stalin	Stockhausen: *Kontrapunkte no 1*	1953	*Chevrolet Corvette:* plastics body Michelin X steel-belted radial-ply tyre
	Françoise Sagan: *Bonjour tristesse*	1954	
	Nabokov: *Lolita* mass vaccination against polio Sony transistor radio	1955	Le Mans disaster *Citroën DS* *Fiat 600*
Suez crisis on nationalisation of canal	Bergman: *The Seventh Seal*	1956	European fuel shortage prompts 'bubble-cars': *Isetta, Messerschmitt &c*
Hungary: USSR quells rebellion	Calder Hall: nuclear power station WSR: 1132mph (Twiss, Fairey Delta 2)		
European Common Market	Sputnik 1 Kerouac: *On the Road* rock and roll	1957	Disaster in last Mille Miglia Pirelli *Cintura* fabric carcass radial-ply tyre
France: de Gaulle president	Galbraith: *The Affluent Society* Lunik 2 first moon-landing rocket	1958	*DAF* with Variomatic transmission *Ford Edsel*
Cuba: Castro revolution succeeds		1959	*Mini* *Lotus type 14 Elite* Cooper begins racing domination of rear-engined cars
European Free Trade Organisation	first working model of laser Niemeyer: Brasilia Fellini: *La Dolce Vita*	1960	cling-rubber tyres Britain: M1 motorway *Chevrolet Corvair* *Ford Anglia 105E*

POLITICS AND ECONOMICS	LIFE AND ART	YEAR	MOTORING
Berlin wall USA: Kennedy president	Gagarin first man in space Heller: *Catch-22*	1961	*Jaguar E-type* *Buick V6* *Honda* begins car manufacture Ferguson 4-wheel-drive
Cuban rocket crisis	Coventry Cathedral contraceptive pill on sale	1962	*BMW Neue Klasse 1500* *Ford Cortina*
French veto British EEC entry	Beatlemania	1963	*Mini Cooper S* *Rover 2000* *Ford Cortina*
	the mini-skirt McLuhan: *Understanding Media*	1964	*Mini* (Hopkirk) wins Monte Carlo Rally *NSU Wankel* *Porsche 911* *Lamborghini 350* LSR: 403mph (D Campbell)
China: cultural revolution heavy US bombing of North Vietnam	natural gas in North Sea	1965	*Ford Mustang* *Rolls-Royce Silver Shadow* low-profile tyres USA: Air Pollution Act
China: *Quotations of Chairman Mao* USA: Black Panthers organised	Hovercraft in service	1966	Chaparral: wing for downforce *Fiat 124* *Lamborghini Miura* Nader: *Unsafe at Any* *Speed*
Israel: Six Days' War US: race riots	flower power Barnard: first heart transplant operation	1967	*NSU Ro80* *Fiat 125:* twin overhead camshaft engine for ordinary domestic car *Ferrari* Dino
USSR invades Czechoslovakia	Kubrick: 2001: *A Space Odyssey*	1968	*Jensen FF*
Ulster: riots	Moon landing by US astronauts Dennis Hopper: *Easy Rider*	1969	*Fiat 128* *Datsun 240Z* *Ford Capri*
USA invades Cambodia	oil in North Sea Women's Liberation Movement Solzhenitsyn awarded Nobel prize for literature Seiko: quartz watch	1970	*Citroën SM* *Citroën GS* *Range Rover* US: Clean Air Act LSR: 622mph (Gabelich) using jet propulsion
Britain joins EEC		1972	*Audi 80* *Fiat X1/9* *Honda Civic*

POLITICS AND ECONOMICS	LIFE AND ART	YEAR	MOTORING
Israel: Yom Kippur War	extensive famine	1973	Arab oil embargo provides excuse for general speed limits
Vietnam War ends	Mike Oldfield: *Tubular Bells*		*Citroën CX*
widespread inflation		1974	*VW Golf*
		1975	*Porsche Turbo*
China: death of Mao tse-tung	world population reaches 4000 million first personal computer (Apple)	1976	
	Paris: Centre Pompidou Lucas: *Star Wars*	1977	*Porsche 928* Pirelli P7 tyre
	first 'test-tube baby' born	1978	Bosch anti-lock brakes
Israel and Egypt sign peace treaty Iran: revolution establishes Islamic rule	USA: nuclear accident at Three Mile Island	1979	*Audi Quattro* first F1 win by turbocharged car (Renault)
	space shuttle begins operation IBM personal computer	1981	
USSR in crisis of direction as Brezhnev dies Falklands war		1982	*Chevrolet Blazer*
USA: economic revival	Internet opens	1983	*Citroën BX* *Mercedes-Benz 190* *Fiat Uno* *Honda Prelude* *Toyota Camry*
	Jeffreys (UK): DNA fingerprinting	1984	4wd becomes prominent in rallying *Renault Espace*
	Chernobyl nuclear accident	1986	anti-lock brakes extend downmarket
		1987	active 4-wheel steering in *Honda* Prelude
	Ishiguro: *The Remains of the Day*	1988	*Lexus LS400*
Glasnost in USSR; Berlin Wall breached	Switzerland: scientists begin work on WorldWide Web	1989	
		1990	*Honda NSX* *Mitsubishi 3000GT* *Nissan Skyline GT-R*
USSR dissolved Gulf war		1991	*Mercedes-Benz S-klasse*
'ethnic' wars	satellite navigation	1992	*McLaren*
	fissile increase in use of Internet and mobile telephones	1997	*Smart*
		1999	drivable fuel-cell prototypes
		2000	*Honda Insight*

We are grateful to the following for permission to reproduce the pictures:

6 Hulton Getty, 9 National Motor Museum, Beaulieu, 12 Topham Picturepoint, 19 The Peter Roberts Collection/Neill Bruce, 20 Science & Society/Science Museum, 22 Mary Evans Picture Library, 45 Imperial War Museum, 46 Citroën, 56 Fiat, 59 Southampton Hall of Aviation, 60 Topham Picturepoint/Press Association, 61 AKG London, 62 British Motor Industry Heritage Trust, 64 LAT, 67 © Corbis/Austrian Archives, 75 Hulton Getty, 78 The Advertising Archives, 82 Fiat, 94 Vauxhall Motors, 100 LAT, 107 BMW Group, 120 LAT, 123, 124 Topham Picturepoint, 145 National Motor Museum, Beaulieu, 154 Giles Chapman Library, 165 AKG London, 171 National Motor Museum, Beaulieu, 173 Fiat, 187 Topham Picturepoint, 190 Citroën, 198 Mary Evans Picture Library, 201 Hulton Getty, 208 Reproduced with permission from Italy 1 © 1993 Lonely Planet Publications, 214 Terry Stevens and KET, 216 Bridgeman Art Library/Museum of London UK, 225 LAT, 240 Fiat, 244 © Corbis/Bettmann, 256 © Dingo/Car en Sac, 270 Dunlop Tyres, 290 Daimler Chrysler, 299 © Corbis/Bettmann, 308 Copyright 2001, American Society of Heating, Refrigerating and Air-Conditioning Engineers, Inc. www.ashrae.org Reprinted by permission from ASHRAE Journal, August/September 2001, 362 The Peter Roberts Collection/Neill Bruce, 364 Fiat, 384 Science & Society/Zoltan Glass/NMPFT, 386 © Corbis, 388 top left The Peter Roberts Collection/Neill Bruce, 388 centre right Publicity poster for cars from the Valencian Regional Exhibition 1909/Private Collection/Bridgeman Art Library, 388 centre left Peugeot Quadrilette Advertisement, Michel Liebeaux (1881-1923)/Private Collection/Bridgeman Art Library, 388 top right Science & Society/Science Museum, 388 bottom The Peter Roberts Collection/Neill Bruce

Cover picture: Science & Society/Zoltan Glass/NMPFT

Picture research by Sandra Assersohn.

INDEX

Figures in *italics* indicate
captions.

AC 97n
Ackermann, Rudolph 356
Ader 279
Adler 83
Adwest 292
AEI 298
Agnelli, Giovanni 68
Alfa Romeo *64*, 89, 98, 255
  1.5-litre 95
  1750 360
Alfonso XIII, King of Spain 74
Allenby, Field Marshal 42n
Alvis 76, 189, 230
Amati, Pietro 320
Andretti, Mario 283
Appert, Nicholas 236, 237
Aquila-Italiana 40
Arlandes, Marquis d' 278
Arlen, Michael 74
Armstrong-Siddeley 262
Arpels, Mme Louis 165
Ascari, Alberto 369
Aston Martin 110, 152, 292,
  360, 380, 387n
Audi 137, 139, 233, 321, 371
  100 139, 144
  Coupé 137
  Quattro 137, 282, 319, 320,
    321
  V8 258
Audi-VW 139, 152
Austin 54, 66, 132, 176, 378,
  387n
  Oxbridge 233n
  Seven 51, 79, 84, 172, 188,
    248, 249
Austin, Herbert 50, 172, 248

Auto-Union *64*, 69, 81, *225*
  P-Wagen 232
Autobianchi 124
Avon 110

Babbage, Charles 299
Bailey, Senator Joseph W 11
Bantam 51, 84
Barnato, Woolf 369
Bartlett, William E 271
Bauer, Wilhelm 29n
Bauhaus 56, 382
Bazin, F 382
Bean 12hp 291
Bédarida, François 19
Bedelia 261
Bedford 77
  Dormobile *94*, 140
  trucks 318
Beeston 25, 56
Beetle *see* Volkswagen
Bel Geddes, Norman 206
Bell 369
Bendix 301
Bentley 54, 271
  3-litre 338, 360
  Mulsanne 137
  Turbo R 137
Benz 10, 15, 68, *225*, 354–8
  tricycles 355
  Viktoria 355–8
Benz, Bertha 354
Benz, Karl 4, 6, 11, 14, 18, 29,
  156, 232, 354, 355, 357
Bertone 389
Betjeman, John 378
Bira, B (Prince Birabongse of
  Siam) 92
Birkigt, Marc 74, 252
Blériot, Louis 49

BMC 106, 108, 110, 112, 124,
  176, 190, 232
BMW 68, 92, *107*, 109, 110,
  136, 148, 152, 174, 234,
  255, 300, 302, 311n, 319,
  357
  328 sports car 82, 83, 192,
    360
  507 387
  Dixi Austin 68
  Neue Klasse 110
Boillot, Georges 372
Booth, Charles 18
Bordino, Pietro 369
Borghese, Prince Scipione
  359
Borgward 265
Bosch 136, 302, 331n
Boudeville 331n
Boulanger, M. 176n
Boulton, Matthew 48, 316
Boulton & Watt ix
Bouton, Georges *19*
Brady, James 23, 246
Briscoe 246
Bristol Aeroplane Company
  145, 234, 255, 280, 292,
  293, 340, 361, 387n
  400 341n
  401 93, *145*
  406 341n
  407 111
British Aerospace 152
British Leyland Metro 140
BRM V16 95
Broadley, Eric 389
Brooks, C A S (Tony) 369
Brown & Sharpe 24
Bruckberger, R L 4
Bucciali 383

Büchi, Dr Alfred J 39, 137, 147n
Budd, Edward Gowan 53, 54, 70, 237, 238, 239
Bugatti 52, 54, 111n, 152, 162, 172, 176, 289, 381, 383
   Type 13 171
   Type 28 racer 289
   Type 35 360
   Type 35B 360
   Type 59 329n
Bugatti, Ettore *171*
Buick 60, 90, 179, 247, 264, 344
   Dynaflow 264
   Roadmaster 78, 386
Buick/Oldsmobile 3.5-litre V8 108
Burnham and Root 205
Bush 300
Butler, Edward 10, 11n, 12

Cadillac 24, 40, 41, 60, 61, 62, 146, 262, 264, 317, 329, 339
   Eldorado Biarritz 180
Cadillac, Antoine de la Mothe 244, 245
Caesar, Emperor Julius 7n, 223
Cagno 368
Calvet, Jacques 125
Canstatt Daimler 24, 29n
Caracciola, Rudolf 368
Carlsson, Erik 368
Carnegie, Andrew 77
Carrier, Willis 309
Castellane, Count Boni de 179
Castle, Dame Barbara 115
Castrol Ltd 291
Caters, Baron Pierre de 33n
Cayley, Sir George 278
Chadwick, Lee 39
Chaparral 119, *120*, 226, 280, 281, 283, 371
Chaplin, Charlie 379
Chaplin, Roy 23, 246, 373
Chapman, Colin 95, 176, 225, 283
Charles, Professor J A 278
Chevrolet 59, 61, 66, *78*, 79, 110, 111, 112, 114, 147
   Blazer 138
   Corvair 108, 113, 181
   Corvette 96, 99, 360
   Impala 112
   Powerglide 264
   trucks 77
Chevrolet, Louis 252
Chiron, Louis *64*
Christie 189, 230
Chrysler Corporation 55, 97n, 112, 130, 151, 152, 292

5.4 litre V8 94
70 *290*, 291
Airflow 79, 153, *154*, 280, 384, 385
Hemi engines 94, 96, 114
Imperial 343
Six 55
Chrysler, Walter P 40, 55
Churchill, Sir Winston 42, 161
Cibié 49
Cisitalia 91
Citroën *46*, 83, 100, 101, 124, 125, 128, 141, 142, 146, 176n, 233n, 265, 295, 371, 382
   2CV 93, *173*, 176n, 244, 255, 293, 380
   5CV Cloverleaf 50, 68, 173, 359n
   7A 189
   7CV *Traction Avant* 70
   BX 141
   CX 100, 127, 128, 256, 294
   DS *100*, 101, 127, 153, 232, 255, 293
   ECO 2000 prototype 172
   GS 125
   Onze Légère (Light 15) 189, *190*, 231, 232, 238
   SM 125, 293, 294
   Type A 50
   XM 294
Citroën, André 50, 54, 226, 238, 239
Clair, René 379
Clark, Jim 369
Clemens family 355
Clement-Bayard 50
Clerk, Sir Dugald, FRS 161n
Cockcroft, Sir John 299
Cockerell 118
Cocteau, Jean 379
Colombo, Gioacchino 95
Colt, Samuel 23
Coolidge, Calvin 44, 47, 58, 164
Cooper Car Company 105, 215n, 280, 371
   500 225
   formula 2 racer 104
Cord, E L 189, 230
Costin, Frank 105n, 280
Cosworth 226, 282, 319
Cottenham, Lord 76
Coulthard, David 344
Coventry Climax 112, 113
Coventry Motor 25
Coventry-Daimler 381
Cripps, Sir Stafford 163
Crosley 97
Crosley, Powell 97
Crossley 42

Cugnot, Nicholas-Joseph 5, 229

Dacia 147
Daewoo 147
DAF 261, 298, 344
Daft, Leo 97n
Daimler, Gottlieb 4, 10, 11, 18, 24, 29
Daimler Motor Company 24, 25, 39, 41, 61, 85, 152, 188, 224, 248, 262, 310, 327, 331, 336, 355, 358
   3 ½ horsepower 25
   Double Six 61
   Scout Car 84
Daimler-Benz 4, 77, 95, 234, 256, 292, 319, 357
   inverted V12 Aero engine 69
   L3000S truck 77
DaimlerChrysler 152
Dalton, Hugh 163
Dalton, John 198
Daninos, Pierre 176
DAT 79, 81
Datson 79, 81
Datsun 51, 79, 81, 97, 114
Daubrée, Edouard 347n
Davy, Sir Humphrey 236
De Dietrich 179
De Dion 14, 21, 32, 82, 230
De Dion, Albert, Marquis *19*
De Dion Bouton quadricycle *20*
De Havilland Comet 96, 105n
De Looze, John 31n
Delage 49, 162, 165, 317, 343n, 378
Delahaye 162
Delamère-Deboutteville 5
Delaunay-Belleville 38, 41n, 381
Delco Light 59
Detroit Automobile company 247
Deutsch & Bonnet 280
Deutz 11
Diesel, Rudolf Christian Karl 36, 311n
Dillinger, John Herbert 74, 75n
Dixi (later BMW) 51, 192, 357
Dixon, F W 320
DKW 189, 231
Dodge 54, 147, 224, 238
   3 ½ litre, 4-cylinder 1917 0
   Stealth 151
Dodge, Horace 23
Dodge, John 23
Dodge brothers 63, 246
Donath, Kurt 92
Donkin, Bryan 236

Doorne, Hubertus van 261, 266
Dubonnet, André 61n, 83
Duesenberg 52, 288, 289, 290, 295
   Model A 290
Dunlop 106, 109, 270
Dunlop, John Boyd 268, 271
DuPont 52, 270
duPont, Pierre 59
Durand, Peter 236
Durant, William 40, 59, 247
Duryea brothers 15, 361

Earl, Harley 78, 385
Eckhardstein, Baron von 179
Edison, Thomas 247
Einstein, Albert 36
Elegant Motors 180
   Phaeton Brougham 180
Elizabeth II, Queen 109n
Ellis, Hon Evelyn, MP 13
EMW 357
ENASA truck company 98
Engels, Friedrich 199
ERA 262
Evans, Oliver 5
Everitt 246

Facel Vega 162, 176n
Fangio 369
Feeley, Frank 387n
Ferguson 105, 282, 299, 318, 319
Ferodo 39
Ferrand, Charles 348, 349
Ferrari 83, 91, 110, 163, 281, 389
   4.5-litre 95
   4.9-litre 96
   Dino 360
Ferrari, Enzo 98
Fiat 37, 51n, 54, 55, 56, 61, 63, 69, 91, 112, 124, 141, 147, 152, 162, 163, 188, 189, 191, 233, *240*, 252, 261, 265, 289, 295, 317, *364*, 368, 371, 378
   1.4 litres 95
   124 112, 147, 360
   126 63n
   128 124, 125, 126, 170, 191, 233
   500 83
   600 172, *173*
   1100 147
   1400 163
   1500 83
   Balilla 69
   Lingotto 55, *56*
   Millecento 82
   Nuova 63n, *64*

Panda 63n, 141
Topolino 83, 172
Uno 141
X1/9 125, 360
Firestone 119, 269, 281
Fleming, Ian 377
Flusser, Dr Vilem 164
Fogarty, Carl 367n
Fonck, Capitaine René P 382, 383n
Ford, Henry 24, 36, 38, 44, 50, 62, 66, 68, 71n, 75n, 83, 129n, 130, 153, 165, 246, 248, 260, 261, 262
   his first car 247
   his 'revolution' 248
   mass production 24
   conscientious objector 44
Ford, Henry, II 206
Ford Motor Company 40, *60*, *61*, 66, 79, 84, 94, 95, 99, 105, 110, 132, 152, 188, 247, 261, 263, 265, 281, 306, 312, 313, 379, 381
   Highland Park plant *245*
   production efficiency 40
   materials 40
   Dagenham factory *60*, 66
   strikebreaking *61*
   Urmiston shadow factory, near Manchester 76
   8 173
   Anglia 111
   Capri 306
   Consul 95
   Cortina 111, 112, 306, 312
   Edsel 153
   Escort 136
   Galaxie 110, 232
   GT40 114, 389
   Ka 172
   Lincoln division 66
   MacPherson strut 95, 256
   Model A 63
   Model AA light truck *60*
   Model N 38, 261
   Model T 39, 44, 62, 63n, 129n, 153, 161, 188, 224, 248, 260, 261, 329n, 339
   Model Y 66, 188
   Mustang 114, 306
   Thunderbird 99
   V8 66
   V12 66
   Zephyr 95
Fornaca, Guido 61, 95
Föttinger, Herman 61, 262, 263
Fougasse 326
Fouillaron 344
Franklin, Benjamin 21n, 154

Frazer Nash 360

Gabelich, Gary 125
Gabriel 363
Gaiman, N 204
Gajal de la Chenaye, Luigi 163
Gallieni, General 41
Geddes, Sir Eric 162
Gendebien, Olivier 369
General Motors 40, 52, 55, 58, 59–63, 66, 68, 77, 78, 90, 94, 96, 108, 112, 118, 119, 123n, 152, 238, 244, 247, 262, 263, 264, 281, 318, 339, 344, 350, 351, 383
   two-ways Champion 90
   V8 90, 138
   V12 90
Ghia 389
Giacosa, Dante 83, 95, 163, 189
Giaur 176
Ginther, Ritchie 281
Giugiaro, Giorgetto 141
Goebbels, Dr Josef 164
Gooch, Daniel 28, 29n
Goodrich, B F 107, 271
Goodyear, Charles 268, 273
Gordini 83, 280
Gould, Jay 179
Graham 79
Graham-Paige 79
Grant, Richard H 59, 60
Gray, Christian H 107, 270, 272
Green, Andy 281
Grégoire, J A 83, 231
Grégoire/Aluminium Français 89
Gregory, B F 231
Gropius, Walter 382
Gurney, Dan 110
Guynemer, Capitaine Georges M L J 382, 383n

Hall, James Ellis 118, 225, 280–83
Hall, John 236
Hammel, A F 5
Hancock, Thomas 7n
Hancock, Walter 7, 8
Hausmann, Raoul 36, 199n
Hayes 262, 266
Healey 360
Heinkel 175
Heinrich, Prinz 363
Hemingway, Ernest 377
Henry, Ernest 337, 338, 339
Heron, Sam 52
Hillman 232, 378, 387n
   Imp 232

Hindustan Motors 147
Hispano-Suiza 74, 97, 252,
    382
  H6B 49
Hitler, Adolf 29, *67*, 69, 70, 71,
    74, 77, 84, 92, 164, 165,
    226, 248, 370
Hobbs, David 264
Hobbs, Dudley 387n
Hobbs, Howard 264
Honda 39n, 109, 114, 122,
    136, 148, 150, 151, 152,
    256, 258, 265, 314, 320
  Accord 136, 148
  Civic 122, 128, 172, 261
  NSX 150, 151, 295, 361
  Prelude 142, 150, 295, 321
  S2000 234
Honda, Soichiro 79
Hooke, Robert 231
Hoover, Herbert 58
Horch 82
Hotchkiss 162
  Grégoire 83
Houdaille 39
Howard, Sir Ebenezer 30, 31
HRG 258
Humber 25, 86, 387n
  12 Vogue 83
Hume, William 268
Hupmobile 378
Hupp 54, 238

Ickx, Jacques-Bernard 369
India Tyre Ltd 270
Iso Isetta 174
Isotta Frascini 317
Issigonis, Sir Alec 106, 112,
    174, 176, 181, 190, 226,
    248
Issigonis Lightweight Special
    95, 176
Itala 368

Jackson 302
Jaguar 93, 95, 97n, 152, 176n,
    234, 255, 280, 292
  C-type 96, 97n
  D-type 280
  E-type 110, 111, 191
  Mk 2 110
  XJ6 119
  XK120 92, 110
Jaray, Paul 280
Jeep 84, 86, 138, 318, 320
Jeep Corporation *CJ-5
    Renegade Roadster* 180
Jellinek, Emil 29
Jellinek, Mercédès 29
Jenatzy, Camille 33n
Jensen 97n
  FF 119, 137, 282, 319

Interceptor 119, 319
Johnson, Claude 32, 31n
Johnson, Leslie 92
Johnson Matthey 123n
Joule, James Prescott 198
Junek, Mme 369n

Kaiser 91
Kamm, Dr 311n
Keene, Foxhall 33n
Keller, Eugene Jnr 92
Keller, Hans 11
Kendall 89
Kendall, Denis, MP 89
Kettering, Charles Franklin
    'Doc' 52, 134, 300
Khamsin 294
Khruschev, Nikita 104
Kimberley 176n
Kipling, Rudyard 376
Kissinger, Henry 126, 156
Kluck 41
Knyff, Chevalier de 32
Kugelfischer 302
Kwaishinsha Co. 81

La Salle, Robert Chevalier,
    Seigneur de 244, 245
Lagonda *75*, 239, 263, 378,
    387n
  M45 saloon 311n
Lalique, René Jules 381
Lamborghini 389
  Miura 309, 389
Lampredi, Aurelio 95
Lanchester 36, 83–4, 97n, 110,
    377
Lanchester, Dr Frederick 30
Lancia 49, 54, 71n, 223, 265,
    371
  Aprilia 83
  Lambda 54, 224, 238, 239
Lancia, Vincenzo 239
Land Rover 138, 152
Lankensperger 356
Lawson, Harry J 13, 22, 24, 25
Ledwinka, Hans 84, 85n, 232,
    238
Leland, Henry Martyn 24, 246
Leland & Faulks 23
Lenin, Vladimir Ilyich 74, 226
Lenoir, Jeanne Etienne 5
Leopold, King of Belgium 28
Levassor, Emile 15, 153, 229,
    234, 361
Levavasseur 39
Levegh (Bouillon), Pierre 99
Liebig, Johann von 355
Liebig, Freiherr Theodor
    Franz von 355
Liebig, Baron Theodor von
    354–9

Lincoln Motors 173
  Zephyr 385
Linn 289n
Lloyd George, David 160, 247
Lockheed 290, 291
  Constellation 280
Loewy, Raymond 90, 385
Lohner 229, 230
Lola 280, 389
London Electrical Cab
    Company 25
Lord, Sir Leonard 176
Lotus 95, 105, 110, 152, 226,
    282, 294, 319, 371
  Lotus 3 95, 176n
  Lotus 18 225
  Lotus 78 283
  Elite 105, 110, 264
  Europa 176n
  F1 373
Loughead, Malcolm 290
Lucas 51n, 302
Ludersdorf 268

MacAdam, John Loudoun 6
McCarthy, Mary 179
MacIntosh, Charles 347
MacIntosh family 271
McLaren 280, 282, 319
MacNeice, Louis 79, 378
Makinen, Timo 369
Marchal 49
Marconi, Guglielmo 47
Marcos coupé 281n
Marinetti, Filippo 378
Markus, Siegfried 5
Marshall, George C 92
Marx, Karl 199, 252, 258, 317,
    318, 319, 321
Maserati 280, 294
Matra 282, 319
Matté-Trucco, Giacomo 56
Mauchly, Dr J W *299*, 300
Maugras, Johabert 342
Maxwell company 55
May, Michael 252
Maybach, Wilhelm 11n, 29,
    83, 263
Mays, Raymond 369
Mazda 119, 152, 226, 320
  MX-5 360
Megy, Leander 342
Mercédès 29, 30, 33n, 39, 42,
    68, 246, 310, 336, 372
  3-litre V12 82
Mercedes-Benz 69, 81, 95, 99,
    100, 136, 141, 142, 148,
    151, 253n, 279, 343n,
    371
  300SL 96, 99, 279, 387
  450 SEL 180
  500K *384*

C-class saloon 141
Type 600 *Grosser
    Prunkwagen* 112
W125 82
Messerschmitt *Kabinenroller*
    175
MG 91
    Midget 91, 95
    TC 91, 360
Michelin 128, 272, 273, 274,
    275
    X 100, 107
Michelin, André 271, 347n
Michelin, Edouard 272, 347n
Michelin family 271
Michelin, James 347n
Midgeley, Walter 52
Mignol, Marius 272
Mikkola, Hannu 369
Miller, Harry 82, 189, 230,
    231
Minerva 132
Mini 106, 108, 110, 111, 113n,
    153, 170, 174, 175, 182,
    190, 232, 248, 249, 371,
    387n
Mini Cooper S 110, 113n, 380
Mitsubishi 147, 151
    3000GT 150
Mitter, Gerhard 369
ML Aviation Company 279
MMC (Motor Manufacturing
    Company) 24, 25
Mohs *Ostentatienne Opera
    Sedan* 180
Montagu of Beaulieu, Lord
    24n
Morgan 3-wheeler 329n
Morris, William *see* Nuffield,
    Viscount
Morris Motors 66, 86, 387n
    8 173, 188
    1100 112
    Minor *62*, 106
    Oxbridge 233n
Mors 50, 363
Moseley, David 270
Moss, Stirling 279, 368
Moulton, Dr Alex 112
Mouton, Mlle 369n
Murdock, William 7n
Muskie, Senator 181
Mussolini, Benito 69, 70, 71,
    84, 252
Mussolini, Bruno 71n

Nader, Ralph 114, 181, 281
Napier 27, 111n
Napoleon Bonaparte 7, 8, 15,
    155, 215, 225
Nardi-Danese 176
Nash, Charles 40, 78, 314

Nasser, Gamal Abdul 104, 121
Nazzaro, Felice *364*
Neander 83
Nelson, Emil 238
Nervi, P L (architect) 98
Neubauer, Alfred 95
Newton, Sir Isaac 268, 278,
    285
Nissan 79, 81, 138, 151, 261
    300ZX 151
    Skyline GT-R 150, 151
Northey, Percy 32
NSU 226, 265, 299
    Ro80 119, 153
Nuffield, Viscount (William
    Morris) 31n, 54, 86, 89,
    239
Nuvolari, Tazio 368

Oakland 238
O'Connor, John *216*
Oldfield, Barney 231
Olds, Ransom Eli 23, 245, 246
Oldsmobile 24, 171, 224, 246,
    264
    'curved-dash' 23
    *Cutlass Luxury Supreme
    Sedan* 180
Olley, Maurice 59, 60, 82, 317
Opel 50, 68, 77, 132, 147, 165,
    173, 280
    Blitz truck 77, 318
    Laubfrosch 50
    P4 165
Opel, Fritz von 279
Otis, Elisha 204, 205
Otto, Dr N A 10, 64

Packard 62, 78, 314
Packard, Colonel James 24
Palmer, J F 258, 270, 271
Panhard 24, 27, 32, 153, 179,
    187, 189, 229, 234, 266,
    280, 311n, 335, 361, 383
    système Panhard 14, 18, 139,
    153, 187, 229, 268
Panhard, Hippolyte 346
Panhard-Levassor 14
Park Ward 311n
Parsons, Sir Charles 10
Pasteur, Louis 236
Pegaso 98, 361
Perbury 262, 266
Peugeot 13n, 40, 50, 125, 317,
    337, 338, 361, 371, 372,
    383, 389
    205 141
    205 GTi 141
    Bébé 171, 172
Peugeot, Armand 14
Peugeot family 14
Philips, Wal 258

Piccard Pictet 317
Piëch, Dr Ferdinand 152
Pinin Farina 389
Pirelli 107, 133, 271, 273, 274,
    275
Plastow, David 132
Porsche *64*, 93, 101, 144, 229,
    255, 262, 265, 371
    356 93, 232
    911 133
    928 133, 144
    Spyder 279
Porsche, Ferdinand 69, 84,
    85n, 230, 248
Porsche family 152
Porsche Lohner 18
Pratchett, T 204
Pressed Steel Company 54,
    239
Prost, Alain 368
Proton 147
Pugh-Barker, Elizabeth 347n
Pullman Company 53, 179,
    238

Renault 28, 70, 83, 140, 147,
    232, 239, 311n, 349, 364
    4CV 97, 111, 172
    45 *350*
    Espace *94*, 139, 140, 141
    R16 232
    Twingo 140
Renault, Louis 28, 32, 50, 91,
    171, 226, 239, *362*
Renault, Marcel 28, *362*
Ricart, Wilfredo 98
Riley 89, 262
Robert brothers 278
Rolls, Hon C S 32
Rolls-Royce 32, 33n, 38, 42,
    49, 52, 59–60, 62, 70, 74,
    89, 119, 132, 152, 226,
    234, 262, 292, 313, 317,
    379, 381
    40/50hp 38, 65n
    emblem 381
    Merlin engine 76
    motto 33n
    Phantom 377
    Silver Ghost 38
Rolt, A P 320
Rommell, Feldmarschall Erwin
    84
Roosevelt, Franklin D 70, 77
Rootes Group 112, 387n
Rosemeyer, Bernd 368
Rosenberger, Adolf *64*, 69
Rosengart 51
Rothschild, Baron Henri de 30,
    247n
Rothschild & Fils, J 348
Rothschild family 357

Rover 138, 152, 340, 341n, 378
Rowntree, B Seebohm 18
Royce, Frederick Henry 25n, 31, 32, 33n, 38, 74
Rozier, Pilatre de 278
Rumpler 231
Rumpler and Benz 'teardrop' cars 69
Rzeppa 232

Saab 340, 341n, 368
Salerni, Commendatore (later Count Teremala) 263
Salomons, Sir David 13
Sayer, Malcolm 280
Sbarro, Franco 252, *256*, 257, 258
Schumacher, Michael 369
Scott-Montagu, J, MP 23n
Seat 152
Serpollet 14, 355
Shanghai 147
Sharp, Hap 281
Siddeley 52
Simca 83
Simms, Frederick R 11n, 24, 331n
Singer 50, 387n
Singh, Joghinder 114
Sitwell, Dame Edith 85
Sizaire 39
SKF 257
Skinner brothers 39
Skoda 152
Sloan, Alfred P Jr 55n, 59, 60, 61n, 63, 262
Sloper, Thomas 107, 270, 272
Smith (Olds' financier) 23, 246
Society of Motor Manufacturers and Traders Ltd (SMM&T) 88, 132, 249
Solomon, Isaac 236
Sopley 96
Southern Railway Company 22
Spallanzani, Lazzaro 236
Spaulding 344
Spencer, Herbert 18, 30
Stanguellini 176
Stanley, Captain F W 342, 343n
Steam Carriage of Scotland Company 8

Steinbeck, John 377
Stephenson, George 11
Stibitz 300
Stirling, Patrick 0
Stransky, Franz 356–8
Studebaker 90, 147, 238
Sturmey, Henry 24, 25
Sturmey-Archer 263
Sturtevant Brothers 342
Stutz 62
Subaru 150
Sullivan, Louis 205
Summers brothers 114
Sunbeam 62, 76, 387n
Swift, Dean Jonathan 215
Sykes, Charles 381
Symington, William 7n

Talbot 162, 262
Tatlin, Vladimir 36, 37n, 38
Tatra 84, 232, 238
Tecalemit 302
Thompson 62
Thomson, Robert W 13n
Thum, Johannes 355
Tilling, Thomas 200
Tocqueville, Alexis de 27, 197, 199
Touring 389
Toyota 79, 97, 138, 142, 148, 149, 150
  Camry 142
  Carina 174
  Lexus 149, 150, 234
  Supra 149
Tracta 83, 189, 230
Trésauguet, Pierre 6
Trevithick, Richard 5, 7n
Triumph 173
Trojan 175
Trotsky, Leon 41, 42
Tucker 91
Tudor, Frederic 306, 307, 308
Turing, A W 300

Uhlenhaut, Rudolf 279

Valéry, Paul 42
Valetta, Dr Vittorio 112
Vandervell 111n
Varzi *64*, 369
Vauquelin, Louis Nicolas 53n

Vauxhall 42, 62, 66, *94*, 132, 241, 262, 317, 381
  30/98 65n
Verbiest, Ferdinand 5
Vergniaud, Pierre 93n, 266
Viotti 389
Voisin, Gabriel 53n, 317n
Volkswagen 63, 84, 86, 91, 147, 152, 164, 165, *187*, 248
  Beetle 93, 95, 108, 113, 128, 129n, 153, 170, 233, 380, 387
  Golf 128
  KdF (*Kraft durch Freude*) 84, 86, 93, 164, 188, 232, 248
  Kübelwagen 84
  Passat 128
  Scirocco/Golf GTi 302
Volvo 114, 152, 173, 265, 281n

Wakefield 291
Walker, Peter 92
Walkerley, Rodney 353
Watt, James 6, 48, 316
Weber 300
Welch 271
Welchman 300
Wellington, Duke of 236, 351n
Werner, Wilhelm 30
Williams 266, 344
Williamson, C N and A M 375, 376
Willys 84, 238
Willys-Overland 84
Wilson 188, 262, 263
Wilson, Major W G 263n
Wilson, Woodrow 32, 260
Wilson-Pilcher 263n
Wimille, Jean-Pierre 369
Winton, Alexander 22
Witzky 302
Wolseley *75*
Wright Brothers 39n, 279, 281

Yates, Dornford 377

Zagato 389
Zeppelin, Ferdinand 278
ZF 292